The Enterprise Linux Administrator

Journey to a New Linux Career

Kenneth Hitchcock

Apress®

The Enterprise Linux Administrator: Journey to a New Linux Career

Kenneth Hitchcock
Hampshire, UK

ISBN-13 (pbk): 978-1-4842-8800-9   ISBN-13 (electronic): 978-1-4842-8801-6
https://doi.org/10.1007/978-1-4842-8801-6

Managing Director, Apress Media LLC: Welmoed Spahr
Acquisitions Editor: Divya Modi
Development Editor: James Markham
Coordinating Editor: Divya Modi

Cover designed by eStudioCalamar

Cover image designed by Freepik (www.freepik.com)

Distributed to the book trade worldwide by Springer Science+Business Media New York, 1 New York Plaza, New York, NY 10004. Phone 1-800-SPRINGER, fax (201) 348-4505, e-mail orders-ny@springer-sbm.com, or visit www.springeronline.com. Apress Media, LLC is a California LLC and the sole member (owner) is Springer Science + Business Media Finance Inc (SSBM Finance Inc). SSBM Finance Inc is a **Delaware** corporation.

For information on translations, please e-mail booktranslations@springernature.com; for reprint, paperback, or audio rights, please e-mail bookpermissions@springernature.com.

Apress titles may be purchased in bulk for academic, corporate, or promotional use. eBook versions and licenses are also available for most titles. For more information, reference our Print and eBook Bulk Sales web page at http://www.apress.com/bulk-sales.

Any source code or other supplementary material referenced by the author in this book is available to readers on GitHub via the book's product page, located at www.apress.com/. For more detailed information, please visit http://www.apress.com/source-code.

Printed on acid-free paper

Dedicated to my nephew Nico Kleinhans. Your quest to change your own career path inspired me to write this book.

Table of Contents

About the Author ....**xvii**

About the Technical Reviewer ....**xix**

Acknowledgments ....**xxi**

Introduction ....**xxiii**

Part I: Requirements and Linux Background 1

Chapter 1: Requirements 3

   Information Technology Basics 3

      Hardware 4

      Software 5

      Networking 6

   Further Reading 7

      Hardware 8

      Software 9

      Network 9

      Storage 10

   Further Study 10

      Free Online Courses 10

      Paid-For Online Courses 11

      Hardware and Software 11

      Networking 11

   Summary 12

Chapter 2: Origins and Brief History **13**

    Unix and Linux History 13

        Unix... 13

        Linux History.. 16

    Evolution of Linux... 18

        Debian 19

        Important Milestones of Linux 20

        Linux Now and in the Future 23

    Summary.. 23

Chapter 3: Linux Explained **25**

    Linux Operating System... 25

        Kernel 25

        Initial Ramdisk... 28

        Everything Is a File, Mostly.. 29

        Utilities 29

    Common Distributions.. 31

        Differences 32

        Upstream Projects 32

        Unique Distributions 33

    Operating System Differences 33

        Windows 33

        Windows vs. Linux... 34

    Uses of Linux.. 34

        Servers 35

        Desktop 35

        Mobile Devices 35

        IoT.. 35

        Future Linux... 36

    Summary.. 36

Part II: Getting Started 37

Chapter 4: Installing Linux for the First Time 39

Where to Get Linux...39

    OpenSource and Free Software...40

    Enterprise Linux..40

    Community 42

Virtualization 44

    What Is Virtualization?..44

    Types of Virtualization...45

    Creating Virtual Machines...53

Installation Media..62

    Burn Image 63

    USB Drive..63

    Network Install 64

Installing Linux...64

    Lab Environment..64

Ubuntu...65

    Installation Media 66

    Basic Installation 66

    Basic Exercise 79

    Custom Installations 80

    Optional Custom Exercise...80

Fedora Server 81

    Installation Media 81

    Basic Installation 81

    Basic Exercise 94

    Custom Installations 95

    Optional Custom Exercise...96

OpenSUSE 96

    Installation Media 97

    Basic Installation 97

Basic Exercise 115

Custom Installations 116

Optional Custom Exercise 116

Upgrading Linux 117

Upgrade vs. Migration 117

Before Upgrading 118

What Distributions Can Be Upgraded 118

Exercise 119

Summary 121

Chapter 5: Using Linux for the First Time **123**

Accessing Linux 123

Console 124

SSH 126

Web Console 133

Exercise 134

Command Line 135

Finding Help 135

Navigating the Filesystem 136

Command-Line Shortcuts 143

Different Commands in Different Distributions 145

Exercise 146

Desktop Basics 147

Installing Different Desktops 147

Enabling and Disabling Desktops 156

Exercise 157

Summary 158

Part III: Basic Configuration **159**

Chapter 6: Access Control **161**

SSH and SSHD Configuration 161

Configuration Files 162

Default Configuration 164

SSH Service 167

Debugging ssh Issues 168

Exercise 170

Users and Groups 171

Local Users and Groups 171

Remote Users and Groups 176

Sudo 177

Exercise 179

File and Directory Permissions 180

Understanding Linux Permissions 180

Managing File and Directory Permissions 182

ACLs 185

Exercise 191

Summary 192

Chapter 7: Package Installation 193

Installing Packages 193

Package Management Systems 194

Manual Package Installation 207

Repository Configuration 211

System Patching 219

Errata 219

System Updates 220

Rollback 226

Exercise 235

Summary 236

Chapter 8: Network Configuration 237

Network Basics in Linux 237

Network Configuration Using Command Line 238

Network Configuration Using Textual Interfaces 250

Network Configuration with Desktop 252

Exercise 261

Network Tools 262

    Default Tools Available.. 262

    Exercise 265

Summary... 266

Chapter 9: Disk Configuration.. 267

Disk Management... 267

    Disk Layers.. 268

    Tools Available 269

    Exercise 292

    LVM... 293

    Exercise 305

Filesystem Management.. 306

    Filesystem Types 306

    Checking Disk Filesystem.. 307

    Creating 307

    Mounting Filesystems 308

    Resizing 309

    Directory Hierarchy.. 310

    Exercise 312

Summary... 312

Chapter 10: Service Management 313

Basic Service Management 313

    Service Management Utilities.. 313

    Starting a Service.. 316

    Stopping a Service 317

    Viewing the Status of a Service... 318

    Enabling/Disabling a Service... 319

    Exercise 320

systemd 321

    Configuration Files.. 321

Utilities 324

Exercise 325

Creating a New Service 326

Example Script 326

Unit File 327

Enable and Start Service 330

Remove a Service 331

Exercise 331

Summary 332

Part IV: Enterprise Linux **333**

Chapter 11: Enterprise Linux Distributions **335**

Red Hat 335

Brief History 335

RHEL 336

Subscriptions and Support 349

Estate Management Basics 355

Training and Certifications 356

Exercise 357

SUSE Linux Enterprise Server 358

Brief History 358

SLES 359

Subscriptions and Support 378

Estate Management Basics 381

Training and Certifications 382

Exercise 383

Ubuntu 384

Brief History 384

Ubuntu 384

Training and Certifications 384

Ubuntu Installation 386

Estate Management Basics 386

Subscriptions and Support 387

Summary.. 389

Chapter 12: Example Use Cases for Linux 391

Building a Web Server... 391

Web Server Options.. 391

Web Server Configuration Overview... 392

Linux Installation and Configuration... 393

Web Server Package Installation.. 394

Configuration Files.. 396

Firewall Configuration 400

SELinux Configuration 401

Exercise 406

Building a File Server.. 406

NFS vs. Samba 407

File Server Configuration Overview.. 408

Linux Installation and Configuration... 408

NFS Server Package Installation 410

Firewall Configuration 411

SELinux Configuration 413

Disk to Share... 414

NFS Server Configuration 415

Exercise 418

Summary.. 419

Chapter 13: Security 421

Firewall 421

Command-Line Configuration... 422

Web UI Configuration... 427

Exercise 429

SELinux 430

SELinux Modes 431

Command-Line Configuration.. 431

Exercise 440

Hardening.. 441

Hardening Standards.. 441

Compliance Scanning... 442

Exercise 449

Encryption... 450

How Does Encryption Work 450

Linux Encryption... 451

Exercise 462

Summary.. 463

Chapter 14: High Availability **465**

Clustering.. 465

Types 465

Cluster Concepts 467

Enterprise Linux Clustering.. 467

Projects 467

RHEL Cluster Example 468

Cluster Troubleshooting... 485

Exercise 486

Summary.. 487

Chapter 15: Scripting and Automation **489**

Shell Scripting... 489

Linux Shell 489

Shell Scripting Basics... 492

Examples 500

Exercise 501

Ansible 502

Explained 502

Ansible Configuration 504

Exercise 513

Summary.. 514

Chapter 16: Deployment at Scale **515**

Deployment Methods 515

Kickstart 515

Image Cloning.. 520

Kickstart vs. Cloning.. 521

Exercise 521

Deployment Tools 522

Enterprise Deployment Tools 523

Automation 525

Training and Certifications.. 528

Summary.. 528

Part V: Troubleshooting and Recovery **531**

Chapter 17: Troubleshooting Linux **533**

Logging 533

Logs.. 534

Journalctl... 540

Remote Logging 543

Exercise 545

Monitoring.. 546

Process-Related Tools 546

Disk-Related Tools... 549

Network-Related Tools 550

Performance Copilot.. 551

Remote Monitoring.. 552

Nagios 552

Prometheus 553

Finding Help 553

    Tools 553

    Asking for Help 555

    Getting Support 557

Summary 558

Chapter 18: Recovering from Disaster **561**

Reinstalling 561

    Things to Consider 561

Recovering 563

    Single-User Mode 563

    Emergency vs. Rescue Mode 573

    Using Rescue Disks 573

    Rescue Examples 576

    Exercise 580

Summary 581

Chapter 19: Backup and Restore **583**

Backups 583

    Backup Methods 583

    Backup Reports 588

Restore 588

    What to Restore 588

    Test Restore 589

Summary 589

Index **591**

About the Author

Kenneth Hitchcock is currently a Senior Architect working for Red Hat, with over 20 years of experience in IT. He has spent the last 12 years predominantly focused on Red Hat products, certificating himself as a Red Hat Architect along the way. The last 12 years have been paramount in his understanding of how large Linux estates should be managed, and in the spirit of openness, he was inspired to share his knowledge and experiences in this book. Originally from Durban, South Africa, he now lives in the South of England where he hopes to not only continue inspiring all he meets but also to continue improving himself and the industry he works in.

About the Technical Reviewer

 **Zeeshan Shamim** has been an IT professional in various capacities from management to DevOps for the past 15 odd years. He has served in roles ranging from support to DevOps/sysadmin in various organizations ranging from big telecom firms to big financial banks and is a big proponent of OpenSource technologies.

Acknowledgments

My own journey into the OpenSource world can be attributed to so many people and the opportunities they afforded me. From my early days working for Justin Garlick and Alasdair Mackenzie to my current and past Red Hat family, you all have inspired and supported my own journey, and I feel very humbled to share my experiences in this book with so many others.

Introduction

Changing careers to IT or switching disciplines within IT can be a difficult journey on its own. Often not knowing where to start or what to learn can end your journey before it begins.

Within this book, we look to guide you through the various elements an enterprise Linux administrator should know, while giving you all the additional breadcrumbs for you to follow on your own. This book strives to equip you with the basic skills to get you started on your new career path and encourage you to learn more about the OpenSource world.

PART I

Requirements and Linux Background

Switching careers or changing your career path by learning more about Linux can be a daunting task for anyone, so being a bit apprehensive can be expected; having been through a similar journey myself, I can fully relate. I will, however, just say, don't try to learn everything at once. Take your time, read in increments, and absorb as much as you can. The goal of this entire book is to help you along with my experience and advice on your journey to becoming an enterprise Linux administrator.

This book will be broken down into multiple parts and will feature exercises for you to practice basic Linux administrative tasks. Part 1, however, is written as a long introduction to give you some indication of what you should know as an IT person and also to act as a knowledge check. If you are completely new to IT, this book is also for you, but you will need to do some further reading or learning to get up to speed on a few basic IT concepts that will be discussed in Chapter 1.

Chapter 2 will then begin your history lesson into Linux, Unix, and OpenSource in general. This section may not teach you the practice skills to becoming an enterprise Linux administrator, but it will give you some good general knowledge about the industry for when you start working with other Linux or OpenSource professionals.

Finally, Chapter 3 will start to dig a bit deeper into what Linux is and what it can be used for; this will hopefully help with some of the questions you may have been asking yourself before you started reading this book or before you knew anything about Linux, like how does Linux work and how is Linux different from Windows.

Further questions you may have, like how is Linux installed and how am I ever going to remember all those long command line arguments, will be covered in later chapters.

For now, let's begin your journey by going through the basic IT requirements you need in order to become an enterprise Linux administrator.

CHAPTER 1

Requirements

When entering the world of IT, there are many things that need to be learned to gain the required knowledge to start a successful IT career. The same is true for becoming an enterprise Linux administrator.

However, before your journey to becoming an enterprise Linux administrator can begin, we need to establish the baseline IT knowledge that is required. Chapter 1 is focused just on that. In this chapter, we will highlight and briefly discuss the basic information technologies and terminologies you are expected to know and understand before you can begin your journey to becoming an enterprise Linux administrator.

If you already have an information technology background or have completed training that has already covered these subjects, feel free to skip through this chapter. If you are not confident in your knowledge or feel like a refresher, double-check what is covered in these first few pages. It is entirely possible that there is something new you may not know.

Information Technology Basics

It goes without saying that Linux, as an operating system, falls within the very broad subject of information technology. Within the information technology (IT henceforth) world, there are many subjects you will need to be familiar with, to enable you to start building your knowledge, thus allowing you to become successful in the IT industry. It is not crucial to be a subject matter expert (SME) on any of these subjects while you are learning. You may just naturally evolve into an SME later as you find a subject that really interests you.

The main areas we need to establish a baseline knowledge on are

- Hardware
- Software
- Networking

3

© Kenneth Hitchcock 2023
K. Hitchcock, *The Enterprise Linux Administrator*, https://doi.org/10.1007/978-1-4842-8801-6_1

Hardware

The very first thing you will need to become familiar with in the IT world is the terminology and understanding of the different IT or computer hardware. It will always be assumed you know computer hardware when you tell people you work in IT. Even if you are a software developer, people will always assume you can fix their computer for some strange reason.

This chapter, and this book for that matter, is not here to teach you how to fix computer or server hardware but to highlight that you may need to learn the basics and be familiar with certain terminologies before moving on.

On that note, let's quickly look at what is expected from you when it comes to IT hardware.

Required Knowledge

None of the following terms in each bullet point should be unknown to you. You do not need to have experience working with each of them, but it is important you understand what they are and their function.

Minimum hardware knowledge requirement list:

- Input and output devices
- CPU
- GPU
- CPU sockets vs. CPU cores
- Motherboards
- System buses
- Spinning disk storage
- Solid-state disk storage
- NVMe storage
- RAID storage
- System memory

- USB, serial, and parallel ports

- Bluetooth and wireless technologies

- Network adapters

In the IT industry, these terms are common knowledge for anyone working in a technical role and are often discussed when building or configuring systems. Not knowing what they are can make your journey more difficult.

If you are someone who is completely new to IT, then don't feel disheartened or discouraged by not knowing anything about computer hardware. Take time from reading this book and broaden your computer hardware knowledge by reading some basic resources on the subject; maybe even consider doing a free online course to give you a better understanding. Recommendations on where to go and what courses you could do can be found a few pages later in this chapter.

STOP   If you are completely new to IT, skip ahead now to the recommended reading and study materials. Read and understand the different articles or training courses; then come back and read further. Building your foundation as we go is more important than getting through this book quickly. If the suggested reading further down in this chapter does not cover everything for you, search the Internet or YouTube for further information.

Software

Knowing what computer hardware is and how all the components work together is important to build a good IT foundation. However, at some point, you will need to know what can make use of computer or server hardware.

As an enterprise Linux administrator, you will spend much of your time working with software in one form or another. Unlike hardware and fixing computers, this book is aimed at trying to help you understand how to install and troubleshoot basic Linux systems. The goal of this book is to give you a basic understanding of what Linux is, how to install it, how to configure Linux to run a workload, and how to resolve some basic issues.

Required Knowledge

The following list of topics is vital for you to understand before you can proceed with the book. Like hardware, these software terms are common knowledge and are expected to be known.

- Operating system

- Kernel

- Compiler

- Application server

- Common development or programming languages, such as Python, Java, and C++. Not necessarily how to program with them, just a basic understanding of them

- Device drivers

- Command-line interface

As previously mentioned with hardware, if any of these terms do not seem familiar, skip to the further reading and study section to get up to speed before continuing.

STOP   If you are completely new to computer software, skip ahead now to the recommended reading and study materials. Once up to speed, return to this book.

Networking

With a good understanding of computer hardware and software, you are well on your way to being successful in IT. However, it is also very important to build on that knowledge with a good foundation of computer networking knowledge.

Networking can be a very complex subject and can be difficult sometimes to grasp or even remember. Focus on learning the basics and build from there. The required knowledge section will highlight the basics you need to understand for this book and when working as an enterprise Linux system administrator.

Required Knowledge

The following list of networking concepts should give you a simple enough foundation to not be completely in the dark when people discuss computer networking.

Make sure you understand what each of these is and how they work with each other. You do not need to be an expert; a basic understanding for now will do.

- OSI model
- Network protocol such as TCP, UDP, and ICMP
- Dynamic and static IP addressing
- Subnetting and how they restrict a network size
- Gateways
- DNS
- DHCP
- Firewall
- Switches
- Routers and routing
- Load balancer

As previously mentioned in the previous sections, if any of these terms do not seem familiar, skip to the further reading and study section to get up to speed before continuing.

Tip   Do not get too hung up on all the networking terms, stick to the list above and be sure you know what each of them are. These are the minimum you should know.

Further Reading

The following are some good starting points to building your knowledge of computers and hardware.

Hardware

The following link is a good a place as any to start understanding the basics about computers. Understanding the history and components explained in a simple Wikipedia page will give you the beginning of your computer hardware foundation.

https://en.wikipedia.org/wiki/Computer

POST

What is post? Why is it important? These questions are explained in the following Wikipedia link:

https://en.wikipedia.org/wiki/Power-on_self-test

Boot Process

The computer boot process is a vital area to understand if you are going to be successful at deploying a Linux or any operating system. Read the content in the following Wikipedia link or search the Internet for another explanation that will make sense to you. Basically, you need to know how a computer boots and how to boot installation media.

https://en.wikipedia.org/wiki/Booting

Computer Memory

What is computer memory, how does it work, and what are the differences between desktop and server memory?

https://en.wikipedia.org/wiki/Computer_memory

System Buses

Understanding the system buses on a computer motherboard might not be crucial to anyone first learning about computers but does add to your overall knowledge. The following is the basic explanation that will help you understand:

https://en.wikipedia.org/wiki/Bus_(computing)

Software

The Operating System

The following is a link that is simple to understand with a sufficient explanation of what an operating system is:

    https://en.wikipedia.org/wiki/Operating_system

Kernel

The following link is a very good breakdown of the operating system kernel. You do not need to understand everything about the kernel as long as you understand the basic function.

    https://en.wikipedia.org/wiki/Kernel_(operating_system)

Device Driver

Device drivers allow computer software to use hardware from the system the software is installed on. The following is a link with further information for your own understanding:

    https://en.wikipedia.org/wiki/Device_driver

Network

Computer Networking

If you know nothing about computer networking, this Wikipedia page will be a good place to start. This page explains everything from computer networking protocols through to different network hardware used today.

    https://en.wikipedia.org/wiki/Computer_network

The OSI Model

The following link explains what the OSI model is and all its layers. Understand and memorize the different layers; it is often referred to in technical discussions.

    https://en.wikipedia.org/wiki/OSI_model

Storage

What are the different storage options for computers and servers today? The following are reading links that explain more about computer storage. Read and understand all; storage is quite important as it can affect the performance of your system if you choose or configure the wrong storage.

Basic computer storage explained

`https://en.wikipedia.org/wiki/Computer_data_storage`

Solid-state storage

`https://en.wikipedia.org/wiki/Solid-state_drive`

NVMe storage

`https://en.wikipedia.org/wiki/NVM_Express`

Redundant array storage

`https://en.wikipedia.org/wiki/RAID`

Further Study

If reading knowledge base articles and general Internet searching is not your preferred method of study, consider enrolling in an online or correspondence training course.

Free Online Courses

There are many different online part-time courses you can do that are free. You may not get a certification, but just having access to the knowledge is a major advantage at this stage of your learning path. Registering with one of the following could help you build your foundation while you are still learning the basics:

- Coursera

- edX

If you do not like any of the aforementioned, you can also search for other providers that offer free training. This link is useful to find training providers:

`www.findcourses.co.uk/search/it-software-training-courses`

Paid-For Online Courses

If you prefer to pay for training, you could look at a few places that offer training, with some actually offering you certifications you can use when applying for jobs.

- LinkedIn

- Amazon

- Cisco

- Red Hat

Warning   Do not pay for anything before you have understood the syllabus and the value you can get from the training. Ensure that you do not skip any small print. Some training providers will want you to provide card details for a subscription and can be quite difficult when you want to cancel.

Hardware and Software

Basic Hardware Courses

At the time of writing, I found a few useful beginner computer courses that are completely free:

www.edx.org/course/computer-hardware-and-operating-systems

www.coursera.org/learn/how-computers-work#syllabus

Networking

Coursera also has useful free courses you can do on computer networking to get started:

www.coursera.org/learn/computer-networking#syllabus

Summary

In this chapter, you were introduced to the following:

- Hardware knowledge requirements that are needed for a successful career in IT

- How software is just as important as hardware and what software knowledge is required to progress as an enterprise Linux administrator

- The importance of networking to understand how computers and servers communicate

- Why storage configuration should never be ignored

CHAPTER 2

Origins and Brief History

In Chapter 1, we discussed the basic IT knowledge required to start working in an enterprise Linux role. These IT basics would give you the foundational knowledge to stay afloat when discussing general technical issues without pushing you too far beyond your limits.

This chapter takes a break from checking what you know and acts as the introduction to Linux. We will look at the history of Unix and Linux without digging too much into the details; we will step through the rough timeline of how Linux came to be and how Linux evolved into what we know today.

We will explore how Linux and the OpenSource world have not only caught up to the enterprise leaders of yesteryear but how they are now paving the path for the future. We will look at some of the possibilities that OpenSource brings and how you as an individual can contribute to be part of the bigger community.

Unix and Linux History

If history is not something you enjoy or care much for, feel free to skip to the OpenSource sections of this chapter. Those are the important bits you should be aware of as an aspiring enterprise Linux administrator. However, I do urge you to consider knowing some basic Unix and Linux history; we OpenSource people do take pride in where we came from, and it often fuels the conversations we have.

Unix

Long before Linux was even thought of, the world had Unix. Unix, very much like Linux, was created out of necessity. The story of Unix, like Linux, started with another product: Multics.

© Kenneth Hitchcock 2023

K. Hitchcock, *The Enterprise Linux Administrator*, https://doi.org/10.1007/978-1-4842-8801-6_2

Multics

Before Unix became the product we know today, we had Multics (Multiplexed Information and Computing Service).

Multics was developed by General Electric, MIT, and AT&T Bell Labs to be a time-sharing operating system in the mid- to late 1960s. Multics was the first operating system to effectively allow multiple users to share resources on the same physical system. All our modern operating systems, microcomputers, and mainframes were influenced by how Multics was designed.

Multics, though far from perfect, had a few limitations. One of these limitations was the sizing of segments. Segments (we know them as files) were limited to no more than 256 kilowords (1MB). It was limitations like the segment sizing that ultimately led to the push for something better.

The dissatisfaction of Multics and the eventual separation of Bell Labs from the Multics project led Ken Thompson, Dennis Ritchie, and a few others to build their own operating system: Unix.

Early Unix

The early version of Unix was relatively simple; it featured a hierarchical file system, device files, editors, and a command-line interpreter. A little while later, another programmer by the name of Douglas McIlroy created the first ever high-level language or "assembler" for Unix. Ken Thompson used this assembler to create his first "B" Unix programming language.

Unix 2, Love Ken

In 1973, the development of Unix version 2 included the first instance of the C programming language. With the introduction of C, it was decided that Unix would be rewritten in the C programming language for the first time. The first official release of Unix written in C was Unix version 4. In the same year Unix 4 was released, Unix was presented publicly. However, due to legal restrictions, Bell Labs was not able to sell Unix as a product.

It was rumored that Ken Thompson received numerous requests for the Unix operating system's code. Eventually after constantly being asked, Ken relinquished and sent media with the Unix code to whoever requested it, often with a note "Love Ken".

First Commercially Available Unix

With Bell Labs improving their development process and efforts on the Unix project, Unix evolved to the extent that Bell Labs was able to publicly release the Unix operating system. This first commercial version of Unix was called IS/1.

Unix Limitation

One major limitation of Unix was that the operating system was limited to the hardware it was written for. In the 1970s, the various Unix operating systems were built for specific hardware like the PDP-11/20 or the DECS PDP-11. It was not until the 1980s that Unix finally became portable, allowing different hardware to be used. This progressive move eventually led to the expansion of Unix and its use.

Unix Variations

Bell labs, with their now publicly released version of Unix, sold licenses for Unix to be used by all who wished to do so. These licenses were relatively inexpensive and largely aided in the spread of Unix. The spread allowed companies to build their own variation of Unix. The new Unix variants contributed more than feature enhancement or different ideas on how Unix should be built; it also allowed better compatibility for newer hardware. Unix was growing and gaining in popularity; during the 1984 Unix expo, it had become clear that Unix was going to need to be taken seriously.

Unix Standards

As with any new development on a new software project, there will always be different developers with different ideas on how things should be done. Unix development was no different. Unix was growing, and the code base was becoming more and more diverse. With the lack of development or operating system standards to follow, the development of Unix was threatening to code itself out of existence.

Three major variations of Unix emerged from these diverse groups of developers and companies. They were System V, BSD, and Xenix. All had their own development and feature path with a different idea of the future of Unix.

These different Unix variants fortunately share a few similarities. These allowed common ground to be established, and in the 1990s, COSE (Common Open Software Environment) standards were established. The Unix operating system was being

15

developed by different companies following a common standard. With these new standards in place, the Unix operating system went from strength to strength. Unix started being developed at a global level and no longer by individuals.

Unix Growth in the 1990s

During the 1990s, a few mergers, acquisitions, and disasters occurred. Some of these mergers turned into serious growth opportunities and helped the Unix community grow the adoption of Unix. The big market leaders HP, Sun Microsystems, and IBM dominated the Unix space and continued to control the server industry through the late 1990s and 2000s. These companies still provide the likes of HP-UX, Solaris, and AIX today in the 2020s.

Linux History

The beginning of Linux is not too different from Unix. Unlike how Unix was a fork of Multics, Linux is Unix reinvented from the ground up. With the rise of Unix and the prices that came with it, variations like Linux were inevitable. You only need to understand the main reasons for any new software to be developed to understand what is about to happen. You either write software because the current solution is too expensive or it doesn't exist. This is exactly what led to the decision to develop Linux in the 1990s.

Linus Torvalds

A Finnish student at the University of Helsinki named Linus Torvalds had been stuck using MS-DOS and MINIX on his 80386 computer. Unhappy with these operating system choices, Linus had the notion to try to use Unix. Unfortunately or fortunately, depending on how you see it, Unix was far too expensive for a student, so left with only one choice, Linus had to build his own. From scratch, Linus "Just for fun"* ended up creating the first Linux kernel.

Kernel

The kernel is the core of the Linux operating system; it is responsible for the communication between computer hardware and software.

Very Early Linux

In 1991, Linus Torvalds finished his early versions of the Linux kernel, and just three years later, in 1994, he "officially" released version 1.0.

The Kernel Is Not Enough

With the new Linux kernel, Linus was well on his way to creating the first editions of Linux, but an operating system would be useless if it were just a kernel. For example, what good would a car be if all you had was the engine and nothing else? You need a steering wheel, seats, doors, a body, and maybe windows for it to be a real car. An operating system is no different. There is more needed to an operating system other[*] than the kernel. Utilities, tools, and software are needed to make use of the kernel and in turn make use of the hardware it controls. Yes, Linus had built the engine of today's Linux, but it needed more.

Free Software Foundation

Fortunately, around the same time as Linus wrote the Linux kernel, an American software developer by the name of Richard Stallman along with the FSF (Free Software Foundation) were developing their own operating system called GNU. Linus and Richard Stallman along with the FSF were ultimately working toward the same goal be it from different ends. Linus built the kernel, and Richard and the FSF were building the utilities. The combination of these utilities and the kernel led to the creation of the first Linux operating system: "GNU/Linux."

OpenSource

Why Linux went from "GNU/Linux" to where it is today can largely be attributed to the software revolution that is OpenSource. Linux is built on OpenSource principles along with almost every utility shipped with it. OpenSource means more than just the source code is open for anyone to view and use. OpenSource is a software movement, promoting collaboration like the world has never seen. Anyone can take a copy of the Linux source code and create their own flavor of Linux.

---

[*] Just for fun is the name of the book written by Linus Torvalds.

OpenSource also means software is "free" in that the software has no monetary cost, which begs the question, if the software is free, then how can someone make money from it?

Enterprise Linux

Companies like SUSE, Canonical, and Red Hat make money from OpenSource products by selling subscriptions. These subscriptions provide a mechanism for organizations to pay for support from the likes of Red Hat, SUSE, and Canonical, the support where technical teams answer questions and help when customers have issues. The subscriptions also allow enterprise companies like Red Hat to develop enterprise-grade products that can be used to manage workload in a supported manner.

It is very important to make the distinction that a subscription is not a license. Subscriptions are only for support and enterprise-level updates, not for the software itself. You can use Red Hat Enterprise Linux, for example, without a subscription, and you can update the operating system from community-provided repositories with no software violations or expectation of recompense. You can't, however, ask Red Hat to support you if you choose to use community-provided updates. For that, you will need to pay for subscriptions and change your systems to update from supported repositories.

Subscriptions don't just provide income for enterprise companies like Red Hat. Subscriptions also drive these enterprise Linux companies to invest in the upstream communities like Fedora or Foreman.

Evolution of Linux

How did Linux go from a kernel and some basic utilities to one of the most widely used operating systems today?

Much like what happened to Unix in the 1980s and 1990s, Linux took a similar path. The current solutions did not work; something else was needed. The only difference, however is that current solutions did not work. Everyone who had an interest in the Linux operating system could create their own without having to build anything from the ground up. The kernel code, which is still maintained by Linus Torvalds, is freely available to the public if you want to build your own kernel. However, if you prefer to collaborate, you can submit merge requests to the Linux kernel. That is, if you are brave enough to face the criticism from Linus.

Note   Linus Torvalds briefly took a small break around 2018 to "work on his understanding of people's emotions and how to respond to them"; this was largely due to him being criticized for his handling of people.

Like the code for the kernel was and still is available, the utilities developed by the FSF also remain available. Ultimately, you could take the kernel and utilities source code, develop your own features, and compile and install your very own distribution.

Many community developers and startups did exactly that. They built their own tools, desktops, and management software.

Debian

Debian, one of the earliest Linux distributions, forked the GNU/Linux distribution and started working on their own distribution around 1993. The FSF was the first sponsor for Debian from November 1994 through to November 1995, giving Debian the support it needed to get off the ground. Debian has since been forked into numerous distributions, of which one of the more commonly used distributions is Canonical's Ubuntu.

Fun Fact   A fun fact about Debian is their early support mailing lists were hosted at Pixar, which makes sense because Debian releases are named after "Toy Story" characters. In fact, the name of the "unstable" trunk is Sid, a character who continuously destroys his toys.

With companies like Debian creating their own flavors and many other companies like Red Hat and VA Linux. The OpenSource journey had truly started gaining momentum. The FSF and the work Linus Torvalds began laid the path to countless projects. These projects along with the companies that supported them changed how we use and manage operating systems today.

Important Milestones of Linux

The early distributions were far from perfect, the desktops were rudimentary, and the utilities were limited. It also didn't help that not everything in the beginning was OpenSource. Linus Torvalds still used proprietary applications like BitKeeper in the beginning, but after the pressure from the community, he remedied his use of proprietary software by developing Git. Linus did maintain, and I agree with him, that the best tool should always be used for the job even if the tool is proprietary.

Kernel 2.0

A major milestone in the history of Linux was in 1996 with the release of kernel version 2.0. This was the first kernel to serve several processors at the same time using symmetric multiprocessing (SMP). This now meant that many companies could seriously consider using Linux as an alternative to Unix or Windows platforms, effectively opening the door to many of the big names today to play a major role in the server operating system space.

Linux Desktop

With the improvements to the Linux kernel, the next logical step had to be the Linux desktop. As history had it, this is exactly what happened around 1998. The KDE desktop was released and ended up being the first advanced desktop for a Linux distribution. The biggest problem with KDE was that it used a proprietary component: "Qt tools."

Desktop Wars

The "desktop wars" between KDE and Gnome started as a direct result of the use of the proprietary "QT tools" component. The feud between the two communities continued for almost a decade until finally both sides released such poor versions; the community was forced to create a "GNOME 3" derivative, called Cinnamon. Cinnamon was released in 2011 by Linux Mint who still maintains the desktop today. Cinnamon like Gnome and KDE can be deployed on almost, if not all, Linux distributions and even on some Unix platforms.

Dell, Oracle, and Red Hat Started to Grow

As desktops were improving and the user base of Linux was growing, companies like Dell and Oracle started investing time and effort into Linux. Red Hat has now become one of the biggest names in the OpenSource world and has just equaled the market value of Sun, a major milestone in the OpenSource world, indicating Linux has become a super power in the server operating system space. Dell, with their own ideas, tried to increase the adoption of Linux in their own way by releasing laptops with Ubuntu preinstalled.

Oracle, not to be outdone, created their own distribution from Red Hat Enterprise Linux. This sparked some very interesting marketing battles of which one always makes me laugh when I hear about it.

Oracle had created their own forked version of Red Hat Enterprise Linux and decided that the best place to launch the product was at a Red Hat Summit event in San Francisco. Oracle decided on an advertising campaign that labelled their distribution as the "Unbreakable Linux," indicating Red Hat's product was not bulletproof. Red Hat, not taking this without a fight, unleashed a marketing campaign of sheer brilliance, and for me, it shows the fighting spirit of the company.

The Red Hat marketing team at Summit saw what Oracle was doing and immediately sprang into action. The Red Hat marketing team responded with the now infamous "Unfakeable Linux" rebuttal campaign, creating tee shirts and marketing materials almost within the same hour. The shirts were distributed, and marketing materials were pasted on any available marketing spots between the airport and the conference center. If there ever was a term "aggressive marketing," Red Hat showed it on that day. One thing for sure not lacking at Red Hat is passion.

Kernel 3.0

While company rivalry grew, Linux kernel development continued with version 3.0 being released in 2011. "Nothing, absolutely nothing" of value came with this version other than the version change. Linus made the quoted comment to ensure the next major release of the kernel was more than a number change and actually included something good. The previous 2.x.y versions were beginning to grow too large and needed to move on, hence the shift to 3.0.

Systemd

One of the bigger controversies in the Linux world happened around the same time as the release of Kernel 3.0. This was the release and distribution of Systemd. Systemd was released to be the replacement of Unix System V and BSD init systems. Both System V and BSD init were the current solutions to manage Linux system components, such as service management.

There were a few disgruntled Linux users to say the least with some even going as far as to send death threats to the developers. Fortunately, these ended up being hollow threats and changed nothing. Roll forward to 2015 and almost every Linux distribution has implemented Systemd as the system component software suite.

Android and Ubuntu Increased in Popularity

During the course of 2013, Google's Linux-based android shipped roughly 75% of all smartphone market share, firmly stating that Android was not going away anytime soon.

Ubuntu also continued to grow and boasted a user base of 22 million users. More users were switching to OpenSource software and operating systems than ever before. Even with the growth of Ubuntu and Android, the year of the "Linux desktop" replacing Windows just never materialized, even after the horrific release of Windows Vista.

Kernel 4.0

Very little to no documentation was written about the changes from 3.19 to 4.0. Even Linus himself admitted there was little in the way of changes, even though there was the promise of something more substantial. The only change of any significance in version 4.0 was the ability to patch the kernel live without a reboot.

Kernel 5.0

As with previous major releases of the Linux kernel, 5.0 was another exercise in just changing the major number instead of incrementing the minor. That is not to say there were no enhancements or improvements, just nothing that would have required a major version release.

An interesting and useful feature that Kernel 5.0 did add was the ability for the kernel to become more energy aware, which meant the kernel could make task scheduling decisions to lower power usage on Symmetric multiprocessing (SMP) systems.

This change has been most useful in smartphones and other battery-powered Linux devices. Other released features in 5.0 included improved amdgpu drivers and support for swap files in btrfs.

Linux Now and in the Future

Linux has evolved vastly from its first kernel written from scratch by a university student to being the dominating server operating system in the world today. Linux is everywhere and in almost everything we use today. Red Hat and its acquisition by IBM have cemented the fact that Linux and its communities will continue to grow and innovate in the OpenSource world.

New cloud technologies continue to emerge along with new and interesting ways to use Linux. Linux is no longer the black box nobody wants to touch. Linux is becoming easier to use and to adopt. More organizations are embracing the fact that Linux is here to stay and are accepting that the OpenSource culture is the way forward. Not only does OpenSource promote open ways of working, it encourages us all to contribute or to start something new. Every one of us can give back or innovate; the code is there for all to see and for all to improve. It is this openness and willingness to contribute that fills me with the confidence to say that Linux and OpenSource are the future.

Summary

In this chapter, you were introduced to the following:

- A brief summary of the Unix operating system's history

- The introduction to where Linux came from and its early history

- A run-through of the Linux road map so far along with some interesting changes along the way

- What OpenSource is and why the future looks bright

CHAPTER 3

Linux Explained

Our final bit of theory that we need to discuss is to give you a clear understanding of what Linux actually is. In Chapter 1, we looked to prepare you for entering the world of Linux and the IT world in general. In Chapter 2, we ran through some Linux history and how Linux came to be.

In this chapter, we will start to delve further into what Linux actually is. We will discuss the basics of the operating system, what the components in Linux are, and some of the terminologies you will need to understand. We will look at what a Linux distribution is and what some of the common distributions are available today. We will also explore the many uses of Linux and finally discuss the differences between Linux and other operating systems available.

Linux Operating System

The Linux operating system has evolved a fair bit over the last two decades, but a few fundamentals still exist. Let's have a look at the core fundamentals of Linux.

Kernel

In Chapter 2, we discussed the history of Linux and discussed how the Linux kernel was developed by Linus Torvalds. We also briefly said that the kernel is the core or the brain of the Linux operating system that allows software to communicate with hardware.

But how does the Linux kernel actually work? How is the Linux kernel architected? How does a kernel actually send requests to hardware to do something, and how does software communicate with the kernel?

© Kenneth Hitchcock 2023
K. Hitchcock, *The Enterprise Linux Administrator*, https://doi.org/10.1007/978-1-4842-8801-6_3

Monolithic and Modular

The Linux kernel is a monolithic modular kernel. The monolithic part means the whole
Linux operating system runs in the kernel space, and the modular part means the Linux
kernel can't load additional modules into itself if required.

Kernel Architecture

To allow the Linux kernel to communicate with different hardware and software
components, the Linux kernel architecture is made up of functionality pillars and layers
that run down the pillars.

Functionality Pillars

To provide the different functionalities of the Linux kernel, the Linux kernel is divided
into six functionality pillars:

- User interface

- System

- Processing

- Memory

- Storage

- Networking

Each pillar handles different functionality for the Linux kernel to communicate
with system hardware. The user interface pillar, for instance, would be responsible for
your mouse to work, whereas the network pillar would be responsible for network-
related tasks.

Layers

Having pillars within the Linux kernel architecture is a nice way to categorize
functionality, but it is still a long way for a user or application to request hardware access.
Along with the functionality pillars, the Linux kernel also has different layers to its
architecture. Each of the following layers runs down each pillar when the Linux kernel is
requested to do something:

- User space interfaces

- Virtual

- Bridges

- Logical

- Device control

- Hardware interfaces

Kernel Map

With the combination of the functionality pillars and layers, the Linux kernel can be viewed as a kernel map, which can demonstrate how the Linux kernel performs its tasks. The link for a site with an interactive Linux kernel map is as follows:

`https://makelinux.github.io/kernel/map/`

This map shows the flow of different tasks the kernel can perform when communicating between software and hardware.

The "user interface" pillar example from a few paragraphs earlier describing how the Linux kernel allows your mouse to work on your desktop can be tracked in the interactive map if you want to know more. Take your time to research each component for a better understanding. The interactive map does give you links for further reading.

System Calls

The Linux kernel map will show you how the end-to-end flow of a Linux kernel task is executed, but in this flow, there is the use of something called a system call. A system call is a programmatic way that software can request services from the Linux kernel.

To give you a slightly better understanding of the Linux kernel, you should be aware what a system call is and the different types of system calls. This will allow you to become a better enterprise Linux administrator as you will gain a deeper understanding of tasks when debugging application issues while troubleshooting.

There are six major categories of system calls.

Process Control

This is used for the creation and management of processes. Creating a process makes use of the fork operation, whereas ending a process would use the kill operation.

File Management

File management is as simple as the name implies, the management of files. This is everything related to files, the opening, closing, deleting, creating, reading, and so forth.

Device Management

As with file management, device management manages the devices and device files on your system. The creation and removal of device files indicates the logical attaching and detaching of physical devices. This would also include the setting and getting of attributes of your devices attached to your system.

Information Management

Information management is the category responsible for getting information from your system, for example, things like date, time, and computer name, or even getting information about files, like the author, who opened the file, and when the file was created.

Communication

The communication category is another self-explanatory category. All the sending and receiving of messages along with communication connections are handled by the communication category. The communication category is also responsible for the attaching and detaching of remote devices.

Protection

Protection is the category responsible for managing the file permissions with the get and set attributes.

Initial Ramdisk

With the need for the Linux kernel to be small and efficient, the Linux kernel must be compiled with only the bare minimum. There is one big glaring issue with this approach, however. The bare minimum would not allow different hardware platforms to be used. The kernel would need to be compiled for individual system hardware and would not be very portable, very much how early Unix worked, if you remember the history lesson of Unix discussed in Chapter 2.

To avoid portability issues, the Linux kernel makes use of what is known as an initial ramdisk. The initial ramdisk can be implemented by either the "initrd" or "initramfs" methodology. Both methods provide an additional file that boots with the Linux kernel. This additional file allows the Linux kernel to boot an extra "root" file system before the main "root" file system is booted. This initial root file system contains additional hardware drivers and any other files a Linux kernel would need to be fully portable.

Missing Drivers

In the rare event of drivers missing from a Linux kernel version. Drivers can be compiled into your current Linux kernel version and used. There are utilities provided by all Linux distributions that can help with this. Hardware vendor documentation has also improved over the last decade to provide step-by-step guidance on getting their hardware to work with your Linux kernel. In most cases, the driver installation package provided by the vendor does this all for you.

Everything Is a File, Mostly

In Linux, very much as with Unix, everything is considered a file. Directories, text files, and image files are all considered a file by the system. This even includes the attaching, and detaching, of physical devices to your system, as each of these devices is represented by a file. The only time something is not a file in Linux is when it is a process.

Utilities

Linux as an operating system is more than just the Linux kernel. This was clear in the early creation of Linux, and it was something we discussed in Chapter 2. Linus Torvalds originally developed the Linux kernel, but as you need to have software that can utilize the kernel to provide functionality to the end user, the development of Linux utilities was required. This was where the free software foundation started by Richard Stallman was crucial.

Shell

One of the first utilities for Linux would have been a shell of some type. As the first iterations of the Linux operating systems would not have desktops available, the user would have to have a way to send requests to the Linux kernel.

Table 3-1 lists the common types of Linux shells available today.

Table 3-1. *Common Linux shells*

Linux Shell	Description
Sh	Bourne shell, originally developed for Unix by Bell AT&T by a developer named Steve Bourne. This was also the first Linux shell to be used.
Bash	Bourne again shell. A Linux variant of the original shell by Steve Bourne
Ksh	Korn shell was developed by David Korn as a hybrid of Bash and Csh.
Csh	C shell, developed by Bill Joy while at the University of California. The Csh was developed to provide more C-type programming language syntax within the shell.
Zsh	Z shell is an Sh shell extension with added features and customizations. A modern shell based on the original Sh shell.

Other Utilities

Once you have your shell, the Linux utilities are far too numerous to list all. Common shell utilities include things like chmod or chown for file permission management. Remember the Protection Linux Kernel category from a few pages back? The chmod and chown utilities aid the user in requesting the Linux kernel to set file protection.

Later in this book, we will discuss more around Linux command-line basics. These basics will all use Linux utilities. Basically, if you run a command on your Linux shell, you are using a utility.

Desktops

Utilities do not end with the command line either. The Linux desktop is also a utility. Within the Linux desktop, there are numerous other utilities that can be used by end users for whatever they wish to do with their system.

There are a number of Linux desktops available today; however, the three main desktops you will encounter are listed in Table 3-2.

Table 3-2. *Commonly used Linux desktops*

Desktop	Description
Gnome	One of the more common desktops used today. Gnome is provided and developed by the GNOME project. The GNOME project is made up of volunteers and larger sponsors like Red Hat. Gnome is the default desktop for a few Linux distributions such as RHEL and Fedora.
KDE	Founded in 1996 by Matthias Ettrich. Unhappy with how the current Unix desktops operated, Matthias Ettrich started the KDE project to create a desktop that was intuitively easy to use.
Cinnamon	Developed as a reaction to the poor release of GNOME 3, which abandoned the traditional desktop layout. The developers of Cinnamon originally forked components from Gnome, but later in Cinnamon 2.0, they moved away entirely from Gnome components.

Common Distributions

Currently, there are over 600 Linux distributions or distros available. Many distros have been copied from other distros to create new distros. This process of copying is known as forking.

To understand the sheer number of distros, you need to see the mind map on the Linux distributions Wikipedia page. The main branches start as expected with Slackware, Red Hat, and Debian. From there, it just explodes with all the forks and variations.

As a small taste to that mind map, Table 3-3 provides a small part of the distro family tree for RPM-based distros. This table does not take into account the forks of forks of forks that have happened from these.

Table 3-3. *Linux distributions from the mind map*

RHEL/CentOS	Fedora	OpenSUSE	Mandrake
Asianux	Berry Linux	SUSE Linux Enterprise Desktop	Mandriva Linux
ClearOS	BLAG Linux	SUSE Linux Enterprise Server	Mageia
Fermi Linux LTS	EnGarde Secure Linux	SUSE Studio	ROSA Linux
Miracle Linux	Fuduntu	GeckoLinux	OpenMandriva
Oracle Linux	Hanthana		Unity Linux
Red Flag Linux	Korora		
Rocks Cluster Distribution	Linpus Linux		
Rocky Linux	Linux XP		
Scientific Linux	MeeGo		
Amazon Linux 2	Russian Fedora Remix		
	Trustix		
	Yellow Dog Linux		

Differences

As discussed already, the Linux distribution is made up of the Linux kernel and utilities. The kernel, however, is one of a few things that is the same across all Linux distros. The differences between distros can vary quite a bit depending on where the distro was forked from and the community developing the distro.

Package Management

One major difference that Linux distros have is around their package management systems. Linux distros like Red Hat Enterprise Linux, Fedora, and CentOS use the RPM-based packaging, while distros like Debian and Ubuntu use the deb-based packaging. Another interesting packaging system that seems to be getting a bit of traction is Pacman. Pacman is used by gaming distros like SteamOS and Manjaro.

Upstream Projects

With all the distros available today, it's important to know where each distro came from and what that distro was originally intended for. A good example is Fedora. Fedora is regarded today as the "upstream" for Red Hat Enterprise Linux, but this is not what it was initially intended for. Fedora was first released in 2002 by Warren Togami as an undergraduate project. The goal of the project was for Fedora to act as a repository for third-party products to be developed and tested on a non-Red Hat platform. Fedora was meant to be a platform to provide a mechanism for collaboration that was hosted on a non-Red Hat product, completely opposite to what it has evolved to today.

Unique Distributions

Some distros have been built for a specific purpose. In the case of Kali, which was purely built for security, it has built-in tools to perform tasks such as penetration testing.

Another unique distro is Puppy Linux, which was built to reduce bloat that can sometimes be shipped with more common distros. This cutdown distro is there to allow the "lighter" Linux to run on older slower hardware.

One of the biggest Linux distros used today is Android. We all know how popular that has become, and we all know exactly what its purpose is.

Operating System Differences

What makes Linux different from Microsoft Windows? This section is just a small window into some of the key differences between Windows and Linux.

Windows

Windows is developed and provided by Microsoft and currently holds around 74% of the personal computer desktop market share. Windows still continues to be an easier operating system to use and configure for people who are not familiar with computers.

Not OpenSource

There is not much I can tell you about Windows that you do not already know, but there are a few points that are worth mentioning. None more important than Microsoft Windows not being OpenSource and being a proprietary software. This means that Microsoft Windows requires a license and that license has a price you need to pay to use it. The code base for Windows is also a proprietary and closed source, meaning you cannot fork or clone Windows to create your own version.

Windows vs. Linux

In Table 3-4, we will look at a few of the basic differences between Windows and Linux.

Table 3-4. *Windows vs. Linux differences*

Windows	Linux
File and folder names are not case sensitive.	File and directories are case sensitive.
Admin user is Administrator.	Admin user is root.
Uses the backslash "\" for file and directory pathing.	Uses the forward slash "/" for file and directory pathing.
Windows makes use of a microkernel that provides little in the way of operating system services.	Uses a monolithic kernel architecture. See the Kernel section in this chapter for more information.
Windows traditionally has been less efficient due to its larger footprint. However, this has improved as Windows can be deployed in a more cutdown version. The resource requirements are still higher than Linux, and newer versions of Windows require newer hardware.	Linux can be optimized and installed to provide the absolute bare minimum to run workloads. Linux can still run efficiently on older hardware without the need for new hardware with each new release.
Less secure, higher risks of being infected by viruses and malware.	Tooling like SELinux combined with less risk of viruses or worms infecting Linux makes Linux the more secure platform.
Windows makes use of drive letters for new disks, remote storage, printers etc.	Linux uses files to represent disks and hardware devices and makes use of a hierarchical file system.

Uses of Linux

The uses of Linux are boundless today as more and more devices like the Raspberry Pi and Arduino have become available for home developers and hobbyists to play with. This has opened new avenues into automated home systems a retro gaming to name just a few. However, Linux is still well used in a few other categories.

Servers

The first place people would think to find Linux would be in a server hidden away in a data center, or in a broom closet behind the IT guys desk. In most cases, this would be true. Not so much in the broom closet but more in the data centers. Today, over 90% of cloud infrastructure runs on Linux. It has also been calculated that over 96% of the world's top one million servers run Linux. Chances are that during the course of today, you accessed a website or downloaded this book (i.e., if you bought the ebook) through a Linux server.

Linux servers can be used for almost anything today from web servers through to massive database platforms that store medical records for an entire country. The security, performance, and scalability have made Linux the platform of choice for many organizations over the years, and with companies like Red Hat, SUSE, and Canonical continuing the development of enterprise platforms, this trend does not look like it will change anytime soon.

Desktop

Probably one of the more contentious areas of Linux usage has been the use of Linux as a desktop replacement. The ongoing argument that Linux desktops are still not as good as products like Windows and Macintosh continues even today with good reason. Linux desktops have traditionally been difficult to use for people accustomed to Windows or Macs. The process of installing new packages and configuring hardware with no native Linux drivers and sometimes the lack of simple end user documentation have caused the adoption of Linux desktops to be slow, to say the least. However, developers and communities continue to listen to feedback and work toward the eventual "year of the desktop."

Mobile Devices

Outside of the server market, the biggest use of Linux is in the mobile device market. Android, the Linux distribution for mobile devices, is on more than half of the world's mobile phones and tablets. Nearly 2.5 billion people are using Linux as you are reading this book. In fact, if you are reading this on an eReader device, you are most likely using Linux yourself.

IoT

One of the newer areas in recent years that has been gaining traction with the use of Linux and OpenSource technologies has been devices used in the "Internet of things" market. These are devices that contain sensors or perform specific tasks. They tend to use cutdown versions of operating systems like Linux to perform their function. Remember, a kernel is still required to speak to hardware and communicate with other systems. Smart home devices are among these types of devices; an example of this could be your smart hub for your smart bulbs in your house. The bulbs communicate with the hub for tasks like turning on or off, or if you have the more expensive versions, adjusting the color.

Future Linux

As our world is becoming smarter and more efficient, the use of IoT, edge, cloud, and on-premise Linux will continue to grow.

Not only will Linux continue to solve IT-related problems, Linux and OpenSource will continue to help create smarter transportation with self-driving cars, buses, and commercial shipping, all while making the planet a safer and greener place. Newer kernel versions continue to work on making our data centers a greener place with less power consumption. Even the food production and the agricultural industry have also started and will continue to harness the power of OpenSource and Linux. By using Linux along with automation and machine learning, large-scale automated farming and smart distribution will work toward solving world hunger problems one day.

Summary

In this chapter, you were introduced to the following:

- How the Linux kernel works and how the Linux kernel can be extended by the use of initrd or initramfs files

- What utilities are in Linux and how they, along with the kernel, make the operating system

- Some examples of different Linux distributions and what makes them different

- Some of the common differences between Windows and Linux

- What Linux can be used for and what the future holds with the use of OpenSource and Linux

PART II

Getting Started

With a baseline of your IT knowledge established and a history lesson endured, we are now ready to get our hands dirty. Part 2 and all subsequent parts will have more around the practical uses of Linux, and in almost all sections, there will be exercises for you to try. Most of these exercises will challenge you to use what you read in the chapter to accomplish your tasks.

Part 2 is your first step into using Linux. In Part 2, there will be two major chapters. The first of these chapters will be Chapter 4, where we will take you through the process of installing three different Linux distributions: Ubuntu, Fedora, and OpenSUSE. This chapter will discuss the installation steps and any nuggets of information that will help you along your journey. You may already be asking the question "why are we installing community products if this is a book on becoming an enterprise administrator?" The answer is as simple as before you can run, you must walk. Remember, we are looking at a marathon and not a sprint. Be patient, read through, run the exercises, and if you are confident enough, skip ahead.

Chapter 5 will complete Part 2 and will feature the beginnings to using Linux for the first time. In this chapter, we will discuss how to access your freshly installed Linux distros, how to use the command line, along with some basics to get started, and finally what the different desktops are, how to install them, and how to enable or disable the desktop when you don't need it anymore.

Once you are through with Part 2, you will be well on your way to using Linux for the first time. You would have gained some experience in installing different distros and how to configure some basic system desktops.

CHAPTER 4

Installing Linux for the First Time

The first steps to learning anything new is to practice and practice. In this chapter, we will start to explore a few hands-on exercises for you to start learning how to use Linux.

We will first look at what Linux distributions we will use and where you can find them; we will then look at platforms where you can practice and build your Linux systems. Once we have established the basics to get started, our first Linux distribution we will install is Ubuntu, followed by Fedora and OpenSUSE. Finally, in this chapter, we will look at what is involved to upgrade your distributions.

Each hands-on section will have an exercise for you to practice and start building your Linux experience.

Where to Get Linux

Linux can be found almost entirely online today with very little option of purchasing Linux install media off the shelf. Nothing is impossible, but it is becoming less and less likely these days. With that said, all you really need to do is know what distribution you wish to use and search the Internet for the vendor and its download page; from there, you will be well on your way to getting your Linux install media.

In this chapter, we will focus on three Linux distributions as the goal is for you to get more of an overall understanding of different Linux distributions than to focus on just one as many other books of this nature do. The idea is that as you learn more about Linux, you will become more aware of the differences and gain the required skills to work for any organization that uses Linux, no matter the distribution used.

However, if you do have a preferred distribution or are slightly biassed and time is an issue, feel free to follow the sections that match the distribution you will be focusing on. After all, you can always return to the book and learn more later.

39

© Kenneth Hitchcock 2023
K. Hitchcock, *The Enterprise Linux Administrator*, https://doi.org/10.1007/978-1-4842-8801-6_4

OpenSource and Free Software

Before we look at any Linux distributions, I just wanted to highlight a very important fact about Linux. In previous chapters, we spoke about OpenSource and the Free Software Foundation, and with that, I just wanted to be 100% clear about what OpenSource means.

Linux, enterprise, or community is free to use; the source code and product are available for everyone, with no licensing requirements preventing the use or functionality.

Nothing that claims to be OpenSource should have a price to use. However, there is a price if you expect a vendor to help you with support cases or fix enterprise issues in line with your organization's SLA. That comes at a premium and requires support subscriptions. You can download and use any Linux distribution as you wish with no license preventing you from using product functionality.

Enterprise Linux

Throughout this book, we will focus only on three distributions at any time as mentioned in the previous paragraphs. In this chapter, we will focus on three community-based distributions, but in later chapters, we will look at the three enterprise vendors you will end up working with if you work for any large organizations with enterprise Linux. The three main enterprise vendors most organizations use are as follows.

Red Hat

Red Hat is one of the largest Linux organizations today with a large portfolio of enterprise products from Red Hat Enterprise Linux all the way through to the OpenShift container platform. Red Hat started in 1993 and has been continuing to develop solutions for enterprise companies that are looking for alternatives to the more expensive Unix platforms. Red Hat is the frontrunner in setting trends in the enterprise with advancements in hybrid cloud and edge computing to name a couple. Red Hat is heavily focused on growth and has not stopped developing new products. In fact, Red Hat continues to make important investments where they see potential, with just one example recently of StackRox to improve the security of OpenShift.

Red Hat Enterprise Linux

Red Hat Enterprise Linux, or RHEL as we will refer to it henceforth, is the enterprise Linux distribution used by many large organizations in the world today. RHEL has been in development since 2001 where it took over from the "Red Hat" Linux distribution. During the process of writing this book, Red Hat released version 9 of RHEL with no indication of slowing down the development. An interesting fact about the latest RHEL 9 release is that it will even run on a Raspberry Pi, be it with some limited functionality. With ARM processors potentially being something of the future, this could be another good move by Red Hat.

RHEL can be downloaded directly from Red Hat:

`https://access.redhat.com/downloads`

You will need to create a Red Hat account; this won't cost you anything, and you can request limited period trials if you want to play with RHEL and have support. There is also a "developer" subscription that will allow you to run up to 16 RHEL systems.

Canonical

Canonical was founded in the UK by a South African businessman named Mark Shuttleworth in 2004. Canonical is better known for their community Linux distribution called Ubuntu. Canonical has a slightly different approach to providing their Linux distribution, as they rely entirely on the community for the product development. Where Canonical adds value to Ubuntu is by providing enterprise-level support. Organizations who choose to use Ubuntu could purchase support subscriptions that would assist in any SLA requirements an organization may have without the risk of waiting for community support. Canonical offers support and break/fix where it can but does not actually have its own distribution like Red Hat or SUSE.

Ubuntu

Ubuntu is not a brand-new or even original Linux distribution that forked from the very first versions of Linux. In fact, Ubuntu is a derivative of a Linux distribution called Debian. Ubuntu was forked from Debian circa 2002 and has since spawned many child projects over the years due to its community and home user adoption.

Ubuntu has a six-month release cycle with a long support version released every two years. This allows cutting edge users to get new features quicker while having enterprise customers getting stable long-term supported releases every two years.

Ubuntu can be downloaded directly from the Ubuntu website:
https://ubuntu.com/download

The site does not require registration and has options to download different Ubuntu versions for server and desktop. For the purpose of this book, stick to downloading server editions. It doesn't matter too much, but as you will be working more with server editions in the future, you may as well get used to them now.

SUSE

Probably the next company after Red Hat to provide a large market share of the enterprise Linux space is SUSE. SUSE, like Red Hat, has a slightly wider portfolio of products than Canonical, but still less than their closest competitor, Red Hat. SUSE, like Red Hat, has their own enterprise Linux distribution called SUSE.

SLES Server and Desktop

SUSE has many Linux variations from desktop through to IBM Power versions. All have different subscriptions that can be purchased, and most, if not all, are driven by the "upstream" OpenSUSE product.

SUSE remains a strong competitor to Red Hat Enterprise Linux in the server operating system market, and it is not uncommon to find data centers with both SUSE and RHEL running.

SUSE Linux Enterprise Server or SLES can be downloaded directly from the SUSE website:
www.suse.com/download/sles/

Just as with Red Hat, you will need to register an account to download. The account will give you access to trial subscriptions for support and patching but is not required to actually use or install the distribution.

Community

Community Linux distributions are Linux distributions that are developed by and supported by communities. These communities are generally made up of volunteers and hobbyists who dedicate their free time to providing a product they feel passionately about. That is the general idea; however, some communities do have the backing of larger organizations like the Fedora project who receives support from Red Hat.

Fedora

One of the community distributions we will use in this chapter is Fedora. Fedora is a fork of Red Hat Enterprise Linux and continues to still be the upstream product. All this lends to the fact that Fedora is a great product to learn some of the basic RHEL functionality while you are still learning.

The Fedora project provides a few different product options with a server, desktop, and IoT version available for download. For this book, we will stick to the server option, but again as mentioned with Ubuntu earlier, the desktop version should work fine too if you absolutely prefer to use that.

Fedora can be downloaded from the following link, or from any other mirrors that are provided on the Fedora website:

```
https://getfedora.org/en/server/download/
```

Being a community product with no subscription support options, there is no need to register or get any trial subscriptions.

OpenSUSE

The second community distribution we will install and configure in this book is the OpenSUSE distribution. OpenSUSE is the community version of SUSE Linux Enterprise and is available for download directly from the OpenSUSE website:

```
https://get.opensuse.org/server/
```

As with most community products, there is no need to register on the site or have any subscriptions to download or get new content. There are also a few options with OpenSUSE when you download. There is a desktop and a server option along with variations in each. For now, stick to the main server release for this book and its exercises.

Ubuntu

The download location for Ubuntu community versions (the same as the enterprise version) remains the same as mentioned in the previous section on Ubuntu under the Enterprise Linux section. The only difference between "community" and "enterprise" is one comes with a support contract from Canonical:

```
https://ubuntu.com/download
```

Virtualization

With a good understanding of what Linux distributions we will be using and where to find them, we can now start looking at how we will install each of the operating systems. For that, we need to start looking at our first bit of hands-on work that will involve some technical skills.

Note   If you are not familiar with the following terminologies or the technical stuff just seems too much over your head, take a few minutes, watch some YouTube videos, or read documentation.

What Is Virtualization?

As we will just about to install Linux, we need a place to install these Linux operating systems. For that, we will use something known as virtualization. I can fully appreciate that most of you reading this book may be aware of what virtualization is, but for those who are not, I will try to give you a quick explanation.

Virtualization is the ability to partition or share resources with different "systems" or virtual machines that run on the same physical hardware. With a well-"specced" server or desktop, you may not always use the 12 cores or the 32GB of memory you have; by using virtualization and what is known as a hypervisor layer, you can create virtual machines that make use of surplus hardware or resources.

In Figure 4-1, you can see a very basic representation of virtualization.

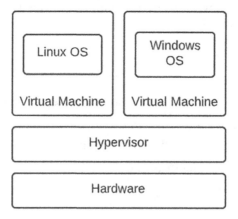

Figure 4-1. *Visualization at a glance*

Types of Virtualization

There are a few options you can use for virtualization both for home use and the enterprise, but as we are looking to start you off slowly, this book will only focus on two virtualization options you can install on a personal laptop or home desktop.

We will look at both Windows virtualization and Linux virtualization, so do not worry if you do not have a Linux system available yet. We still are working our way to installing Linux.

Hardware Requirement

For the next bit, you will need either a Windows system or Linux desktop (if you are already ahead of the curve) with enough resources to install a virtual machine with at least 2 virtual CPUs, 4GB of memory, and 10GB of disk space available.

If you have a dedicated system or laptop you will install on, then feel free to skip this section. You will need to ensure you have installed media available for the installs we will do in later chapters.

BIOS Requirements

On your laptop or desktop that will be used to host your virtualization environment, you will need to ensure that the BIOS has been configured to allow virtualization. Without this configured, your virtualization hypervisor installation will fail and give you an error saying something along the lines of "your hardware does not support virtualization." If you see this error, reboot and configure the virtualization options in your BIOS.

New to computers tip   Some motherboards will hide your POST screen. Normally, you need to press the escape button or tab for the POST screen to show. From there, you can see what button you need to press for your BIOS setup. Once in the BIOS, search for your CPU or virtualization settings.

Windows Virtualization

As many people reading this book will either not be coming from an IT background or may be coming from a Windows-related background, it is important that we explore how virtual machines can be created on a Windows system.

VirtualBox

The most common hypervisor used for home or personal use is the OpenSource product provided by Oracle called VirtualBox. The following is the link for VirtualBox:

www.virtualbox.org/

VirtualBox is relatively easy to install and use. For your first exercise of this book, you will be challenged to do a Windows-related task.

Exercise

The exercise for VirtualBox will have the following steps. Not everything will be shown, so be sure to read the options carefully and select what best suits you.

1. Open a web browser and download VirtualBox for Windows hosts.

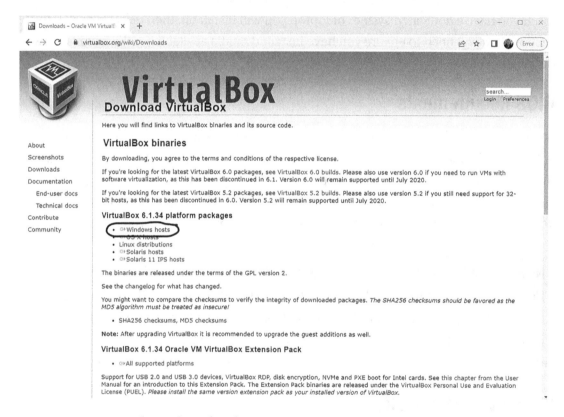

Figure 4-2.   *VirtualBox download site*

2. Double-click the downloaded file and install VirtualBox.

Figure 4-3. *First VirtualBox install scree*

3. Ensure that the bridge networking options are selected.

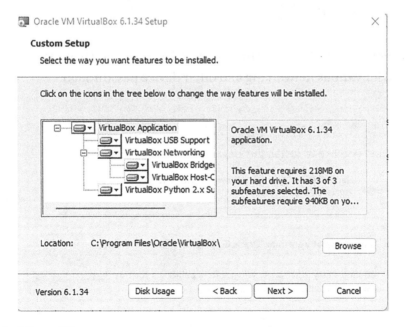

Figure 4-4. *VirtualBox custom setup screen*

4. Be prepared that during the install, you will have a drop in
    network connectivity. This is where your network card is linked
    with any virtual networking that is created.

Figure 4-5. *Adding network interfaces with VirtualBox*

5. Accept and install devices that Oracle tries to install. These will be
    used for various networking and other device passthrough.

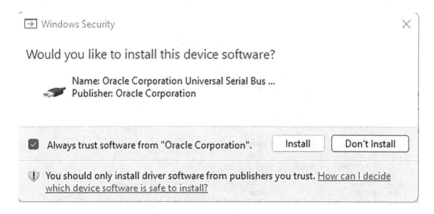

Figure 4-6. *VirtualBox virtual driver installation*

6. Once installed, VirtualBox should look similar to Figure 4-7.

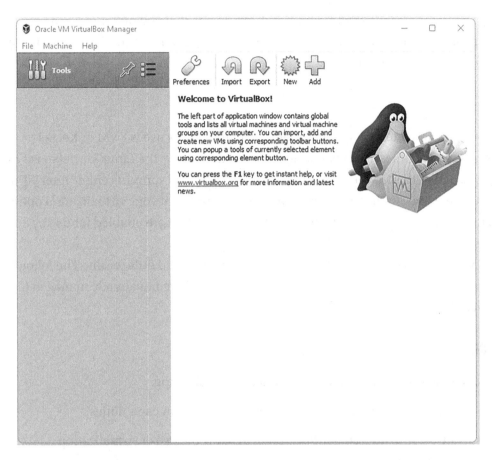

Figure 4-7. *VirtualBox main screen when opened*

Note   For now, we will leave VirtualBox as is and explain more about its configuration when required. If you want to break from the book and have a bit of a play, I would recommend trying to install another Windows virtual machine or whichever operating system you are comfortable with. This is really just for you to get used to the concept of creating virtual machines.

Linux Virtualization

Once you are more familiar with Linux and you decide that you prefer to use a Linux desktop for your continued learning, you will want to install and configure your Linux virtualization environment.

KVM

The common and often the default option that Linux users use is KVM or Kernel-based virtual machines. KVM is a kernel module that allows the Linux kernel to act as a hypervisor. For this to work, KVM requires that your CPU supports either Intel VT or AMD-V extensions. Earlier in this section, we discussed that your virtualization options need to be enabled in your BIOS. It is these extensions that are enabled for use by a hypervisor.

KVM is native to Linux as it can be installed and enabled quite easily. The following exercise is going to step you through the process if you have not already managed to figure it out.

Exercise

This exercise assumes that you have completed the following:

- Linux installed on a system that has virtualization capabilities.

- BIOS configuration has been done to allow the use of virtualization on your system.

- Your system has access to the Internet or repositories that will allow the installation of packages.

To install and configure your Linux system to be used as a virtualization platform, follow these steps:

1. Open a terminal screen that can be used for typing commands.
    This can be seen in Figure 4-8.

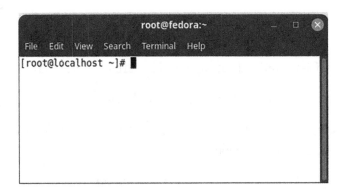

Figure 4-8. *Linux terminal screen*

2. The first command we will run is to verify that your CPU and system are capable of being used as a virtualization platform. In your terminal window, run the following command:

```
# cat /proc/cpuinfo | egrep "vmx|svm"
```

If your output does not look similar to Figure 4-9 or does not show that vmx or svm flags are present in your CPU, you either have not enabled the features in your BIOS or your system does not have the capability.

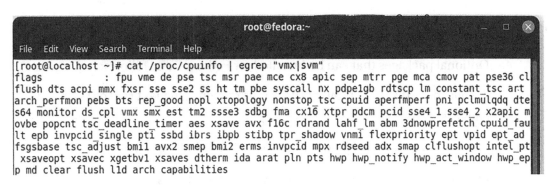

Figure 4-9. *Output from cat /proc/cpuinfo command*

3. Provided step 2 was successful, you can now run the following commands to install the basic packages required to use KVM.

3.1 Install required packages.

On Fedora or similar distros, you can run the following:

```
# sudo dnf -y install bridge-utils libvirt virt-install qemu-kvm
```

On Ubuntu or similar, you can run the following:

```
# sudo apt -y install bridge-utils cpu-checker libvirt-clients
libvirt-daemon qemu qemu-kvm
```

3.2 Verify that kernel modules have been loaded.

```
# lsmod | grep kvm
```

Your output for the lsmod command should look similar to Figure 4-10.

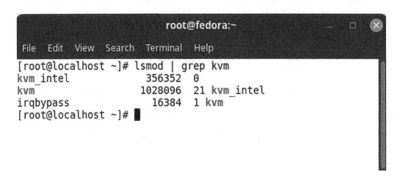

Figure 4-10. *lsmod output*

4. Optional packages that can be installed for Fedora are as follows:

```
# sudo dnf install libvirt-devel virt-top libguestfs-tools
guestfs-tools
```

For Ubuntu or similar, you will need to use the following command:

```
# sudo apt -y install virt-top libguestfs-tools
```

Note   As you will notice, there is a difference between the packages for Fedora and Ubuntu. Currently, the Ubuntu repositories on my system do not have all the packages that the Fedora repositories have. It could be that the tools have been packaged differently or do not exist in Ubuntu at this stage.

4.1 It is advised to install virt-manager as a minimum so you can create virtual machines with a graphical tool later.
For Fedora, you can use the following:

```
# sudo dnf -y install virt-manager
```

For Ubuntu or similar, you can use the following:

```
# apt -y install virt-manager
```

5. The final commands you will need to run on both Fedora and Ubuntu are as follows:

```
# sudo systemctl start libvirtd & sudo systemctl enable libvirtd
```

Creating Virtual Machines

Before we can start the exercises where we will be installing our different community Linux distributions, we must ensure that we all know how to create virtual machines.

As this book has targeted the use of VirtualBox and KVM, we will use these to create some very basic VMs for you to understand the process.

In the following exercises, we will use an Ubuntu ISO image that will be used in the Ubuntu installation section. Feel free to use any image you have available. The purpose of these exercises is only here to show you how to create a basic virtual machine. The operating system install will follow shortly after this section.

VirtualBox

If you choose to use Windows as your learning platform, this section is for you.

Exercise

1. Open VirtualBox by finding it in your start menu. If you cannot find VirtualBox, double-check that it was installed correctly.

2. To create a new virtual machine in VirtualBox, you need to click on the light blue circle shape icon named "New". This can be seen in Figure 4-11.

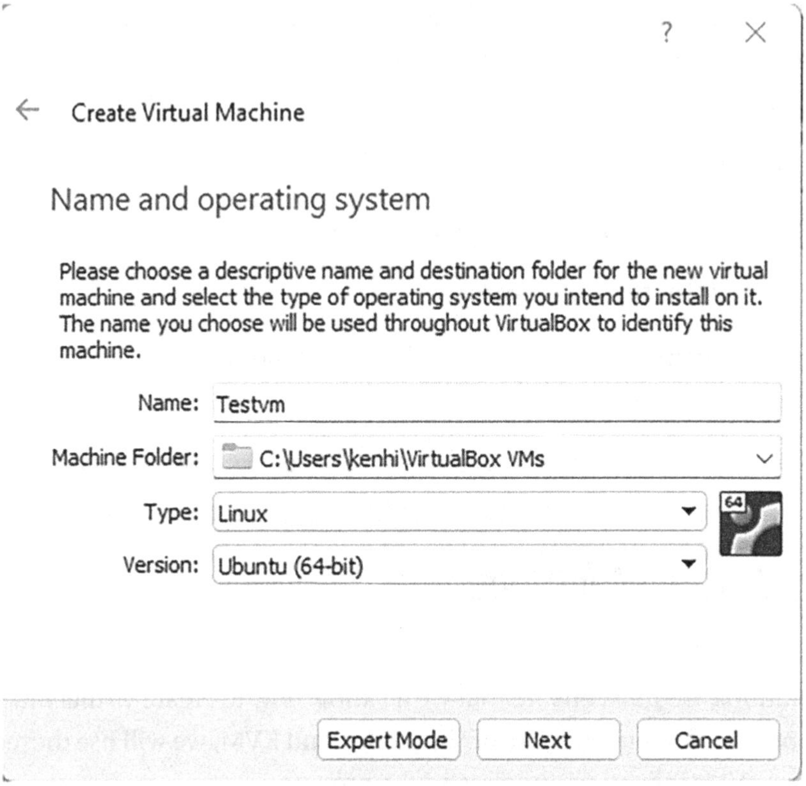

Figure 4-11. *VirtualBox screen to create a virtual machine*

3. Give your virtual machine a name; choose the operating system type and the version of the operating system you are installing, and if you want to change where the virtual machine is stored, you can change the location in the Machine Folder drop-down. When you are done, click Next.

4. Select how much memory you wish to give your virtual machine, then click Next.

5. The next four screens are all about the hard disk you wish to use for your virtual machine. Select the defaults until you reach the disk sizing options. You can leave it at 10GB for this exercise, but in the future, you may want to adjust for larger virtual machine requirements.

6. Once you are done, click the Create button. This will create the back virtual machine environment. This can be seen in Figure 4-12.

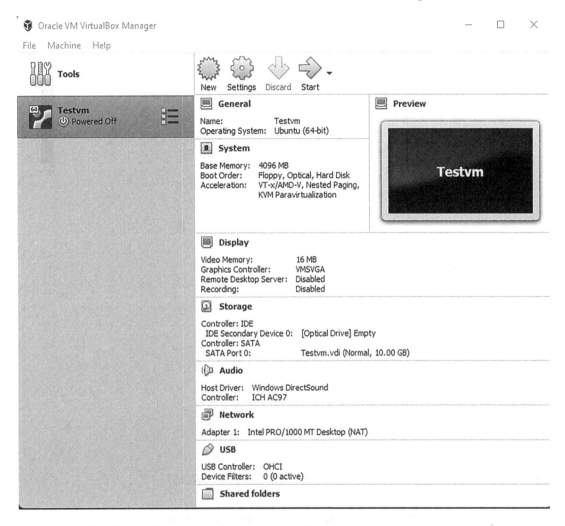

Figure 4-12. *VirtualBox virtual machine information*

7. The final step you will need to do is to attach install media to your virtual CDROM. To do this, you need to click the "settings" icon, and click the Storage side menu. In the Storage settings, you will be able to see the Controller:IDE. By clicking the Empty CDROM, you will expose the Optical Drive settings, where you will see another blue disk icon. By clicking this icon, you will be able to browse where you have downloaded your install media. Click Ok once you have attached your install media.

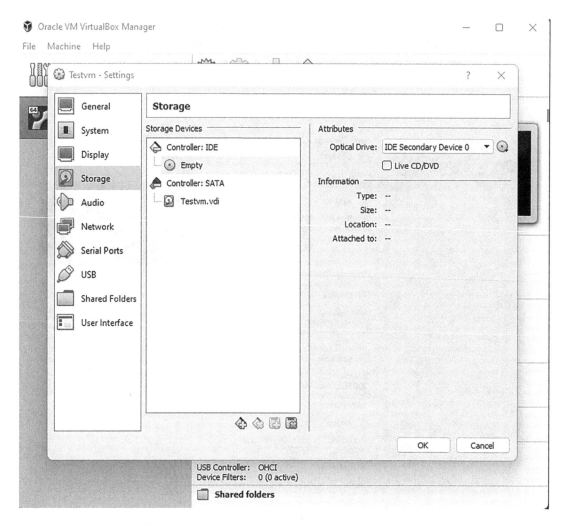

Figure 4-13. *VirtualBox connects the ISO image to CDROM*

8.   The only thing left to do is to start your virtual machine. To do this, click the green arrow icon appropriately named Start. This will open a virtual machine console for you to see your virtual machine boot process.

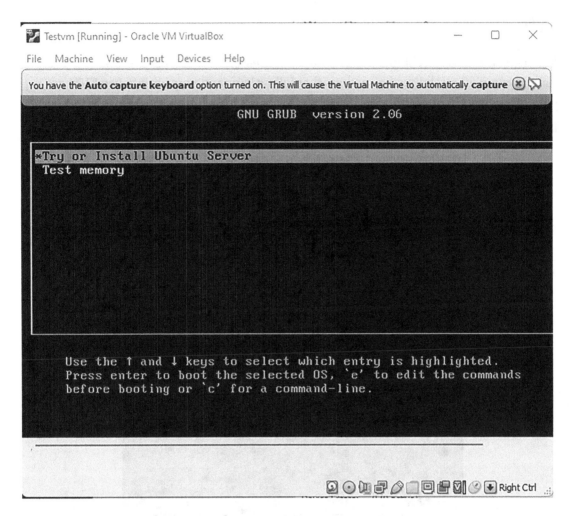

Figure 4-14. *VirtualBox console*

Note   The virtual machine boot process is very quick and will often be too quick for you to trigger any boot menu. If you want to change your boot order, you will need to set your virtual machine settings to boot the virtual machine into the boot menu.

KVM

If you are already using Linux or if you started by using Windows and built your own Linux system after reading the sections that follow later and now wish to use KVM as your virtualization platform, these steps are for you. If you still choose to use Windows, please feel free to skip this section and read further on.

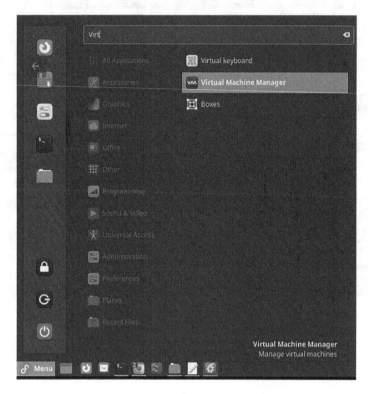

Figure 4-15. *Finding Virtual Machine Manager in Fedora*

Exercise

1. For KVM virtual machines, we will be using the Virt-Manager tool. Find virt-manager and open it.

    If you cannot find anything in your system by the name of virt-manager, you more than likely did not install the package. Go back a few pages and run the package installation, then return here.

2. Virt-manager should look similar to Figure 4-16 when opened.

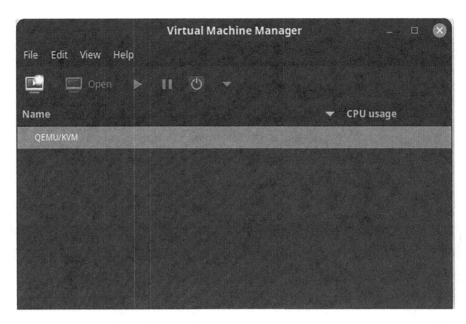

Figure 4-16. *Virtual Machine Manager*

3. Create a new virtual machine by clicking the icon that is circled in Figure 4-17.

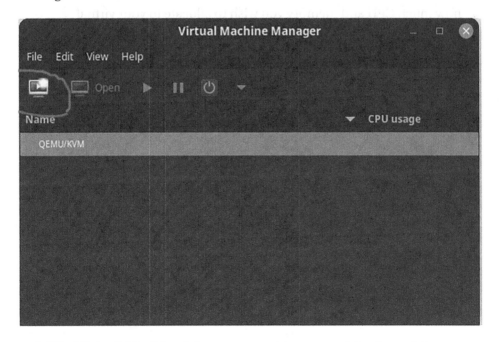

Figure 4-17. *Virtual Machine Manager creates a new virtual machine*

4. On the first screen, you will be presented with options on how you would like to install your operating system. For now, we will only use the first option "Local install media (ISO image or CDROM)". The other options you can experiment with later if you want. Once done, click forward.

5. On the next screen, you will need to browse to where you downloaded or saved your installed ISO image. Select the image and then click forward.

Warning   The location for images will sometimes default to where your actual VM disks will appear. Selecting the wrong disk can sometimes corrupt your running VM. Be sure to carefully select the downloaded or saved ISO images.

---

6. If the operating system cannot be detected automatically, you can deselect the check box that automatically will detect. You will need to then find the operating system or select "Generic OS".

7. The screen shown in Figure 4-18 will be where you configure how much CPU and memory you wish to allocate to your virtual machine. For this exercise, I will allocate 2 CPUs and 4GB of memory.

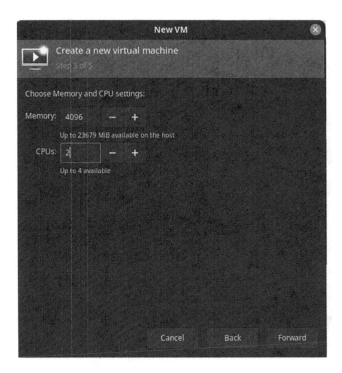

Figure 4-18. *Virtual machine resources*

8. Click forward once you have set your resource sizing.

9. The next screen in Figure 4-19 will determine how large you want to set your virtual machine's boot disk. Set the size you wish, then click forward.

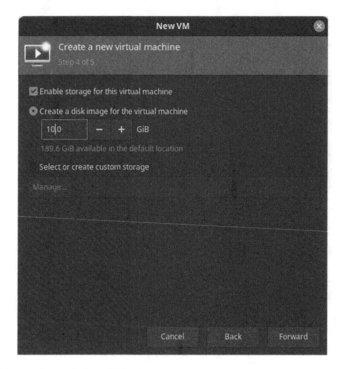

Figure 4-19. Virtual machine disk size

10.   The final screen is where you can make any last customizations if
       you prefer. If you don't want to do anything else, you can click the
       Finish button. This will then start your virtual machine and attach
       the ISO image to boot first in your VM. From there, you can then
       run through your operating system installation, something we will
       do in the next section.

Installation Media

So far in the chapter, we have mostly spoken about virtual machines and how to
create them. We also discussed how to attach downloaded ISO images to those virtual
machines. What do you do though if you prefer to not use a virtual machine?

For this, you have a couple of options.

Burn Image

The first and probably the least likely option to be used these days is to "Burn" your ISO image to a blank DVD disk. Most operating systems that install media these days are pushing the limits of what will fit on a blank DVD, which is why this option is less likely. However, if you do have the blank disks and you do prefer this method, feel free to "Burn" away.

USB Drive

The most likely of all of the install media options is to make a USB drive bootable with your operating system install media. As this is the most common option, let's look at how you would do this.

MediaWriter

Fortunately, the Fedora community has been kind enough to develop a graphical tool that can be used to make a USB drive bootable from an ISO image. In the following link, you can download or follow the installation procedure to use the MediaWriter tool:

```
https://docs.fedoraproject.org/en-US/fedora/latest/install-guide/
install/Preparing_for_Installation/
```

Ventoy

Another tool I was recently shown for bootable USB installations is Ventoy. Ventoy is an extremely useful tool if you wish to deploy multiple operating systems from a single USB drive. No need to wipe the drive and recreate install media when you want to build a different operating system.

Ventoy can be downloaded from the following link:

```
www.ventoy.net/en/index.html
```

Learning Exercise

As your first learning exercise, I challenge you to learn about building install media on a USB drive on your own. Attempt to do the following:

1. Download both the MediaWriter tool and the Ventoy ISO image.

2. Using MediaWriter, write the Ventoy ISO image to a USB drive.

3. Follow Ventoy instructions on how to add more ISO images to the USB drive.

4. Test your new Ventoy bootable USB drive and see if you can add the Ubuntu Server, OpenSUSE Server, and Fedora Server ISO images to the drive. This will help with the next few sections if you choose to install via USB.

Network Install

The last method that can be used for installing operating systems is to use a network boot server of some kind. There are a few options available that can be used such as Cobbler, Foreman, or Red Hat Satellite Server, but as these systems do involve a fair degree of complexity to install and configure, they are out of scope for this book and not advisable yet to spend too much time while you are learning.

In my book *Linux System Administration for the 2020s*, you can learn more about these types of systems, as the book gives a high-level overview of many things an enterprise Linux administrator should know in today's Linux administration world.

If you do still want to know more about network boot systems, it is recommended to read the official installation documentation.

Installing Linux

Now that we have covered a fair amount of preparation work required to install an operating system, we are finally ready to install a Linux environment.

Lab Environment

Before we install our first Linux environment, it is necessary to share my working environment specifications with you in case you wish to follow exactly what I have done.

Hypervisor

All of my Linux environments for this book will be hosted on the following:

- Fedora 34 as the Linux operating system

- KVM as the hypervisor environment

- Virt-manager used for graphical interface configuration of virtual machines

Installation Media

All operating system installations will be done using ISO images attached to virtual machines; the exercises in this book will tell you to do this, but if you choose to install via a different method, adjust accordingly. The installation steps for the operating systems should still be the same no matter which installation media option you choose.

Virtual Machine Sizing

All virtual machines for this book will default to the following specifications:

- 2 CPUs

- 4GB memory

- 20GB disk

If you choose to use a dedicated system, ensure the specifications are similar to the virtual machine specifications I will be using. Any systems under-specced may still work but could be slower and more frustrating to use.

Ubuntu

As our first Linux environment, I have decided to go with Ubuntu. Ubuntu is one of the more popular Linux distributions available today. Ubuntu has a couple different versions that can be installed; for this section, we will focus on installing the Ubuntu server variant.

Installation Media

Depending on where and how you want to install your Ubuntu server will determine how you prepare your installation media. You will still need to first download the Ubuntu server ISO image. This can be found at the following location:

`https://ubuntu.com/download/server`

Once downloaded, prepare your installation USB, DVD, or virtual machine to start the Ubuntu installation.

Basic Installation

When installing Linux, there are quite a few default options you can use and quite a few customizations you can perform. For the basic installation and what we will only focus on in this section is to install a basic deployment of Ubuntu server. You will need to do the following in the next few steps:

- Create a virtual machine to install your Ubuntu server in.

- Boot from your downloaded Ubuntu server ISO in your virtual machine.

If you decided to use a physical system instead of a virtual machine, ensure you have all your installation media prepared.

Create a Virtual Machine

For the first basic installation of the Ubuntu server, you will need to create a virtual machine. For this book, I am building my virtual machines using a KVM installation on my Fedora system.

1. Open virt-manager and create a new virtual machine by clicking the "Create virtual machine" button.

2. The virtual machine operating system will be installed using a downloaded ISO image for the Ubuntu server.

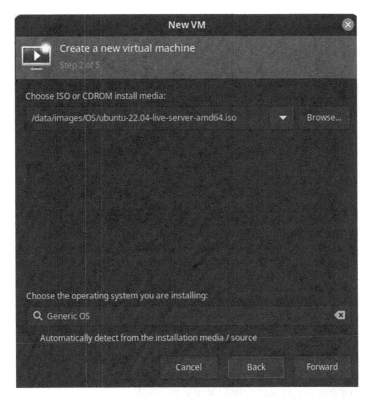

Figure 4-20. *Creating a virtual machine with an Ubuntu ISO image*

The operating system needs to be set to Generic OS as the latest version of the Ubuntu server has not appeared yet in the version of KVM I have installed.

3. For the virtual machine resources, set 4096 for memory and 4 vCPUs.

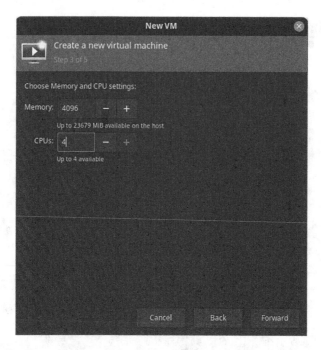

Figure 4-21. *Virtual machine resource sizing*

4.   For the operating system disk, leave at 20GB.

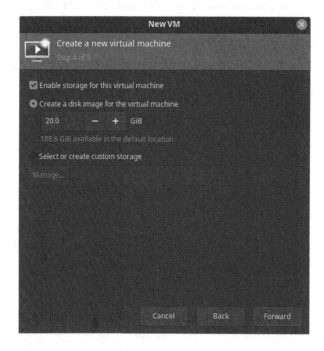

Figure 4-22. *Virtual machine disk sizing for an Ubuntu virtual machine*

5. The final stage of the virtual creation is to give your virtual machine a name and to ensure you are using the correct network. At this stage, you can also select if you wish to do any further customizations. In these early system builds, we will not be adding any customizations.

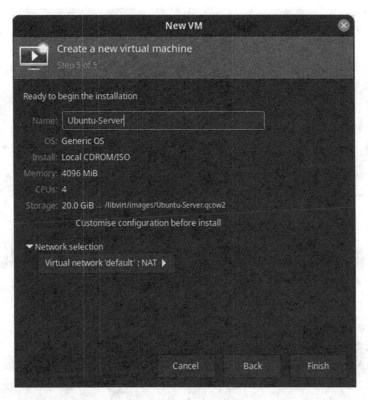

Figure 4-23. *Virtual machine name*

6. Click Finish; a console window will appear, which we will use to install our Ubuntu server.

Ubuntu Server Installation

If you are using a physical system to install the Ubuntu server, you will need to ensure that you have your installed media created and your system configured to boot from your media.

1. Once your physical system or virtual machine has been turned on, you will see the install media boot menu. If your boot process has been configured correctly and your install media is working as intended, you will see a screen similar to Figure 4-24. Select the first option, "Try or Install Ubuntu Server", and hit the Enter key.

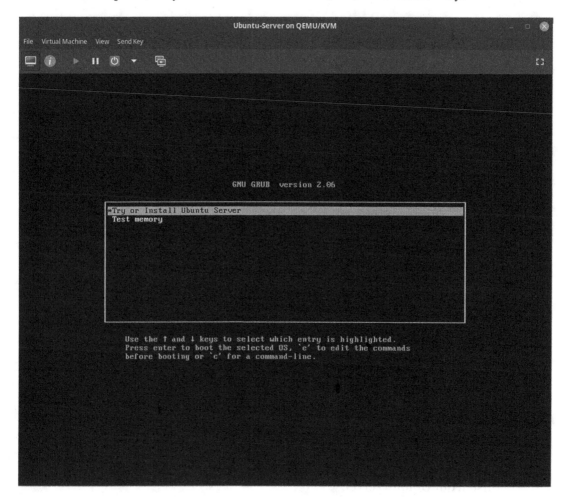

Figure 4-24. *Virtual Machine Manager console with an Ubuntu install option*

2. On the next text screen similar to Figure 4-25, choose the language you would like to use for your environment.

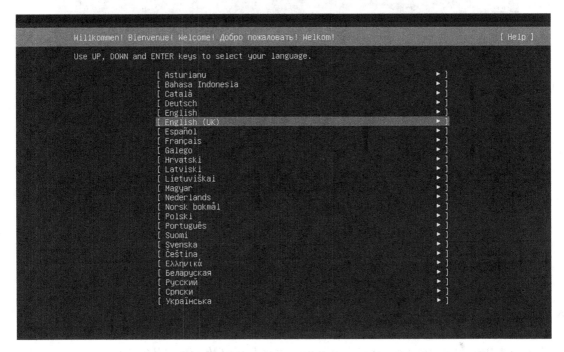

Figure 4-25. *Ubuntu language type*

3. Figure 4-26 shows that you may be prompted to use a newer version of the installer on the next step of the installation. This is purely up to you. For this book, I will continue without updating.

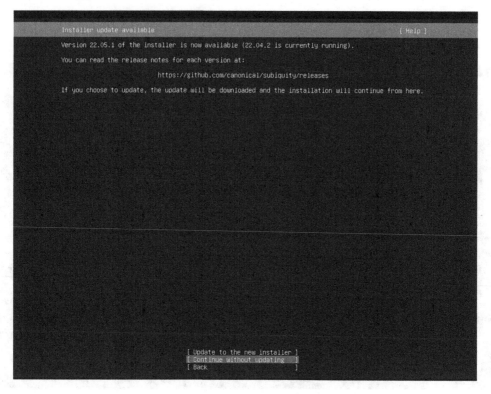

Figure 4-26. Ubuntu prompt for a newer version of the installer

4. On the next screen of the installer, select the keyboard layout you
   prefer and then select the "Done" option followed by pressing the
   Enter key.

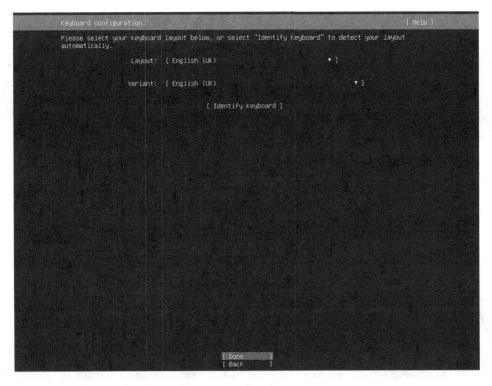

Figure 4-27. *Ubuntu keyboard layout selection*

5. On the next screen, you will be asked the kind of installation you wish to install. For now, we will use the default option selected and press the Enter key.

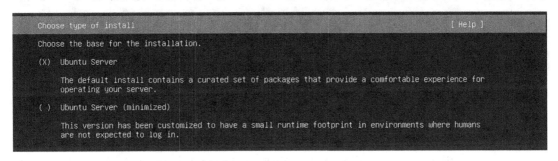

Figure 4-28. *Kind of Ubuntu installation*

6. The screen shown in Figure 4-29 will allow you to make network-related changes to your Ubuntu server. At this stage, we will stick with a DHCP IP address allocation.

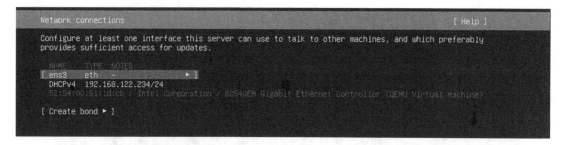

Figure 4-29. *Network configuration*

7. On the next screen, you will be asked if you want to use a proxy; for this basic installation, we will leave as is and press Enter.

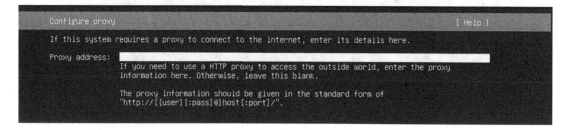

Figure 4-30. *Use a proxy with the Ubuntu installation*

8. On this screen similar to Figure 4-31, leave the default option selected and press the Enter key.

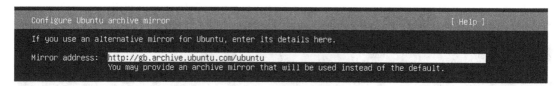

Figure 4-31. *Ubuntu archive mirror configuration*

9. The next screen should look similar to Figure 4-32. This is for you to configure the operating system disk partitions. For now, use the default options and press Enter.

Guided storage configuration
[Help]
Configure a guided storage layout, or create a custom one:
(X) Use an entire disk
[QEMU_HARDDISK_QM00001 local disk 20.000G ▾]
[X] Set up this disk as an LVM group
[ ] Encrypt the LVM group with LUKS
Passphrase:
Confirm passphrase:
( ) Custom storage layout

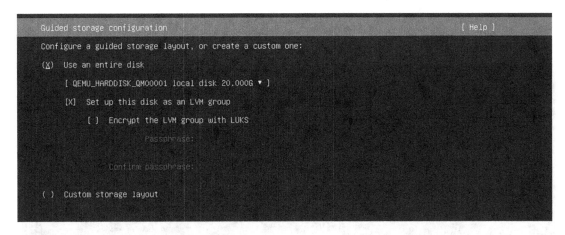

Figure 4-32. *Virtual machine disk partitioning*

10. A screen similar to Figure 4-33 will give you a summary of the disk configuration. We will continue to use the default values for now and press Enter.

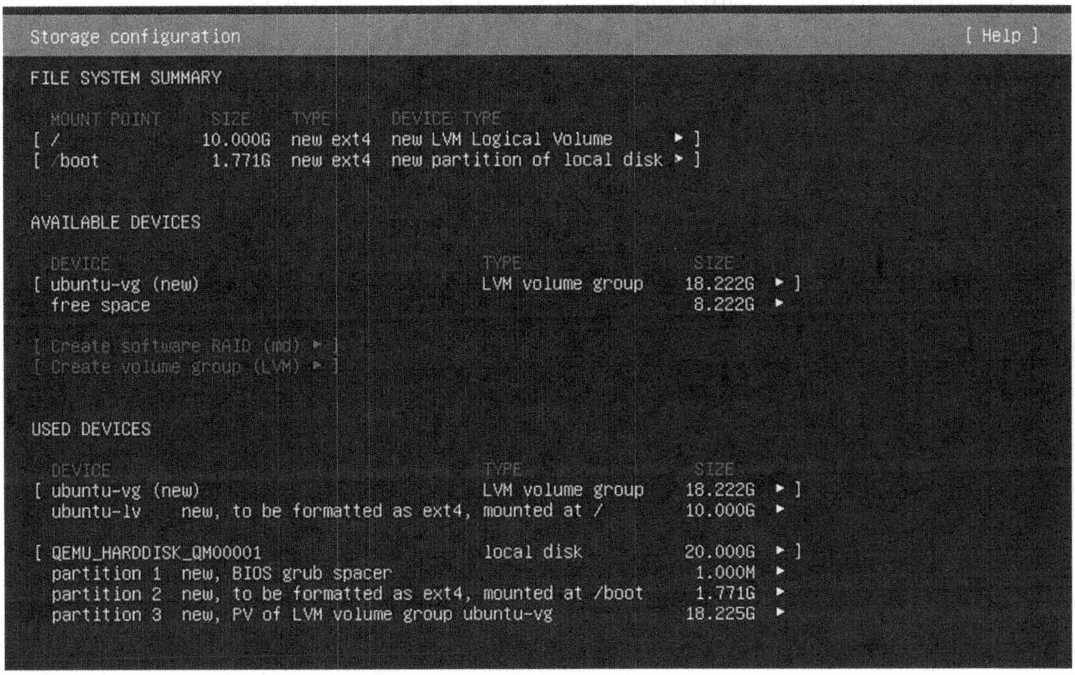

Storage configuration
[Help]
FILE SYSTEM SUMMARY
MOUNT POINT SIZE TYPE DEVICE TYPE
[/ 10.000G new ext4 new LVM Logical Volume ▸]
[/boot 1.771G new ext4 new partition of local disk ▸]
AVAILABLE DEVICES
DEVICE TYPE SIZE
[ubuntu-vg (new) LVM volume group 18.222G ▸]
free space 8.222G ▸
[Create software RAID (md) ▸]
[Create volume group (LVM) ▸]
USED DEVICES
DEVICE TYPE SIZE
[ubuntu-vg (new) LVM volume group 18.222G ▸]
ubuntu-lv new, to be formatted as ext4, mounted at / 10.000G ▸
[QEMU_HARDDISK_QM00001 local disk 20.000G ▸]
partition 1 new, BIOS grub spacer 1.000M ▸
partition 2 new, to be formatted as ext4, mounted at /boot 1.771G ▸
partition 3 new, PV of LVM volume group ubuntu-vg 18.225G ▸

Figure 4-33. *Summary of disk configuration*

11. When presented with a screen similar to Figure 4-34, select
    Continue and press Enter.

```
┌──────────────────────── Confirm destructive action ────────────────────────┐
│                                                                             │
│ Selecting Continue below will begin the installation process and            │
│ result in the loss of data on the disks selected to be formatted.           │
│                                                                             │
│ You will not be able to return to this or a previous screen once the        │
│ installation has started.                                                   │
│                                                                             │
│ Are you sure you want to continue?                                          │
│                                                                             │
│                         [ No            ]                                   │
│                         [ Continue      ]                                   │
│                                                                             │
└─────────────────────────────────────────────────────────────────────────────┘
```

Figure 4-34. *Confirm the destructive action*

12. When presented with a screen similar to Figure 4-35, you can
    create a username you wish to use and what name you want to call
    your server. It helps to match the virtual machine name, but this is
    up to you. Once done with the details, select the Done option and
    press Enter.

```
Profile setup                                                        [ Help ]

Enter the username and password you will use to log in to the system. You can configure SSH access on
the next screen but a password is still needed for sudo.

         Your name: Ken

  Your server's name: ubuntu-server
                      The name it uses when it talks to other computers.

    Pick a username: ken

   Choose a password: ***********

  Confirm your password: ***********_
```

Figure 4-35. *Create a new user screen*

13. The next screen similar to Figure 4-36 will ask if you wish to install the OpenSSH server. Tick the box by pressing the up arrow and pressing the spacebar.

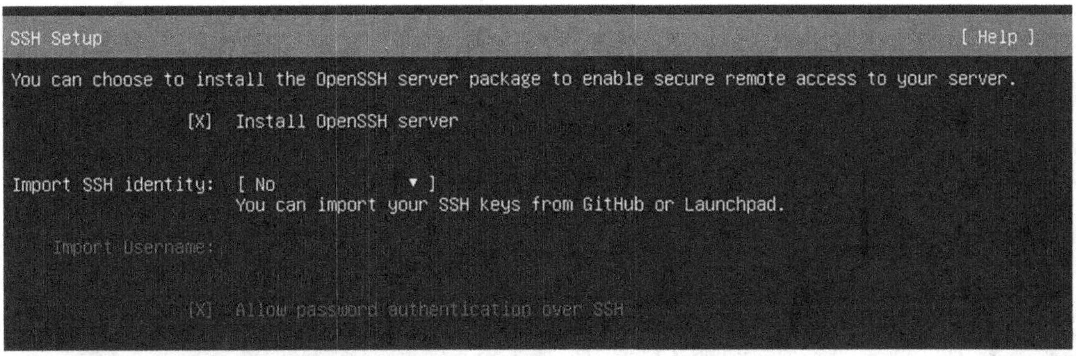

Figure 4-36. *Install the OpenSSH server*

14. For this basic installation, we will leave all the boxes unchecked. These are for configuring applications and services on your Ubuntu server.

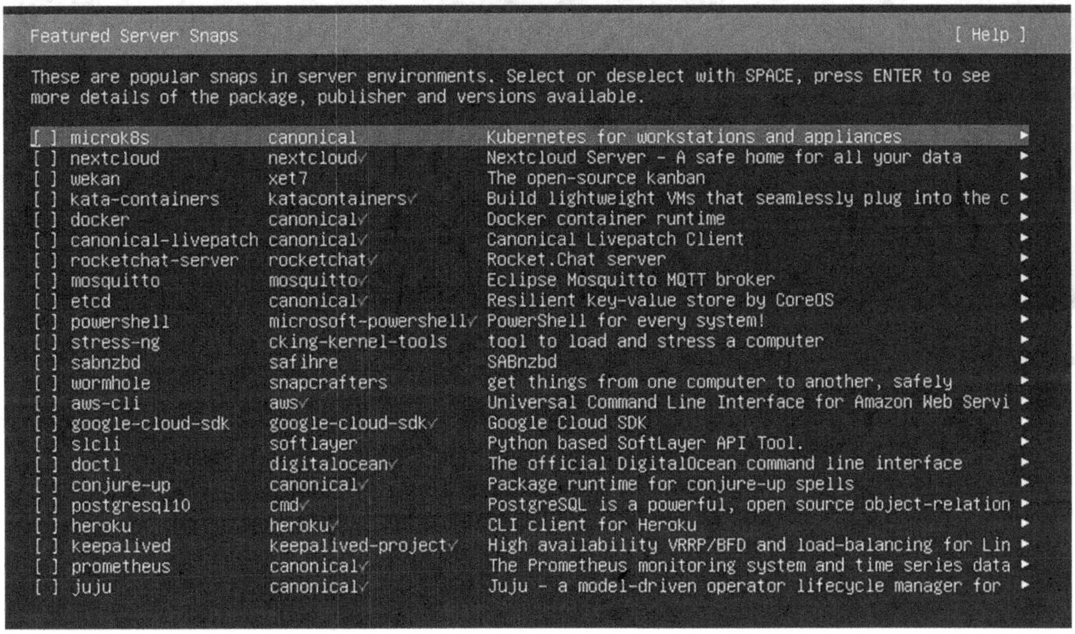

Figure 4-37. *Package installation options for Ubuntu*

15. Select the "Done" option and press Enter.

16. Your installation will begin.

17. Figure 4-38 shows what the installation process looks like.

```
Install complete!                                                       [ Help ]

            configuring partition: partition-2
            configuring lvm_volgroup: lvm_volgroup-0
            configuring lvm_partition: lvm_partition-0
            configuring format: format-1
            configuring mount: mount-1
            configuring mount: mount-0
    writing install sources to disk
       running 'curtin extract'
          curtin command extract
             acquiring and extracting image from cp:///tmp/tmpcqi1wfxy/mount
    configuring installed system
       running 'mount --bind /cdrom /target/cdrom'
       running 'curtin curthooks'
          curtin command curthooks
             configuring apt configuring apt
             installing missing packages
             configuring iscsi service
             configuring raid (mdadm) service
             installing kernel
             setting up swap
             apply networking config
             writing etc/fstab
             configuring multipath
             updating packages on target system
             configuring pollinate user-agent on target
             updating initramfs configuration
             configuring target system bootloader
             installing grub to target devices
       finalizing installation
          running 'curtin hook'
             curtin command hook
       executing late commands
final system configuration
   configuring cloud-init
   calculating extra packages to install
   installing openssh-server
      curtin command system-install
   downloading and installing security updates
      curtin command in-target -
```

Figure 4-38. *Ubuntu installation process*

18. When the installation completes, select the "Reboot now" option
     and press Enter. Your system will now reboot into your installed
     Ubuntu server.

> **Warning**   If your Ubuntu server installation complains that the CDROM could not be unmounted, you may need to manually disconnect your virtual CDROM. Once you have done that, return to your console and press Enter.

Basic Exercise

For your first hands-on exercise installing a Linux operating system, you are going to install your own Ubuntu server.

Your Ubuntu server must be built with the following configuration.

Virtual Machine

Create a virtual machine in KVM or VirtualBox with the following specifications:

- 4096MB of memory

- 4 vCPUs

- 10GB disk

- Default network

Ubuntu Server

Your Ubuntu server must be installed with the following configuration options:

- The server name must be "ubuntu-server".

- Your network must use DHCP; if you do not have DHCP, set a static address.

- Do not install any applications and services and do not install using the minimal option.

- Use the default disk layout from the installer.

> **Important**   Do not delete this virtual machine; it will be used in future exercises.

Exercise Outcome

At the end of the exercise, you should have a working Fedora server system that you can log in to with your username and password created during the installation.

Custom Installations

From the previous basic installation screens, you will have noticed a few opportunities for customizations. It really is in these areas where you can tweak and configure your Ubuntu server to match your expectations.

Some of the customizations you can consider for future installs are as follows:

- Network adapter configured with a static IP address.

- Disk configuration changed to match a better recommended layout. This could include a separate /home or /var partition. There are many hardening standards available today that require these kinds of changes.

- Applications or services installed. Or simply a minimal installation.

Optional Custom Exercise

As an optional exercise, install the Ubuntu server again with the following differences.

Virtual Machine

Create a virtual machine in KVM or VirtualBox with the following specifications:

- 4096MB of memory and 4 vCPUs

- 20GB disk

- Default network

Ubuntu Server

Your Ubuntu server must be installed with the following configuration options:

- The server name should be "ubuntu-server".

- Create a static IP address.

- Create a disk layout with a separate /home or /var partition. Both should be no smaller than 5GB.

- Ensure that Docker and Keepalived are installed.

Important   Do not delete this virtual machine if you deleted the basic installation; it will be used in future exercises.

Fedora Server

After a successful first installation of Ubuntu, let's continue the momentum and have a look at what a Fedora server looks like. Fedora may not be as popular a desktop as Ubuntu but Fedora does have one quality that makes it extremely important to learn in today's Linux world. Fedora is the upstream to Red Hat Enterprise Linux, the most widely used enterprise Linux distribution today. Getting a good understanding of Fedora and how it can be used will definitely help you in any future Linux roles.

Installation Media

As with the Ubuntu server installation, you will need to download your installation media for your Fedora server before you can continue with this section. The Fedora install media can be found at the following location:

    https://getfedora.org/en/server/download/

Once downloaded, prepare your installation USB, DVD, or virtual machine to start the Fedora installation.

Basic Installation

As with Ubuntu, Fedora has quite a few default options you can use and quite a few customizations you can perform. For our basic installation, we will need to do the following:

- Create another virtual machine to install your Fedora server in.

- Boot from your downloaded Fedora server ISO in your virtual machine.

If you decided to use a physical system instead of a virtual machine, ensure you have all your installation media prepared.

> **Important**   If you have limited resources on your KVM system, feel free to shut
> down your Ubuntu server. When we need it later, we can start it up again.

Create a Virtual Machine

For the basic installation of Fedora, you will need to create a new virtual machine. For
this book, I will be building all my virtual machines with KVM on my Fedora working
environment.

1. Open virt-manager and create a new virtual machine by clicking
   the "Create virtual machine" button.

2. The virtual machine operating system will be installed using a
   downloaded ISO image for the Fedora server.

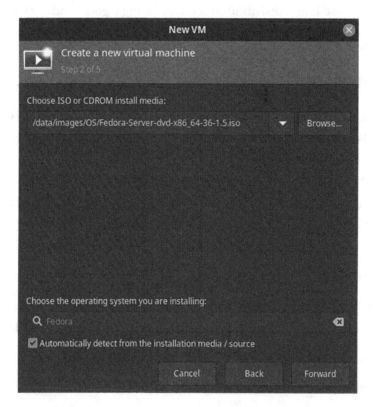

Figure 4-39. *Virtual Machine Manager new virtual machine with a Fedora
ISO image*

Unlike the Ubuntu installation, the operating system is able to be automatically detected. Feel free to tick the box to automatically detect the operating system. If you prefer to use Generic OS, you can do that too.

3. For the virtual machine resources, set 4096 for memory and 4 vCPUs.

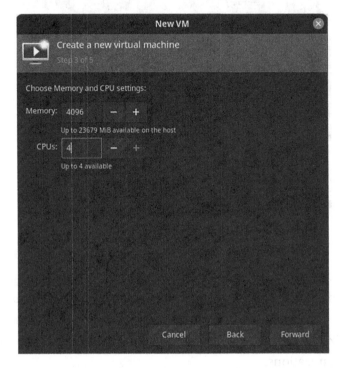

Figure 4-40. *Fedora virtual machine resource configuration*

4. For the operating system disk, leave at 20GB.

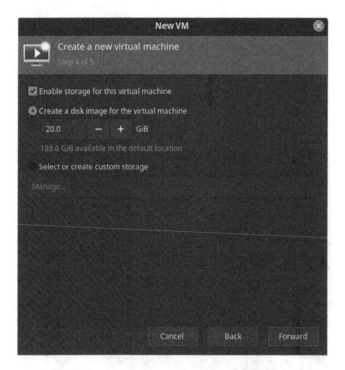

Figure 4-41. *Setting the Fedora virtual machine disk size*

5. End the virtual creation process by giving your virtual machine a
    name, and very much like the Ubuntu installation, ensure you are
    using the correct network. If you wish, you can select to do further
    customizations. In these early system builds, we will not be adding
    any customizations.

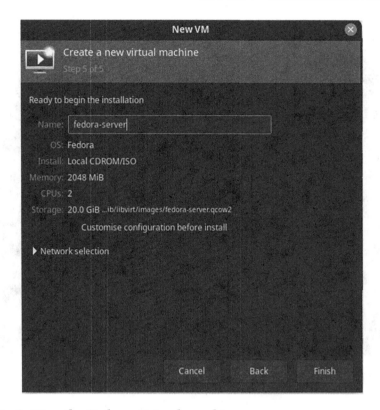

Figure 4-42. *Setting the Fedora virtual machine name*

6. Click Finish; a console window will appear, which we will use to install our Fedora server.

Fedora Server Installation

The following steps will demonstrate the basic Fedora server installation. We will avoid doing any customizations and stick to defaults where possible.

1. Turn on your physical or virtual system that will be used for your Fedora server installation. You should be prompted with a screen similar to Figure 4-43 if your boot process on your physical system or virtual machine was configured correctly.

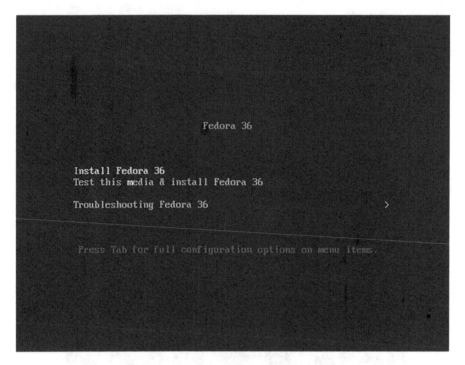

Figure 4-43. *Fedora installation screen from boot media*

2. If you decide to use a physical system with a DVD disk or any removal media that could potentially have issues, select the "Test this media & install Fedora 36". However, if you are installing into a virtual machine with the downloaded ISO mounted in your virtual machine, you will be fairly safe to skip the check and just select the "Install Fedora 36" option.

Important   If you do have problems with the media, download a new copy and transfer to your preferred installation media.

---

3. Once you choose to install the Fedora server, you will see a graphical screen similar to Figure 4-44. Select your preferred language option and click continue. Yes, you can use your mouse. If you do not have a mouse attached, you can tab to the button you wish to use and press the spacebar.

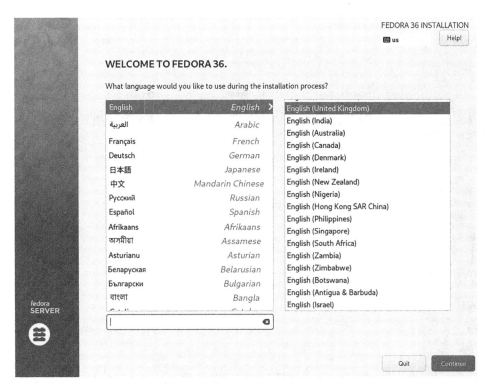

Figure 4-44. *Fedora installation welcome screen*

4. The next screen will look similar to Figure 4-45. You will need to
    make a few changes, but all will be using default options.

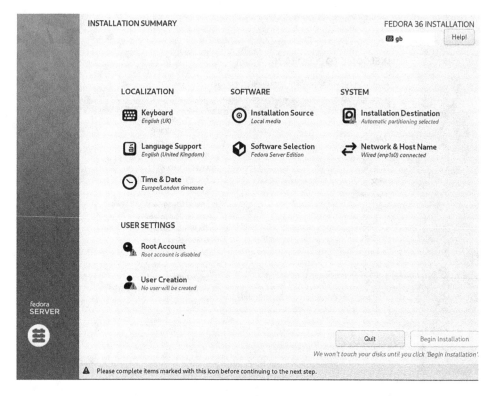

Figure 4-45. *Fedora installation main screen*

5.   The first customization, or lack of customization in this case, will
be the installation destination. Click the "Installation Destination"
button. The new screen will appear similar to Figure 4-46.

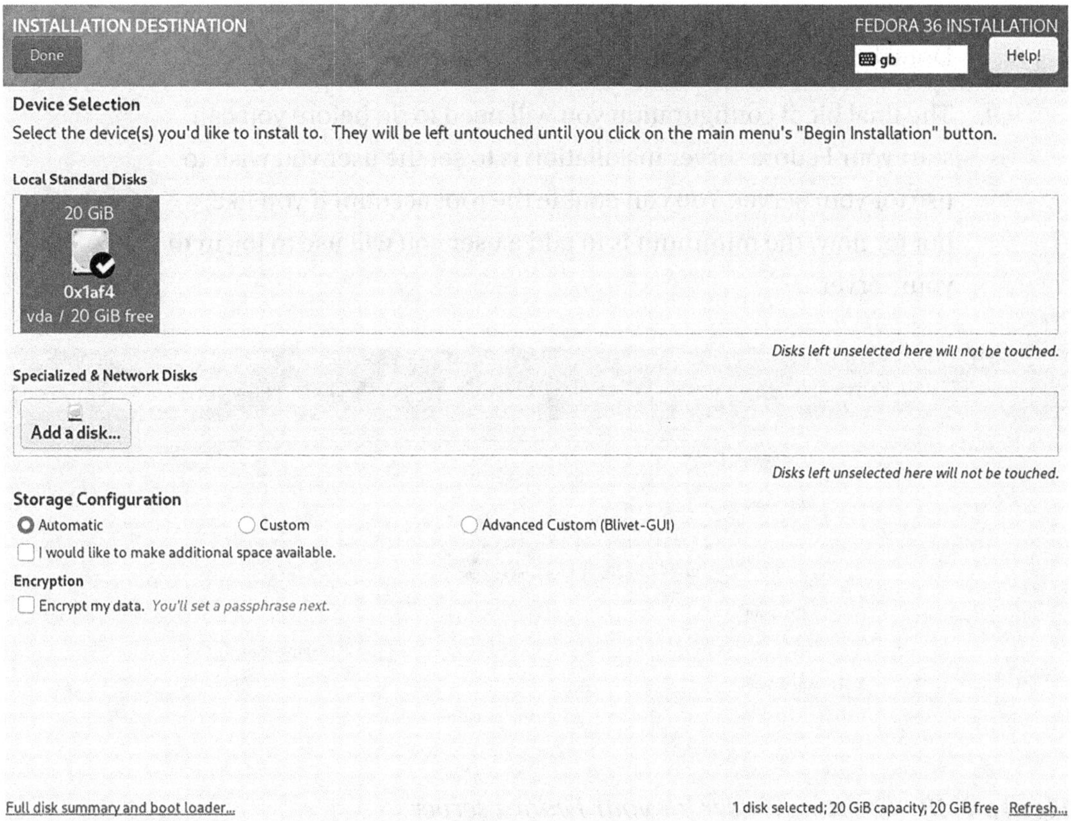

INSTALLATION DESTINATION   FEDORA 36 INSTALLATION

Done   ⌨ gb   Help!

Device Selection

Select the device(s) you'd like to install to. They will be left untouched until you click on the main menu's "Begin Installation" button.

Local Standard Disks

20 GiB

0x1af4
vda / 20 GiB free

Disks left unselected here will not be touched.

Specialized & Network Disks

Add a disk...

Disks left unselected here will not be touched.

Storage Configuration

○ Automatic   ○ Custom   ○ Advanced Custom (Blivet-GUI)

☐ I would like to make additional space available.

Encryption

☐ Encrypt my data. *You'll set a passphrase next.*

Full disk summary and boot loader...   1 disk selected; 20 GiB capacity; 20 GiB free   Refresh...

Figure 4-46. *Select the destination disk for installation*

6. Click the disk you wish to use for your installation until you see a tick appear. For the tick to appear for me, I had to click twice. Once done, click the Done button.

7. Once you are back on the main installation screen, the next bit of configuration you will do is setting the hostname of your new server. Click the "Network & Hostname" button and fill in your hostname in the box that looks similar to that shown in Figure 4-47.

Host Name: Apply

Figure 4-47. *Setting a system hostname*

8. Once you have added a hostname, click apply and then the Done button.

9. The final bit of configuration you will need to do before you can start your Fedora server installation is to set the user you wish to use for your server. You can enable the root account if you like, but for now, the minimum is to add a user you will use to log in to your server.

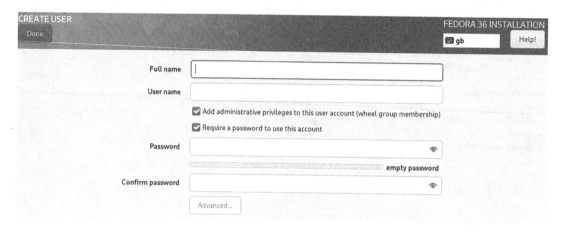

Figure 4-48. Creating a user for your Fedora server

10. Click the "Begin Installation" button to start your server installation.

11. Let your installation run through all the steps it needs to complete to have your server up and running.

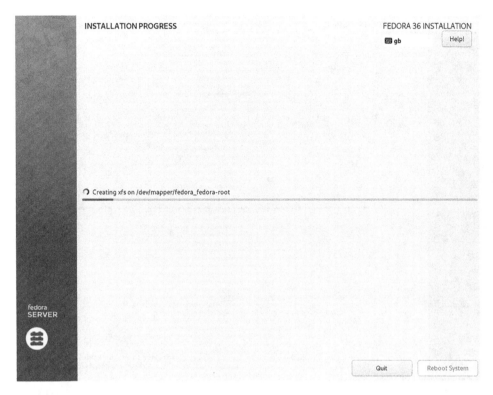

Figure 4-49. *Fedora installation progress*

12. When the installation has completed, click the "Reboot System" button.

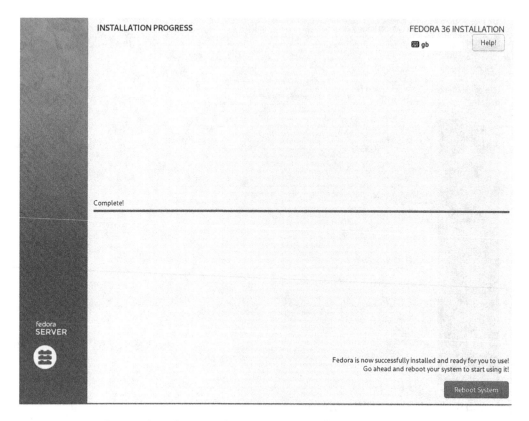

Figure 4-50. *Reboot after the installation screen*

13. Once your system has rebooted, you can now log in with the user
     account you created during the installation.

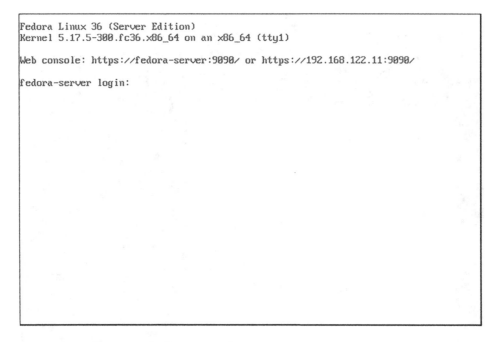

```
Fedora Linux 36 (Server Edition)
Kernel 5.17.5-300.fc36.x86_64 on an x86_64 (tty1)

Web console: https://fedora-server:9090/ or https://192.168.122.11:9090/

fedora-server login:
```

Figure 4-51. *Fedora ready for you to log in*

14. You can also manage your Fedora server via a web browser; if you noticed in the previous screen, there is a URL you can use to open your Fedora system's configuration.

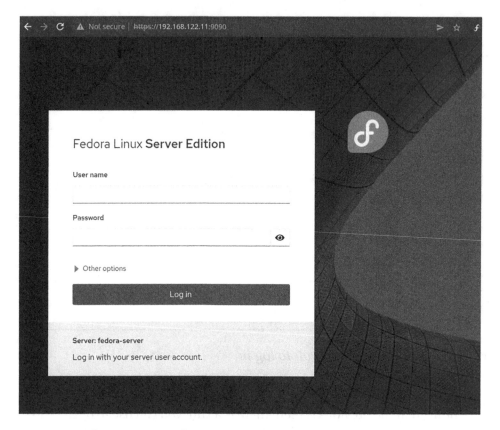

Figure 4-52. *Fedora server web management page*

Note   You will get a browser warning that the site is not safe, click the advanced button and then click the "proceed to website" option.

Basic Exercise

After doing your first basic exercise, installing an Ubuntu server should be straight forward. Since all the steps have been explained already, it is just up to you now to learn them for yourself.

For this exercise, you will need to build your own Fedora server; this again can be in a virtual machine or physical system, whichever you have decided to do.

Your Fedora server must be built with the following configuration if you choose to use a virtual machine.

Virtual Machine

Create a virtual machine in KVM or VirtualBox with the following specifications:

- 4096MB of memory, 4 vCPUs

- 10GB disk

- Default network

Fedora Server

Your Fedora server must be installed with the following configuration options:

- The server name must be "fedora-server".

- Your network IP address must use DHCP; if you do not have DHCP, then set a static IP address.

- Do not install any applications and services and do not install using the minimal option. Use all default package installation options.

- Use the default disk layout provided by the installer.

Important   Do not delete this virtual machine; it will be used in future exercises.

Exercise Outcome

At the end of the exercise, you should have a working Fedora server system that you can log in to with your username and password created during the installation.

Custom Installations

Customizing your Fedora server installation is a little less complicated than the Ubuntu server installation. The options are all driven by a graphical installer with more than intuitive options. Where customizations could be slightly trickier could be around disk configuration layout. Even then, if you read the options carefully, you can easily make sense of what is available.

As previously with the Ubuntu server installation, Fedora server does give you the following customization options during the installation:

- Network configuration

- Disk layout configuration

- Package installation options

- Date/time and time zone settings

- Keyboard and language options

Optional Custom Exercise

As an optional custom exercise, repeat the installation of your Fedora server, but this time customize the following.

Fedora Server

Your Fedora server must be installed with the following configuration options:

- The server name should be "fedora-server".

- Create a static IP address.

- Create a disk layout with a separate /home and /var partition. Both should be no smaller than 2GB.

- Ensure that your Fedora server is configured to be a web server.

Important   Do not delete this virtual machine if you deleted the basic installation; it will be used in future exercises.

OpenSUSE

The third Linux distribution worth learning how to install is OpenSUSE. OpenSUSE is the upstream to another popular enterprise Linux distribution: SUSE Linux Enterprise Server (SLES). Most major Linux-using organizations will be either using RHEL, SLES, or Ubuntu.

Installation Media

All Linux operating system installation will need installation media. You will need to download you own media for your openSUSE server before you continue. For the installations in this section and for all our OpenSUSE install we will do from here onward, we will be using the Leap version of OpenSUSE. The OpenSUSE install media can be found at the following location:

`https://get.opensuse.org/leap/15.3/#download`

When downloading your ISO images for your installation media, make sure you are downloading the correct version for your system architecture. If you are using x86_64 hardware, be sure you download the x86_64 version. Once downloaded, prepare your installation USB, DVD, or virtual machine to start the OpenSUSE installation.

Basic Installation

As with both Ubuntu and Fedora, there are again quite a few default options you can use during the installation and a few customizations you can perform. For our basic OpenSUSE installation, we will need to do the following:

- Create another virtual machine to install an OpenSUSE server in.

- Boot from the downloaded OpenSUSE server ISO mounted in a virtual machine.

Important   If you have limited resources on your KVM system, feel free to shut down your Ubuntu and Fedora servers. When we need them later, we can start them up again.

Create a Virtual Machine

For the basic installation of OpenSUSE, we will need to create a new virtual machine. For this book, I will be building all my virtual machines with KVM on my Fedora working environment.

1. Open virt-manager and create a new virtual machine by clicking the "Create virtual machine" button.

2. The virtual machine operating system will be installed using a downloaded ISO image for OpenSUSE server.

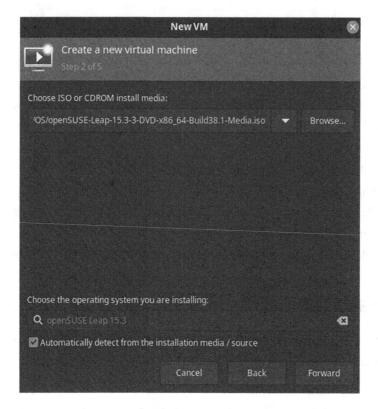

Figure 4-53. *Create a new virtual machine with an OpenSUSE ISO image*

Very much like the Fedora installation, the operating system is able to be automatically detected. Feel free to tick the box to automatically detect the operating system. If you prefer to use Generic OS, you can do that too.

3. For the virtual machine resources, set 4096 for memory and 4 vCPUs.

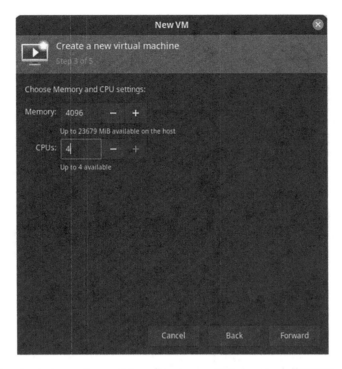

Figure 4-54. *Setting virtual machine resources for the OpenSUSE virtual machine*

4. For the operating system disk, leave at 20GB.

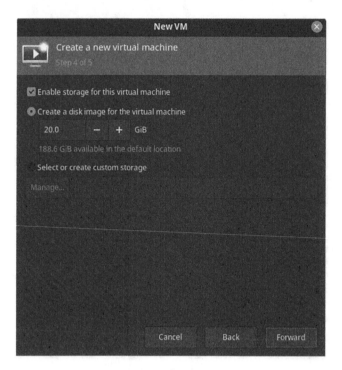

Figure 4-55. *Setting disk size for the OpenSUSE virtual machine*

5.   End the virtual machine creation process by giving your virtual machine a name like we did with the Fedora and Ubuntu installations; also make sure you are using the correct network if you have more than one. If you wish, you can select to do further customizations. However, like our other installations, we will not be adding any customizations.

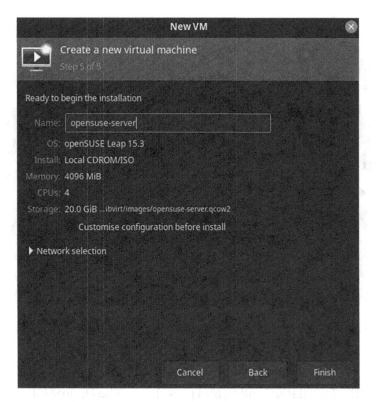

Figure 4-56. Set the virtual machine name for the OpenSUSE virtual machine

6. Click "Finish"; a console window will appear, which we will use to install our Fedora server.

OpenSUSE Server Installation

The following steps will demonstrate the basic OpenSUSE server installation. We will avoid doing any customizations and stick to defaults where possible.

1. Turn on your physical or virtual system that will be used for your OpenSUSE server installation. Your console or system screen should be similar to Figure 4-57 if your boot process is correct.

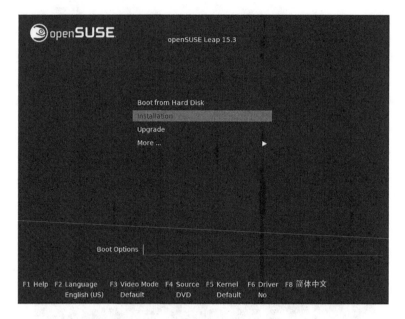

Figure 4-57. *OpenSUSE initial installation screen when booting from install media*

2. Select the Installation option and press Enter. The OpenSUSE installer will start the installation process by loading drivers and preparing the installation environment. This should look similar to Figure 4-58.

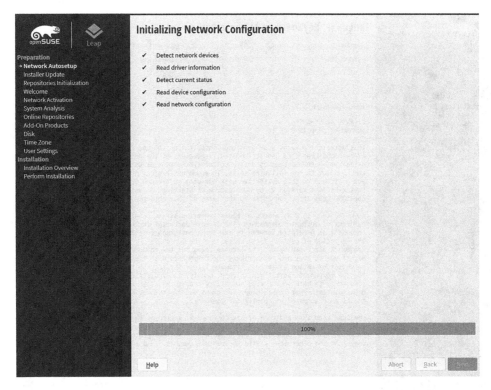

Figure 4-58. *OpenSUSE installation process beginning*

3. As soon as you see the screen similar to Figure 4-59, you will be
    ready to start the installation steps. Select the keyboard layout and
    language you prefer, then click next.

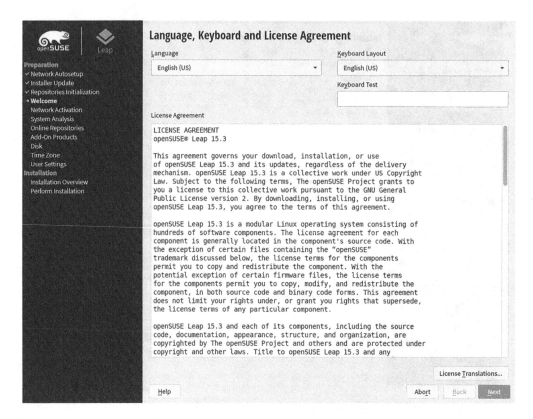

Figure 4-59. *OpenSUSE keyboard type configuration*

4. If you are connected to the Internet with your system, you will be
    given the option to activate online repositories. Click Yes.

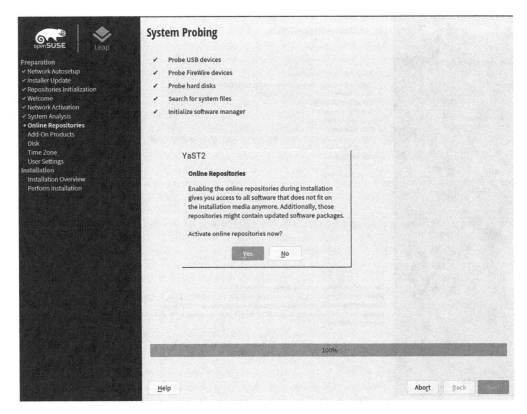

Figure 4-60. *OpenSUSE online repository configuration*

5. If you are selected to activate online repositories, you will see a
    screen similar to Figure 4-61. Once you have enabled or disabled
    any repositories, click Next.

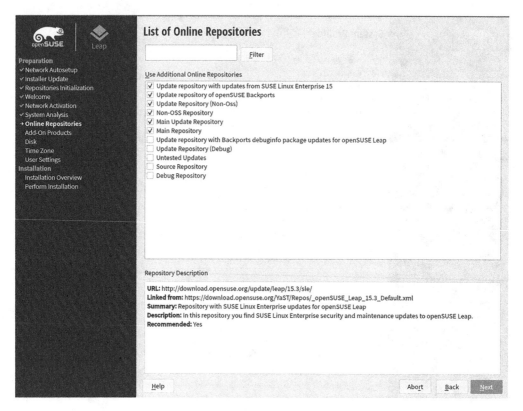

Figure 4-61. *Online repository activation*

6.   The online repositories can take a few minutes to activate; just be patient and let them complete. If your Internet is a bit slow it can take a bit longer.

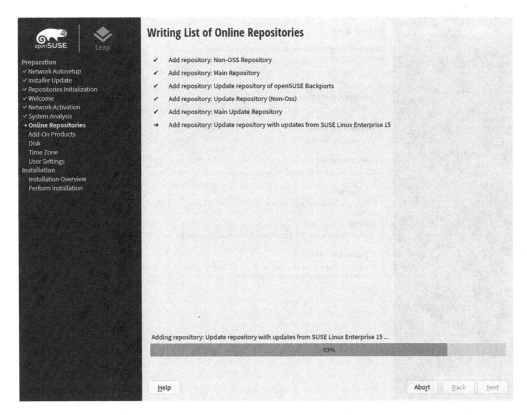

Figure 4-62. *Online repositories updating*

7. Once all online repositories have finished activating, select the
    "Server" radio button, then click the Next button.

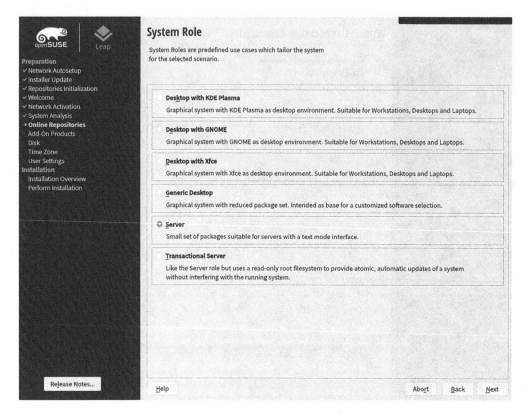

Figure 4-63. *OpenSUSE system type selection screen*

8. Very much like we did on all our other basic installations, we
    will stick with the default disk layout provided by the OpenSUSE
    installer. Click the Next button.

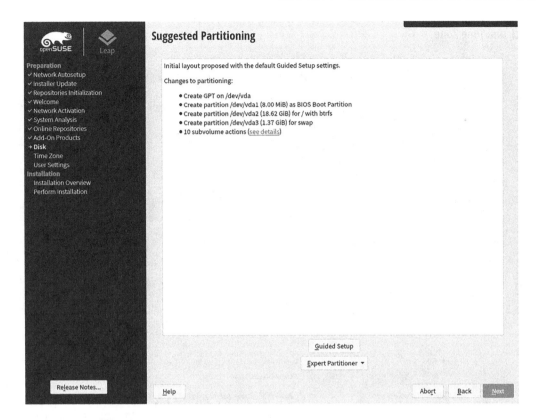

Figure 4-64. *Disk partitioning screen*

9.   Set your time zone and click the Next button.

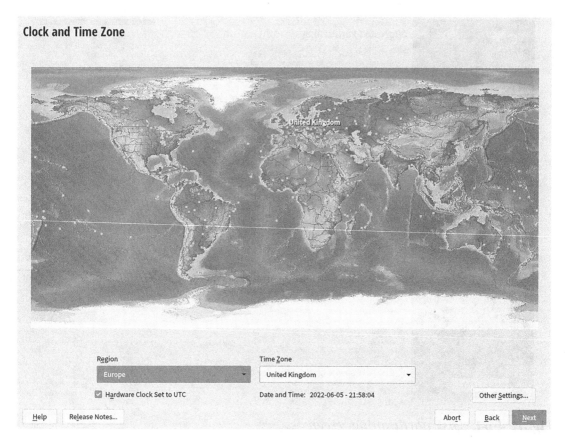

Figure 4-65. *Time zone configuration screen*

10. Create a user account that will be used to log in to your OpenSUSE server. Then click the Next button.

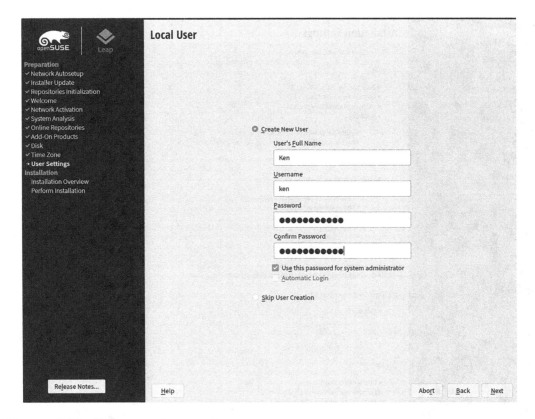

Figure 4-66. *User account creation screen*

11. Review all your installation options that you selected during the
     installer wizard, and if you are happy, click the "Install" button.

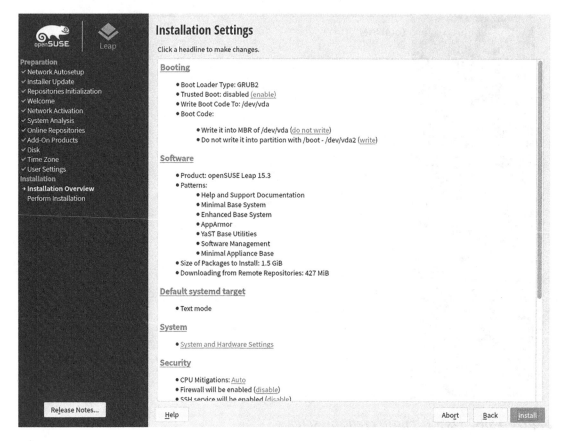

Figure 4-67. *Final installation configuration screen*

12. To accept the installation confirmation screen, click the
     "Install" button.

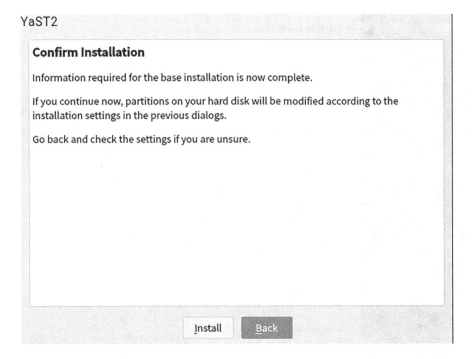

Figure 4-68. *Confirm installation screen*

13. The OpenSUSE installation should then start and look similar to Figure 4-69. The OpenSUSE installation is by far the slowest of the three to complete and comes with a very nice time indicator showing how much time is remaining. This is mostly due to packages being downloaded. If you decided to go with a disconnected installation, this could potentially be quicker.

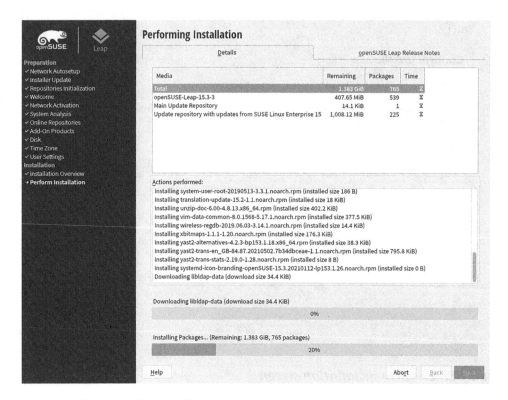

Figure 4-69. OpenSUSE installation progress

14.   Once the installation has completed, your system will be rebooted
into your OpenSUSE server.

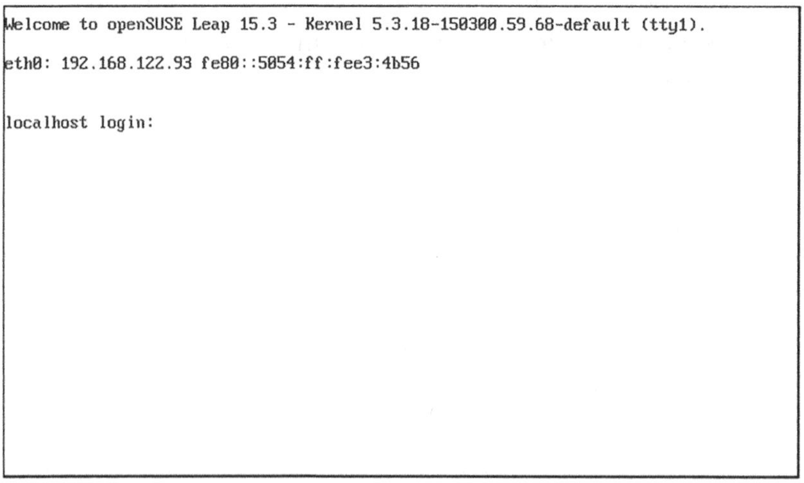

```
Welcome to openSUSE Leap 15.3 - Kernel 5.3.18-150300.59.68-default (tty1).

eth0: 192.168.122.93 fe80::5054:ff:fee3:4b56


localhost login:
```

Figure 4-70. OpenSUSE ready for user login

Basic Exercise

With two Linux operating system installations complete, you are probably feeling quite confident about this one and with good reason. These Linux installations are not that difficult if you take your time to understand the install process and pay attention to the messages.

To continue your learning momentum, you'll be tasked with building your own OpenSUSE server like the previous Ubuntu and Fedora systems. As previously stated, you can use either a virtual machine or physical system; it really is up to you.

Your OpenSUSE server must be built with the following configuration if you choose to use a virtual machine. If you prefer to use a physical system, ensure the specs are close to the virtual machine specifications.

Virtual Machine

Create a virtual machine in KVM or VirtualBox with the following specifications:

- 4096MB of memory, 4 vCPUs

- 10GB disk

- Default network

OpenSUSE Server

Your OpenSUSE server must be installed with the following configuration options:

- Your network IP address must use DHCP; if you do not have DHCP, then set a static IP address.

- Install OpenSUSE as a server.

- Use the default disk layout provided by the installer.

Important   Do not delete this virtual machine; it will be used in future exercises.

Exercise Outcome

At the end of the exercise, you should have a working OpenSUSE server that you can log in to with your username and password created during the installation.

Custom Installations

Customizing your OpenSUSE server installation is similar in a way to Fedora as you do most of the customization before the installation begins.

As previously with the Fedora and Ubuntu server installations, OpenSUSE server does give you the following customization options during the installation:

- Disk layout configuration

- Package installation options

- Date/time and time zone settings

- Keyboard and language options

Optional Custom Exercise

As an optional custom exercise, repeat the installation of your OpenSUSE server, but this time, customize the following.

OpenSUSE Server

Your OpenSUSE server must be installed with the following configuration options:

- Create a disk layout with a separate /home and /var partition. Both should be exactly 5GB.

- Ensure that your OpenSUSE server is configured to include the Gnome Desktop.

Important   Do not delete this virtual machine if you deleted the basic installation; it will be used in future exercises.

Upgrading Linux

Most Linux distributions can be upgraded from minor version to minor version quite simply and do not require too much configuration. However, major version to major version will often require extra steps and could be slightly riskier if the system is a production server.

Upgrade vs. Migration

The need to upgrade a Linux system is really dependent on what the Linux system is used for and if the upgrade process is far more of a risk than a migration. In some cases, it may be quicker to build a new server and migrate than to upgrade.

A few questions you should ask yourself when deciding between upgrading and migrating are as follows:

- Can my distribution be upgraded in place?

  Pointless thinking about upgrades if it is not even possible. Some Linux distributions do not support in-place upgrades, meaning your only option is a migration.

- How many versions do I have to upgrade before I get to my target version?

  This question is very important as not all upgrades can skip minor upgrades in between. Some require upgrades to be done in sequence, which will consume further time.

- What is the server used for? Is the workload small enough that it can be migrated quicker than an upgrade can be done?

Basically, if you are just running a small web server that hosts an internal intranet site, rebuilding and redeploying your application may be far quicker than upgrading. However, a database server running 1TB of data might take a bit longer, which would make more sense to upgrade.

There are many more of these questions you can ask yourself. Take your time and work out what the best option would be. Ideally, you should have an environment that does not require upgrading as you should be running a platform that can be rebuilt from code, but that is a conversion for another time or another book.

Before Upgrading

In situations where upgrades are absolutely required, there are a few things you should always do before upgrading.

Backup

Sounds very obvious but it still needs to be said. Ensure you have a working backup of your system before upgrading. Always make sure you have a way out if something goes wrong.

If you are upgrading a virtual machine, take a snapshot or backup the operating system storage disk. Just be 100% sure you have a way back if something goes wrong.

If you are upgrading a physical server, the backup and recovery process could be more complicated and could involve rebuilding and then restoring your data, in which case you could have just done a migration in the first place. There are many backup and restore options these days; just be sure that you have a working solution before you upgrade.

Check Disk Space

Another obvious thing to check is the available disk space for your main partitions. If you do not have enough space during the upgrade process, you could be left in a situation where the upgrade fails and it leaves you in a defunct state. Best to avoid this by cleaning up storage or increasing disk sizing where possible.

Confirm Your Version Can Be Upgraded

Not all distributions can be upgraded from major to major versions. Do not attempt to force an upgrade or try workarounds to circumvent guardrails. This will leave you in a situation where you will need to restore from backups.

Take your time and read upgrade documentation before you start.

What Distributions Can Be Upgraded

Before upgrading any Linux distribution, you will first need to understand your distribution's upgrade process. Each distribution will have its own instructions that you will need to follow and read very carefully. In almost every case, there has been quite a bit of effort put in to document the upgrade process. This has been tested and should work if you follow the instructions as directed.

Ubuntu

One of the more simpler Linux distributions to upgrade is Ubuntu. The process might be easier to do than others but still requires some effort on your part. As an example, have a look at the Desktop upgrade process. The server upgrade process is not too dissimilar. The following is the link to the Ubuntu upgrade process for the Desktop variant:

`https://ubuntu.com/tutorials/upgrading-ubuntu-desktop#1-before-you-start`

Fedora

The Fedora upgrade process is slightly more complicated but not too difficult if you follow the instructions to the letter. Fortunately, the documentation provided by the Fedora community is very good and to the point. I personally have used it a few times with my own upgrades over the years. Take your time and read the upgrade process if you ever need to upgrade Fedora versions:

`https://docs.fedoraproject.org/en-US/quick-docs/dnf-system-upgrade/`

OpenSUSE

Like the Fedora upgrade process, OpenSUSE does involve a few steps, and very much like the Fedora documentation, the OpenSUSE documentation is very good. If the need does arise for you to upgrade your OpenSUSE server, make sure you read the latest documentation and confirm that the documentation steps you through the upgrade process for your version. The current OpenSUSE documentation for upgrades can be found at the following link:

`https://en.opensuse.org/SDB:System_upgrade`

Exercise

From all that you have learned about installing different Linux distributions and how different Linux distributions have different upgrade processes, you should be in a good position to install and upgrade an older Linux distribution version on your own.

The following are three exercises you could do on your own to practice upgrades. If you do not want to do all three, choose one that you think you will stick with and practice that upgrade.

Upgrade Ubuntu

For this Ubuntu upgrade exercise, you will need to do the following:

- Create a new virtual machine with the following specs:

    - 4 vCPUS

    - 4096MB of memory

    - 20GB disk

- Download the Ubuntu server 21.10 ISO and install the operating system into the virtual machine you created.

    - The link for Ubuntu server 21.10 is as follows:

    - `https://releases.ubuntu.com/21.10/`

- Read the upgrade documentation and upgrade your Ubuntu server to 22.04.

Upgrade Fedora

For this Fedora upgrade exercise, you will need to do the following:

- Create a new virtual machine with the following specs:

    - 4 vCPUS

    - 4096MB of memory

    - 20GB disk

- Download the Fedora server 35 ISO and install the operating system into the virtual machine you created.

    - The link for older Fedora releases is as follows:

    - `https://fedora.mirrorservice.org/fedora/linux/releases/`

- Read the upgrade documentation and upgrade your Fedora server to version 36.

Upgrade OpenSUSE

For this OpenSUSE upgrade exercise, you will need to do the following:

- Create a new virtual machine with the following specs:

    - 4 vCPUS

    - 4096MB of memory

    - 20GB disk

- Download the OpenSUSE server 15.0 ISO and install the operating system into the virtual machine you created.

    - Older versions of OpenSUSE can be found at the following link:

    - `https://download.opensuse.org/distribution/leap/`

- Read the upgrade documentation and upgrade your Fedora server to version 36.

Summary

In this chapter, you were introduced to the following:

- Where you can get Linux distributions from

- What enterprise and community Linux distributions are

- What virtualization is and how it can be used to learn about Linux

- Installation media and how to create a USB disk that will allow multiple operating systems to be deployed from it

- How to install Ubuntu server

- How to install Fedora server

- How to install OpenSUSE server

- What it means to upgrade or migrate your Linux server to new versions

- What is involved in upgrading your Linux distribution

CHAPTER 5

Using Linux for the First Time

In Chapter 4, we started to explore how Linux distributions are installed and how to upgrade them. This chapter is the next logical step where we start to learn how to use and customize our Linux distributions. We will first look at how a Linux system can be accessed and run through some exercises to get fully up to speed on how to log in to a Linux system.

Once logged in, you will need to learn how to use a Linux system and understand what some of the basic commands are. This chapter will take you through some of these basic command-line commands you should know and will explore differences in the different Linux distributions.

Finally, in this chapter, we will look at using the desktop on your Linux server platforms. We will explore how to install different desktops and look at how these desktops can be enabled or disabled.

Accessing Linux

To make use of a Linux system, you will need to know how to log in to your Linux environment. This sounds like a simple enough task. However, what happens when you have not installed a desktop? Or you don't have direct access to a console? What happens when you cannot open an ssh session? For these reasons, it is important to know all methods of gaining access to your Linux environment.

© Kenneth Hitchcock 2023
K. Hitchcock, *The Enterprise Linux Administrator*, https://doi.org/10.1007/978-1-4842-8801-6_5

Console

The first and probably the most important method of accessing a Linux system is by direct console. The console is vital for resolving issues related to your Linux environment that cannot be resolved with other access methods. There are two console types you should be aware of.

Virtualization

Virtualization software layers like KVM have graphical management tools similar to virt-manager. These graphical tools have consoles that are used to simulate a screen attached to the virtual machine. In Chapter 4, when we created virtual machines that were used to install the different Linux operating systems, we used the KVM console.

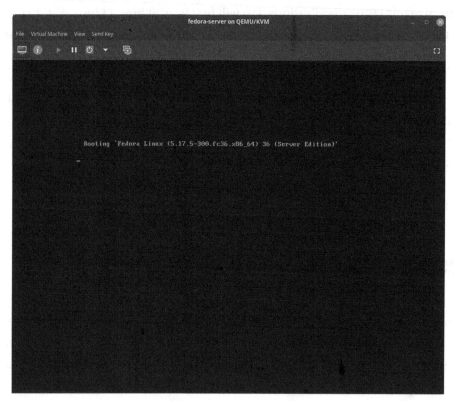

Hardware Consoles

Hardware consoles like "ILO" or "DRAC" are provided by hardware manufacturers like HP and Dell. These consoles are configured on a dedicated network interface and are configured when the physical server is being prepared for the operating system to be installed.

These consoles are normally accessed via a web browser by entering the IP address configured on the "ILO" or "DRAC" network interface. With this web interface, you are able to open a console to the physical system (Figure 5-1).

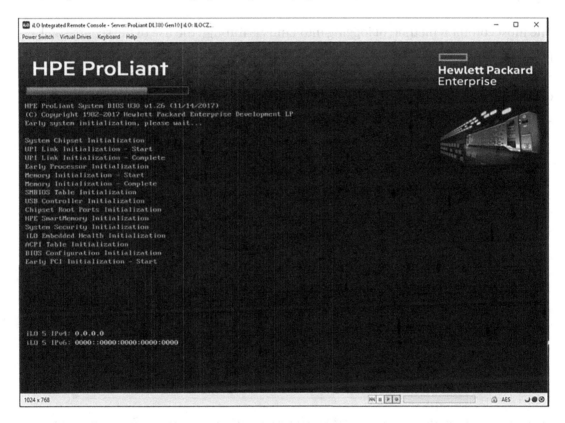

Figure 5-1. An example of a hardware console provided by HP iLO systems

Why Is the Console Important?

Console access becomes vitally important when you have forgotten your root password or you have a system boot issue. Being able to see the boot process can assist you during your troubleshooting process, often allowing you to see where the issue lies and allowing you to resolve the problem remotely instead of making a trip to your data center. Not ideal if you have a problem in the early hours of the morning.

SSH

The most common method of logging into Linux is through the use of the secure shell protocol, almost always referred to as "SSH". SSH is a secure way of connecting to a Linux system on an unsecure network. SSH operates over port 22 and is typically enabled by default on most Linux distros. SSH is controlled by the sshd daemon and configured through the configuration files generally found in the /etc/ directory.

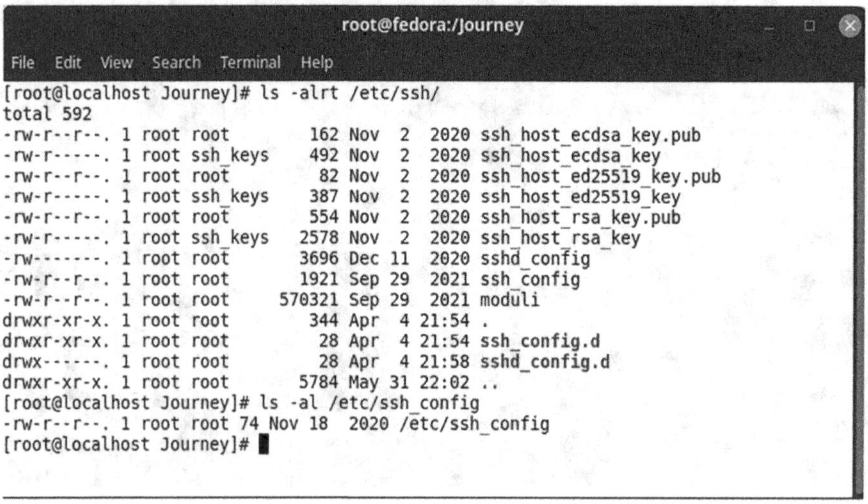

Figure 5-2. An example of an active ssh session with the ssh configuration file

Logging into Another Linux System

Figure 5-3 is a basic flow of how you would log in to another Linux system. In Chapter 4, we created a Fedora server virtual machine with a DHCP-configured network address. In my lab, this network address was 192.168.122.11. I created a user account called ken with a password of "password123".

```
                            ken@fedora-server:~                    —  □  ⊗

  File  Edit  View  Search  Terminal  Help
 [root@localhost Journey]# ssh ken@192.168.122.11
 The authenticity of host '192.168.122.11 (192.168.122.11)' can't be established.
 ED25519 key fingerprint is SHA256:cL7BdTLc/cT2hB2qwBs95PPk2A2rfUaLxThYxk8sMtI.
 This key is not known by any other names
 Are you sure you want to continue connecting (yes/no/[fingerprint])? yes
 Warning: Permanently added '192.168.122.11' (ED25519) to the list of known hosts.
 ken@192.168.122.11's password:
 Web console: https://fedora-server:9090/ or https://192.168.122.11:9090/

 Last login: Sun Jun 12 21:33:00 2022 from 192.168.122.1
 [ken@fedora-server ~]$ █
```

Figure 5-3. *ssh session with user ken logged in*

In Figure 5-3, you can see the steps followed.

- From a Fedora desktop, a terminal window was opened.

- In the terminal window, the command "ssh ken@192.168.122.11" was executed.

- Immediately after the command was run, there was a prompt asking if we wanted to continue connecting to the system. This message is there to let us know that we have never logged into this system before and is there to confirm we are sure we wish to connect.

- Finally, the password for the user account was entered.

There is much more that happens on the Fedora system to allow the login process to occur, but for now, just be familiar with the preceding process to log in to another Linux system from a Linux system. This will be done on a regular basis going forward.

Putty

Not all organizations like employees use Linux systems for their working environments. What happens more than most of us would like is we are relegated to using Windows, which means you will need to have applications installed that allow you to work with Linux systems.

The common Windows SSH tool used is called Putty. If you have ever been in the situation where you needed to log in to a Linux system from Windows, you are probably familiar with it. Putty can typically be found at the following link:

www.putty.org/

WinSCP

There is another tool very useful if you have to work from a Windows base. This is WinSCP. WinSCP allows the easy transfer of files to and from a Linux system. This is a very useful tool if you need to get logs or configuration files.

https://winscp.net/eng/download.php

Warning   Editing files in Windows text editors and transferring to a Linux system can result in services not starting. This is large due to Windows editors adding additional invisible characters to your file. Using utilities like "dos2unix" can help resolve any issues you may encounter.

SSH Configuration Files

There are a number of configuration files you will use with your ssh configuration. The most important files you will need to understand are as follows.

sshd_config

The main configuration file for the ssh daemon is the sshd_config. This file in previous versions of Fedora could be found at /etc/sshd_confg, but with newer versions, the configuration files are stored in the /etc/ssh/sshd_config.d/ directory. The /etc/ssh/ sshd_config file is still used as a system-wide configuration file.

Read the man page for the sshd_config configuration file for parameters you can use. This will be covered more in detail in Chapter 6.

```
# man sshd_config
```

Note   As a Linux system administrator, it is crucial that you know how to configure ssh and more importantly how to restrict access to your Linux system by configuring the ssh daemon.

SSH Keys

In Figure 5-4, you can see the manual process of logging into another Linux system. In this manual login process, a password had to be provided.

```
ken@fedora-server:~
File  Edit  View  Search  Terminal  Help
[root@localhost Journey]# ssh ken@192.168.122.11
The authenticity of host '192.168.122.11 (192.168.122.11)' can't be established.
ED25519 key fingerprint is SHA256:cL7BdTLc/cT2hB2qwBs95PPk2A2rfUaLxThYxk8sMtI.
This key is not known by any other names
Are you sure you want to continue connecting (yes/no/[fingerprint])? yes
Warning: Permanently added '192.168.122.11' (ED25519) to the list of known hosts.
ken@192.168.122.11's password:
Web console: https://fedora-server:9090/ or https://192.168.122.11:9090/

Last login: Sun Jun 12 21:33:00 2022 from 192.168.122.1
[ken@fedora-server ~]$ █
```

Figure 5-4. *An example of logging into an ssh session with a password*

By using what is known as "ssh" keys or public/private keys, we can log in to another Linux system without providing a password. Not only is this process more convenient, it actually is more secure.

To create your own set of ssh keys, you can use the following steps:

1. Power on the Fedora Linux server we built in Chapter 4. If you deleted or do not have access to it anymore, quickly build a new system to work with.

2. Log in to your now powered-on Fedora server system as a standard user instead of root; the reason for not using root will be discussed in a later chapter. To get the IP address of your Fedora server, open the virt-manager console of your virtual machine.

Log in with your user you created during the installation and you will see the IP address of your system in the URL that can be used to access your Fedora server via the web console. See Figure 5-4 for an example.

3. As the user you created during the operating system install (in my case, this was "ken"), run the following command:

```
# ssh-keygen
```

4. Press enter to choose the default values or type what changes you would like to make.

5. Type a passphrase if you want to use one; confirm the passphrase.

6. That's it; you have generated a new ssh key pair.

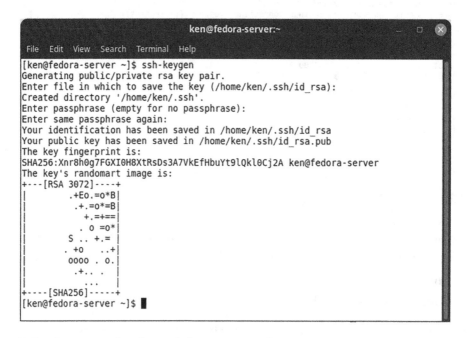

Figure 5-5. *An example of an ssh keys generation*

To test your ssh key pair and configure passwordless access to another system, let us explore what you would need to accomplish this.

1. Leave your previous Linux system powered on and power on your Ubuntu server Linux system. Again, if you deleted or do not have access to the system, quickly build another server to use. If you are having resource constraints, feel free to drop the CPU and memory by half for both your virtual machines.

2. Open your console to your newly powered-on Linux system and log in with the user you created during the install.

3. Run the following command on your newly powered Ubuntu server virtual machine:

```
# ip a
```

4. From the output, look for the IP address assigned to your virtual machine. Figure 5-6 shows an example of this.

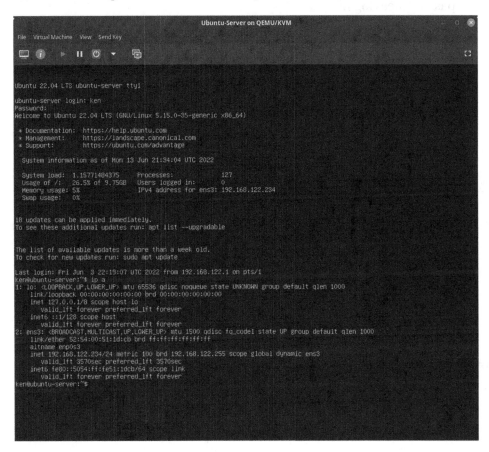

Figure 5-6. *Working out the IP address of a linux system*

5. Make a note of this IP address as we will be using it in the next step.

6. Open a new Putty or terminal ssh session to your Fedora server system. If you forgot the IP address, repeat steps 2 to 5 on your Fedora server.

7. From your Fedora server, run the following command. Change the user and IP address to match your environment.

```
# ssh-copy-id -i ~/.ssh/id_rsa.pub <user>@<ip address>
```

8. Type "yes" to confirm you wish to connect to your Ubuntu server system.

9. Type the password for your user and press enter.

10. Your ssh key will now be configured on your Ubuntu server for passwordless logins.

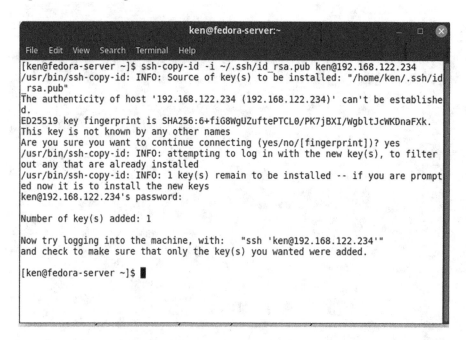

Figure 5-7. *An example of ssh keys being copied to another Linux system*

11. To test your passwordless login, run the following command. Remember to change the details to match your environment.

```
# ssh <user>@<ip address>
```

It is not only vital to know how your Linux systems use ssh keys but also it is crucial to know how these keys are generated. As a system administrator, you need to know where these keys are stored and how you secure access to them.

Often as a system administrator, you will need to allow access to systems; one of the safest methods is by allowing users to log in with their own ssh keys, which means you will need to know how to add new keys to your system to allow user access. Users will also not be added to the sudoers group by default and need to be added manually or through automation. Without configuring the sudoers, your user will not have elevated permissions and will be restricted to the content owned by them.

Web Console

Newer Linux distributions like Fedora server 36 and Red Hat Enterprise Linux 8 and 9 have the ability to install a web interface utility called "Cockpit." This web interface allows the user to configure a number of things on the system that you normally did from the command-line or desktop environments. Another very nice feature of the "Cockpit" web console is that it provides a terminal window. This terminal window can be used to unlock user accounts or restart services like sshd. It, however, cannot show you the boot process or help you with single user mode issues.

It should go without saying, though, if you don't know the password or have not configured a password for the system, you won't be able to log in to the Cockpit console either.

Installing Cockpit

To install the Cockpit web console on a system that does not have it installed, you will need to do something very similar to the following.

Fedora Server by default has the "Cockpit" web console installed. So for this example, I will install the "Cockpit" environment on my Ubuntu server. To do this, I will be using the following steps:

1. Ssh to the Ubuntu server from Chapter 4. If you forgot how to do this, go back a few pages to remind yourself.

2. Run the following command:

```
# sudo apt install cockpit -y
```

3. Type your user's password to enable the command to run.

4. Provided you do not have any Internet connectivity issues, the command should install a number of packages for the "Cockpit" utility.

Accessing Cockpit

With "Cockpit" now installed, you can access your system's "Cockpit" web interface by opening an Internet browser, and in the address bar, enter the following URL. Be sure to change the values to match your environment.

```
https://<ip address or hostname>:9090/
```

Exercise

For the first exercise of this chapter, you will need to power on your OpenSUSE server. If your server has been deleted or not available, quickly build a new one based on the instructions from Chapter 4.

Enable Passwordless ssh

The purpose of this exercise is to configure ssh access to your OpenSUSE server from your Fedora server.

1. Start your OpenSUSE server if you have not already done so.

2. Start your Fedora server if you have not already done so.

3. Determine the IP address of your Fedora server.

4. Determine the IP address of your OpenSUSE server.

5. Ssh into your Fedora server using the user you created during the server installation in Chapter 4.

6. From your Fedora server, configure passwordless ssh access to your OpenSUSE server. This should be the same as how the Ubuntu server ssh configuration was done a few pages back.

Configure Cockpit

The purpose of this exercise is to ensure that Cockpit is running on your OpenSUSE server.

On your OpenSUSE server, run the following commands to install the Cockpit utility on OpenSUSE:

```
zypper addrepo https://download.opensuse.org/repositories/
home:ecsos:server:cockpit/15.3/home:ecsos:server:cockpit.repo
```

```
zypper refresh
zypper install cockpit
systemctl start cockpit
firewall-cmd --add-port=9090/tcp --permanent
firewall-cmd --reload
```

Command Line

Once you are logged into your Linux server, you will need to know fundamental basics to navigate the operating system. For that, you will need to know some basic commands to get started.

Finding Help

The first thing to learn about the Linux command line is how to find more information and help on commands you will use. It does not help if all you know is the command. There are important switches and parameters that all commands come with, and as there are so many commands and utilities available today, you will need to know how to find those parameters without having to remember them all.

Man Pages

The first and most important thing to understand about Linux and its utilities is that almost everything has a manual. These are referred to as man pages. Often when asking questions on technical forums, you may be referred back to the man pages if the answer is straightforward enough, so always ensure you check them first.

Man pages are typically installed by default on standard Linux distributions. Smaller cutdown installs for cloud images may not always have man pages installed, typical to save space and resources. If man pages for a utility are missing, they normally can be installed with supplementary packages. If a package for a utilities man page is not available, it typically can also be installed manually.

Table 5-1 lists the basic packages required for man pages.

Table 5-1. *The basic packages required for man pages*

Linux Package	Description
man-db	The database of caches where man pages are kept.
manpages-posix	Basic man pages for POSIX-related Linux commands.

Navigating the Filesystem

Being presented with a command prompt is no fun if you do not know what commands to run. So to get you started, let's start by looking at how you list files and directories, how you find files, and how you go about editing files when you do find them.

Listing Files

The first ever Unix/Linux command I learned when starting to use Linux for the first time was "ls -al". Coming from a predominately Microsoft Windows background, my first instinct was to use the "dir" command, which technically can work in Linux if you configure an alias for it. We will cover what an alias is shortly.

To list all the files in the current directory, run the following command:

```
# ls -al
```

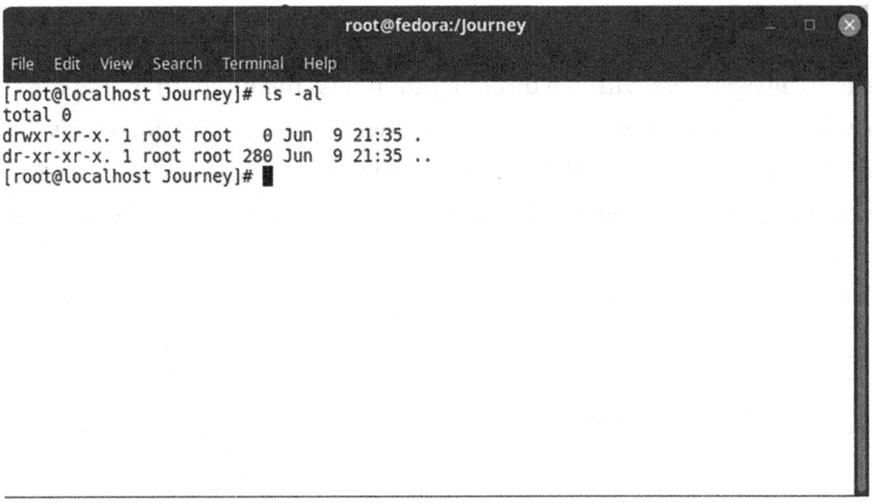

Figure 5-8. *An example of the ls -al command*

The "ls" utility has many parameters you can use to format your file listing. Check the following command for all the options you can use:

```
# ls --help
```

You can also list files and directories not within the current directory. This is done by specifying the path to where you wish to list files and directories. An example of this can be seen in Figure 5-9.

```
# ls -al /home
```

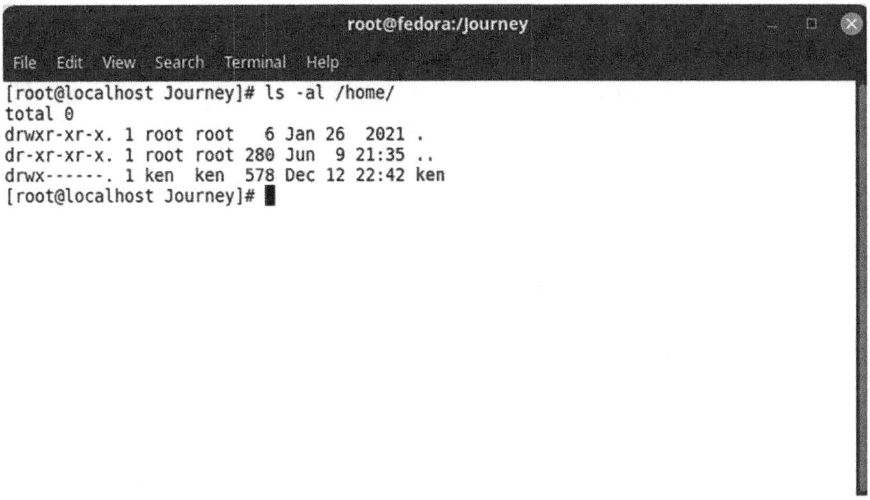

Figure 5-9. *An example of the ls -al command on the /home directory*

Changing Directories

If you prefer to always work within a directory than pass the full path of that directory each time you want to use it, you will need to know how to change directories.

Fortunately, this is not much different than what you would have done in the Windows or Unix world. The only difference with Linux from the Windows world is that Linux and Unix are case sensitive.

To change directories, simply do the following.

```
# cd /path/to/directory
```

or as an example to get to your home directory, you can use either of the following:

```
# cd /home/ken
# cd ~/
```

To change to the parent directory of where you currently are, you can run the following command:

```
# cd ..
```

Don't Know Where Are You?

If you do not know what directory you currently are in, you can use the "pwd" utility or command.

```
# pwd
```

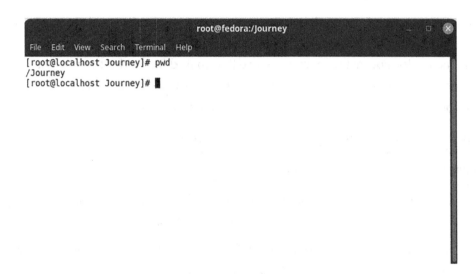

Figure 5-10. *An example of the pwd command*

Summary of the Very Basics

The following is the absolute bare minimum you will need to know to navigate a Linux or Unix system.

Table 5-2 lists the basic commands for navigating a Linux filesystem.

Table 5-2. *A basic list of commands for navigating the Linux filesystem*

Linux Command	Description
ls -al	Lists all the files in a directory in a list format.
cd /path/dir	Changes directory to a different directory using the full path.
pwd	Shows the current directory location the user is in.

Finding Files

Once you know how to see what's in your current directory and once you know how to change directories, the next logical thing will be to understand how to find files. More often than you think, you will forget where files are located and will need to do a search.

In the past, people have used the "locate" utility or command, but today, most use the "find" command. Both have their uses, but "find" is the better one to use for filesystem files.

Being familiar with "find" will help with more than just finding a file by name. You are able to search for files based on age too. Find is then able to execute commands based on its results. For instance, you can use find to find files older than five days and delete them. It is useful when you need to clean out files in a large directory.

Table 5-3 lists some useful examples of the find command.

Table 5-3. *Some useful examples of the find command*

Find Command	Description
find / -name tmp	This example will look for anything that has the name "tmp" that exists on the entire root filesystem.
find / -name test.txt -exec rm -i {} \;	This example file searches for any files with the name "test. txt" and forcibly removes it.
find /tmp -empty	This example will search for any files in the /tmp directory that are empty.
find / -perm 777	This example is very useful when looking for files that have very insecure permissions configured.
find /var/log -iname "*.log" -atime +30 -type f	Find all log files in the /var/log directory that were last accessed more than 30 days ago.
find /var/log -iname "*.log" -mtime +60 -exec rm -i {} \;	Find all logs in the /var/log directory that were last modified over 60 days ago, then delete these files.

It is not expected for you to know all of these find commands. I personally had to double-check many of them myself for this book.

Tip   Albert Einstein once said, "Never memorize something that you can look up."

Editing Files

Once you know where your files are, you need to know how to edit them. There are a few methods of editing files on your Linux platform.

Desktop Utilities

The simplest method would be to use the desktop if you have it installed; on the Linux desktop, you have tools available like gedit that can be used to edit your files. However, as we are more focused on the command line as system administrators, we will stick to using the command-line options.

Command-Line Editing

The editing tool you use is down to preference. I myself am a "vi" or "vim" user, but many others prefer emacs or nano. Prior to 2019, "vi" was installed by default on almost all GNU/Linux-type distributions, but today, you will need to install it if it is not available. Similarly with "emacs," if you wanted to use "emacs," you would have to install it post installation.

For this book and in general, I personally prefer to use "vim". Feel free to use whichever editor you prefer and adjust accordingly where I say to edit a file.

Table 5-4 lists a few different Linux file editors that you can use.

Table 5-4. *List of Linux file editors*

Linux Command	Description
vi or vim	Developed as a visual mode for an old line editor called ex.
emacs	A family of text editors with over 10 000 commands available.
nano	Text editor for Unix-like systems. Emulation of Pico text editor.

Note   Decide on the editor you would like to learn and get familiar with its subcommands. vi and vim, for example, have some really nice tips and tricks that can speed up configuration.

Using vi and vim

As this book will only focus on using vi or vim, it may be worth explaining the very basics of using this text editor.

vi and vim are command-based text editors, which basically means you need to tell the editor when you want to edit, search, and save files. This typically means you need to switch between two different modes.

Command Mode

The default mode is the command mode where vi or vim is expecting you to send a command. These commands could be to enter edit mode, to save the file, or to search for a string.

Table 5-5 lists the basic vi command options you should know.

Table 5-5. *List of vi command options*

vi/vim Commands	Description
I	Enters vi or vim into edit mode.
press escape	Exits the current edit mode.
:"searchtext"	By using the ":" character followed by text you wish to search for, you can search your currently opened file.
!q	The command will exit without saving your changes.
:wq	This command will tell vi/vim to save and exit your file.

Edit Mode

By pressing the "i" key, you will tell vi/vim to enter edit mode. This is where you can type and delete text as you would normally do in a text editor.

When you have finished creating your file content, press the escape key and type ":wq" to exit and save your file.

Example

To create and edit a new file, simply run the following command. This will create a new file in memory and open a text editor utility.

```
# vi test.txt
```

Press the "i" key and add content to your file. Once you are done, press the escape key and enter the command ":wq" to exit and save your file.

Command-Line Shortcuts

This section is a very small discussion around how you can reduce some of the commands you run to save time when you need to get things done quickly.

Alias

Alias is a utility that allows you to create a shortcut to a command. To see what alias commands your system has, run the following command:

```
# alias
```

To create your own alias commands, we can use the "find" command examples previously discussed.

As a basic example, let's create a new alias command called kenfind and link the command to the following longer find command:

```
# find / -name ken
```

The command to create the new alias can be seen as follows:

```
# alias kenfind='find / -name ken'
```

```
                                    ken@fedora-server:~                    —   □   ⊗

  File  Edit  View  Search  Terminal  Help
 opensuse-server:~ # alias
 alias +='pushd .'
 alias -- -='popd'
 alias ..='cd ..'
 alias ...='cd ../..'
 alias beep='echo -en "\007"'
 alias cd..='cd ..'
 alias dir='ls -l'
 alias egrep='egrep --color=auto'
 alias fgrep='fgrep --color=auto'
 alias grep='grep --color=auto'
 alias ip='ip --color=auto'
 alias kenfind='find / -name ken'
 alias l='ls -alF'
 alias la='ls -la'
 alias ll='ls -l'
 alias ls='_ls'
 alias ls-l='ls -l'
 alias md='mkdir -p'
 alias o='less'
 alias rd='rmdir'
 alias rehash='hash -r'
 alias unmount='echo "Error: Try the command: umount" 1>&2; false'
 alias you='if test "$EUID" = 0 ; then /sbin/yast2 online_update ; else su - -c "/sbin/yast2 online_update"
  ; fi'
 opensuse-server:~ # █
```

Figure 5-11. *An example of the alias command*

Scripts

Sometimes, you may have the need to run a few commands quite often. This would be best served by creating a new shell script. In a later chapter, we will discuss shell scripting and how to create some basic scripts. For now, the following is a basic example of the steps you would follow to create a simple shell script:

1. Log in to a Linux system.

2. Run the following commands:

    a. `touch test.sh`

    b. `vi test.sh`

    c. Inside the file, add the following lines. Be sure to add no spaces in the beginning of each line:

    ```
    #!/bin/bash
    echo "helloworld"
    ```

3. Press escape and save your file. The instructions to do this are in the vi/vim section a couple pages back.

4. Finally, configure the script to have execute permissions with the following command. Later in the book, we will explain this a bit more in detail.

```
# chmod 0750 test.sh
```

5. To test and run the script, run the following command:

```
# ./test.sh
```

Do not forget to include the "."; this just tells the shell to run the script from the current directory and not look for any commands that are the same in the system path configured.

Different Commands in Different Distributions

The three Linux distributions we have chosen for the beginning of this book are all very similar, and most have the same command or utilities available. For this reason, you have not seen too many times where I have specifically mentioned this command is for Ubuntu or Fedora or OpenSUSE. This is largely due to the fact that these distributions are using common packages and utilities.

For now, there is only one area that should be addressed for these three distributions. This is around how packages are installed and the commands you will use to install them. There is a chapter a bit later that will go more into detail with examples, but for now, all I want to do is make you aware of the utilities you will need to use on the different Linux servers.

As a usable example, let's install the "tmux" package. With each command, we will also use the "sudo" command prefixed to our different installation commands. This command will elevate permissions for the current user (this too will be discussed in more detail later in the book).

With each command included, there will be a "-y" switch, which will install the "tmux" package without prompting the user to confirm if they wish to install.

Fedora – dnf

On Fedora, to install the "tmux" package, we use either of the following commands:

```
# sudo dnf install tmux -y
# sudo yum install tmux -y
```

Ubuntu – apt

On Ubuntu, to install the "tmux" package, we will use the following command:

```
# sudo apt install tmux -y
```

OpenSUSE – zypper

On OpenSUSE, to install the "tmux" package, we will use the following command:

```
# sudo zypper install tmux -y
```

Exercise

The following are some exercises to test your command-line knowledge you have just gained from the last few pages.

Finding Files

Old Files

On any of your Linux servers that have been installed, look for any files that are older than five days. Do not delete them; just make sure you are comfortable with finding older files.

Files with Permissions

On any of your Linux servers that have been installed, look for any files that have the permission of 750. Do not delete or change anything with these files. Just check your knowledge to confirm you know how to find files based on permissions.

Creating File with Content

On any Linux server of your choosing, create a very simple file in your user's home directory called "exercise.txt" with the following content:

"This is my first exercise working with a command-line text editor."

Make sure you save the file.

Installing a Package

On all your Linux servers that have been created so far, confirm that the following packages have been installed:

- screen

- wget

- vim

Desktop Basics

So far in this chapter, we have focused on command-line utilities and briefly discussed that some things can be done on the Linux desktop. However, with our Linux servers we have built so far, we do not have any desktops installed.

This is common practice with Linux servers to not have a desktop installed, mostly due to the fact that most Linux systems are accessed through the command line or via a web console like "Cockpit."

Installing Different Desktops

For this section, we will look at how the desktop can be installed for the various different distributions and how we go about enabling the desktop to start as the default environment.

Fedora Server

The steps to install a desktop on Fedora are relatively simple. The following are the steps I have used to install the "Cinnamon Desktop":

1. Open a new ssh session to your Fedora server and run the
   following command:

   `"sudo dnf group list | grep -i Desktop"`

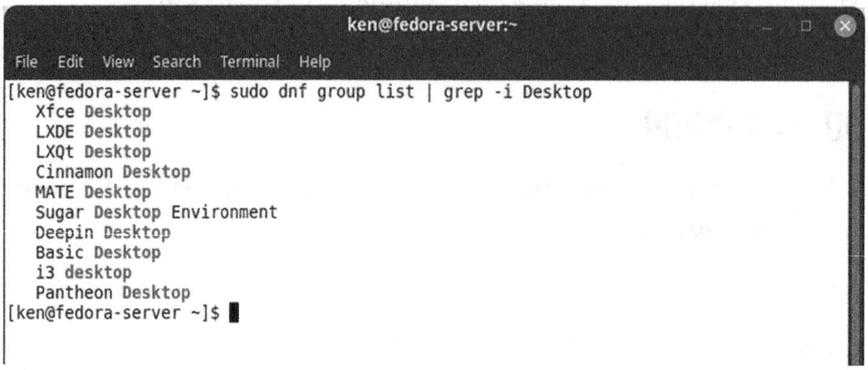

Figure 5-12. *An example of the dnf group list command*

From the output in Figure 5-12, you can see all the different desktops available
to install. For this book, I will mostly install the Cinnamon Desktop, mainly
because it's my own preference. Feel free to adjust to your own if you like.

2. To install the "Cinnamon Desktop," run the following command.
   Or adjust to the desktop of your choice. You will notice the case
   and name are exactly as the output from step 1.

   `# dnf groupinstall "Cinnamon Desktop"`

```
                        ken@fedora-server:~                    _  □  ⊗
 File  Edit  View  Search  Terminal  Help
 perl-Math-BigInt                   noarch 1:1.9998.30-1.fc36   updates 199 k
 perl-Mozilla-CA                    noarch 20211001-2.fc36      fedora   12 k
 perl-NDBM_File                     x86_64 1.15-486.fc36        fedora   27 k
 pinentry-gnome3                    x86_64 1.2.0-2.fc36         fedora   41 k
 pipewire-jack-audio-connection-kit x86_64 0.3.52-2.fc36       updates 135 k
 python3-pygit2                     x86_64 1.7.1-3.fc36         fedora  202 k
 python3-regex                      x86_64 2022.4.24-1.fc36     updates 348 k
 python3-simpleaudio                x86_64 1.0.4-6.fc36         fedora  1.8 M
 sane-backends-drivers-cameras      x86_64 1.1.1-3.fc36         fedora   32 k
 tracker-miners                     x86_64 3.3.1-1.fc36         updates 905 k
 xdg-desktop-portal-gtk             x86_64 1.12.0-5.fc36        fedora  131 k
 Installing Environment Groups:
  Cinnamon Desktop
 Installing Groups:
  base-x
  Cinnamon
  Core
  Dial-up Networking Support
  Fonts
  Guest Desktop Agents
  Hardware Support
  Input Methods
  Multimedia
  Common NetworkManager Submodules
  Printing Support
  Standard

 Transaction Summary
 =================================================================================
 Install  887 Packages
 Upgrade   12 Packages

 Total download size: 1.0 G
 Is this ok [y/N]: y
```

Figure 5-13. *An example of the groupinstall command for the Cinnamon Desktop*

3. Type "y" and press enter for the packages to install.

4. Once the packages are installed, set the environment to be
    graphical. This will boot into a graphical desktop when rebooted.

    ```
    # systemctl set-default graphical.target
    ```

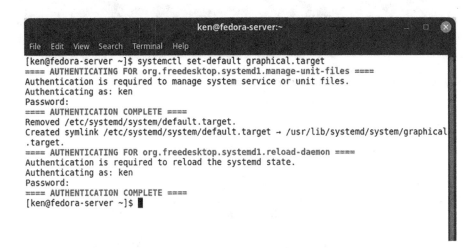

```
                        ken@fedora-server:~                    _  □  ⊗
 File  Edit  View  Search  Terminal  Help
 [ken@fedora-server ~]$ systemctl set-default graphical.target
 ==== AUTHENTICATING FOR org.freedesktop.systemd1.manage-unit-files ====
 Authentication is required to manage system service or unit files.
 Authenticating as: ken
 Password:
 ==== AUTHENTICATION COMPLETE ====
 Removed /etc/systemd/system/default.target.
 Created symlink /etc/systemd/system/default.target → /usr/lib/systemd/system/graphical
 .target.
 ==== AUTHENTICATING FOR org.freedesktop.systemd1.reload-daemon ====
 Authentication is required to reload the systemd state.
 Authenticating as: ken
 Password:
 ==== AUTHENTICATION COMPLETE ====
 [ken@fedora-server ~]$ ■
```

Figure 5-14. *An example of setting the graphical target in a Linux system*

If you run the command without the sudo prefix, you will need to type your user's password twice. To avoid this, just add sudo in front of the command.

5.   Reboot by running the command "`reboot -f`".

6.   If all is installed correctly, you will see a graphical desktop on your virtual machine console.

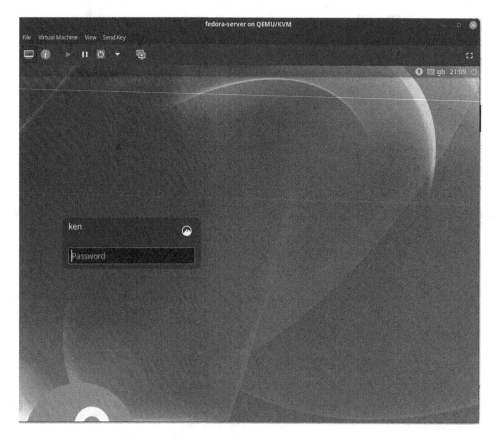

Figure 5-15. *A Linux desktop environment*

7.   If you encounter any errors along the line of "service not found," you may need to run the following command and reboot:

```
# systemctl enable gdm.service
```

Some desktops require the additional service to be enabled.

8.   You can log in to your server with the user account you created during your installation, or switch if you created any other users.

Ubuntu Server

The Ubuntu desktop installation is slightly different to the Fedora install, but not too difficult if you follow the instructions carefully.

There are a number of desktops available to install, including the Cinnamon Desktop that we installed for Fedora, but to change things slightly and to stick to the Ubuntu environment, we will install the Ubuntu Desktop.

1. Open a new ssh session to your Ubuntu server.

2. As an optional step, you can see what desktops are available to install. As the user you created during your Ubuntu server installation, run the following command:

```
# sudo apt list | grep -i desktop
```

3. To install the ubuntu-desktop environment, run the following command:

```
# sudo apt install ubuntu-desktop
```

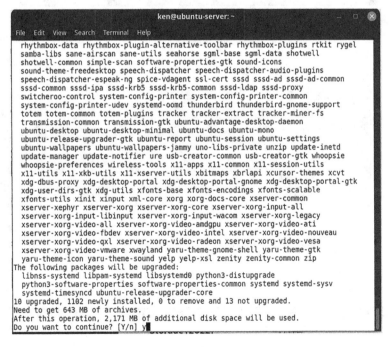

Figure 5-16. *The installation of a desktop on Ubuntu*

4. As with the Fedora install, type "y" and then press enter to install
    the packages for your Ubuntu Desktop.

5. Once the installation has completed, you may see a similar message,
    just select the <ok> options and press enter that you accept.

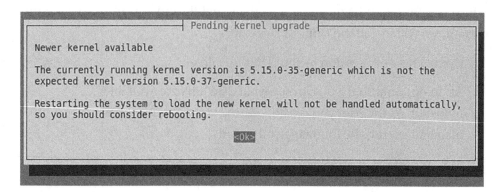

Figure 5-17. *A prompt to install a new kernel version*

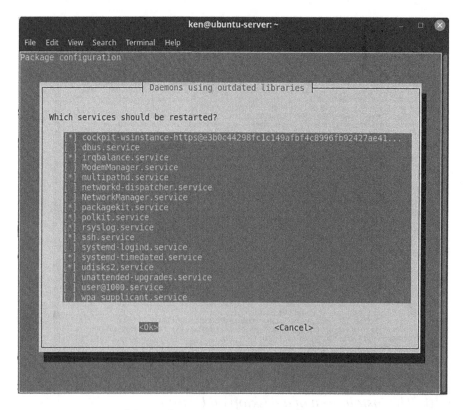

Figure 5-18. *A screen asking what services you wish to restart*

6.   Reboot by running the following command:

```
# reboot -f
```

7.   Open your virtual machine console.

8.   If your installation has succeeded, you will now see a graphical
     desktop appear in your virtual machine console.

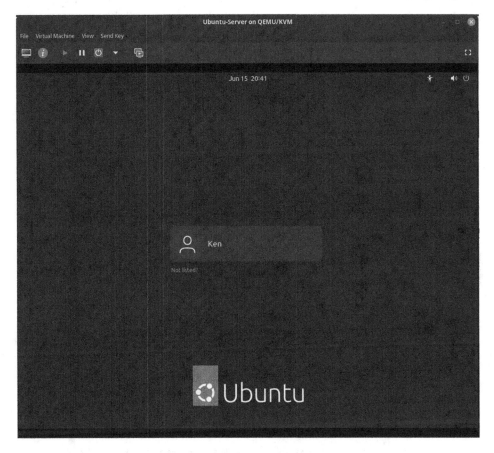

Figure 5-19.   *The Ubuntu graphical desktop login prompt*

9.   If your Ubuntu server has not booted into the graphical
     environment, you may need to run the following command from a
     new ssh session to your Ubuntu server:

```
# systemctl set-default graphical.target
```

OpenSUSE Server

The final Linux distribution we will install a desktop on is OpenSUSE server. The process remains very similar to both Fedora and Ubuntu.

For our OpenSUSE server, we will install the KDE Desktop.

1. The first step is to open a new ssh session to your OpenSUSE server.

2. As an optional step, you can see what desktops are available to install by running the following command:

   ```
   # sudo zypper packages | grep -i desktop
   ```

3. To install the KDE Desktop on your OpenSUSE server, run the following command:

   ```
   # zypper install -t pattern kde kde_plasma
   ```

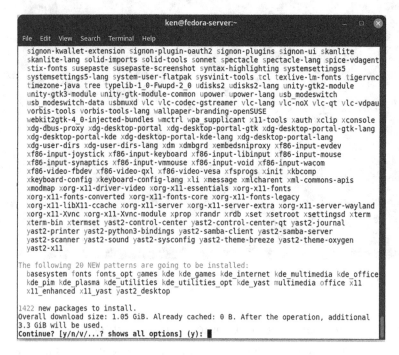

Figure 5-20. *OpenSUSE graphical desktop installation*

4. As with the Fedora and Ubuntu installs, type "y" and then press enter to install the packages for your OpenSUSE KDE Desktop.

5. Reboot by running the following command:

    ```
    # reboot -f
    ```

6. Run the following command to set the graphical environment to start on reboot:

    ```
    # systemctl set-default graphical.target
    ```

7. Open your virtual machine console:

8. If your installation has succeeded, you will now see a graphical desktop appear in your virtual machine console.

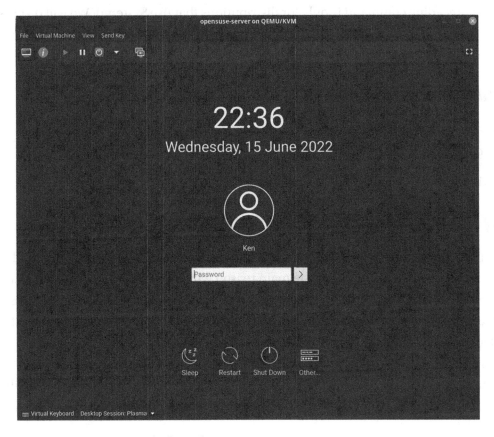

Figure 5-21. *OpenSUSE desktop login prompt*

9. You should now be able to log in with the user that you created when you installed your OpenSUSE server.

Enabling and Disabling Desktops

It may sometimes happen that your desktop environment was not set to start on boot or you may decide that you do not want your graphical interface to be default. To switch between the multi-user and graphical modes, you can do the following on each of your Linux distributions.

Enable Graphical Desktop

To enable and set your graphical interface as default, you will need to run the following command on your Linux server:

```
# systemctl set-default graphical.target
```

The preceding command is only for distributions that use Systemd. We will discuss that a bit later in this book, but for now, the three distributions we have been working with all support the commands.

Disable Graphical Desktop

To disable your graphical desktop as default, you will need to run the following command on your Linux server:

```
# systemctl set-default multi-user.target
```

Why Not Install Desktop During Installation

The multi-user mode is the default mode that is installed when you install a minimal Linux server installation. This was the main reason why in Chapter 4 we installed all our servers as minimal. Not only did it allow us to learn how to install the desktops in this chapter, it also ensured that our Linux installs were as small as possible with the least "surface area" available for security vulnerabilities.

As enterprise Linux system administrators, it is crucial to always install the absolute minimum and then add what content is required. This reduces as much risk as possible for anything to be installed that could be a potential backdoor into your environment.

Exercise

To practice installing different desktops, run through the following exercises to get a feel for what the other desktops look like and how to install them.

As Fedora was the quickest to install its desktop for me, we will use the Fedora server as our test system.

Remove Cinnamon

Open a new ssh session to your Fedora server and do the following.

1. Set your Fedora server to boot into a nongraphical mode.

2. Reboot.

3. Remove the "Cinnamon Desktop" packages with the following command:

```
# sudo dnf remove "" -y
```

Install the MATE Desktop

Open a new ssh session to your Fedora server if you are not still logged in.

1. Install all packages for "MATE Desktop".

2. Ensure that your new desktop will be started on reboot.

3. Reboot and have a look at the new desktop.

Optional – Try Another Desktop

Open a new ssh session to your Fedora server if you are not still logged in.

1. Remove packages for the "MATE Desktop".

2. Install all packages for the new desktop you wish to install.

3. Ensure that your new desktop will be started on reboot.

4. Reboot and have a look at the new desktop.

Summary

In this chapter, you were introduced to the following.

- How you can log in to your Linux system from an ssh client and how you can manage your Linux system if you cannot ssh to it

- How Linux can be managed via the Cockpit web console

- Basic introduction to Linux commands, including how to navigate and find files on the filesystem

- How shortcuts can be made for long commands and how scripts can be useful

- How to edit files using vi and vim

- Different Linux desktops and how to install them

- What to do when a Linux system does not boot into its graphical environment

PART III

Basic Configuration

The basics of installing your first Linux distributions were covered in Part 2, these being your first steps into using Linux. Part 3 expands on the knowledge gained as well as starts to look at some of the basic Linux usage concepts.

In Part 3, we will start by understanding how users can log in to their Linux distributions and how they can restrict access using ssh. We will delve into how users and groups are created and managed. We then continue on the same path of user management by exploring how files and directories can be protected and shared with different users.

With a solid foundation of user management covered, we will continue to explore package installation along with how systems are patched for the different distribution types you could be expected to manage as a Linux system administrator.

Part 3 will not end with these basic configuration options but will continue on to explain disk management, network configuration, and service management, giving you all you will need to know to manage basic Linux system configuration.

Where Part 2 was all about getting you to understand the Linux system deployment process, Part 3 is all about system configuration, taking you from system login to service configuration.

## CHAPTER 6

Access Control

In Chapter 5, we learned how to access a Linux environment, what some of the basic commands you need to know to navigate around the Linux command-line interface, and finally how to manage the graphical desktop for a Linux distribution.

In this chapter, we will dig a little further into how you will control the ssh access you allow to your system, how you could restrict access, and some of the important configuration you should be aware of. We will also briefly touch on how you would configure your local firewall to allow ssh if it were to be restricted.

With control on how and who can ssh into your Linux system, we will then delve into local users and groups on your Linux distributions. We will also discuss sudo and how you can configure sudo for your privileged users.

Finally, in this chapter, we will look at restricting files and directories based on the users allowed to use your system.

This chapter is your first step into Linux system administration; by stepping through the various layers of security, you will start to understand how you can protect your Linux systems from unwanted guests.

SSH and SSHD Configuration

Excluding users and firewall restrictions, controlling who and what can access your Linux system via ssh is extremely important to get right the first time. With the incorrect configuration, you could either lock yourself out of your system or allow unrestricted access to anyone with a user account.

© Kenneth Hitchcock 2023
K. Hitchcock, *The Enterprise Linux Administrator*, https://doi.org/10.1007/978-1-4842-8801-6_6

Configuration Files

For ssh configuration with modern Linux distributions, there are a few configuration files you need to be aware of. These will allow you to configure the access you wish to grant to users connecting to your system and how you would connect to other systems. Confusing? Let me explain.

There are two different configuration file types in the /etc/ssh directory. There are the ssh_config and sshd_config configuration files. Both look similar but serve very different purposes.

ssh_config

The ssh_config file and any subsequent ".conf" files in the ssh_config.d directory are related to configuration for your ssh client. This is where you would configure your ssh client configuration that may be required by the host you wish to ssh into. As an example, if an ssh host decided to use a different port for its ssh daemon, you could configure your ssh client to connect on the correct port.

sshd_config

Where the ssh_config configuration file is used for your ssh client, the sshd_config and any ".conf" files in the sshd_config.d directory are used to configure your ssh daemon running on your host. If you did not want to use your system as an ssh host, you can ignore this file and disable the sshd service.

ssh_config.d and sshd_config.d

The ssh_config.d and sshd_config.d are directories that can be used to store additional configuration files for each configuration type. If you wanted to create individual configuration files for different networks or hosts, you could create them here. The most important thing to remember is that all files created in this location must be saved with the .conf extension. This is the default configuration in the ssh_config and sshd_config files. You can of course change this to whatever else you want, but it is recommended to stick to the standard when working with many systems.

Important ssh Parameters

There are many different configuration parameters you can use for your ssh environments. To spend time going through all of them in this book would not be best served in this book; instead, we will only look at a few examples of important parameters that are used in enterprise environments and leave you to read the rest from the sshd_ config man page.

PermitRootLogin

A very simple parameter that allows you to block users logging in as root. This should always be set to "no" in a secure environment.

PasswordAuthentication

Another important parameter to set if you want to lock your systems down to only authorized users. By setting PasswordAuthentication to "no", you force users to log in with public-private keys.

Port

Rarely, there is a need to change the port used for ssh. The Port parameter can be used to adjust the port required to ssh into your system.

ListenAddress

As with the Port parameter, the ListenAddress parameter can be used to change which local network address would be listed for ssh connections. Useful if you want to keep ssh traffic down a secured network.

MaxAuthTries

A simple parameter to restrict the maximum number of auth attempts. Useful to prevent a brute-force attack.

UsePam

You may have noticed this parameter in some of the default ssh configurations. This parameter is normally set by default to "yes". All this does is allow ssh to make use of the pluggable authentication module. This is used for more advanced authentication configuration. For now, ensure it is always set to "yes" unless you have a good reason to set it to "no".

AllowUsers and DenyUsers

The AllowUsers and DenyUsers are, as the names imply, a way to allow users or deny them from logging into a system. The DenyUsers parameter is read before the AllowUsers parameter; be sure you have configured the users correctly to not have problems where users are blocked from logging in.

AllowGroups and DenyGroups

The AllowGroups and DenyGroups parameters are very much like the users equivalent but for groups. The same rule applies for Deny before Allow.

LogLevel

Used for debugging ssh issues. The parameter can be set to different degrees of verbosity from QUIET to DEBUG3. Step through the levels one by one if you ever need to resolve ssh issues.

Tip   Go through the man page for sshd_config and briefly get yourself familiar with some of the other parameters. Over time, you may need to use them for different systems.

Default Configuration

Even though all our Linux distributions we have used so far share similarities with configuration files for ssh, each has a different default configuration configured.

Fedora

The Fedora server is the upstream distribution for Red Hat Enterprise Linux, and it won't surprise you to find files on the Fedora filesystem with the Red Hat name. This is evident with the sshd configuration in the /etc/ssh/sshd_config.d directory, as a 50-redhat.conf exists with ssh configuration recommended for Fedora and potentially a newer RHEL version.

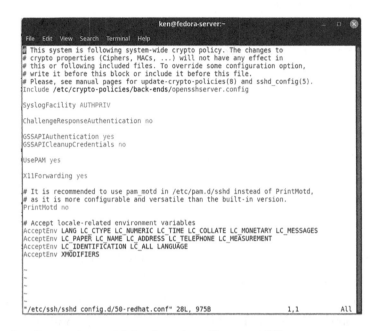

Figure 6-1. *Configuration within the 50-redhat.conf file*

A few default configuration lines do also exist in the ssd_config file, which include the following uncommented lines:

```
Include /etc/ssh/sshd_config.d/*.conf
AuthorizedKeysFile    .ssh/authorized_keys
Subsystem  sftp  /usr/libexec/openssh/sftp-server
```

Ubuntu

The Ubuntu server, unlike the Fedora server, does not have any configuration files by default in the /etc/ssh/sshd_config.d/ directory. Instead, the default configuration exists purely in the /etc/ssh/sshd_config file. The following is an output of all uncommented lines in a default Ubuntu server installation:

```
ken@ubuntu-server:~$ sudo cat /etc/ssh/sshd_config | grep -v "#" | uniq
[sudo] password for ken:

Include /etc/ssh/sshd_config.d/*.conf

KbdInteractiveAuthentication no

UsePAM yes

X11Forwarding yes
PrintMotd no

AcceptEnv LANG LC_*

Subsystem sftp  /usr/lib/openssh/sftp-server

PasswordAuthentication yes
```

OpenSUSE

The OpenSUSE server's sshd configuration is very limited in what is configured. One parameter, which may have been configured during the installation, is the ability to permit root to log in. Fedora and Ubuntu both do not permit root login with a default installation. The OpenSUSE server also does not have any sshd_config.d or ssh_config.d directories for configuration files. You most likely could copy the syntax from Fedora or Ubuntu to configure it if you like.

```
ken@opensuse-server:~> sudo cat /etc/ssh/sshd_config | grep -v "#" | uniq
[sudo] password for root:

PermitRootLogin yes

AuthorizedKeysFile     .ssh/authorized_keys

UsePAM yes

X11Forwarding yes

Subsystem      sftp    /usr/lib/ssh/sftp-server

AcceptEnv LANG LC_CTYPE LC_NUMERIC LC_TIME LC_COLLATE LC_MONETARY LC_MESSAGES
AcceptEnv LC_PAPER LC_NAME LC_ADDRESS LC_TELEPHONE LC_MEASUREMENT
AcceptEnv LC_IDENTIFICATION LC_ALL
```

SSH Service

The sshd daemon is controlled by a service appropriately named "sshd". Any configuration changes that are made to the sshd_config file or files in the sshd_config.d directory will not be applied unless you restart the sshd service or restart your system.

Test Syntax

To test the syntax of your sshd configuration files, you can run the test command provided by the sshd daemon:

```
# sudo /usr/sbin/sshd -t
```

If the preceding command does not return anything, your configuration files are configured without error.

Restart sshd

To restart the sshd daemon, you run the following command:

```
# sudo systemctl restart sshd
```

Check Status

To validate that your sshd daemon is running, run the following command:

```
# sudo systemctl status sshd
```

It is important to make sure that the sshd daemon is running and not reporting as dead. A dead service will mean no one can ssh into your system.

Warning   Always test your ssh configuration by restarting the sshd daemon. Rebooting your system and finding you are not able to ssh into it because of a syntax issue is just a terrible waste of time. It takes less than a few seconds to test.

Debugging ssh Issues

There are a number of things that can go wrong with your sshd daemon. The following are a few examples of things to look at.

Service Dead

The first thing to always check if a user reports they cannot log in to a system via ssh is whether the sshd service is running. The service should be reporting to be running and not dead. If the service has crashed for whatever reason, attempt to restart it. If the service fails to start, look at the output from the following command for more help:

```
# journalctl -xe
```

If you have any syntax issues, the journal output should help.

Syntax Error

Human error happens all the time; if the sshd service will not start, more than likely you have a syntax error. Run the following syntax check command or the journal -xe command to help identify the error:

```
# sudo /usr/sbin/sshd -t
```

Firewall Rule

The next major configuration that could prevent ssh access to your system is the local firewall or network firewall. The first step is to check if your firewall is enabled.

```
# sudo systemctl status firewalld
```

```
ken@opensuse-server:~> sudo systemctl status firewalld
▶ firewalld.service - firewalld - dynamic firewall daemon
    Loaded: loaded (/usr/lib/systemd/system/firewalld.service; enabled; vendor preset▊
    Active: active (running) since Wed 2022-06-15 22:36:24 BST; 2 days ago
      Docs: man:firewalld(1)
  Main PID: 1027 (firewalld)
     Tasks: 2 (limit: 4683)
    CGroup: /system.slice/firewalld.service
            └─1027 /usr/bin/python3 /usr/sbin/firewalld --nofork --nopid

Jun 15 22:36:23 opensuse-server systemd[1]: Starting firewalld - dynamic firewall daem▊
Jun 15 22:36:24 opensuse-server systemd[1]: Started firewalld - dynamic firewall daemo▊
lines 1-11/11 (END)
```

Figure 6-2. *Firewall status*

If you have your firewall enabled and it is running, you will need to confirm that the ssh daemon port is configured to allow access. The following command will list all firewall ports currently open:

```
# sudo firewall-cmd --list-all
```

```
ken@opensuse-server:~> sudo firewall-cmd --list-all
public (active)
  target: default
  icmp-block-inversion: no
  interfaces: eth0
  sources:
  services: dhcpv6-client ssh
  ports: 9090/tcp
  protocols:
  forward: no
  masquerade: no
  forward-ports:
  source-ports:
  icmp-blocks:
  rich rules:
ken@opensuse-server:~> ▮
```

Figure 6-3. *Firewall configuration listed with ssh included in the list*

In the event that your system has not been configured to allow ssh access, you will need to add the service or port. The following command will add the TCP port 22 to the allowed ports:

```
# sudo firewall-cmd --add-port=22/tcp --permanent
# sudo firewall-cmd --reload
```

Network and Port

If the firewall is configured correctly and your ssh service is running, you may need to confirm that the correct network and port have been configured in your ssh configuration. It is less likely this is the case but is definitely an area to validate.

Incorrect Allow or Deny

Finally, if your users are still not able to connect. Check that you have not added any users or groups incorrectly to the AllowUsers, DenyUsers, AllowGroups, and DenyGroups parameters.

Exercise

Now with a good understanding of the sshd environment and how to configure different parameters, it's time to practice what you have learned. The following are two exercises you can attempt on your own.

Change Port

This exercise is simply for you to change the listening port of sshd of your Ubuntu server and then configure your Fedora server to be able to ssh to it.

1. On your Ubuntu server, change the sshd listening port to 2222.

2. On your Fedora server, configure the ssh client to be able to access your Ubuntu server on the new port.

Tip   There is more to this exercise than what meets the eye. Think back to what you read in the last few pages.

Create custom_sshd.conf

This exercise requires that you create your own custom_ssd.conf file and configure it with all the configuration from exercise one. This needs to be done on your Ubuntu server.

1. In the host section, change the * to the IP address of your Fedora server.

```
Host *
#    ForwardAgent no
#    ForwardX11 no
#    ForwardX11Trusted yes
#    PasswordAuthentication yes
```

Figure 6-4. *Syntax example of custom_sshd.conf*

2. Remove any configuration from the main configuration files you may have created.

3. Reboot your Ubuntu server.

4. Ensure that users can still log in to your Ubuntu server.

Users and Groups

With access into your Linux system secured with ssh, the next step as a Linux administrator is to manage the users and groups that are allowed to log in to your system.

Local Users and Groups

As a Linux system administrator, you will from time to time need to create local users and groups; the general commands are straightforward but can be more complex if you wish them to be.

Configuration Files

The following files are used on most Linux platforms to store local user account information. These files should not be edited manually and should only be updated using the commands that will be discussed shortly.

Table 6-1 lists the files used to manage local Linux user accounts.

Table 6-1. *Linux files used to manage local user accounts*

Linux File	Description
/etc/passwd	Stores all the details about the user account, except the password.
/etc/shadow	Stores the password for the user.
/etc/group	Contains all the groups and group membership.

Creating Users

To create local users on most Linux distributions, you would use the following command:

```
# sudo useradd <username>
```

The useradd command has a fair few parameters you can use as can be in Figure 6-5. The only parameter you are forced to add is the name of the user you wish to create.

```
Options:
      --badnames                    do not check for bad names
  -b, --base-dir BASE_DIR           base directory for the home directory of the
                                    new account
      --btrfs-subvolume-home        use BTRFS subvolume for home directory
  -c, --comment COMMENT             GECOS field of the new account
  -d, --home-dir HOME_DIR           home directory of the new account
  -D, --defaults                    print or change default useradd configuration
  -e, --expiredate EXPIRE_DATE      expiration date of the new account
  -f, --inactive INACTIVE           password inactivity period of the new account
  -g, --gid GROUP                   name or ID of the primary group of the new
                                    account
  -G, --groups GROUPS               list of supplementary groups of the new
                                    account
  -h, --help                        display this help message and exit
  -k, --skel SKEL_DIR               use this alternative skeleton directory
  -K, --key KEY=VALUE               override /etc/login.defs defaults
  -l, --no-log-init                 do not add the user to the lastlog and
                                    faillog databases
  -m, --create-home                 create the user's home directory
  -M, --no-create-home              do not create the user's home directory
  -N, --no-user-group               do not create a group with the same name as
                                    the user
  -o, --non-unique                  allow to create users with duplicate
                                    (non-unique) UID
  -p, --password PASSWORD           encrypted password of the new account
  -r, --system                      create a system account
  -R, --root CHROOT_DIR             directory to chroot into
  -P, --prefix PREFIX_DIR           prefix directory where are located the /etc/* files
  -s, --shell SHELL                 login shell of the new account
  -u, --uid UID                     user ID of the new account
  -U, --user-group                  create a group with the same name as the user
  -Z, --selinux-user SEUSER         use a specific SEUSER for the SELinux user mapping
      --extrausers                  Use the extra users database
```

Figure 6-5. *The help options of the useradd command*

Setting a Password

If during your user creation process you fail to use the -p or --password parameter, you can set your user's password with the following command:

```
# sudo passwd <user>
```

```
ken@ubuntu-server:~$ sudo useradd ken2
ken@ubuntu-server:~$ sudo passwd ken2
New password:
BAD PASSWORD: The password fails the dictionary check - it is based on a dictionary wor
d
Retype new password:
passwd: password updated successfully
```

Figure 6-6. *Example of updating a password for a user*

Modifying a User

Once a user has been created, you can make any future changes with the usermod command. The usermod command has parameters you can use (see Figure 6-7).

```
Options:
  -b, --badnames             allow bad names
  -c, --comment COMMENT      new value of the GECOS field
  -d, --home HOME_DIR        new home directory for the user account
  -e, --expiredate EXPIRE_DATE  set account expiration date to EXPIRE_DATE
  -f, --inactive INACTIVE    set password inactive after expiration
                             to INACTIVE
  -g, --gid GROUP            force use GROUP as new primary group
  -G, --groups GROUPS        new list of supplementary GROUPS
  -a, --append              append the user to the supplemental GROUPS
                             mentioned by the -G option without removing
                             the user from other groups
  -h, --help                display this help message and exit
  -l, --login NEW_LOGIN     new value of the login name
  -L, --lock                lock the user account
  -m, --move-home           move contents of the home directory to the
                             new location (use only with -d)
  -o, --non-unique          allow using duplicate (non-unique) UID
  -p, --password PASSWORD   use encrypted password for the new password
  -R, --root CHROOT_DIR     directory to chroot into
  -P, --prefix PREFIX_DIR   prefix directory where are located the /etc/* files
  -s, --shell SHELL         new login shell for the user account
  -u, --uid UID             new UID for the user account
  -U, --unlock              unlock the user account
  -v, --add-subuids FIRST-LAST  add range of subordinate uids
  -V, --del-subuids FIRST-LAST  remove range of subordinate uids
  -w, --add-subgids FIRST-LAST  add range of subordinate gids
  -W, --del-subgids FIRST-LAST  remove range of subordinate gids
  -Z, --selinux-user SEUSER  new SELinux user mapping for the user account
```

Figure 6-7. *Additional parameters that can be used with the usermod command*

The usermod command is often used to add users to new or existing groups. Another common use could be to lock the user account if you need to secure it for a while.

Removing Users

Removing users when they are no longer needed is often a task that gets neglected and could potentially be an unwanted security hole in the future. To remove users, you can use the following command. Figure 6-8 shows additional parameters you can use.

```
# sudo userdel <user>
```

```
Options:
  -f, --force               force some actions that would fail otherwise
                             e.g. removal of user still logged in
                             or files, even if not owned by the user
  -h, --help                display this help message and exit
  -r, --remove              remove home directory and mail spool
  -R, --root CHROOT_DIR     directory to chroot into
  -P, --prefix PREFIX_DIR   prefix directory where are located the /etc/* files
  -Z, --selinux-user        remove any SELinux user mapping for the user
```

Figure 6-8. *Additional parameters for the userdel command*

User Password Management

Setting age limits on user passwords is highly recommended. You can view the age of a user's password by running the following command:

```
# sudo chage --list <user>
```

```
[ken@rhel9-server ~]$ chage --list ken
Last password change                                    : never
Password expires                                        : never
Password inactive                                       : never
Account expires                                         : never
Minimum number of days between password change          : 0
Maximum number of days between password change          : 99999
Number of days of warning before password expires       : 7
```

Figure 6-9. *The output of a user's password settings*

From Figure 6-9, you can see that the password for the user ken never expires. To change this behavior for any new users that are created, you will need to adjust the parameters in the "/etc/login.defs" file.

```
[ken@rhel9-server ~]$ sudo cat /etc/login.defs | grep PASS
#         PASS_MAX_DAYS   Maximum number of days a password may be used.
#         PASS_MIN_DAYS   Minimum number of days allowed between password changes.
#         PASS_MIN_LEN    Minimum acceptable password length.
#         PASS_WARN_AGE   Number of days warning given before a password expires.
PASS_MAX_DAYS   99999
PASS_MIN_DAYS   0
PASS_WARN_AGE   7
```

Figure 6-10. *A snippet of the /etc/login.defs file*

To adjust the password age for any users that have already been created, you can use a command similar to the following:

```
# sudo chage --mindays 7 --maxdays 90 --warndays 5 <user>
```

The preceding command will ensure that all the same configuration changes that are in the "/etc/login.defs" file are applied to the current user.

Creating Groups

Similar to how users are created, groups can be created with the following command:

```
# sudo groupadd <groupname>
```

Figure 6-11 is a list of the parameters you can use with the groupadd command.

```
Options:
  -f, --force                   exit successfully if the group already exists,
                                and cancel -g if the GID is already used
  -g, --gid GID                 use GID for the new group
  -h, --help                    display this help message and exit
  -K, --key KEY=VALUE           override /etc/login.defs defaults
  -o, --non-unique              allow to create groups with duplicate
                                (non-unique) GID
  -p, --password PASSWORD       use this encrypted password for the new group
  -r, --system                  create a system account
  -R, --root CHROOT_DIR         directory to chroot into
  -P, --prefix PREFIX_DIR       directory prefix
      --extrausers              Use the extra users database
```

Figure 6-11. *Additional options for the groupadd command*

Like the useradd command, the only mandatory parameter is the name of the group
you wish to create.

Modifying a Group

Just as with the ability to modify a user, you can modify a group with the following
command:

sudo groupmod <group>

```
Options:
  -g, --gid GID                 change the group ID to GID
  -h, --help                    display this help message and exit
  -n, --new-name NEW_GROUP      change the name to NEW_GROUP
  -o, --non-unique              allow to use a duplicate (non-unique) GID
  -p, --password PASSWORD       change the password to this (encrypted)
                                PASSWORD
  -R, --root CHROOT_DIR         directory to chroot into
  -P, --prefix PREFIX_DIR       prefix directory where are located the /etc/* files
```

Figure 6-12. *The groupmod command parameters that can be used to
modify a group*

The most common use of the groupmod command is to change the name of
the group.

Removing Groups

Similar to how users can be removed, groups can also be removed with their own
groupdel command:

sudo groupdel <group>

Figure 6-13 shows the additional parameters that can be used with the preceding command.

```
Usage: groupdel [options] GROUP

Options:
  -h, --help                  display this help message and exit
  -R, --root CHROOT_DIR       directory to chroot into
  -P, --prefix PREFIX_DIR     prefix directory where are located the /etc/* files
  -f, --force                 delete group even if it is the primary group of a user
```

Figure 6-13. *Additional parameters for the groupdel command*

Remote Users and Groups

Managing users and groups on a single Linux system is painless enough for most system administrators. However, when you have hundreds if not thousands of systems to manage, it can become a problem. This is most efficient when users or groups need to be added or removed. For this reason, having a way to centrally manage users is the recommended approach.

There are two common practices among most organizations; they are as follows.

Windows Active Directory

Windows Active Directory is one of the more common central user management tools used for Linux today. This is not a Linux tool nor is it OpenSource, but it still requires that you understand the basics if you are to become an Enterprise Linux administrator. You do not need to know how to install or configure Active Directory, you just need to know the basic concepts.

For more understanding on Active Directory, I would recommend watching a few YouTube videos or running through some of the free courses available on sites like Coursera.

FreeIPA

FreeIPA is an OpenSource alternative to the Windows Active Directory. Enterprise companies like Red Hat use the FreeIPA project as the upstream for their Enterprise equivalent of their product called Identity management or IdM. For more information on FreeIPA, have a look at the product documentation:

www.freeipa.org/

Using Remote Users and Groups

Whether you decide to use Windows Active Directory or IdM to manage your users, you will need to configure your Linux systems to authenticate to your central user management system if you want to log in with centrally managed users. For this functionality, there are different ways to configure this based on your central user management system.

Windows Active Directory

To connect to a Windows Active Directory from your Linux systems we installed, you will need to install a package called "realmd". With the "realmd" utility, you can join an Active Directory and configure which users and groups are allowed to log in to your system. More about "realmd" can be found in the following:

www.freedesktop.org/software/realmd/

IPA-Client

Similar to the "realmd" process of joining a system to the Windows Active Directory, FreeIPA or IdM, requires a client to be installed on each Linux system. The client that needs to be installed is the "ipa-client" package. The "ipa-client" would then be used to connect the Linux system to the central IdM or FreeIPA server. More of IdM can be read on the Red Hat documentation site:

https://access.redhat.com/documentation/en-us/red_hat_enterprise_
linux/8/html/installing_identity_management/assembly_installing-an-idm-
client_installing-identity-management

Unfortunately, the upstream documentation for the IPA-client is no longer being maintained. All efforts are being put into the Red Hat documentation.

Sudo

With the ability now for users to log in to your Linux environments. You will need to know how to restrict what users can do, or at very least have a way to audit what happens. This is where the use of sudo comes in.

All users no matter their skill level should log in with their own user account and never directly log in with the root user. To elevate permissions to enable users to run privileged commands, users should use the sudo command as a prefix, as you would have done in a few of the exercises or seen in some of the examples. This is the recommended security practice and should be followed as much as possible. Using sudo from our individual accounts allows for better auditing, a common practice for larger organizations.

Sudo Commands and Tools

As the Linux system administrator, it is your responsibility to ensure users have the appropriate permissions and access rights. Sudo is one of the simplest ways to ensure users can do what they are authorized to. A list of all the basic information you need to know about sudo is shown in Table 6-2.

Table 6-2 lists the basic information for using the sudo command.

Table 6-2. *Linux sudo information*

Linux Command	Description
sudo <command>	Running sudo before a privileged command will elevate the user's permissions so the command runs successfully.
sudo -i	Elevates the user to root. Same as the "sudo su -" command
visudo	Command to edit the sudoers file. Typically uses the vi editor.
/etc/sudoers	Default sudoers file; this is where permissions can be added or removed. Same file is edited using the visudo command.
/etc/sudoers.d	A directory for custom sudoers files to be stored. The sudo system will treat all the files in this directory as it would the sudoers file.

Managing Sudo

As a simple example of managing sudo, Figure 6-14 shows the configuration for my user that was created on my OpenSUSE server.

```
... . ........ ......
Defaults targetpw   # ask for the password of the target user i.e. root
ALL   ALL=(ALL) ALL   # WARNING! Only use this together with 'Defaults targetpw'!

##
## Runas alias specification
##

##
## User privilege specification
##
root ALL=(ALL) ALL

## Uncomment to allow members of group wheel to execute any command
# %wheel ALL=(ALL) ALL

## Same thing without a password
# %wheel ALL=(ALL) NOPASSWD: ALL

## Read drop-in files from /etc/sudoers.d
@includedir /etc/sudoers.d
```

Figure 6-14. *Example of a /etc/sudoers file*

But my user is nowhere to be seen? This is because the following line catches all the user's permission escalations and prompts them to insert the root or destination account's password:

```
ALL   ALL=(ALL)   ALL
```

If I wanted to save myself the pain of entering my password each time, I could add the following line to the /etc/sudoers file:

```
ken  ALL=(ALL)  NOPASSWD: ALL
```

Exercise

As a recently skilled Linux system administrator in the ways of managing users and groups, try and do the following exercises on your own to test your knowledge.

These exercises should be done on your Fedora server where possible.

Create a New User

Create a new user with the following:

- The user must be called testuser.

- Set the password to "password123" (without the quotes).

- Set the users shell to /bin/bash.

- Set the user's home directory to /newusershome/testuser.

Create a New Group

Create a new group and ensure the following conditions have been met:

- The group must be called newtestusers.

- The new user testuser must be part of this group.

- Set the group's gid to 5000.

Elevate Permissions

Configure your system to ensure that all users that are part of the newtestusers group can run privileged commands.

File and Directory Permissions

With a multitude of users on your Linux systems, there will always be the need to ensure that files and directories on your servers are kept secure. For this, there are a number of utilities that can be used. Each of these utilities is used on most, if not all, Linux distributions available today. This is only possible due to the standard that was created called POSIX. Most Linux distributions are POSIX compliant, but it is always worth checking if you decide to use something different.

Understanding Linux Permissions

Before you can learn to change file and directory permissions, you should have a good understanding of how to read the current permissions.

In Figure 6-15, when you run an "ls -al" command on your Linux system, you will see a listing of files and directories in your current location.

```
ken@opensuse-server:~> ls -al
total 24
drwxr-xr-x 1 ken   users  164 Jun 17 21:49 .
drwxr-xr-x 1 root  root     6 Jun  5 22:15 ..
-rw------- 1 ken   users  436 Jun 17 22:40 .bash_history
-rw-r--r-- 1 ken   users 1177 Jun  5 22:15 .bashrc
drwxr-xr-x 1 ken   users    0 Jun  5 22:15 bin
drwx------ 1 ken   users    0 Jun  5 22:15 .cache
drwx------ 1 ken   users    0 Jun  5 22:15 .config
-rw-r--r-- 1 ken   users 1637 Jun  5 22:15 .emacs
drwxr-xr-x 1 ken   users    0 Jun  5 22:15 .fonts
-rw-r--r-- 1 ken   users  861 Jun  5 22:15 .inputrc
-rw------- 1 ken   users   62 Jun 17 21:49 .lesshst
drwx------ 1 ken   users    0 Jun  5 22:15 .local
-rw-r--r-- 1 ken   users 1028 Jun  5 22:15 .profile
drwx------ 1 ken   users   30 Jun 14 20:05 .ssh
```

Figure 6-15. *Directory listing of the current directory*

There are a few important bits you need to understand. What access permissions have been set and who can access the content? If you are completely new to Linux, this may not make any sense, so let's explain how to interpret the data presented to you.

Directory Listing Explained

In the image shown in Figure 6-15, you have nine columns of information presented. Let's break each column down so they make more sense.

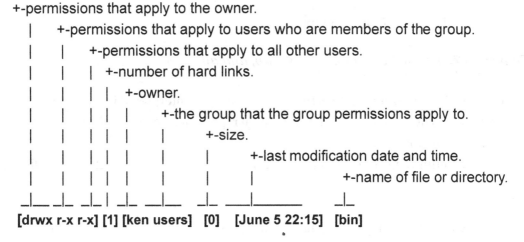

Figure 6-16. *Directory and file information broken down*

Managing File and Directory Permissions

With a basic understanding of file and directory permissions, the next logical step is to understand how to manage them. There are two main file and directory management utilities. Each has their own parameters and will feature quite highly on your day-to-day management of your Linux systems.

Chmod

The first utility is the "chmod" utility; this utility allows you to set the access properties of a file or directory. These properties are what is presented in the first column in your directory listing command. The access permissions are displayed as follows:

```
drwx rwx rwx
d = directory, r = read, w = write, x= execute
```

The access permissions column can also be further divided into three further columns of data.

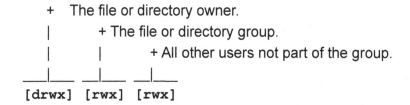

Figure 6-17. *Permissions for owner, group, and all other*

The permissions format of "rwx rwx rwx" can also be interpreted in a numerical format of "777". The d does not have a numerical representation as it indicates that the line item is a directory.

The maximum value for each set of "rwx" is 7. The value of 7 is calculated as follows:

```
r = 4, w = 2, x = 1
```

Using what we now know about file permissions and how values are calculated, if you wanted to set a permission of "rwx r-x r-x", you would need to set a permission value of "755", which brings us to how you would set file permissions.

The chmod utility has a few parameters that can be used and can also be seen in Figure 6-18, of which only one is often used: the -R for recursive, setting permissions to all child files and directories.

```
ken@opensuse-server:~> chmod --help
Usage: chmod [OPTION]... MODE[,MODE]... FILE...
  or:  chmod [OPTION]... OCTAL-MODE FILE...
  or:  chmod [OPTION]... --reference=RFILE FILE...
Change the mode of each FILE to MODE.
With --reference, change the mode of each FILE to that of RFILE.

  -c, --changes          like verbose but report only when a change is made
  -f, --silent, --quiet  suppress most error messages
  -v, --verbose          output a diagnostic for every file processed
      --no-preserve-root  do not treat '/' specially (the default)
      --preserve-root    fail to operate recursively on '/'
      --reference=RFILE  use RFILE's mode instead of MODE values
  -R, --recursive        change files and directories recursively
      --help     display this help and exit
      --version  output version information and exit

Each MODE is of the form '[ugoa]*([-+=]([rwxXst]*|[ugo]))+|[-+=][0-7]+'.

GNU coreutils online help: <https://www.gnu.org/software/coreutils/>
Full documentation <https://www.gnu.org/software/coreutils/chmod>
or available locally via: info '(coreutils) chmod invocation'
```

Figure 6-18. *Chmod command help menu*

To set new file permissions or to modify current file permissions, you would use the following command. You would of course need to adjust the permissions you wish to set based on what was discussed previously.

Example

If we created a new script file called test.sh, you will see in Figure 6-19 that it has been created with default permissions set by your Linux configuration.

```
ken@opensuse-server:~> touch test.sh
ken@opensuse-server:~> ls -al
total 24
drwxr-xr-x 1 ken  users  178 Jun 21 21:37 .
drwxr-xr-x 1 root root     6 Jun  5 22:15 ..
-rw------- 1 ken  users  436 Jun 17 22:40 .bash_history
-rw-r--r-- 1 ken  users 1177 Jun  5 22:15 .bashrc
drwxr-xr-x 1 ken  users    0 Jun  5 22:15 bin
drwx------ 1 ken  users    0 Jun  5 22:15 .cache
drwx------ 1 ken  users    0 Jun  5 22:15 .config
-rw-r--r-- 1 ken  users 1637 Jun  5 22:15 .emacs
drwxr-xr-x 1 ken  users    0 Jun  5 22:15 .fonts
-rw-r--r-- 1 ken  users  861 Jun  5 22:15 .inputrc
-rw------- 1 ken  users   62 Jun 17 21:49 .lesshst
drwx------ 1 ken  users    0 Jun  5 22:15 .local
-rw-r--r-- 1 ken  users 1028 Jun  5 22:15 .profile
drwx------ 1 ken  users   30 Jun 14 20:05 .ssh
-rw-r--r-- 1 ken  users_   0 Jun 21 21:37 test.sh
```

Figure 6-19. Example of script permissions being incorrect to run

The permissions set would be sufficient if we only wanted to store text in the file that could only be written to by its owner. However, as this is a script, we are missing an important execute permission. Without this permission, we could not execute the script and render it useless.

To fix this, we can run the following command:

```
# chmod 755 test.sh
```

```
ken@opensuse-server:~> chmod 755 test.sh
ken@opensuse-server:~> ls -al test.sh
-rwxr-xr-x 1 ken users 0 Jun 21 21:37 test.sh
```

Figure 6-20. Example of the correct permissions for a script to run

---

Note   There are alternative ways to run a script if the execute permissions are not set, but for the sake of this section, let's just pretend there are not.

Chown

The second important file and directory permission management utility is the chown tool. Chown is used to set the owner of a file or directory. Chown can also be used to set the group of the file or directory, but if you prefer, you can also use the chgrp utility.

In the directory listing explanation, the owner and group can be found in the third and the fourth column.

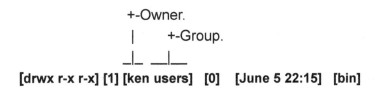

+-Owner.

| +-Group.

_|_ _|_

[drwx r-x r-x] [1] [ken users]   [0]   [June 5 22:15]   [bin]

Figure 6-21. *Directory listing explanation for the third and the fourth column*

Example

In the test.sh example where we created the test.sh file and set the correct execute permissions. Let us now change the owner and group to something different.

First, I created a new user and group.

```
ken@opensuse-server:~> sudo useradd ken2
[sudo] password for root:
ken@opensuse-server:~> sudo groupadd scriptusers
```

Figure 6-22. *Create a new user*

To change the script test.sh to use the new user and group, I run the following command:

```
# chown ken2:scriptusers test.sh
```

```
ken@opensuse-server:~> sudo chown ken2:scriptusers test.sh
ken@opensuse-server:~> ls -al test.sh
-rwxr-xr-x 1 ken2 scriptusers 0 Jun 21 21:37 test.sh
```

Figure 6-23. *Permissions updated for the new user*

From the output shown in Figure 6-23, you can now see that the test.sh is owned by the user ken2 and the group is now set to scriptusers.

ACLs

With your newly gained knowledge around file and directory permissions, you may be asking, "how can I add multiple users or groups with different permissions to a directory or file?" The answer for this is ACLs.

ACLs or access control lists can give you the ability to add additional users and groups to a file or directory. You can also set what default permissions are applied to any new files or directories.

There are two utilities that you need to know to be able to use ACLs.

getfacl

"getfacl" will give you all the ACL information for a directory or file.

```
ken@opensuse-server:/testacls> pwd
/testacls
ken@opensuse-server:/testacls> ls -al
total 0
drwxr-xr-x 1 root root   0 Jun 22 21:23 .
drwxr-xr-x 1 root root 172 Jun 22 21:23 ..
ken@opensuse-server:/testacls> getfacl .
# file: .
# owner: root
# group: root
user::rwx
group::r-x
other::r-x

ken@opensuse-server:/testacls> █
```

Figure 6-24. *Output of the getfacl command*

In Figure 6-25, a new directory called "testacls" was created on the base root filesystem. The owner and group for this directory are both root. Because the r-x permissions are on other users, we are able to access this directory as the "ken" user. However, new files cannot be created.

```
ken@opensuse-server:/> cd testacls/
ken@opensuse-server:/testacls> touch test
touch: cannot touch 'test': Permission denied
```

Figure 6-25. *Example of not being able to create new files*

To fix the permission issue from the previous screen, we can either create a group and assign it to the directory with my user as a member or change the ownership of the directory. Both would work but would be no good if we wanted to add more complex permissions to the directory, that is, allowing only certain users or groups to write or even view content.

setfacl

To set ACL permissions, we use the utility called "setfacl". As the name implies, setfacls will set values and getfacls will get values. Simple enough.

The setfacl utility has options you can use when setting ACL permissions (see Figure 6-26).

```
ken@opensuse-server:/testacls> setfacl --help
setfacl 2.2.53 -- set file access control lists
Usage: setfacl [-bkndRLP] { -m|-M|-x|-X ... } file ...
  -m, --modify=acl          modify the current ACL(s) of file(s)
  -M, --modify-file=file    read ACL entries to modify from file
  -x, --remove=acl          remove entries from the ACL(s) of file(s)
  -X, --remove-file=file    read ACL entries to remove from file
  -b, --remove-all          remove all extended ACL entries
  -k, --remove-default      remove the default ACL
      --set=acl             set the ACL of file(s), replacing the current ACL
      --set-file=file       read ACL entries to set from file
      --mask                do recalculate the effective rights mask
  -n, --no-mask             don't recalculate the effective rights mask
  -d, --default             operations apply to the default ACL
  -R, --recursive           recurse into subdirectories
  -L, --logical             logical walk, follow symbolic links
  -P, --physical            physical walk, do not follow symbolic links
      --restore=file        restore ACLs (inverse of `getfacl -R')
      --test                test mode (ACLs are not modified)
  -v, --version             print version and exit
  -h, --help                this help text
ken@opensuse-server:/testacls> █
```

Figure 6-26. *setfacl options*

The important parameters are modify "-m", remove "-x", default "-d", and the recursive parameter "-R".

With the example from the getfacl screenshot, if we wanted to set a new user to write in the testacls directory, we can use the following command:

```
# setfacl -m ken:rwx .
```

The output for this command can be seen in Figure 6-27.

```
ken@opensuse-server:/testacls> sudo setfacl -m ken:rwx .
ken@opensuse-server:/testacls> touch test.ken
ken@opensuse-server:/testacls> ls -al
total 0
drwxrwxr-x+ 1 root root    16 Jun 22 21:39 .
drwxr-xr-x  1 root root   172 Jun 22 21:23 ..
-rw-rw-r--+ 1 ken  users    0 Jun 22 21:39 test.ken
ken@opensuse-server:/testacls> getfacl .
# file: .
# owner: root
# group: root
user::rwx
user:ken:rwx
group::r-x
mask::rwx
other::r-x
default:user::rwx
default:user:ken:rwx
default:group::r-x
default:mask::rwx
default:other::r-x
```

Figure 6-27. *setfacl command output*

From the output in Figure 6-27, you can now see that the user has been added as a user with rwx permissions and is able to create a new file.

Example

If we were working with multiple users and we wanted to restrict access to directories or subdirectories, we could further make use of ACLs. With utilities like chmod and chown, we can set the owner and group of the base directory. This would normally be sufficient, but what if we wanted to add users that were not part of the aclgroup group and give them access not only to the testacl directory but also allow them to have their own directory that no one else can see but them? We would accomplish this with the following steps:

1. Using the testacl directory, we set the owner to root and the group to aclgroup:

    ```
    # sudo chown root:aclgroup /testacl
    ```

    We also set the chmod permissions to 750 so only users who are part of the aclgroup and root can access the directory.

    ```
    drwxr-x---+  1 root aclgroup   34 Jun 22 22:00 testacls
    ```

Figure 6-28. *Chmod 750 permissions*

2. With the permissions shown in Figure 6-28, you either need to be part of the aclgroup or root to access the directory. The only other way is to add users to the ACL of the testacl directory. To enable the new ken2 user to access the /testacl directory, we need to add ken2 to the testacl directory acl.

```
# sudo setfacl -m ken2:rwx /testacl
```

```
ken2@opensuse-server:/> getfacl /testacls/
getfacl: Removing leading '/' from absolute path names
# file: testacls/
# owner: root
# group: aclgroup
user::rwx
user:ken:rwx                         #effective:r-x
user:ken2:rwx                        #effective:r-x
group::r-x·
mask::r-x
other::---
default:user::rwx
default:user:ken:rwx
default:group::r-x
default:mask::rwx
default:other::r-x
```

Figure 6-29. *Output of the setfacl command*

3. Next, we create a new directory in the /testacl directory for ken2 called ken2.

```
# mkdir ken2
```

At this point, we don't have the permissions to do this as ken2, so we use the sudo command. In other environments, you more than likely would not have this permission, in which case you would do it with a user that does have permission.

```
ken2@opensuse-server:/testacls> mkdir ken2
mkdir: cannot create directory 'ken2': Permission denied
ken2@opensuse-server:/testacls> ls -alrt
total 0
drwxr-xr-x 1 root root      172 Jun 22 21:23 ..
-rw-rw-r--+ 1 ken  users      0 Jun 22 21:39 test.ken
-rw-rw-r--+ 1 ken2 users      0 Jun 22 22:00 test.ken2
drwxr-x---+ 1 root aclgroup   34 Jun 22 22:00 .
ken2@opensuse-server:/testacls> sudo mkdir ken2
[sudo] password for root:
ken2@opensuse-server:/testacls> ls -al
total 0
drwxr-x---+ 1 root aclgroup   42 Jun 22 22:36 .
drwxr-xr-x 1 root root      172 Jun 22 21:23 ..
drwxrwxr-x+ 1 root root        0 Jun 22 22:36 ken2
-rw-rw-r--+ 1 ken  users      0 Jun 22 21:39 test.ken
-rw-rw-r--+ 1 ken2 users      0 Jun 22 22:00 test.ken2
```

Figure 6-30. *Errors occurring due to lack of permissions*

4. Now with sudo again, we set the owner of the new ken2 directory
    to be owned by ken2 and the group to be set to aclgroup. We also
    set the permissions to 700.

```
ken2@opensuse-server:/testacls> sudo chown ken2:aclgroup ken2
ken2@opensuse-server:/testacls> ls -al
total 0
drwxr-x---+ 1 root aclgroup   42 Jun 22 22:36 .
drwxr-xr-x 1 root root      172 Jun 22 21:23 ..
drwxrwxr-x+ 1 ken2 aclgroup    0 Jun 22 22:36 ken2
-rw-rw-r--+ 1 ken  users      0 Jun 22 21:39 test.ken
-rw-rw-r--+ 1 ken2 users      0 Jun 22 22:00 test.ken2
ken2@opensuse-server:/testacls> chmod 700 ken2
ken2@opensuse-server:/testacls> ls -al
total 0
drwxr-x---+ 1 root aclgroup   42 Jun 22 22:36 .
drwxr-xr-x 1 root root      172 Jun 22 21:23 ..
drwx------+ 1 ken2 aclgroup    0 Jun 22 22:36 ken2
-rw-rw-r--+ 1 ken  users      0 Jun 22 21:39 test.ken
-rw-rw-r--+ 1 ken2 users      0 Jun 22 22:00 test.ken2
```

Figure 6-31. *Adjusting the permissions using sudo*

5. With the permissions shown in Figure 6-31, only ken2 has
    access. However, this is supposed to be a collaborative team, and
    sometimes, people will need to access some of ken2's files or
    directories. This is where additional ACLs can be added. In the
    following, we will add the user ken to also have rwx permissions
    on the ken2 directory:

```
# setfacl -m ken:rwx ken2
```

```
ken2@opensuse-server:/testacls> setfacl -m ken:rwx ken2
ken2@opensuse-server:/testacls> getfacl ken2
# file: ken2
# owner: ken2
# group: aclgroup
user::rwx
user:ken:rwx
group::r-x
mask::rwx
other::---
default:user::rwx
default:user:ken:rwx
default:group::r-x
default:mask::rwx
default:other::r-x
```

***Figure 6-32.** Results from the setfacl command*

6. With the configuration shown in Figure 6-32, both ken and ken2
   now have the ability to access and write files in the /testacl/ken2
   directory. New users like ken3 are denied access.

7. For added security on the directory, the sticky bit can be used:

   ```
   # sudo chmod +t directory
   ```

Exercise

With the knowledge gained from this section to manage file permissions, attempt the
following exercise.

File and Directory Permissions

Create the following on any one of your Linux servers that were created in the server
deployment chapter.

1. Create a new directory on your root filesystem called
   "testpermissions".

2. Create a new group called testgroup.

3. Create the following users:

   a. user1

   b. user2

   c. user3

4. Set passwords for the users if you like, but you can switch to them without passwords if you are already logged in.

5. Add only user1 and user2 to the testgroup.

6. Set file and directory ownership of the testpermissions directory to the root user and the group to testgroup.

7. Within the testpermissions directory, create the following directories:

   a. user1 owned by the user1 user and the group set to testgroup

   b. user2 owned by the user2 user and the group set to testgroup.

ACLs

To restrict the access of the testpermissions directory created in the previous exercise, configure the following.

1. user1 and user2 must be able to create files in the testpermissions directory. user2 should not have access at all.

2. user1 should only have access to the user1 directory.

3. user2 should be able to rwx in both the user1 and user2 directory.

Summary

In this chapter, you were introduced to the following:

- How ssh configuration works on a Linux system and how you can control access with ssh

- How users and groups are created

- What the correct methods of elevating permissions are and why it's never a good idea to log in directly as root

- Finally, how to manage file and directory permissions with the various Linux utilities available

CHAPTER 7

Package Installation

With a well-built and configured Linux system, there will come a time when maintenance or further system configuration will be needed. For that, as a Linux system administrator, it is very important to understand the system patching and Linux package installation process for the three major distributions used today.

In this chapter, we will work through the different package management systems used by the different Linux distributions we have used so far and look to understand how they differ from each other. We will also look to understand how packages can be downloaded manually and installed in a best practices manner. Finally, we will explore how your Linux distribution package installation options can be extended by adding new resource repositories.

Once done with this chapter, you will be well on your way to installing new content on any of the three Linux distributions we have used so far.

Installing Packages

Installing packages on your Linux system is often required when customizing Linux systems for their intended purpose. This could be as simple as installing a new text editor or adding a group of packages required for a desktop.

© Kenneth Hitchcock 2023
K. Hitchcock, *The Enterprise Linux Administrator*, https://doi.org/10.1007/978-1-4842-8801-6_7

Package Management Systems

If you recall from previous chapters, we run a few commands to install packages but did not expand much on the commands. In this section, we will look at the different package management systems that are available on the three different Linux distributions we have been using so far. Internet connectivity is required for these early exercises. However, local repositories can also be configured.

Fedora

On a Fedora desktop or server, the method to install packages remains the same. Packages can be installed through the command line using utilities like "dnf", "yum", and "rpm", and if you really want, you can build from source and deploy. Packages can also be installed on the graphical desktop using the desktop utilities.

Command Line

For almost all Linux administrators, the command line is almost always the first choice. For this reason, I will go through all the various options you are more than likely to use.

dnf

The most common package installation utility you will use on any of the new versions of Fedora is a utility called "dnf". As a replacement for the "yum" utility, "dnf" was introduced due to performance issues, dependency resolution delays, and occasional high memory usage problems with "yum" .

"dnf" is also the main package installation utility for Red Hat Enterprise Linux 8; being familiar with "dnf" is quite important if you are to work for any organization that uses RHEL.

There are a number of useful commands that "dnf" has that can help you find any packages you may need. Table 7-1 is a breakdown on the important options you should be aware of when using "dnf".

Table 7-1 lists the basic dnf command options.

Table 7-1. *Basic dnf options*

dnf Option	Description
Install	Tells dnf to install the package or packages that follow the "install" parameter.
Remove	Instructs dnf to remove the package or packages that follow the remove parameter.
whatprovides	If you need to install a package that contains a file but you are unsure of the package name, you can use the "whatprovides" parameter to query the various repositories for any packages that contain the file. To use the "whatprovides" parameter effectively, you give the full path to where the file exists or you can use the "*" wildcard to replace the path or extension.
repolist	All packages come from a repository of some kind. To query what repositories you have enabled, use the repolist parameter.
list	Lists all the packages available. The list parameter can be followed by the "installed" parameter to list all the installed packages on your system.

Using dnf

Using the "dnf" utility is fairly straightforward. Figures 7-1 and 7-2 show a basic example of installing, removing, and querying packages on a Fedora server.

```
[ken@fedora-server ~]$ sudo dnf install tmux -y
Last metadata expiration check: 0:44:42 ago on Mon 27 Jun 2022 21:12:02 BST.
Dependencies resolved.
================================================================================
 Package          Architecture        Version              Repository      Size
================================================================================
Installing:
 tmux             x86_64              3.2a-3.fc36           fedora          475 k

Transaction Summary
================================================================================
Install  1 Package

Total download size: 475 k
Installed size: 1.1 M
Downloading Packages:
tmux-3.2a-3.fc36.x86_64.rpm                         561 kB/s | 475 kB   00:00
--------------------------------------------------------------------------------
Total                                               279 kB/s | 475 kB   00:01
Running transaction check
Transaction check succeeded.
Running transaction test
Transaction test succeeded.
Running transaction
 Preparing        :                                                         1/1
 Installing       : tmux-3.2a-3.fc36.x86_64                                 1/1
 Running scriptlet: tmux-3.2a-3.fc36.x86_64                                 1/1
 Verifying        : tmux-3.2a-3.fc36.x86_64                                 1/1

Installed:
 tmux-3.2a-3.fc36.x86_64

Complete!
[ken@fedora-server ~]$ ▮
```

Figure 7-1. *An example of installing tmux using "dnf"*

```
[ken@fedora-server ~]$ sudo dnf remove tmux -y
Dependencies resolved.
===========================================================================================
 Package              Architecture        Version             Repository          Size
===========================================================================================
Removing:
 tmux                 x86_64              3.2a-3.fc36          @fedora             1.1 M

Transaction Summary
===========================================================================================
Remove  1 Package

Freed space: 1.1 M
Running transaction check
Transaction check succeeded.
Running transaction test
Transaction test succeeded.
Running transaction
  Preparing        :                                                              1/1
  Erasing          : tmux-3.2a-3.fc36.x86_64                                      1/1
  Running scriptlet: tmux-3.2a-3.fc36.x86_64                                      1/1
  Verifying        : tmux-3.2a-3.fc36.x86_64                                      1/1

Removed:
  tmux-3.2a-3.fc36.x86_64

Complete!
[ken@fedora-server ~]$ █
```

Figure 7-2. *An example of removing tmux*

With both of the commands, you will notice I used the "-y" switch; this is to automatically answer yes to any questions if I am sure I want to install the package.

Getting More out of dnf

To understand more about any command, it is always advisable to read the manual or man pages. "dnf" is no different.

man dnf or # dnf --help

Desktop

If the command line is not for you yet, the Linux desktop is another option that can be used to install packages. For this installation method, you will need to install or have your Linux desktop installed during the installation of your operating system.

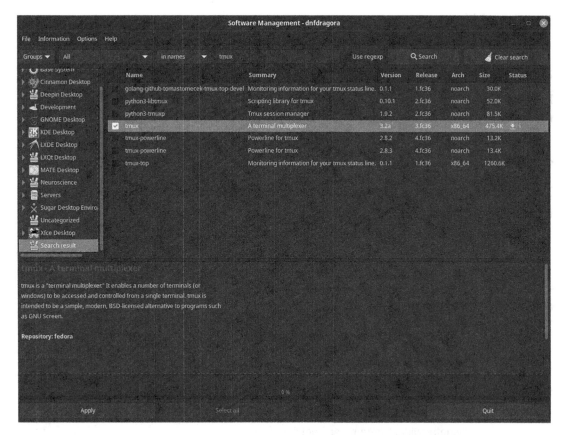

Figure 7-3. *To install packages on your Linux desktop, you can use the "dnfdragora" utility*

With dnfdragora, you can search and install any packages that are available to your system.

Ubuntu

Ubuntu, like Fedora, has its own package installation tooling to install packages manually or automatically. As Ubuntu is based on Debian, the package management system is the same as Debian, which is the Debian package management or "deb" for short. The package files normally have the ".deb" extension. These files can be installed manually or through a package installation tool called "apt" or the older "apt-get" utility. Packages can also be installed through the Linux desktop if you prefer not to use the command line.

Command Line

The command-line Ubuntu package installation utility that most use is called "apt". "apt" is a simplified version of the "apt-get" utility and does a few things other than just install packages. This includes the ability to act as an interface to the "dpkg" utility and assist in resolving dependency issues, very similar to how "dnf" does for Fedora.

apt

The "apt" utility has a few parameters you will need to be familiar with. Table 7-2 shows a basic list of parameters to get you started.

Table 7-2 lists the basic apt command options.

Table 7-2. *Basic apt options*

dnf Option	Description
install	Tells apt to install the package or packages that follow the "install" parameter.
remove	Instructs apt to remove the package or packages that follow the remove parameter.
search	apt has the ability to search for string values in package descriptions, allowing you to find any packages that contain files you may be looking for. Very similar to the "whatprovides" parameter from "dnf".
show	Describes the details of a package that is listed in the search option.
list	Will list packages available; if followed by the "--installed" parameter, it will list all installed packages.
autoremove	Removes all unused packages.

Using apt

Figures 7-4 and 7-5 are examples of installing and removing packages using the apt utility.

```
ken@ubuntu-server:~$ sudo apt install tmux -y
Reading package lists... Done
Building dependency tree... Done
Reading state information... Done
The following packages were automatically installed and are no longer required:
  pastebinit python3-newt run-one
Use 'sudo apt autoremove' to remove them.
The following NEW packages will be installed:
  tmux
0 upgraded, 1 newly installed, 0 to remove and 76 not upgraded.
Need to get 428 kB of archives.
After this operation, 1,051 kB of additional disk space will be used.
Get:1 http://gb.archive.ubuntu.com/ubuntu jammy/main amd64 tmux amd64 3.2a-4build1 [428 kB]
Fetched 428 kB in 0s (1,117 kB/s)
Selecting previously unselected package tmux.
(Reading database ... 197336 files and directories currently installed.)
Preparing to unpack .../tmux_3.2a-4build1_amd64.deb ...
Unpacking tmux (3.2a-4build1) ...
Setting up tmux (3.2a-4build1) ...
Processing triggers for man-db (2.10.2-1) ...
Scanning processes...
Scanning candidates...
Scanning linux images...

Restarting services...
 /etc/needrestart/restart.d/systemd-manager
 systemctl restart packagekit.service ssh.service systemd-journald.service systemd-networkd.service sys
temd-oomd.service systemd-resolved.service systemd-timesyncd.service systemd-udevd.service udisks2.serv
ice upower.service
Service restarts being deferred:
 systemctl restart NetworkManager.service
 systemctl restart systemd-logind.service
 systemctl restart user@1000.service
 systemctl restart wpa_supplicant.service

No containers need to be restarted.

No user sessions are running outdated binaries.

No VM guests are running outdated hypervisor (qemu) binaries on this host.
```

Figure 7-4. *An example of installing the "tmux" package using apt*

```
ken@ubuntu-server:~$ sudo apt remove tmux -y
Reading package lists... Done
Building dependency tree... Done
Reading state information... Done
The following packages were automatically installed and are no longer required:
  libevent-core-2.1-7 pastebinit python3-newt run-one
Use 'sudo apt autoremove' to remove them.
The following packages will be REMOVED:
  tmux
0 upgraded, 0 newly installed, 1 to remove and 76 not upgraded.
After this operation, 1,051 kB disk space will be freed.
(Reading database ... 197344 files and directories currently installed.)
Removing tmux (3.2a-4build1) ...
Processing triggers for man-db (2.10.2-1) ...
ken@ubuntu-server:~$ 
```

Figure 7-5. *An example of removing the "tmux" package using apt*

Getting More out of apt

To learn more about the "apt" utility, you can read the man pages or look at the help.

```
# man apt
```

or

```
# apt --help
```

```
ken@ubuntu-server:~$ apt --help
apt 2.4.5 (amd64)
Usage: apt [options] command

apt is a commandline package manager and provides commands for
searching and managing as well as querying information about packages.
It provides the same functionality as the specialized APT tools,
like apt-get and apt-cache, but enables options more suitable for
interactive use by default.

Most used commands:
  list - list packages based on package names
  search - search in package descriptions
  show - show package details
  install - install packages
  reinstall - reinstall packages
  remove - remove packages
  autoremove - Remove automatically all unused packages
  update - update list of available packages
  upgrade - upgrade the system by installing/upgrading packages
  full-upgrade - upgrade the system by removing/installing/upgrading packages
  edit-sources - edit the source information file
  satisfy - satisfy dependency strings

See apt(8) for more information about the available commands.
Configuration options and syntax is detailed in apt.conf(5).
Information about how to configure sources can be found in sources.list(5).
Package and version choices can be expressed via apt_preferences(5).
Security details are available in apt-secure(8).
                              This APT has Super Cow Powers.
```

Figure 7-6. *Apt utility help*

Desktop

Installing packages using the Linux desktop is one of the easier options available, that is, if you have the desktop installed. With most server environments, this won't always be the case, but if you prefer, you can use the software center tool for Ubuntu.

On a minimal installation of Ubuntu server, software center will not be available. To install the software center, you will first need to install it on the command line.

```
# sudo apt install gnome-software -y
```

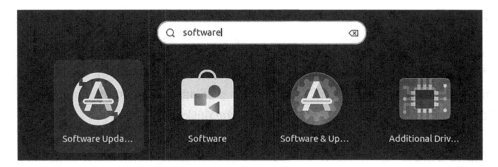

Figure 7-7. *An example of the software utility on the desktop called "Software"*

With the "software center" utility, you will be able to search and install packages available to your Ubuntu server. Figure 7-8 is an example of installing the tmux package.

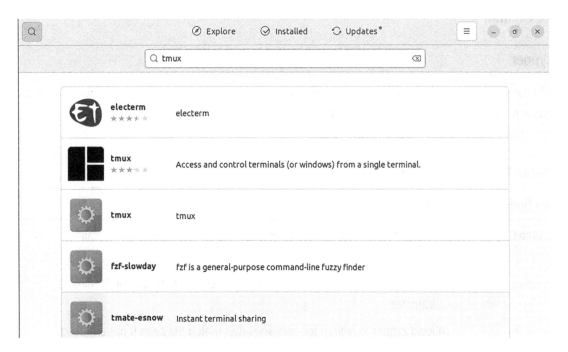

Figure 7-8. *An example of installing tmux using the desktop utilities*

OpenSUSE

Very much how Ubuntu's package management system is different from Fedora, OpenSUSE is different again from both Ubuntu and Fedora. OpenSUSE uses a package management system called "ZYpp". "ZYpp" is the package management engine that is used by the command-line utility "zypper" and the desktop utility "YaST".

Command Line

The command-line OpenSUSE package installation utility is the "zypper" utility. "Zypper" acts as a conduit to the "ZYpp" package engine. "ZYpp" does all the heavy lifting and feeds back the results to "zypper"; this includes the ability to resolve dependency issues, very similar to how "dnf" does for Fedora and "dpkg" does for Ubuntu.

Zypper

The "zypper" utility has a few parameters you will need to be familiar with. Table 7-3 is a basic list of parameters to get you started.

Table 7-3 lists the basic zypper options.

Table 7-3. *Basic zypper options*

dnf Option	Description
install	Tells zypper to install the package or packages that follow the "install" parameter.
remove	Tells zypper to remove the package or packages that follow the "remove" parameter.
search	Allows zypper to search for packages that match the search pattern used.
info	Gives information of the package specified.
packages	Will list all packages available in currently enabled repositories.
purge-kernels	Removes all unused kernels.

Using Zypper

Figures 7-9 and 7-10 are examples of installing and removing packages using the zypper utility.

```
ken@opensuse-server:~> sudo zypper install tmux
Loading repository data...
Reading installed packages...
Resolving package dependencies...

The following NEW package is going to be installed:
  tmux

1 new package to install.
Overall download size: 379.5 KiB. Already cached: 0 B. After the operation, additional 936.4 KiB will
be used.
Continue? [y/n/v/...? shows all options] (y): y
Retrieving package tmux-3.1c-bp153.1.16.x86_64                            (1/1), 379.5 KiB (936.4 KiB unpacked)
Retrieving: tmux-3.1c-bp153.1.16.x86_64.rpm ....................................................[done]

Checking for file conflicts: ...................................................................[done]
(1/1) Installing: tmux-3.1c-bp153.1.16.x86_64 ..................................................[done]
ken@opensuse-server:~> █
```

Figure 7-9. *An example of installing the "tmux" package using zypper*

```
ken@opensuse-server:~> sudo zypper remove tmux
Reading installed packages...
Resolving package dependencies...

The following package is going to be REMOVED:
  tmux

1 package to remove.
After the operation, 936.4 KiB will be freed.
Continue? [y/n/v/...? shows all options] (y): y
(1/1) Removing tmux-3.1c-bp153.1.16.x86_64 .....................................................[done]

ken@opensuse-server:~> █
```

Figure 7-10. *An example of removing the "tmux" package using zypper*

Compared to other package installation utilities, zypper's output is far less.

Getting More out of Zypper

To learn more about the "zypper" utility, you can read the man pages or look at the help.

man zypper or # zypper --help

```
ken@opensuse-server:~> zypper --help

Usage:

    zypper [--GLOBAL-OPTIONS] <COMMAND> [--COMMAND-OPTIONS] [ARGUMENTS]
    zypper <SUBCOMMAND> [--COMMAND-OPTIONS] [ARGUMENTS]

Global Options:

    --help, -h              Help.
    --version, -V           Output the version number.
    --promptids             Output a list of zypper's user prompts.
    --config, -c <FILE>     Use specified config file instead of the default.
    --userdata <STRING>     User defined transaction id used in history and plugins.
    --quiet, -q             Suppress normal output, print only error messages.
    --verbose, -v           Increase verbosity.
    --color
    --no-color              Whether to use colors in output if tty supports it.
    --no-abbrev, -A         Do not abbreviate text in tables. Default: false
    --table-style, -s <INTEGER>
                            Table style (0-11).
    --non-interactive, -n   Do not ask anything, use default answers automatically. Default: false
    --non-interactive-include-reboot-patches
                            Do not treat patches as interactive, which have the rebootSuggested-flag
                            set. Default: false
    --xmlout, -x            Switch to XML output.
    --ignore-unknown, -i    Ignore unknown packages. Default: false
    --terse, -t             Terse output for machine consumption. Implies --no-abbrev and
                            --no-color.
```

Figure 7-11. *Zypper additional parameters and help*

```
Commands:

    help, ?                 Print zypper help
    shell, sh               Accept multiple commands at once.

Repository Management:

    repos, lr               List all defined repositories.
    addrepo, ar             Add a new repository.
    removerepo, rr          Remove specified repository.
    renamerepo, nr          Rename specified repository.
    modifyrepo, mr          Modify specified repository.
    refresh, ref            Refresh all repositories.
    clean, cc               Clean local caches.

Service Management:

    services, ls            List all defined services.
    addservice, as          Add a new service.
    modifyservice, ms       Modify specified service.
    removeservice, rs       Remove specified service.
    refresh-services, refs
                            Refresh all services.

Software Management:

    install, in             Install packages.
    remove, rm              Remove packages.
    verify, ve              Verify integrity of package dependencies.
    source-install, si      Install source packages and their build dependencies.
    install-new-recommends, inr
                            Install newly added packages recommended by installed packages.
```

Desktop

The desktop utility for package installation on OpenSUSE is called "YaST" (Yet another Setup Tool). As with other package installation tools, it is quite simple to use and relatively self-explanatory.

To open YaST, click the utility menu and search for "YaST". This will open the "YaST" control center. From there, you can open the Software Management part of "YaST".

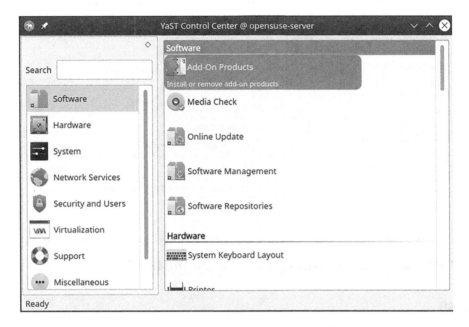

Figure 7-12. *OpenSUSE YaST screen for software installations*

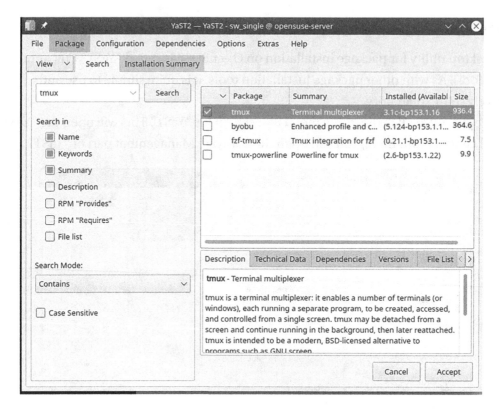

Figure 7-13. *The search for packages to install using YaST*

Exercise

To continue practicing how packages are installed, removed, and investigated, the following exercise is going to require that you install packages on all three of your Linux distributions you have installed so far.

   If you have deleted your virtual machines or if you are using a physical system for your testing, it would be advisable to create virtual machines for each of the distributions we are using.

Installing Packages via Command Line

Log in to each of your Fedora, Ubuntu, and OpenSUSE systems and install the package "figlet". To test if the package is working, run the following command on each of your systems:

```
# figlet test
```

```
ken@ubuntu-server:~$ figlet test
```

Figure 7-14. *An example output that your tests should be similar to*

Removing Packages Using the Desktop

Now that the figlet package is installed on each of your Linux systems, remove the figlet package with the desktop utility for each distribution.

To verify that all the figlet packages are removed, run the figlet test again:

```
# figlet test
```

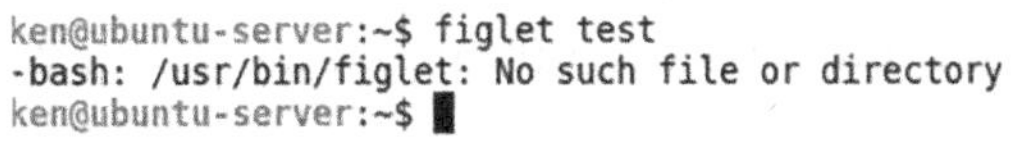

```
ken@ubuntu-server:~$ figlet test
-bash: /usr/bin/figlet: No such file or directory
ken@ubuntu-server:~$ ▮
```

Figure 7-15. *An example output that your tests should be similar to*

Manual Package Installation

There sometimes comes a time when packages are not available in your package management system like "dnf", "apt", or "zypper". When this happens, you are only left with installing packages manually.

The two package types that are commonly used across most Linux distributions are RPM and Deb. There are other methods of package installation, but for now, focus on understanding these two.

RPM

The Red Hat package manager (rpm) is the package management system for Fedora, Red Hat Enterprise Linux, and OpenSUSE to name a few. "rpm" files always contain a .rpm extension and are installed using the "rpm" utility.

"rpm" files are effectively a packaged set of files, scripts, and binaries that are copied and configured according to the rpm spec file. This spec file is the recipe that details where files are copied and what file permissions they are configured with.

Instead of writing a script each time you need your application deployed, you can bundle everything with an rpm file. "rpm" files can also be versioned and stored in central repositories for other systems to access, very useful if you need to do mass deployments.

Installing an rpm Package

As mentioned, "rpm" files are installed using the "rpm" utility. The following is a common example of installing an "rpm" file. Some rpm files may have dependencies to other rpm files. When installing your rpm, take note of what other rpms may be required.

```
# rpm -ivh /path/to/testrpm.rpm
```

Uninstalling an rpm Package

To remove an rpm file from your system, you can use a command similar to the following:

```
# rpm -e testrpm.rpm
```

Learning More About rpm

The "rpm" utility has a number of switches that can be viewed using the man page or the help page.

```
# man rpm
# rpm --help
```

We could dedicate an entire chapter to the functionality of "rpm", but as you are still learning, understanding how to install and erase is enough to know for now.

Warning   If you ever need to install a kernel from rpm, *never* use the "-u" parameter. This will update the current kernel and not install a separate kernel. The problem with this is if your new kernel has an issue, you will not be able to boot into your previous kernel, potentially leaving you in a position where you will need to boot your system into rescue mode.

Deb

The Ubuntu and other Debian forked Linux distributions all use the "deb" packaging format. "deb" files contain two tar files: one for the information that determines where files, binaries, and scripts are stored and configured and one tar file that stores the actual files.

Unlike the "rpm" package installer, deb files are installed using the "dpkg" utility.

Installing a "deb" Package

As mentioned, "deb" files are installed using the "dpkg" utility. The following is a common example of installing a "deb" package:

```
# dpkg -i /path/to/testdeb.deb
```

Uninstalling a "deb" Package

To remove a "deb" package from your system, you can use a command similar to the following:

```
# dpkg -r testdeb.deb
```

Learning More About dpkg

The "dpkg" utility has a number of switches that can be viewed using the man page or the help page.

```
# man dpkg
# dpkg --help
```

Installing Manually Using dnf, apt, and zypper

A better approach to installing "rpm" or "deb" packages manually would be through the use of the various package installation utilities distributed with your Linux system.

Dependencies

The reason why these package installation utilities are better is largely due to their ability to resolve dependencies. Not all packages are packaged with all binaries, utilities, or scripts required for them to run. For this reason, packages are often configured to request or stop when another package is required. This is where the package installation utility helps the most. If the package installation utility detects the dependency, it will go and attempt to download and install any requirements your package may have, saving you time and effort from searching and downloading packages manually.

Installing a Package Using a Package Installation Utility

To install a package using "dnf", "apt", or "zypper", you can use a similar command:

```
# dnf install testrpm.rpm
# apt install testbed.deb
# zypper install testrpm.rpm
```

Removing a Package Using a Package Installation Utility

The removal process is very much the same as if you were installing and removing a package from a repository. See the previously discussed sections on the different package installation utilities.

Exercise

To start installing packages manually on your Linux systems, let's continue with our previously used package: figlet.

Install figlet Manually

On each of the Linux distributions you have deployed, download and install the figlet rpm or deb file on each system.

Feel free to download the latest version of figlet, but at the time of writing, the current rpm version was

http://rpmfind.net/linux/RPM/fedora/devel/rawhide/x86_64/f/figlet-2.2.5-23.20151018gita565ae1.fc36.x86_64.html

Current deb package

https://packages.debian.org/sid/amd64/figlet/download

Download from any mirror you choose.

Tip   Copy the URL from your browser and use the "wget" utility: wget
`http://ftp.uk.debian.org/debian/pool/main/f/figlet/`
`figlet_2.2.5-3+b1_amd64.deb`.

Remove figlet

Using your package management utility, remove figlet from all your systems.

Confirm that figlet is no longer installed by running the following command:

```
# figlet test
```

Repository Configuration

So far in this chapter, we have only spoken about how packages can be installed, both
automatically and manually. We have even touched on how dependencies are managed.
However, we have not mentioned where packages come from that are installed via
package management systems like "dnf", "apt", or "zypper". I suppose technically we did
cover manual package installations using these tools but we did not discuss where the
dependencies come from.

This is where repositories come into the picture. When writing this book, I purposely
decided to start with community-driven Linux distributions for many reasons. One
of those reasons is that these distributions come preconfigured with community
repositories. There is no need for subscriptions to enable these repositories, and they are
available "out of the box."

These "out-of-the-box" repositories are often more than enough for package
installations. It really is only in certain situations you may need additional repositories
or have an environment that is not connected to the Internet to automatically download
packages. For these situations, it is very important to understand how repositories are
configured.

Fedora

Fedora uses the "rpm" package installation utility that is generally controlled using the "dnf" package management system. "dnf" makes use of repositories that are configured in files stored in the location shown in Figure 7-16.

```
[ken@fedora-server ~]$ ls -alrt /etc/yum.repos.d/
total 44
-rw-r--r--.   1 root root 1344 Apr 11 20:09 fedora-updates-testing.repo
-rw-r--r--.   1 root root 1391 Apr 11 20:09 fedora-updates-testing-modular.repo
-rw-r--r--.   1 root root 1286 Apr 11 20:09 fedora-updates.repo
-rw-r--r--.   1 root root 1349 Apr 11 20:09 fedora-updates-modular.repo
-rw-r--r--.   1 root root 1239 Apr 11 20:09 fedora.repo
-rw-r--r--.   1 root root 1302 Apr 11 20:09 fedora-modular.repo
-rw-r--r--.   1 root root  728 Apr 11 20:09 fedora-cisco-openh264.repo
drwxr-xr-x.   2 root root 4096 Jun  4 22:57 .
drwxr-xr-x. 140 root root 8192 Jul  3 22:50 ..
```

Figure 7-16. *Directory location for dnf repo files*

Within this directory, files with the extension ".repo" are stored. These files contain the connection details for the repositories that "dnf" or "yum" will use.

Example of a Repository File

Each repository within the file shown in Figure 7-17 starts with a repository name in square brackets, that is, [fedora]. Under these repositories are a few important parameters that should always be included with any repository:

- name
- metalink or baseurl
- enabled

```
[fedora]
name=Fedora $releasever - $basearch
#baseurl=http://download.example/pub/fedora/linux/releases/$releasever/Everything/$basearch/os/
metalink=https://mirrors.fedoraproject.org/metalink?repo=fedora-$releasever&arch=$basearch
enabled=1
countme=1
metadata_expire=7d
repo_gpgcheck=0
type=rpm
gpgcheck=1
gpgkey=file:///etc/pki/rpm-gpg/RPM-GPG-KEY-fedora-$releasever-$basearch
skip_if_unavailable=False

[fedora-debuginfo]
name=Fedora $releasever - $basearch - Debug
#baseurl=http://download.example/pub/fedora/linux/releases/$releasever/Everything/$basearch/debug/tree/
metalink=https://mirrors.fedoraproject.org/metalink?repo=fedora-debug-$releasever&arch=$basearch
enabled=0
metadata_expire=7d
repo_gpgcheck=0
type=rpm
gpgcheck=1
gpgkey=file:///etc/pki/rpm-gpg/RPM-GPG-KEY-fedora-$releasever-$basearch
skip_if_unavailable=False

[fedora-source]
name=Fedora $releasever - Source
#baseurl=http://download.example/pub/fedora/linux/releases/$releasever/Everything/source/tree/
metalink=https://mirrors.fedoraproject.org/metalink?repo=fedora-source-$releasever&arch=$basearch
enabled=0
metadata_expire=7d
repo_gpgcheck=0
type=rpm
gpgcheck=1
gpgkey=file:///etc/pki/rpm-gpg/RPM-GPG-KEY-fedora-$releasever-$basearch
skip_if_unavailable=False
```

Figure 7-17. *An example of a Fedora repository file*

Creating Your Own Repository File

In most situations, you will have the example repo files in the /etc/yum.repos.d/ directory, but in the rare occasion where someone has deleted them, you can recreate them manually. All the parameter options you can use are available to view in the man pages for dnf.conf.

```
# man dnf.conf
```

List Available Repositories

To view what repositories are available to your Fedora system, you can use the command shown in Figure 7-18.

```
# dnf repolist
```

```
[ken@fedora-server ~]$ dnf repolist
repo id                              repo name
fedora                               Fedora 36 - x86_64
fedora-cisco-openh264                Fedora 36 openh264 (From Cisco) - x86_64
fedora-modular                       Fedora Modular 36 - x86_64
updates                              Fedora 36 - x86_64 - Updates
updates-modular                      Fedora Modular 36 - x86_64 - Updates
```

Figure 7-18. *An example of the output for the dnf repolist command*

Ubuntu

Ubuntu being based on Debian is quite different in how repositories are configured. Unlike Fedora and OpenSUSE, Ubuntu makes use of the deb package method, which manages its repositories from the /etc/apt directory. Within this directory, there is the sources.list configuration file that contains all the repository information.

```
ken@ubuntu-server:~$ ls -alrt /etc/apt/
total 48
drwxr-xr-x    2 root root  4096 Apr  8 10:22 sources.list.d
drwxr-xr-x    2 root root  4096 Apr  8 10:22 preferences.d
drwxr-xr-x    2 root root  4096 Apr  8 10:22 keyrings
drwxr-xr-x    2 root root  4096 Apr  8 10:22 auth.conf.d
drwxr-xr-x    2 root root  4096 Apr 21 01:00 trusted.gpg.d
-rw-r--r--    1 root root  2403 Apr 21 01:01 sources.list.curtin.old
-rw-r--r--    1 root root  2437 Jun  3 21:54 sources.list
drwxr-xr-x    8 root root  4096 Jun  3 21:54 .
drwxr-xr-x    2 root root  4096 Jun 15 20:36 apt.conf.d
drwxr-xr-x  145 root root 12288 Jun 28 21:09 ..
ken@ubuntu-server:~$
```

Figure 7-19. *Ubuntu directory where repository files are stored*

The sources.list.d directory can also contain files with a ".list" extension for any custom repositories. These files can be cloned from the sources.list file for an example of the syntax.

Example of a repository file

```
⍰ See http://help.ubuntu.com/community/UpgradeNotes for how to upgrade to
# newer versions of the distribution.
deb http://gb.archive.ubuntu.com/ubuntu jammy main restricted
# deb-src http://gb.archive.ubuntu.com/ubuntu jammy main restricted

## Major bug fix updates produced after the final release of the
## distribution.
deb http://gb.archive.ubuntu.com/ubuntu jammy-updates main restricted
# deb-src http://gb.archive.ubuntu.com/ubuntu jammy-updates main restricted

## N.B. software from this repository is ENTIRELY UNSUPPORTED by the Ubuntu
## team. Also, please note that software in universe WILL NOT receive any
## review or updates from the Ubuntu security team.
deb http://gb.archive.ubuntu.com/ubuntu jammy universe
# deb-src http://gb.archive.ubuntu.com/ubuntu jammy universe
deb http://gb.archive.ubuntu.com/ubuntu jammy-updates universe
# deb-src http://gb.archive.ubuntu.com/ubuntu jammy-updates universe

## N.B. software from this repository is ENTIRELY UNSUPPORTED by the Ubuntu
## team, and may not be under a free licence. Please satisfy yourself as to
## your rights to use the software. Also, please note that software in
## multiverse WILL NOT receive any review or updates from the Ubuntu
## security team.
deb http://gb.archive.ubuntu.com/ubuntu jammy multiverse
# deb-src http://gb.archive.ubuntu.com/ubuntu jammy multiverse
deb http://gb.archive.ubuntu.com/ubuntu jammy-updates multiverse
# deb-src http://gb.archive.ubuntu.com/ubuntu jammy-updates multiverse

## N.B. software from this repository may not have been tested as
## extensively as that contained in the main release, although it includes
## newer versions of some applications which may provide useful features.
## Also, please note that software in backports WILL NOT receive any review
## or updates from the Ubuntu security team.
deb http://gb.archive.ubuntu.com/ubuntu jammy-backports main restricted universe multiverse
# deb-src http://gb.archive.ubuntu.com/ubuntu jammy-backports main restricted universe multiverse

deb http://gb.archive.ubuntu.com/ubuntu jammy-security main restricted
# deb-src http://gb.archive.ubuntu.com/ubuntu jammy-security main restricted
deb http://gb.archive.ubuntu.com/ubuntu jammy-security universe
# deb-src http://gb.archive.ubuntu.com/ubuntu jammy-security universe
deb http://gb.archive.ubuntu.com/ubuntu jammy-security multiverse
# deb-src http://gb.archive.ubuntu.com/ubuntu jammy-security multiverse
~
~
```

Figure 7-20. *An example of the sources.list file that is supplied with Ubuntu by default*

Repository Lines Explained

The format of the sources.list file is quite different from Fedora and OpenSUSE. There are a few parameters that are as follows:

<package type> <url to packages> <version of distribution> <components>

The *<package type>* parameter determines if the package repository contains deb packages or deb source packages.

The *<url to packages>* parameter is the location of the packages.

The *<version of distribution>* is the Ubuntu version you are using.

Finally, the *<components>* parameter is the names of the repositories you wish to enable.

Creating Your Own Repository File

As with Fedora, you will have the example or "out-of-the-box" repository files in the /etc/apt/ directory, but in the rare occasion where they are missing, you can recreate it manually. All the parameter options you can use are available to view in the man pages for sources.list.

```
# man sources.list
```

List Available Repositories

To view what repositories are available to your Ubuntu system is not as easy as Fedora or OpenSUSE. There is no "apt" parameter to list repositories, only the ability to edit the repository sources file.

To see what repositories are uncommented, you can use a simple command similar to the following:

```
# cat /etc/apt/sources.list | grep -v '#'
```

```
root@ubuntu-server:~# cat /etc/apt/sources.list | grep -v '#'
deb http://gb.archive.ubuntu.com/ubuntu jammy main restricted

deb http://gb.archive.ubuntu.com/ubuntu jammy-updates main restricted

deb http://gb.archive.ubuntu.com/ubuntu jammy universe
deb http://gb.archive.ubuntu.com/ubuntu jammy-updates universe

deb http://gb.archive.ubuntu.com/ubuntu jammy multiverse
deb http://gb.archive.ubuntu.com/ubuntu jammy-updates multiverse

deb http://gb.archive.ubuntu.com/ubuntu jammy-backports main restricted universe multiverse

deb http://gb.archive.ubuntu.com/ubuntu jammy-security main restricted
deb http://gb.archive.ubuntu.com/ubuntu jammy-security universe
deb http://gb.archive.ubuntu.com/ubuntu jammy-security multiverse
```

Figure 7-21. *The output of the cat command*

OpenSUSE

Repository configuration for OpenSUSE is not very different from Fedora except for a few basics you need to know.

```
ken@opensuse-server:~> ls -alrt /etc/zypp/repos.d/
total 80
-rw-r--r-- 1 root root 208 Mar  4 10:35 repo-sle-update.repo
-rw-r--r-- 1 root root 234 Mar  4 10:35 repo-sle-debug-update.repo
-rw-r--r-- 1 root root 199 Mar  4 10:35 repo-backports-update.repo
-rw-r--r-- 1 root root 254 Mar  4 10:35 repo-backports-debug-update.repo
drwxr-xr-x 1 root root 250 Jun  5 22:11 ..
-rw-r--r-- 1 root root 176 Jun  5 22:15 openSUSE-Leap-15.3-3.repo
-rw-r--r-- 1 root root 178 Jun  5 22:15 repo-non-oss.repo
-rw-r--r-- 1 root root 167 Jun  5 22:15 repo-oss.repo
-rw-r--r-- 1 root root 199 Jun  5 22:15 repo-backports-update.repo_1
-rw-r--r-- 1 root root 165 Jun  5 22:15 repo-update.repo
-rw-r--r-- 1 root root 183 Jun  5 22:15 repo-update-non-oss.repo
-rw-r--r-- 1 root root 208 Jun  5 22:15 repo-sle-update.repo_1
-rw-r--r-- 1 root root 200 Jun  5 22:15 repo-backports-debug-update.repo_1
-rw-r--r-- 1 root root 209 Jun  5 22:15 repo-sle-debug-update.repo_1
-rw-r--r-- 1 root root 157 Jun  5 22:15 repo-debug.repo
-rw-r--r-- 1 root root 162 Jun  5 22:15 repo-debug-update.repo
-rw-r--r-- 1 root root 179 Jun  5 22:15 repo-debug-non-oss.repo
-rw-r--r-- 1 root root 160 Jun  5 22:15 repo-source.repo
-rw-r--r-- 1 root root 183 Jun  5 22:15 repo-debug-update-non-oss.repo
-rw-r--r-- 1 root root 295 Jun 14 20:21 home_ecsos_server_cockpit.repo
-rw-r--r-- 1 root root 234 Jun 14 20:26 home_stawidy.repo
drwxr-xr-x 1 root root 928 Jul  4 21:34 .
```

Figure 7-22. *The location of repository files stored on OpenSUSE*

Example of a Repository File

```
[repo-oss]
name=Main Repository
enabled=1
autorefresh=1
baseurl=http://download.opensuse.org/distribution/leap/$releasever/repo/oss/
path=/
type=rpm-md
keeppackages=0
~
~
```

Figure 7-23. *An example of an OpenSUSE repository file*

Each repository within the file shown in Figure 7-23, like Fedora's repository files, starts with a repository name in square brackets, that is, [repo-oss]. Under these repositories are a few important parameters that should always be included with any repository:

- name
- metalink or baseurl
- enabled

Creating Your Own Repository File

OpenSUSE, like Fedora, does come with a few repositories configured "out of the box" from the installer. OpenSUSE, if you can remember, actually gives you the option to install more repositories during your installation. If you chose to skip those, it is not too much of an issue as you can configure them at a later stage.

If you do want to configure a repository manually and need to know the parameters, you can read the following man page for zypper. These man pages are quite lengthy and will require a fair bit of scrolling before you find the repository parameters.

```
# man zypper
```

List Available Repositories

To view what repositories are available to your OpenSUSE system, you can use the following command:

```
# zypper repos
```

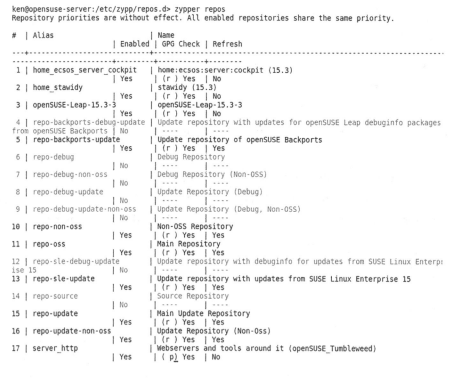

```
ken@opensuse-server:/etc/zypp/repos.d> zypper repos
Repository priorities are without effect. All enabled repositories share the same priority.

 #  | Alias                      | Name
                             | Enabled | GPG Check | Refresh
---+----------------------------+-----------------------------------------------------------------
-------------------------------+---------+-----------+--------
 1 | home_ecsos_server_cockpit  | home:ecsos:server:cockpit (15.3)
                             | Yes     | (r ) Yes  | No
 2 | home_stawidy               | stawidy (15.3)
                             | Yes     | (r ) Yes  | No
 3 | openSUSE-Leap-15.3-3       | openSUSE-Leap-15.3-3
                             | Yes     | (r ) Yes  | No
 4 | repo-backports-debug-update| Update repository with updates for openSUSE Leap debuginfo packages
from openSUSE Backports | No     |  ....    |  ....
 5 | repo-backports-update      | Update repository of openSUSE Backports
                             | Yes     | (r ) Yes  | Yes
 6 | repo-debug                 | Debug Repository
                             | No      |  ....     |  ....
 7 | repo-debug-non-oss         | Debug Repository (Non-OSS)
                             | No      |  ....     |  ....
 8 | repo-debug-update          | Update Repository (Debug)
                             | No      |  ....     |  ....
 9 | repo-debug-update-non-oss  | Update Repository (Debug, Non-OSS)
                             | No      |  ....     |  ....
10 | repo-non-oss               | Non-OSS Repository
                             | Yes     | (r ) Yes  | Yes
11 | repo-oss                   | Main Repository
                             | Yes     | (r ) Yes  | Yes
12 | repo-sle-debug-update      | Update repository with debuginfo for updates from SUSE Linux Enterpr
ise 15 | No     |  ....     |  ....
13 | repo-sle-update            | Update repository with updates from SUSE Linux Enterprise 15
                             | Yes     | (r ) Yes  | Yes
14 | repo-source                | Source Repository
                             | No      |  ....     |  ....
15 | repo-update                | Main Update Repository
                             | Yes     | (r ) Yes  | Yes
16 | repo-update-non-oss        | Update Repository (Non-Oss)
                             | Yes     | (r ) Yes  | Yes
17 | server_http                | Webservers and tools around it (openSUSE_Tumbleweed)
                             | Yes     | ( p) Yes  | No
```

Figure 7-24. *Output of zypper repos*

System Patching

System patching is the second major part of this chapter. Understanding how to install packages and configure repositories is your first step to adding content to your Linux environments. Learning how to maintain and patch your Linux systems is equally important.

The most important thing to take away from this section is to understand how systems can be patched, upgraded, and, in some cases, rolled back.

Errata

Errata is a list of errors or corrections to be made in a published text. It is typically used by publishers when notifying the public of issues in a published work. The same is used for Linux packages. When a package has a known bug or security issue, errata is released, which can be applied to your Linux environment.

Community vs. Enterprise

So far, we have only been using community-based Linux distributions that are solely reliant on the various Linux communities to provide any bug or package updates. These patches and updates are really only on best endeavors and could sometimes be delayed due to lack of people to do the work.

With enterprise platforms, the patch development is done more frequently and typically addresses security vulnerabilities before they become public knowledge, or at least as soon as the vendor has been made aware of an issue. This is largely due to those subscriptions that organizations pay for. That and the support they offer. The main driving force for why larger organizations pay for subscriptions is because they cannot afford security breaches and thus are more inclined to opt for enterprise support.

Note   Remember Linux is OpenSource and free. Support and enterprise patching are not. No one will or should ever sell you Linux software, only the support for it.

System Updates

To apply errata or system updates to each of your Linux distributions is not as difficult as it sounds. In fact, you may already have an idea on what to do.

So far, we have looked at the various package installation tools such as "dnf", "apt", and "zypper". For system patching and updates, we will continue to use these tools with one minor change. Instead of using the "install" parameter, we will be using the "update" parameter.

As you have been working through this book, you may have been taking breaks and reading over time. During that time, the systems we deployed in our early chapters may have received new updates. Hopefully, this will be the case for you with the following steps. If not, do not worry. In a few days, you will most likely have updates available again.

Warning   Please don't update your systems yet. Wait for the exercise before doing this. There is an important reason that will be explained.

Fedora

Our first system we will attempt to update is a Fedora server. As with the package installation steps we have used so far for Fedora, we will use the "dnf" utility. The following is the command to use to update your Fedora server:

```
# dnf update -y
```

```
[ken@fedora-server ~]$ sudo dnf update -y
[sudo] password for ken:
Last metadata expiration check: 0:26:59 ago on Tue 05 Jul 2022 20:58:13 BST.
Dependencies resolved.
================================================================================
 Package                    Arch      Version                 Repository   Size
================================================================================
Installing:
 kernel                     x86_64    5.18.9-200.fc36         updates     252 k
Upgrading:
 ImageMagick                x86_64    1:6.9.12.52-1.fc36      updates      78 k
 ImageMagick-libs           x86_64    1:6.9.12.52-1.fc36      updates     2.3 M
 ModemManager               x86_64    1.18.8-1.fc36           updates     1.1 M
 ModemManager-glib          x86_64    1.18.8-1.fc36           updates     301 k
 NetworkManager             x86_64    1:1.38.0-2.fc36         updates     2.1 M
 NetworkManager-adsl        x86_64    1:1.38.0-2.fc36         updates      26 k
 NetworkManager-bluetooth   x86_64    1:1.38.0-2.fc36         updates      53 k
 NetworkManager-libnm       x86_64    1:1.38.0-2.fc36         updates     1.7 M
 NetworkManager-ppp         x86_64    1:1.38.0-2.fc36         updates      36 k
 NetworkManager-team        x86_64  · 1:1.38.0-2.fc36         updates      30 k
 NetworkManager-wifi        x86_64    1:1.38.0-2.fc36         updates     127 k
 NetworkManager-wwan        x86_64    1:1.38.0-2.fc36         updates      59 k
 alsa-lib                   x86_64    1.2.7.1-1.fc36          updates     502 k
 alsa-sof-firmware          noarch    2.1.1-1.fc36            updates     3.2 M
 alsa-ucm                   noarch    1.2.7.1-1.fc36          updates      95 k
 at                         x86_64    3.2.5-3.fc36            updates      61 k
 authselect                 x86_64    1.4.0-1.fc36            updates     139 k
 authselect-libs            x86_64    1.4.0-1.fc36            updates     234 k
 bind-libs                  x86_64    32:9.16.30-1.fc36       updates     1.2 M
 bind-license               noarch    32:9.16.30-1.fc36       updates      16 k
 bind-utils                 x86_64    32:9.16.30-1.fc36       updates     208 k
 blueman                    x86_64    1:2.2.5-1.fc36          updates     1.4 M
```

Figure 7-25. *Output of the Fedora update process*

.....(reduced output)

```
Installing dependencies:
 cronie                     x86_64    1.5.7-5.fc36            updates     114 k
 cronie-anacron             x86_64    1.5.7-5.fc36            updates      32 k
 grub2-tools-efi            x86_64    1:2.06-42.fc36          updates     543 k
 grub2-tools-extra          x86_64    1:2.06-42.fc36          updates     843 k
 kernel-core                x86_64    5.18.9-200.fc36         updates      49 M
 kernel-modules             x86_64    5.18.9-200.fc36         updates      57 M
 kernel-modules-extra       x86_64    5.18.9-200.fc36         updates     3.6 M
 mtools                     x86_64    4.0.40-1.fc36           updates     210 k
 python3-gobject-base-noarch  noarch  3.42.1-1.fc36           updates     154 k
Installing weak dependencies:
 reportd                    x86_64    0.7.4-8.fc36            fedora       48 k
 rpm-plugin-systemd-inhibit x86_64    4.17.0-10.fc36          fedora       21 k

Transaction Summary
================================================================================
Install   12 Packages
Upgrade  266 Packages

Total download size: 703 M
Downloading Packages:
(1/278): evolution-data-server-langpacks-3.44.2-1.fc36_3.44.3-1.fc36.n  58 kB/s |  23 kB   00:00
(2/278): reportd-0.7.4-8.fc36.x86_64.rpm                               109 kB/s |  48 kB   00:00
(3/278): rpm-plugin-systemd-inhibit-4.17.0-10.fc36.x86_64.rpm         451 kB/s |  21 kB   00:00
(4/278): cronie-anacron-1.5.7-5.fc36.x86_64.rpm                       624 kB/s |  32 kB   00:00
(5/278): cronie-1.5.7-5.fc36.x86_64.rpm                               1.0 MB/s | 114 kB   00:00
```

.....(reduced output)

```
(278/278): thunderbird-91.11.0-1.fc36.x86_64.rpm                      6.0 MB/s |  97 MB   00:16
[DRPM 1/2] evolution-data-server-langpacks-3.44.2-1.fc36_3.44.3-1.fc36.noarch.drpm: done
[DRPM 2/2] evolution-data-server-3.44.2-1.fc36_3.44.3-1.fc36.x86_64.drpm: done
--------------------------------------------------------------------------------
Total                                                                 11 MB/s | 700 MB   01:01
Delta RPMs reduced 702.8 MB of updates to 699.6 MB (0.5% saved)
Running transaction check
Transaction check succeeded.
Running transaction test
Transaction test succeeded.
Running transaction
  Running scriptlet: selinux-policy-targeted-36.10-1.fc36.noarch                            1/1
  Running scriptlet: firefox-102.0-1.fc36.x86_64                                            1/1
  Running scriptlet: alsa-sof-firmware-2.1.1-1.fc36.noarch                                  1/1
  Preparing        :                                                                        1/1
  Upgrading        : libgcc-12.1.1-1.fc36.x86_64                                          1/544
  Running scriptlet: libgcc-12.1.1-1.fc36.x86_64                                          1/544
  Upgrading        : linux-firmware-whence-20220610-135.fc36.noarch                      2/544
  Upgrading        : grub2-common-1:2.06-42.fc36.noarch                                  3/544
  Upgrading        : selinux-policy-36.10-1.fc36.noarch                                  4/544
  Running scriptlet: selinux-policy-36.10-1.fc36.noarch                                  4/544
  Running scriptlet: selinux-policy-targeted-36.10-1.fc36.noarch                         5/544
  Upgrading        : selinux-policy-targeted-36.10-1.fc36.noarch                         5/544
  Running scriptlet: selinux-policy-targeted-36.10-1.fc36.noarch                         5/544
  Upgrading        : vim-data-2:8.2.5172-1.fc36.noarch                                   6/544
```

.....(reduced output)

```
vim-common-2:8.2.5172-1.fc36.x86_64
vim-data-2:8.2.5172-1.fc36.noarch
vim-default-editor-2:8.2.5172-1.fc36.noarch
vim-enhanced-2:8.2.5172-1.fc36.x86_64
vim-filesystem-2:8.2.5172-1.fc36.noarch
vim-minimal-2:8.2.5172-1.fc36.x86_64
yum-4.13.0-1.fc36.noarch
zchunk-libs-1.2.2-1.fc36.x86_64
Installed:
  cronie-1.5.7-5.fc36.x86_64                 cronie-anacron-1.5.7-5.fc36.x86_64
  grub2-tools-efi-1:2.06-42.fc36.x86_64      grub2-tools-extra-1:2.06-42.fc36.x86_64
  kernel-5.18.9-200.fc36.x86_64              kernel-core-5.18.9-200.fc36.x86_64
  kernel-modules-5.18.9-200.fc36.x86_64      kernel-modules-extra-5.18.9-200.fc36.x86_64
  mtools-4.0.40-1.fc36.x86_64                python3-gobject-base-noarch-3.42.1-1.fc36.noarch
  reportd-0.7.4-8.fc36.x86_64                rpm-plugin-systemd-inhibit-4.17.0-10.fc36.x86_64

Complete!
```

Explanation

The preceding screenshots have given you a basic look at what the update process looks like. You would have noticed packages being downloaded and then applied to the system. Some of the packages required scripts to be run, and some packages would have been upgraded. In cases where dependencies were required, they were downloaded and installed.

Once the downloads and installs were completed, the package installation utility (dnf) verified that everything was working as expected.

Ubuntu

Updating Ubuntu is as simple as Fedora; again we will be replacing the install parameter with the update parameter. The following is the command to update your Ubuntu server:

```
# sudo apt update -y
```

```
ken@ubuntu-server:~$ sudo apt update -y
[sudo] password for ken:
Hit:1 http://gb.archive.ubuntu.com/ubuntu jammy InRelease
Get:2 http://gb.archive.ubuntu.com/ubuntu jammy-updates InRelease [114 kB]
Get:3 http://gb.archive.ubuntu.com/ubuntu jammy-backports InRelease [99.8 kB]
Get:4 http://gb.archive.ubuntu.com/ubuntu jammy-security InRelease [110 kB]
Get:5 http://gb.archive.ubuntu.com/ubuntu jammy-updates/main amd64 Packages [340 kB]
Get:6 http://gb.archive.ubuntu.com/ubuntu jammy-updates/main Translation-en [85.7 kB]
Get:7 http://gb.archive.ubuntu.com/ubuntu jammy-updates/main amd64 DEP-11 Metadata [90.9 kB]
Get:8 http://gb.archive.ubuntu.com/ubuntu jammy-updates/universe amd64 Packages [141 kB]
Get:9 http://gb.archive.ubuntu.com/ubuntu jammy-updates/universe Translation-en [50.8 kB]
Get:10 http://gb.archive.ubuntu.com/ubuntu jammy-updates/universe amd64 DEP-11 Metadata [94.9 kB]
Get:11 http://gb.archive.ubuntu.com/ubuntu jammy-updates/multiverse amd64 Packages [7,032 B]
Get:12 http://gb.archive.ubuntu.com/ubuntu jammy-updates/multiverse Translation-en [2,112 B]
Get:13 http://gb.archive.ubuntu.com/ubuntu jammy-updates/multiverse amd64 DEP-11 Metadata [940 B]
Get:14 http://gb.archive.ubuntu.com/ubuntu jammy-backports/universe amd64 DEP-11 Metadata [12.5 kB]
Get:15 http://gb.archive.ubuntu.com/ubuntu jammy-security/main amd64 DEP-11 Metadata [11.4 kB]
Get:16 http://gb.archive.ubuntu.com/ubuntu jammy-security/universe amd64 DEP-11 Metadata [608 B]
Fetched 1,162 kB in 1s (1,284 kB/s)
Reading package lists... Done
Building dependency tree... Done
Reading state information... Done
89 packages can be upgraded. Run 'apt list --upgradable' to see them.
```

Figure 7-26. *Output of the apt update command*

Once the preceding command completes, run the upgrade command. This will now apply all the potential upgrades and errata available for your system. Unlike Fedora, you will need to run the second command:

sudo apt upgrade -y

```
ken@ubuntu-server:~$ sudo apt upgrade -y
Reading package lists... Done
Building dependency tree... Done
Reading state information... Done
Calculating upgrade... Done
The following packages were automatically installed and are no longer required:
  pastebinit python3-newt run-one
Use 'sudo apt autoremove' to remove them.
The following NEW packages will be installed:
  linux-headers-5.15.0-40 linux-headers-5.15.0-40-generic linux-image-5.15.0-40-generic
  linux-modules-5.15.0-40-generic linux-modules-extra-5.15.0-40-generic
The following packages will be upgraded:
  apparmor base-files evolution-data-server evolution-data-server-common fonts-opensymbol
  gir1.2-gnomedesktop-3.0 gir1.2-gtk-4.0 gir1.2-mutter-10 gir1.2-nm-1.0 gnome-control-center
  gnome-control-center-data gnome-control-center-faces gnome-desktop3-data gnome-keyring
  gnome-keyring-pkcs11 gnome-shell gnome-shell-common gvfs gvfs-backends gvfs-common gvfs-daemons
  gvfs-fuse gvfs-libs isc-dhcp-client isc-dhcp-common ldap-utils libapparmor1 libcamel-1.2-63
  libebackend-1.2-10 libebook-1.2-20 libebook-contacts-1.2-3 libecal-2.0-1 libedata-book-1.2-26
  libedata-cal-2.0-1 libedataserver-1.2-26 libedataserverui-1.2-3 libfreerdp-client2-2
  libfreerdp-server2-2 libfreerdp2-2 libgnome-bg-4-1 libgnome-desktop-3-19 libgnome-desktop-4-1
  libgtk-4-1 libgtk-4-bin libgtk-4-common libjson-c5 libldap-2.5-0 libldap-common libmutter-10-0
  libnautilus-extension1a libnm0 libpam-gnome-keyring libreoffice-base-core libreoffice-calc
  libreoffice-common libreoffice-core libreoffice-draw libreoffice-gnome libreoffice-gtk3
  libreoffice-impress libreoffice-math libreoffice-pdfimport libreoffice-style-breeze
  libreoffice-style-colibre libreoffice-style-elementary libreoffice-style-yaru libreoffice-writer
  libuno-cppu3 libuno-cppuhelpergcc3-3 libuno-purpenvhelpergcc3-3 libuno-sal3 libuno-salhelpergcc3-3
  libusb-1.0-0 libwinpr2-2 linux-generic linux-headers-generic linux-image-generic motd-news-config
  mutter-common nautilus nautilus-data network-manager network-manager-config-connectivity-ubuntu
  python3-uno snapd ubuntu-advantage-tools uno-libs-private ure wpasupplicant
89 upgraded, 5 newly installed, 0 to remove and 0 not upgraded.
Need to get 265 MB of archives.
```

Figure 7-27. *Output of the apt upgrade command*

.....(reduced output)

```
Generating grub configuration file ...
Found linux image: /boot/vmlinuz-5.15.0-40-generic
Found initrd image: /boot/initrd.img-5.15.0-40-generic
Found linux image: /boot/vmlinuz-5.15.0-39-generic
Found initrd image: /boot/initrd.img-5.15.0-39-generic
Found linux image: /boot/vmlinuz-5.15.0-37-generic
Found initrd image: /boot/initrd.img-5.15.0-37-generic
Found memtest86+ image: /memtest86+.elf
Found memtest86+ image: /memtest86+.bin
Warning: os-prober will not be executed to detect other bootable partitions.
Systems on them will not be added to the GRUB boot configuration.
Check GRUB_DISABLE_OS_PROBER documentation entry.
done
Processing triggers for initramfs-tools (0.140ubuntu13) ...
update-initramfs: Generating /boot/initrd.img-5.15.0-40-generic
Processing triggers for libc-bin (2.35-0ubuntu3) ...
Scanning processes...
Scanning candidates...
Scanning linux images...

Restarting services...
 /etc/needrestart/restart.d/systemd-manager
 systemctl restart colord.service cups-browsed.service cups.service packagekit.service spice-vdagent.s
rvice ssh.service udisks2.service
Service restarts being deferred:
 /etc/needrestart/restart.d/dbus.service
 systemctl restart gdm.service
 systemctl restart systemd-logind.service
 systemctl restart user@1000.service
 systemctl restart user@132.service

No containers need to be restarted.

No user sessions are running outdated binaries.

No VM guests are running outdated hypervisor (qemu) binaries on this host.
```

Explanation

Ubuntu has a very similar approach to the Fedora upgrade process. Packages are downloaded, updated, and upgraded; scripts are run, followed by any service restarts. It is generally recommended to reboot your system once patched. Ubuntu is quite good at reminding you when you complete your updates.

OpenSUSE

Very much the same with Fedora and Ubuntu, OpenSUSE has a similar update command. Again, we will replace the install parameter with the update parameter in the package installation tool; in the case of OpenSUSE, this is the "zypper" utility.

The following is the update command that is used to initiate the operating system update process:

```
# zypper update -y
```

```
ken@opensuse-server:~> sudo zypper update -y
Retrieving repository 'Update repository of openSUSE Backports' metadata .......................[done]
Building repository 'Update repository of openSUSE Backports' cache ...........................[done]
Retrieving repository 'Update repository with updates from SUSE Linux Enterprise 15' metadata ...[done]
Building repository 'Update repository with updates from SUSE Linux Enterprise 15' cache ........[done]

New repository or package signing key received:

  Repository:       Webservers and tools around it (openSUSE_Tumbleweed)
  Key Fingerprint:  F9F2 2DA4 3BD1 5B00 05E5 5C53 B268 0E8E 08D1 D8B3
  Key Name:         server:http OBS Project <server:http@build.opensuse.org>
  Key Algorithm:    DSA 1024
  Key Created:      Sat 22 May 2021 16:04:40 BST
  Key Expires:      Mon 31 Jul 2023 16:04:40 BST
  Rpm Name:         gpg-pubkey-08d1d8b3-60a91d88


    Note: Signing data enables the recipient to verify that no modifications occurred after the data
    were signed. Accepting data with no, wrong or unknown signature can lead to a corrupted system
    and in extreme cases even to a system compromise.

    Note: A GPG pubkey is clearly identified by it's fingerprint. Do not rely the keys name. If you
    are not sure whether the presented key is authentic, ask the repository provider or check his
    web site. Many provider maintain a web page showing the fingerprints of the GPG keys they are
    using.

Do you want to reject the key, trust temporarily, or trust always? [r/t/a/?] (r): r
Error building the cache:
[server_http|https://download.opensuse.org/repositories/server:/http/openSUSE_Tumbleweed/] Valid metada
ta not found at specified URL
History:
 - Signature verification failed for repomd.xml
 - Can't provide /repodata/repomd.xml
```

Figure 7-28. *The output of the zypper update command*

.....(reduced output)

```
The following 2 package updates will NOT be installed:
  net-tools net-tools-lang

The following 33 packages are going to be upgraded:
  binutils curl fwupd fwupd-lang grub2 grub2-i386-pc grub2-snapper-plugin grub2-systemd-sleep-plugin
  ImageMagick ImageMagick-config-7-SUSE libctf0 libctf-nobfd0 libcurl4 libfwupd2 libfwupdplugin1
  libgcc_s1 libMagickCore-7_Q16HDRI6 libMagickWand-7_Q16HDRI6 libopenssl1_1 libstdc++6
  libstdc++6-pp-gcc11 MozillaFirefox MozillaFirefox-translations-common openssl-1_1
  openSUSE-signkey-cert os-prober qemu-guest-agent typelib-1_0-Fwupd-2_0 vim vim-data vim-data-common
  xen-libs yast2-network

The following 3 NEW packages are going to be installed:
  kernel-default-5.3.18-150300.59.76.1 kernel-default-extra-5.3.18-150300.59.76.1
  kernel-default-optional-5.3.18-150300.59.76.1

The following package requires a system reboot:
  kernel-default-5.3.18-150300.59.76.1
```

.....(reduced output)

```
dracut: *** Resolving executable dependencies done ***
dracut: *** Hardlinking files ***
dracut: *** Hardlinking files done ***
dracut: *** Stripping files ***
dracut: *** Stripping files done ***
dracut: *** Generating early-microcode cpio image ***
dracut: *** Constructing GenuineIntel.bin ***
dracut: *** Store current command line parameters ***
dracut: Stored kernel commandline:
dracut:   resume=UUID=bf51cdde-7069-4bb9-b594-da0e672443b2
dracut:   root=UUID=3634dc64-e554-4a24-ad0b-f9222c247110 rootfstype=btrfs rootflags=rw,relatime,space_ca
che,subvolid=268,subvol=/@/.snapshots/1/snapshot,subvol=@/.snapshots/1/snapshot
dracut: *** Creating image file '/boot/initrd-5.3.18-150300.59.76-default' ***
dracut: *** Creating initramfs image file '/boot/initrd-5.3.18-150300.59.76-default' done ***
Executing %posttrans scripts ...............................................................[done]
There are running programs which still use files and libraries deleted or updated by recent upgrades. T
hey should be restarted to benefit from the latest updates. Run 'zypper ps -s' to list these programs.

Since the last system boot core libraries or services have been updated.
Reboot is suggested to ensure that your system benefits from these updates.
```

Explanation

Compared to Ubuntu and Fedora, OpenSUSE has the most verbose output. There will sometimes also be errors that occur that can be ignored, so it will be important to read the output carefully.

During the update process, OpenSUSE will start by updating repositories where required, followed by a description of what packages will be updated and what will not be updated. The zypper utility will then go on to download all the packages required for the updates followed by the installation. The final phase of the update process is where the update process updates any kernel modules and rebuilds any kernel dependencies.

Note   Read the output carefully to determine if any errors are in fact a problem. With a supported platform, you may need these outputs for support cases. If you are using the community distributions we are using in the beginning of this book, you will also need these outputs for any community questions if you have a problem.

Rollback

Rolling back system updates can be a bit tricky with some Linux distributions. In the past, not all distributions or package installation tools supported a rollback facility. To work around this issue, you typically would have to make a backup before you begin and restore if you had an issue. Another way would have been to run a virtual machine snapshot, to which you could revert if the worse were to happen.

In the following, we will look at what rollback options are available for your Linux distributions and also discuss how to create a virtual machine snapshot.

Fedora

Fedora is one of the easiest systems to use when rolling back package installations. The "dnf" and "yum" utilities have built-in rollback functionality you can use if you ever encounter issues.

To view the history of package installations, you can use the following command:

```
# dnf history
```

```
[root@fedora-server ~]# dnf history
ID   | Command line                        | Date and time    | Action(s) | Altered
--------------------------------------------------------------------------------------
   8 | update                              | 2022-07-07 21:33 | Upgrade   |     47
   7 | update -y                           | 2022-07-05 21:26 | I, U      |    278 EE
   6 | install figlet                      | 2022-07-03 22:50 | Install   |      1
   5 | remove tmux -y                      | 2022-06-27 21:58 | Removed   |      1
   4 | install tmux -y                     | 2022-06-27 21:56 | Install   |      1
   3 | remove tmux -y                      | 2022-06-27 21:56 | Removed   |      2
   2 | groupinstall Cinnamon Desktop       | 2022-06-15 20:58 | I, U      |    912 E<
   1 |                                     | 2022-06-04 22:55 | Install   |    620 >E
```

Figure 7-29. *The output of the dnf history command*

From the output shown in Figure 7-29, you can see all the successfully run dnf commands. The latest command was an update command that was run to show the rollback capability of dnf.

In the update, a number of new packages were updated. The output can be seen in Figure 7-30.

```
[root@fedora-server ~]# dnf update
Last metadata expiration check: 0:26:18 ago on Thu 07 Jul 2022 21:05:26 BST.
Dependencies resolved.
================================================================================
 Package                            Architecture  Version          Repository   Size
================================================================================
Upgrading:
 glibc                              x86_64        2.35-14.fc36     updates      2.1 M
 glibc-common                       x86_64        2.35-14.fc36     updates      330 k
 glibc-gconv-extra                  x86_64        2.35-14.fc36     updates      1.6 M
 glibc-langpack-en                  x86_64        2.35-14.fc36     updates      585 k
 gnupg2                             x86_64        2.3.6-2.fc36     updates      2.5 M
 hwdata                             noarch        0.361-1.fc36     updates      1.5 M
 libipa_hbac                        x86_64        2.7.3-1.fc36     updates      32 k
 libsss_certmap                     x86_64        2.7.3-1.fc36     updates      75 k
 libsss_idmap                       x86_64        2.7.3-1.fc36     updates      37 k
 libsss_nss_idmap                   x86_64        2.7.3-1.fc36     updates      40 k
 libsss_sudo                        x86_64        2.7.3-1.fc36     updates      30 k
 meanwhile                          x86_64        1.1.1-1.fc36     updates      102 k
 mesa-dri-drivers                   x86_64        22.1.3-1.fc36    updates      18 M
 mesa-filesystem                    x86_64        22.1.3-1.fc36    updates      18 k
 mesa-libEGL                        x86_64        22.1.3-1.fc36    updates      125 k
 mesa-libGL                         x86_64        22.1.3-1.fc36    updates      175 k
 mesa-libgbm                        x86_64        22.1.3-1.fc36    updates      44 k
 mesa-libglapi                      x86_64        22.1.3-1.fc36    updates      53 k
 mesa-libxatracker                  x86_64        22.1.3-1.fc36    updates      1.9 M
 mesa-vulkan-drivers                x86_64        22.1.3-1.fc36    updates      4.8 M
 openssl1.1                         x86_64        1:1.1.1p-1.fc36  updates      1.5 M
 pipewire                           x86_64        0.3.53-4.fc36    updates      40 k
 pipewire-alsa                      x86_64        0.3.53-4.fc36    updates      63 k
 pipewire-gstreamer                 x86_64        0.3.53-4.fc36    updates      61 k
 pipewire-jack-audio-connection-kit x86_64        0.3.53-4.fc36    updates      136 k
 pipewire-libs                      x86_64        0.3.53-4.fc36    updates      1.6 M
 pipewire-pulseaudio                x86_64        0.3.53-4.fc36    updates      28 k
 pipewire-utils                     x86_64        0.3.53-4.fc36    updates      332 k
 setroubleshoot                     x86_64        3.3.30-1.fc36    updates      70 k
 setroubleshoot-server              x86_64        3.3.30-1.fc36    updates      320 k
```

Figure 7-30. *The output of the dnf update command*

If there were to be any problems on the Fedora system due to one of these packages being updated, a rollback of the update can be done with the following command:

```
# dnf history undo 8
```

In the preceding command, you can see I have specified the "ID" of the update command from the previous screenshot. This will now instruct "dnf" to remove all the updated packages and revert to prior versions. The output should look similar to that shown in Figure 7-31.

```
[root@fedora-server ~]# dnf history undo 8
Last metadata expiration check: 0:34:54 ago on Thu 07 Jul 2022 21:05:26 BST.
Error: The following problems occurred while running a transaction:
  Cannot find rpm nevra "glibc-2.35-12.fc36.x86_64".
  Cannot find rpm nevra "glibc-common-2.35-12.fc36.x86_64".
  Cannot find rpm nevra "glibc-gconv-extra-2.35-12.fc36.x86_64".
  Cannot find rpm nevra "glibc-langpack-en-2.35-12.fc36.x86_64".
  Cannot find rpm nevra "gnupg2-2.3.6-1.fc36.x86_64".
  Cannot find rpm nevra "hwdata-0.360-1.fc36.noarch".
  Cannot find rpm nevra "libipa_hbac-2.7.1-2.fc36.x86_64".
  Cannot find rpm nevra "libsss_certmap-2.7.1-2.fc36.x86_64".
  Cannot find rpm nevra "libsss_idmap-2.7.1-2.fc36.x86_64".
  Cannot find rpm nevra "libsss_nss_idmap-2.7.1-2.fc36.x86_64".
  Cannot find rpm nevra "libsss_sudo-2.7.1-2.fc36.x86_64".
  Cannot find rpm nevra "mesa-dri-drivers-22.1.2-1.fc36.x86_64".
  Cannot find rpm nevra "mesa-filesystem-22.1.2-1.fc36.x86_64".
  Cannot find rpm nevra "mesa-libEGL-22.1.2-1.fc36.x86_64".
  Cannot find rpm nevra "mesa-libGL-22.1.2-1.fc36.x86_64".
  Cannot find rpm nevra "mesa-libgbm-22.1.2-1.fc36.x86_64".
  Cannot find rpm nevra "mesa-libglapi-22.1.2-1.fc36.x86_64".
```

Figure 7-31. *The output of the dnf rollback performed*

If you think the output does not look good, you will be correct. The rollback will not always work if there are repository issues or dependency issues. In this case, there would be a fair bit of work to find out what has gone wrong. Using an alternative method of rollback would be required to restore your system to its previous state. We will cover that in the next few pages.

Ubuntu

Fedora with the use of "dnf" or "yum" supports the ability to roll back in most situations. However, Ubuntu does not have a native utility that does the same. There is a "apt-rollback" utility that has been written in the community that gives some ability to roll back, but overall not as feature rich as "dnf". To install the rollback utility for Ubuntu, you can use the following command:

```
# sudo apt-get -y install apt-rollback
```

The apt-rollback utility has quite limited functionality, which can be viewed with the help command.

```
ken@ubuntu-server:~$ apt-rollback --help
apt-rollback ver. 1.0.16
Undo the last APT commands or a specified one

Usage: apt-rollback [--last <n>] [--remove/--reinstall package-name] [--help]

    --last      Undo the last <n> APT commands
                Supports the undo of the only Install, Remove and Purge commands

    --remove    Remove an INSTALLED package and related configuration files
                Removing also all its first installed dependencies

    --reinstall  Reinstall a REMOVED package,
                and all its first installed dependences
                Reproducing exactly its first installation

    --help      Print this help
```

Figure 7-32. *Apt rollback help options*

Unfortunately, one major drawback for this utility is the inability to roll back update commands. The rollback only supports the rollback of install commands. To roll back an install command, you specify the "--last" parameter with the number of install commands you wish to roll back.

```
ken@ubuntu-server:~$ apt-rollback --last 1
apt-rollback ver. 1.0.16
Undo the last APT commands or a specified one

The last APT command, performed the following Package operation...

#1: 2022-07-07 20:47:57 - Install of figlet:amd64

Do you wish to Undo it? [y/N]? y

#1 UNDOING: Install of figlet:amd64 ...
.........

Successfully Undone!
```

Figure 7-33. *The apt-rollback --last output*

OpenSUSE

From the "almost" always ability to roll back with "dnf" to the "we can only roll back installs" with Ubuntu, we come to OpenSUSE where there unfortunately is no option available to roll back without writing your own custom scripts.

For rollback in OpenSUSE, you will need to make a note of all packages updated and removed and any new packages installed for you to manually uninstall, reinstall, and potentially remove, a painful and slow process, especially if you have more than one system to maintain.

There fortunately is hope, that is, if you are using virtual machines.

Virtual Machine Snapshots

Virtual machine snapshots are effectively a fork in the timeline of a virtual machine's content that is being written. Imagine a timeline of data being written to your virtual machine's disk.

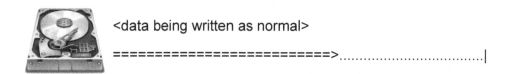

```
<data being written as normal>
=============================>..................................|
```

Figure 7-34. *Data being written to a disk*

A snapshot would effectively be a break in the timeline, with a new timeline continuing below the break now recording all new changes without updating the existing timeline.

```
============================X <Snapshot>
<data being written as normal>
===============================>...........................|
```

Figure 7-35. *Data written to a disk after a snapshot*

When or if a problem occurs to your system and you need to recover, you can delete the new timeline (snapshot), and your system will revert back to where the snapshot was originally created. Roll back any changes made to the disk, and in the process, revert back any issues or problems on your Linux system.

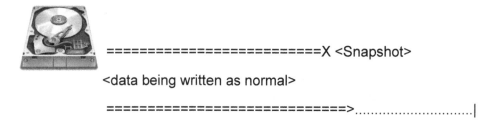

```
<data being written as normal>
=============================>..................................|
            (deleted)     |===>..........................|
```

Figure 7-36. *Delete or roll back to a snapshot*

Creating Snapshots

Any hypervisor that has been around for long enough will have the ability to take snapshots. Some platforms are a bit easier to understand and will have all the tools in one place, and then some tools require a bit more understanding. For the latter reason, we will only look at the libvirt process of creating and reverting snapshots. VirtualBox is all graphically driven with menus that should be self-explanatory once you understand the basics of snapshots.

libvirt Snapshots

To create a snapshot of a virtual machine in libvirt, you will need to do the following steps:

1. Open Virtual Machine Manager.

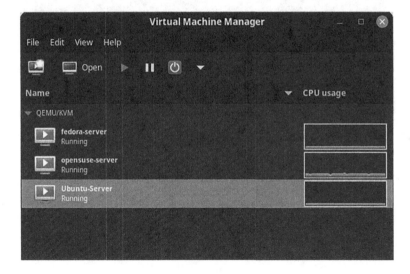

2. Open the virtual machine you wish to snapshot and click the
    "View" menu and click "snapshots".

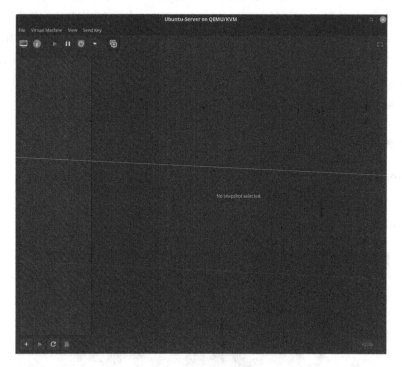

Figure 7-37. Snapshot screen in Virtual Machine Manager

3. Click the "+" on the bottom left of the screen.

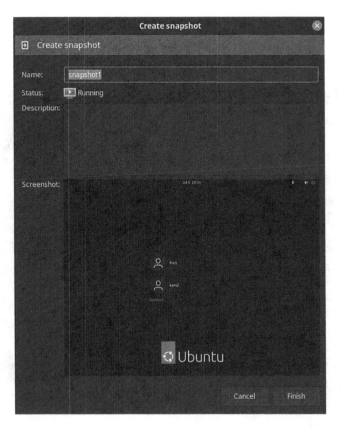

Figure 7-38. *Create a snapshot of the Ubuntu virtual machine*

4.   Give the snapshot a name and click "Finish". You will see the snapshot being created and then see the new snapshot available on the left of the snapshot window.

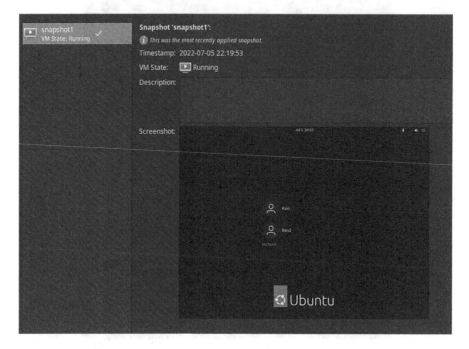

Figure 7-39.   *List of snapshots on the current virtual machine*

Roll Back a Snapshot with libvirt

If the worst happens and you need to recover your system from a snapshot, you will need to do the following.

The virt-manager utility unfortunately is not very clear on how to revert a snapshot, only giving options to create and delete snapshots. To revert the snapshot created in the previous section, the following command can be run:

```
# sudo virsh snapshot-revert --domain Ubuntu-Server --snapshotname
snapshot1 --running
```

The "--domain" parameter is the name of my virtual machine. This is case sensitive so be sure to put the name exactly as it is in your virt-manager list.

The "--snapshotname" is the snapshot name that was used to create the snapshot in the previous section.

The "--running" parameter is the state you wish the virtual machine to be in when the revert is complete.

Exercise

With a good understanding of how your different Linux distributions can be updated, patched, and potentially rolled back, attempt to do the following exercises.

Update Your Linux Environments

On each of your different systems installed, do the following:

1. Take any precautions to revert your system if any problem were to occur.

2. Update your distributions to the latest version.

3. Verify that all packages have been updated.

4. Reboot your systems.

Rolling Back

On any of your Linux systems, do the following.

Prerequisite

Remove the "figlet" package if installed.

Tasks

1. Install the "figlet" package.

2. Confirm "figlet" is working as we did previously.

3. Roll back your system to the point before figlet was installed.

4. Confirm figlet is not working anymore.

Note   This exercise can be repeated over if you forgot to do anything. Just remember to clean up the figlet app before you start. It might not be a long exercise, but it is a simple example that could save you many hours in the future.

Summary

In this chapter, you were introduced to the following:

- How packages are installed in the various Linux distributions discussed in this book so far

- How new locations can be added where packages can be installed from

- What system patching is and how patching can be done on the various Linux distributions

- What Errata is and how it differs from package updates

- How to recover from failed system updates or problematic packages

## CHAPTER 8

Network Configuration

Networking is a very important subject in any IT environment. If you cannot connect to your system or have connectivity out of the system, it does not really serve that much of a purpose, at least in most environments.

This chapter is our first chapter that focuses on the network configuration of your systems. In this chapter, we will look at all the various methods that can be used to configure your system's network configuration. We will then look at some of the useful network tooling you can use to better understand what is happening at your system's network layer.

Network Basics in Linux

In Chapter 1, we very briefly discussed what the network knowledge requirements you will need when starting to work in the IT industry. This knowledge is required to enable you to have a solid foundation of computer and server networking. Most of the knowledge is only there for you to understand networking. This chapter will not push the limits of your knowledge but may occasionally have terminology that will not make sense if you have not gained that networking foundational knowledge.

The general configuration discussed in this chapter should be simple enough to follow, but it is still highly recommended to get that networking knowledge behind you as soon as you can.

In this chapter, we will look at the hands-on configuration of your Linux systems. Where the configuration is drastically different between the Linux distributions, there will be additional explanations to cover any differences, so do not worry too much if you have decided to stick with one distribution for this book.

© Kenneth Hitchcock 2023
K. Hitchcock, *The Enterprise Linux Administrator*, https://doi.org/10.1007/978-1-4842-8801-6_8

Network Configuration Using Command Line

I'm sure you have noticed by now that command-line configuration ends up being the first area this book tends to focus on and for good reason. It has already been mentioned that in some, if not most, situations, you will not have anything except the command line to use. For this reason, it is extremely important you have a very good understanding on how to configure your systems through the command line.

Current System Networking Information

In Chapter 5, we discussed how to connect to your Linux systems through ssh. We discussed how you could determine what your IP address was, but we never went into much detail on what the commands were, only the output.

To typically get a very basic summary of your Linux system's network configuration, there are a few utilities you can use. Some are no longer used, and some are designed to make things a bit easier.

ifconfig

The original tool used to determine IP address information was the "ifconfig" tool. This tool stems from Unix configuration and has a similar command on Windows called "ipconfig".

```
[ken@fedora-server ~]$ ifconfig
enp1s0: flags=4163<UP,BROADCAST,RUNNING,MULTICAST>  mtu 1500
        inet 192.168.122.11  netmask 255.255.255.0  broadcast 192.168.122.255
        inet6 fe80::5054:ff:fe89:755b  prefixlen 64  scopeid 0x20<link>
        ether 52:54:00:89:75:5b  txqueuelen 1000  (Ethernet)
        RX packets 83  bytes 10460 (10.2 KiB)
        RX errors 0  dropped 15  overruns 0  frame 0
        TX packets 82  bytes 11147 (10.8 KiB)
        TX errors 0  dropped 0 overruns 0  carrier 0  collisions 0

lo: flags=73<UP,LOOPBACK,RUNNING>  mtu 65536
        inet 127.0.0.1  netmask 255.0.0.0
        inet6 ::1  prefixlen 128  scopeid 0x10<host>
        loop  txqueuelen 1000  (Local Loopback)
        RX packets 10  bytes 1612 (1.5 KiB)
        RX errors 0  dropped 0  overruns 0  frame 0
        TX packets 10  bytes 1612 (1.5 KiB)
        TX errors 0  dropped 0 overruns 0  carrier 0  collisions 0
```

Figure 8-1. *The output of the "ifconfig" command*

```
# ifconfig
```

The ifconfig utility tends to not be used anymore and in most distributions is not installed by default. This is due to the fact that the "net-tools" package is not installed and regarded by some distributions as deprecated.

ip

The "ip" utility is available on all if not almost every Linux distribution available today, both modern and legacy. "ip" is regarded as the replacement for "ifconfig":

```
# ip a
```

The preceding "ip" command displays the very basic IP address information about your system's network interfaces. The parameter "a" of the command is an abbreviation for "address." This is why the output of this command will list your system's IP address, MAC address, and network interface.

```
root@ubuntu-server:~# ip a
1: lo: <LOOPBACK,UP,LOWER_UP> mtu 65536 qdisc noqueue state UNKNOWN group default qlen 1000
    link/loopback 00:00:00:00:00:00 brd 00:00:00:00:00:00
    inet 127.0.0.1/8 scope host lo
       valid_lft forever preferred_lft forever
    inet6 ::1/128 scope host
       valid_lft forever preferred_lft forever
2: ens3: <BROADCAST,MULTICAST,UP,LOWER_UP> mtu 1500 qdisc fq_codel state UP group default qlen 1000
    link/ether 52:54:00:51:1d:cb brd ff:ff:ff:ff:ff:ff
    altname enp0s3
    inet 192.168.122.234/24 metric 100 brd 192.168.122.255 scope global dynamic ens3
       valid_lft 1856sec preferred_lft 1856sec
    inet6 fe80::5054:ff:fe51:1dcb/64 scope link
       valid_lft forever preferred_lft forever
```

Figure 8-2. *Output of the ip a command*

Getting More Information

As always, read the man pages and help for any and all utilities that you use. Knowing all the parameters and switches is not as important as knowing where to find them when you need them. No need to memorize this information if it is freely available.

```
# man ip
```

   or

```
# ip --help
```

Network Manager

The "ip" and "ifconfig" commands are not the only ways to get information about your system's network interfaces. Most modern Linux systems have the Network Manager package installed, which comes with a host of network tools you can use. One of the utilities that Network Manager has is a command-line utility that can be used to display and configure your network interface. For now, the following command will display the network configuration for all your network interfaces on your Linux system:

```
# nmcli d show
```

If you remove the "show" parameter from the preceding command, it will only list the interfaces you have on your system and not the IP address information. A reduced output version of the preceding command can be used:

```
# nmcli d show | grep IP4
```

```
root@ubuntu-server:~# nmcli d show | grep IP4
IP4.ADDRESS[1]:                         192.168.122.234/24
IP4.GATEWAY:                            192.168.122.1
IP4.ROUTE[1]:                           dst = 192.168.122.0/24, nh = 0.0.0.0, mt = 100
IP4.ROUTE[2]:                           dst = 192.168.122.1/32, nh = 0.0.0.0, mt = 100
IP4.ROUTE[3]:                           dst = 0.0.0.0/0, nh = 192.168.122.1, mt = 100
IP4.ADDRESS[1]:                         127.0.0.1/8
IP4.GATEWAY:                            --
```

Figure 8-3. *Output of the nmcli command*

Configure Your Interface Adapter

In this book, when we deployed our systems, we used DHCP assigned IP addresses, which in most environments is perfectly acceptable if DHCP has been configured and managed correctly. However, this is not always the case, and in most secure data centers, DHCP is not even allowed. With these environments, you will need to set your IP addresses to be static. To configure your network interfaces, you can do the following.

Set Network During Installation

The quickest method would be to configure your network during your system deployment. Using automated deployment or configuring your system to use a reserved IP address would be the most robust method, but as already mentioned, this is not always possible.

Manual Configuration

Your Linux system's network configuration can be configured manually by editing the network configuration files for each network interface. These files unfortunately do differ from Linux distribution to distribution. For this reason, we will look at our Linux systems we have installed so far and configure each of them to use static IP addresses.

Fedora

In the past, network configuration files have been saved in the following directory, but as the ifcfg format in Fedora has been deprecated, these are no longer used. Instead you will find a readme file explaining all of this for you.

```
# /etc/sysconfig/network-scripts
```

```
[ken@fedora-server network-scripts]$ ls -alrt
total 8
-rw-r--r--. 1 root root 1244 May 30 13:27 readme-ifcfg-rh.txt
drwxr-xr-x. 2 root root   33 Jul  5 21:28 .
drwxr-xr-x. 3 root root 4096 Jul  5 21:29 ..
[ken@fedora-server network-scripts]$ █
```

Figure 8-4. *The old location for where network scripts used to be configured*

To configure your network manually with modern versions of Fedora, the following directory is now used to store configuration files:

```
# /etc/NetworkManager/system-connections/
```

The files stored in this directory are configured using the keyfile methodology, allowing for better parsing and general use. To understand the parameters used for the new keyfile method, read the man pages for "nm-settings-keyfile":

```
# man nm-settings-keyfile
```

On a standard Fedora server with a single network interface, you should have a file in the "/etc/NetworkManager/system-connections/" similar to that shown in Figure 8-5.

```
[ken@fedora-server system-connections]$ ls -alrt
total 4
drwxr-xr-x. 7 root root 134 May 30 13:27 ..
-rw-------. 1 root root 229 Jun  4 22:59 enp1s0.nmconnection
drwxr-xr-x. 2 root root  33 Jul 12 20:16 .
[ken@fedora-server system-connections]$ ▉
```

Figure 8-5. *Location of network interface files on Fedora*

```
[connection]
id=enp1s0
uuid=191be02e-0d15-340f-a4fe-3db164cc4a8b
type=ethernet
autoconnect-priority=-999
interface-name=enp1s0
timestamp=1654378559
▉
[ethernet]

[ipv4]
method=auto

[ipv6]
addr-gen-mode=eui64
method=auto

[proxy]
~
~
~
```

Figure 8-6. *An example of the contents of the file from Figure 8-5*

To configure a static IP address, the following parameters would need to be added to the "[ipv4]" section:

```
address1=<your ip address>/<network range>
gateway=<your gateway address>
dns=<dns1>,<dns2>
```

To set a static IP address for your Fedora server, your configuration should look similar to that shown in Figure 8-7.

```
[ipv4]
method=manual
address1=192.168.122.101/24
gateway=192.168.122.1
dns=192.168.122.▉
```

Figure 8-7. *Manual IP address configuration in the interface file from Figure 8-5*

Once your configuration has been changed and saved, restart your system. You can restart the "NetworkManager" service, but that will end up with your "ssh" session hanging as it is still trying to connect to your old DHCP address. Of course, if you are logged in to the physical system or via the virtual machine console, this should not happen. To restart the "NetworkManager" service, you can run the following command:

```
# systemctl restart NeworkManager
```

Ubuntu

Similar to Fedora, Ubuntu has moved away from using the ifcfg configuration methodology for configuring network configuration. Instead, Ubuntu has moved to a yaml-based configuration called "netplan".

```
root@ubuntu-server:/etc/netplan# ls -alrt
total 20
-rw-r--r--   1 root root   115 Jun  3 22:00 00-installer-config.yaml
drwxr-xr-x 145 root root 12288 Jul  7 20:05 ..
drwxr-xr-x   2 root root  4096 Jul 12 19:45 .
root@ubuntu-server:/etc/netplan# █
```

Figure 8-8. *The network configuration files for Ubuntu*

```
# This is the network config written by 'subiquity'
network:
  ethernets:
    ens3:
      dhcp4: true
  version: 2
~
~
```

Figure 8-9. *The file "00-installer-config.yaml" has the following content*

This file can either be edited or a new file can be created with your new static IP address information. As a precaution, I never delete any files until I am satisfied with the configuration.

```
network:
  version: 2
  renderer: networkd
  ethernets:
    ens3:
      dhcp4: no
      addresses:
        - 192.168.122.103/24
      nameservers:
          addresses: [192.168.122.1]
      routes:
        - to: 0.0.0.0/0
          via: 192.168.122.1
          metric: 100
          on-link: true
```

Figure 8-10. *To set a static IP address for an Ubuntu server*

If you noticed in the configuration shown in Figure 8-10 that there is no "gateway" parameter, that is because the use of "gateway4" is now deprecated and you should now instead configure "routes". In the configuration, all network traffic on the ens3 interface will route traffic through the "192.168.122.1" address, which is the gateway.

The configuration was also created in a new file called "01-netcfg.yaml".

```
root@ubuntu-server:/etc/netplan# ls -alrt
total 24
-rw-r--r--   1 root root   115 Jun  3 22:00 00-installer-config.yaml
drwxr-xr-x 145 root root 12288 Jul  7 20:05 ..
-rw-r--r--   1 root root   299 Jul 12 20:07 01-netcfg.yaml
drwxr-xr-x   2 root root  4096 Jul 12 20:11 .
root@ubuntu-server:/etc/netplan# █
```

From the preceding image, you can see that the existing "00-installer-config.yaml" file still exists. If there were to be a problem with the 01-netcfg.yaml file, the new file could be deleted to restore the system back to the previous network configuration.

One more important thing to note with this configuration method is how the configuration is applied to the system. You can as before just restart the system, but if you wish to change the network configuration while logged in, you will need to run the following command:

netplan apply

As the examples were run as root, there is no need to use "sudo". However, if you decide to configure your system as your user, be sure to add "sudo".

openSUSE

To configure your network interfaces manually on OpenSUSE, you will need to create or edit files stored in the following directory. For each interface in your system, there should be a file prefixed with "ifcfg". Unlike Fedora, OpenSUSE is still using the ifcfg configuration methodology.

```
ken@opensuse-server:~> ls -al /etc/sysconfig/network/
total 64
drwxr-xr-x 1 root root   212 Jul 10 20:49 .
drwxr-xr-x 1 root root   676 Jul  3 22:49 ..
-rw-r--r-- 1 root root  9691 Jun  5 22:15 config
-rw-r--r-- 1 root root 14968 Jun 15 22:19 dhcp
-rw------- 1 root root    46 Jun 14 20:04 ifcfg-eth0
-rw------- 1 root root    40 Jun  5 22:29 ifcfg-eth0.bak
-rw------- 1 root root   147 Jun  5 22:15 ifcfg-lo
-rw-r--r-- 1 root root 21738 Jul  7  2021 ifcfg.template
drwxr-xr-x 1 root root     0 Mar 15 11:35 if-down.d
-rw-r--r-- 1 root root     0 Jun  5 22:15 ifroute-eth0
drwxr-xr-x 1 root root    24 Jun 15 22:21 if-up.d
drwx------ 1 root root     0 Mar 15 11:35 providers
-rw-r--r-- 1 root root     0 Jun  5 22:15 routes
drwxr-xr-x 1 root root    76 Jun  5 22:13 scripts
ken@opensuse-server:~
```

Figure 8-11. *OpenSUSE network scripts in the /etc/sysconfig/network directory*

As the OpenSUSE system deployed has an interface by the name of "eth0", there is a file named "ifcfg-eth0".

```
BOOTPROTO='dhcp'
STARTMODE='auto'
ZONE=public
~
~
```

Figure 8-12. *The contents of a network script file*

The two most important parameters in the configuration shown in Figure 8-12 to pay attention to are the BOOTPROTO parameter, which is set to "dhcp", as this was the option that was selected during the installation, and the STARTMODE parameter, which is set to "auto". This ensures that the network interface starts on boot.

```
BOOTPROTO='static'
STARTMODE='auto'
IPADDR='192.168.122.100'
NETMASK='255.255.255.0'
GATEWAY='192.168.122.1'
DNS1='192.168.122.1'
MTU='1500'
ZONE=public
~
```

Figure 8-13. *Minimum parameters needed in a network interface configuration file for a static IP address*

Additional Parameters

There are many more parameters that can be used; examples of these parameters can be found in the following file:

/etc/sysconfig/network/ifcfg.template

You can also see all the parameters in the manual page for ifcfg (5). To view this man page, refer to Figure 8-14.

```
opensuse-server:~ # man ifcfg
Man: find all matching manual pages (set MAN_POSIXLY_CORRECT to avoid this)
 * ifcfg (8)
   ifcfg (5)
Man: What manual page do you want?
Man: 5
```

Figure 8-14. *Man pages for ifcfg*

All the parameters are listed with an explanation for each one. Work through them when you need to set manual network configuration.

Applying Network Configuration

Once you have finished configuring your network interface manually, you will need to restart your system or restart the "NetworkManager" service, which can be done with the following command:

systemctl restart NetworkManager

Remember that if you are logged into your system using ssh and if you change your IP address to something different from your DHCP assigned address, your connection will be interrupted and your ssh session will hang.

Network Manager

An alternative method to configuring your network configuration manually on all three of the distributions discussed so far is through the use of NetworkManager. We briefly discussed how NetworkManager can be used to determine what IP address has already been allocated on your system.

NetworkManager can also be used to configure your Network Interface. The following are the steps and commands you can use to configure your system's network interface with NetworkManager.

Managed or Not

The first thing to check with NetworkManager is to see if your network interface is being managed by NetworkManager.

```
[root@fedora-server ~]# nmcli d
DEVICE  TYPE      STATE      CONNECTION
enp1s0  ethernet  connected  enp1s0
lo      loopback  unmanaged  --
[root@fedora-server ~]#
```

Figure 8-15. *nmcli shows that the interface is being managed by NetworkManager*

If your interface is not being managed, you will need to ensure your network configuration is set to use NetworkManager.

```
root@ubuntu-server:/etc/netplan# nmcli d
DEVICE  TYPE      STATE      CONNECTION
ens3    ethernet  unmanaged  --
lo      loopback  unmanaged  --
```

Figure 8-16. *Interfaces being managed by NetworkManager*

Fedora

With Fedora, this is done by default and should not require any additional configuration.

Ubuntu

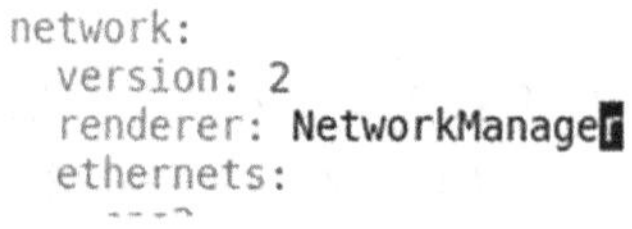

```
network:
  version: 2
  renderer: NetworkManager
  ethernets:
```

Figure 8-17. *With Ubuntu, you will need to set the network configuration "renderer" to "NetworkManager" in the interface file*

Note   If you look back at the Ubuntu network configuration a few pages back, you will see that I purposely set the "renderer" to "networkd". This was to demonstrate what an unmanaged interface looks like.

OpenSUSE

By default, OpenSUSE has the NetworkManager service enabled and configured to manage all interfaces. If something is different with your configuration, ensure that the NetworkManager service is started. If you still have problems, stop the "wicked" service and test again. An alternative would be to use the "YaST" network tool in your OpenSUSE desktop to change your Network Setup Method.

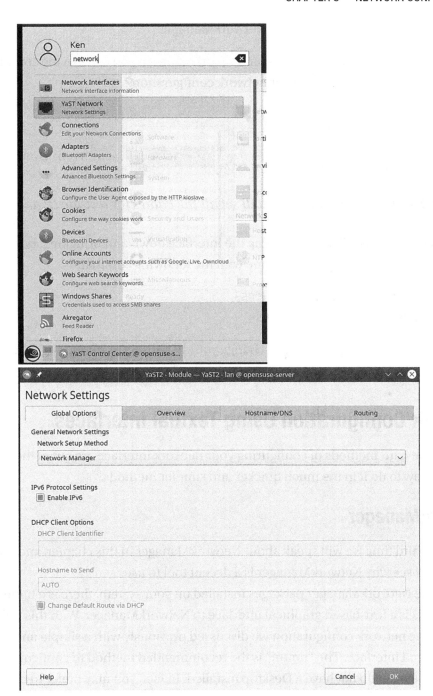

Figure 8-18. *Using YaST to configure NetworkManager settings*

Change Network Configuration with NetworkManager

With your interface under the control of NetworkManager, you can use the commands shown in Figure 8-19 to change your network configuration.

```
root@ubuntu-server:~# nmcli d
DEVICE  TYPE       STATE       CONNECTION
ens3    ethernet   connected   netplan-ens3
lo      loopback   unmanaged   --
root@ubuntu-server:~# nmcli connection mod netplan-ens3 ipv4.method manual
root@ubuntu-server:~# nmcli connection mod netplan-ens3 ipv4.addresses 192.168.122.104/24
root@ubuntu-server:~# nmcli connection mod netplan-ens3 ipv4.gateway 192.168.122.1
root@ubuntu-server:~# nmcli connection mod netplan-ens3 ipv4.dns 192.168.122.1
```

Figure 8-19. *The commands that will set all the values for a static IP address*

nmcli commands will require taking the interface down and bringing it back up to apply to configuration. This can be done with the following commands:

```
# nmcli connection down netplan-ens3
# nmcli connection up netplan-ens3
```

The usual warning applies; if you change your IP address to something other than the current IP address, your ssh session will need to be restarted.

Network Configuration Using Textual Interfaces

Now that the hard methods of configuring your network interface are out of the way, you can learn how to do it in the much quicker and simpler methods.

NetworkManager

This is the third time we will speak about NetworkManager in this chapter, and it is now that you will see why NetworkManager is a decent tool to use.

With the NetworkManager packages installed on your system, there is a utility called "nmtui". This is a text-based graphical interface to NetworkManager. With this utility, you can do all the network configuration we discussed previously with a simple and easy-to-understand interface. The "nmtui" is the recommended method to configure your network when you do not have a Desktop installed. In fact, you may prefer to use the "nmtui" utility even if you have access to the Desktop as it is quicker.

To use the "nmtui" utility, you will need to open an ssh session to your system and run the following command:

```
# nmtui
```

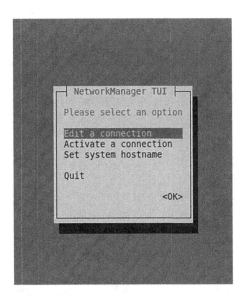

Figure 8-20. *Textual utility for NetworkManager*

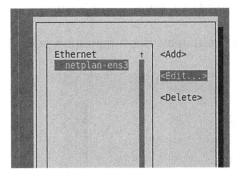

Figure 8-21. *"Edit a connection"*

Select the name of your interface under the "Ethernet" list and then select the "<Edit..>" option on the right.

In the new screen, make any changes you require.

```
┤ Edit Connection ├
            Profile name netplan-ens3
                  Device ens3 (52:54:00:51:1D:CB)

 = ETHERNET                                                      <Show>

 = IPv4 CONFIGURATION <Manual>                                  <Hide>
          Addresses 192.168.122.103/24          <Remove>
                    <Add...>
            Gateway
        DNS servers 192.168.122.1               <Remove>
                    <Add...>
     Search domains <Add...>

            Routing One custom route <Edit...>
 [ ] Never use this network for default route
 [ ] Ignore automatically obtained routes
 [ ] Ignore automatically obtained DNS parameters

 [ ] Require IPv4 addressing for this connection


 = IPv6 CONFIGURATION <Ignore>                                  <Show>

 [X] Automatically connect
 [X] Available to all users

                                            <Cancel> <OK>
```

Figure 8-22. *Screen to update network configuration*

Once you are done with your network configuration, select the <OK> option.

Figure 8-23. *You can change your system's hostname with this utility too*

As always, when done, restart your system or services depending on your preference.

Network Configuration with Desktop

The final method of configuring your network configuration is through the various Linux desktops.

Fedora

To configure your network configuration on a Fedora desktop like GNOME, left-click the network icon on the bottom right-hand corner of your screen.

Figure 8-24. *Network icon in Fedora's desktop*

Click Network Settings to show the screen displayed in Figure 8-25.

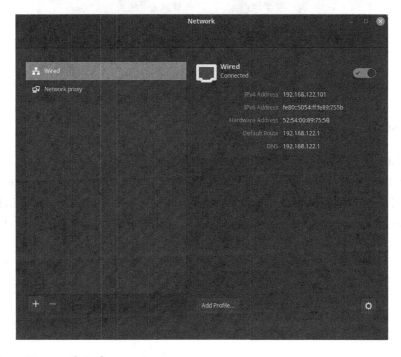

Figure 8-25. *Network information screen*

Click the Network you wish to edit on the left and then click the icon that looks like a "cog".

Figure 8-26. *Network configuration screen*

This will allow you to edit your network configuration.

Click the IPv4 menu on the left for the network configuration we have been configuring throughout this chapter. Make any changes you wish and then click "Apply".

To apply the network configuration to your running environment, toggle the "Wired" option in the Network Icon menu on your desktop.

Figure 8-27. *Wired network icon*

Ubuntu

To configure your network configuration with the Ubuntu desktop "Unity", you will need to click the network icon in the top right-hand corner of your desktop.

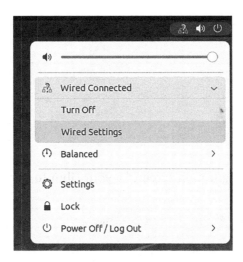

Figure 8-28. *Ubuntu desktop network configuration menu item*

From there, you will need to click the "Wired Settings" menu item.

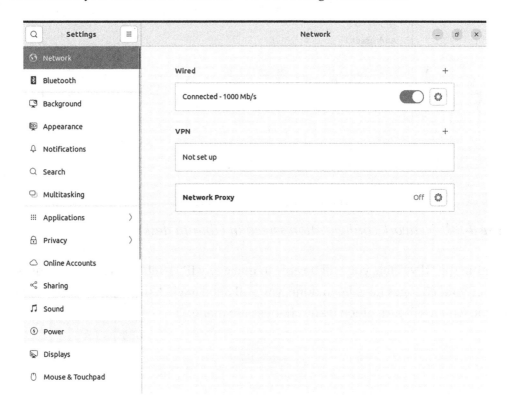

Figure 8-29. *Network information screen*

On the "Wired Settings" screen, you will need to click the Settings button under your "Wired" network.

This will open the configuration screen for your Ubuntu server's network settings.

Figure 8-30. *Network configuration screen in Ubuntu desktop*

Within the "IPv4" tab, you will be able to make any IPv4-related network changes.

Once your changes have been done, you will need to click the "Apply" button on the top right, which will turn green if any changes are made.

OpenSUSE

As OpenSUSE uses the YaST utility to control much of its configuration, you will need to use the "YaST" network configuration utility within the OpenSUSE desktop environment. To find this utility, click the YaST menu and search for "network".

Figure 8-31. *Finding network options on OpenSUSE*

You will need to authenticate to elevate your privileges.

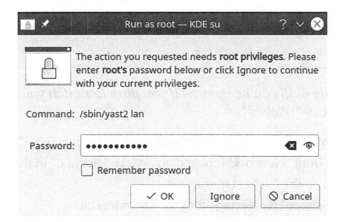

Figure 8-32. *Elevate permissions window*

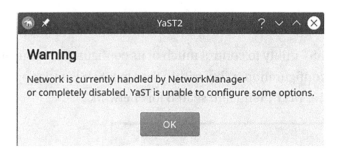

Figure 8-33. *This error will appear if you are using NetworkManager to control your network configuration*

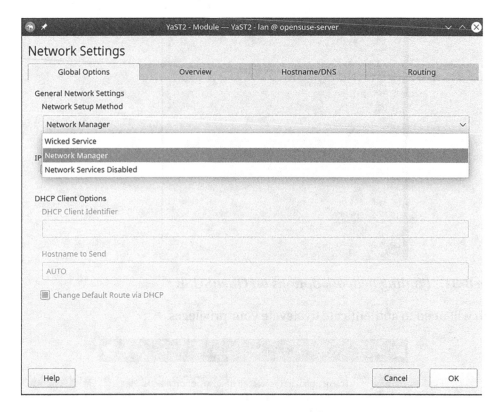

Figure 8-34. *Figure 8-33 can be ignored if you plan to switch your network management back to "Wicked".*

If you wish to change your network configuration with OpenSUSE YaST utilities, you will need to change from "NetworkManager" to "Wicked Service" in the Network Setup Method drop-down on the Global Options tab.

Once "Wicked Service" is selected, click the Overview tab.

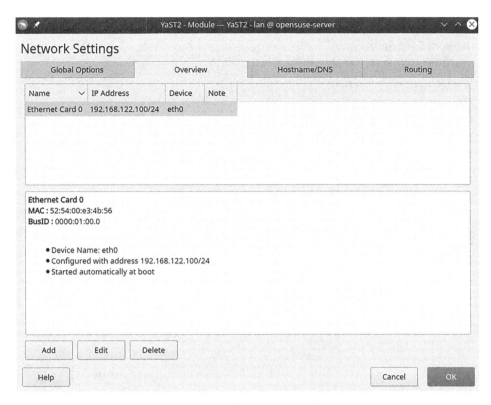

Figure 8-35. *Network information screen for OpenSUSE*

To change the current network configuration of your OpenSUSE system, click the "Edit" button.

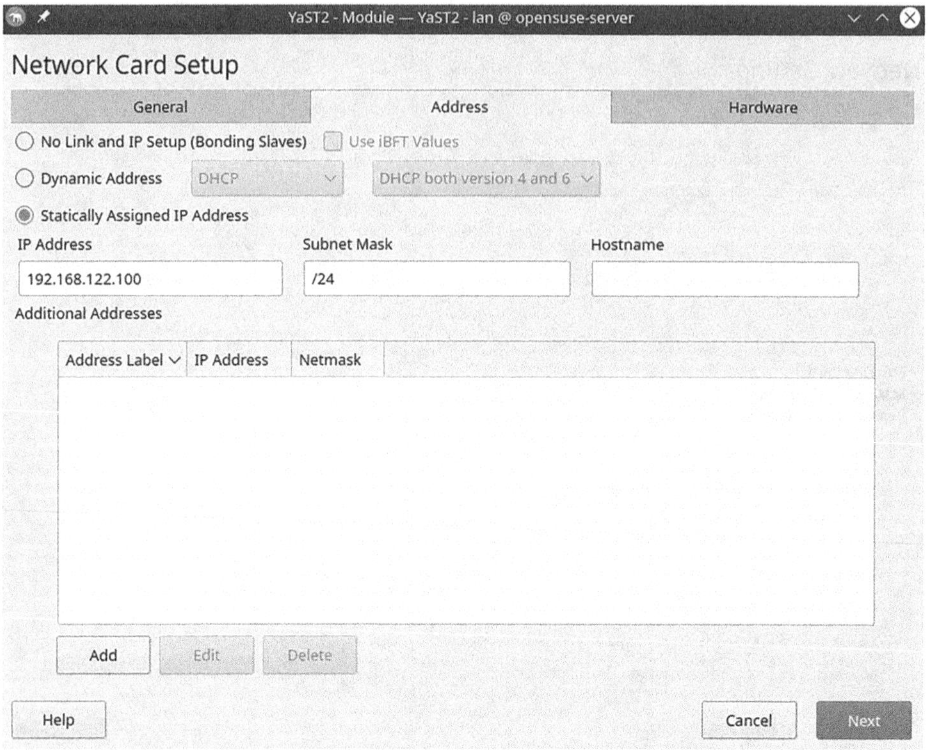

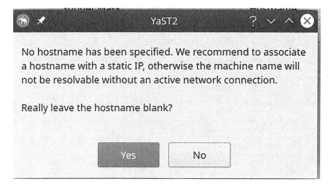

Figure 8-36. *Network configuration screen*

Once your changes have been completed, click the "Next" button.

Figure 8-37. *If you have not configured a hostname for your system, you may get this message*

Click "Yes", then click "OK".

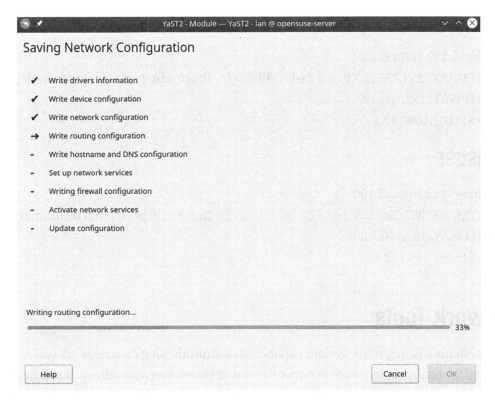

Figure 8-38. *This screen will appear that will apply your network configuration*

Exercise

As a very simple exercise on network configuration, configure all your systems with a series of IP addresses that match your network.

On the lab environments that were used for the examples in this book, I configured the following network configuration on each.

Fedora

IP Address: 192.168.122.101

NETMASK: 255.255.255.0 or a 24-bit subnet for those who prefer that terminology

GATEWAY: 192.168.122.1

DNS1: 192.168.122.1

Ubuntu

IP Address: 192.168.122.102

NETMASK: 255.255.255.0 or a 24-bit subnet for those who prefer that terminology

GATEWAY: 192.168.122.1

DNS1: 192.168.122.1

OpenSUSE

IP Address: 192.168.122.100

NETMASK: 255.255.255.0 or a 24-bit subnet for those who prefer that terminology

GATEWAY: 192.168.122.1

DNS1: 192.168.122.1

Network Tools

Linux systems like any other system capable of communicating on a network will need to be tested for connectivity or other network-related issues. Occasionally, you will need to make use of various network utilities and tools to help you diagnose any of these issues.

There are a number of tools that can be useful to you as an enterprise Linux administrator. Some are very simple, and some require further tooling to understand the output. As this is only the introduction into Linux system administration in the enterprise, we will only look at what the tools are and their general use. For more information, it is always recommended to read man pages or do some further training into the network tooling where they end up being more complicated.

Default Tools Available

On standard Linux systems, the following network tools are available to use. These tools should be your first call when attempting to diagnose network-related queries or issues.

Ping

This is the most basic of basic tools available to check general connectivity. This does require that the "ICMP" protocol is allowed on your network and between your devices but can be a quick tool to determine if you can see another device on your network.

```
ken@ubuntu-server:~$ ping 192.168.122.100
PING 192.168.122.100 (192.168.122.100) 56(84) bytes of data.
64 bytes from 192.168.122.100: icmp_seq=1 ttl=64 time=1.39 ms
64 bytes from 192.168.122.100: icmp_seq=2 ttl=64 time=1.45 ms
64 bytes from 192.168.122.100: icmp_seq=3 ttl=64 time=1.35 ms
^C
--- 192.168.122.100 ping statistics ---
3 packets transmitted, 3 received, 0% packet loss, time 2004ms
rtt min/avg/max/mdev = 1.346/1.392/1.445/0.040 ms
```

Figure 8-39. *Example of the ping command*

The example shown in Figure 8-39 shows connectivity between the Ubuntu server used in this book and the OpenSUSE server. The network between these two systems does not have any restrictions, hence why the ping command has worked.

On a Linux system, the ping command will also run until killed if you do not specify how many counts you wish to run. On a Windows system, this defaults to four counts and stops.

SS

It is not always enough to confirm connectivity between your systems. In some cases, you may need to determine that your system is actually providing a service for another system to connect to. This is done by confirming your "socket statistics." Tools like "ss" and "netstat" will list all ports and services that are listening on your system.

The following command will list all sockets listening for traffic on all network interfaces on your system using the TCP protocol:

```
# ss -l | grep 0.0.0.0 | grep tcp
```

```
[ken@localhost ~]$ ss -l | grep 0.0.0.0 | grep tcp
tcp    LISTEN 0    32                                              192.168.122.1:doma
in                       0.0.0.0:*
tcp    LISTEN 0    4096                                          127.0.0.53%lo:doma
in                       0.0.0.0:*
tcp    LISTEN 0    128                                                 0.0.0.0:ssh
                         0.0.0.0:*
tcp    LISTEN 0    128                                               127.0.0.1:ipp
                         0.0.0.0:*
tcp    LISTEN 0    5                                                 127.0.0.1:4432
1                        0.0.0.0:*
tcp    LISTEN 0    5                                                 127.0.0.1:dey-
sapi                     0.0.0.0:*
tcp    LISTEN 0    4096                                                0.0.0.0:host
mon                      0.0.0.0:*
tcp    LISTEN 0    4096                                              127.0.0.1:rfb
                         0.0.0.0:*
tcp    LISTEN 0    4096                                              127.0.0.1:5901
                         0.0.0.0:*
tcp    LISTEN 0    4096                                              127.0.0.1:5902
                         0.0.0.0:*
```

Figure 8-40. *Output of the ss -l command*

The output shown in Figure 8-40 lists all the services available to receive requests. You will notice this includes the ssh service that is controlled by the sshd daemon. If you killed the sshd daemon on your system, the socket would not show on the output. This is how you could determine if your system is actively listening for requests on a particular port or service.

dig

From time to time, you will need to debug issues where hostnames are not resolving IP addresses. For this, a useful tool to use is the dig utility. "dig" will attempt to resolve hostnames using the configured DNS settings for your network interface.

```
ken@ubuntu-server:~$ dig opensuse-server

; <<>> DiG 9.18.1-1ubuntu1.1-Ubuntu <<>> opensuse-server
;; global options: +cmd
;; Got answer:
;; ->>HEADER<<- opcode: QUERY, status: NOERROR, id: 57969
;; flags: qr aa rd ra ad; QUERY: 1, ANSWER: 1, AUTHORITY: 0, ADDITIONAL: 1

;; OPT PSEUDOSECTION:
; EDNS: version: 0, flags:; udp: 65494
;; QUESTION SECTION:
;opensuse-server.                IN      A

;; ANSWER SECTION:
opensuse-server.        0       IN      A       192.168.122.100

;; Query time: 0 msec
;; SERVER: 127.0.0.53#53(127.0.0.53) (UDP)
;; WHEN: Wed Jul 13 21:54:28 UTC 2022
;; MSG SIZE  rcvd: 60
```

Figure 8-41. *Results of a successful query for the opensuse-server*

```
ken@ubuntu-server:~$ dig fedora-server

; <<>> DiG 9.18.1-1ubuntu1.1-Ubuntu <<>> fedora-server
;; global options: +cmd
;; Got answer:
;; ->>HEADER<<- opcode: QUERY, status: SERVFAIL, id: 18357
;; flags: qr aa rd ra; QUERY: 1, ANSWER: 0, AUTHORITY: 0, ADDITIONAL: 1

;; OPT PSEUDOSECTION:
; EDNS: version: 0, flags:; udp: 65494
;; QUESTION SECTION:
;fedora-server.                  IN      A

;; Query time: 0 msec
;; SERVER: 127.0.0.53#53(127.0.0.53) (UDP)
;; WHEN: Wed Jul 13 21:58:08 UTC 2022
;; MSG SIZE  rcvd: 42
```

Figure 8-42. *This demonstrates when DNS does not resolve a hostname*

The important section on the basic "dig" output is the "ANSWER" section. This will normally result in the successful resolution of the hostname to IP address.

Exercise

Prerequisites

On all of your Linux systems deployed so far, edit the /etc/hosts file and add lines for each of your systems with their IP addresses and hostnames.

```
127.0.0.1 localhost
127.0.1.1 ubuntu-server

# The following lines are desirable for IPv6 capable hosts
::1     ip6-localhost ip6-loopback
fe00::0 ip6-localnet
ff00::0 ip6-mcastprefix
ff02::1 ip6-allnodes
ff02::2 ip6-allrouters

192.168.122.100          opensuse-server.local    opensuse-server
~
```

Figure 8-43. *An example of a /etc/hosts file*

Network Testing

On each of your Linux systems, check that they can communicate with each other by using the ping command. Attempt to ping by both IP address and system hostname that you may have configured.

For successful connectivity and DNS resolution, you should be able to ssh to each of your systems from each other using the system's hostname.

For this, you will need to ensure hostnames are configured, "/etc/hosts" files are updated, and static IP addresses are configured.

Summary

In this chapter, you were introduced to the following:

- How network configuration can be done on a Linux system using command-line utilities and how command-line graphical utilities can reduce configuration complexity

- How network configuration can also be done using the desktop on most Linux systems

- The various networking tools available and how to use them

## CHAPTER 9

Disk Configuration

When running any operating system over a long time, one functional thing generally tends to happen. Storage space runs out. In this chapter, we will look at the various methods to manage Linux disk storage from command-line utilities through to graphical or desktop-based utilities.

This chapter will look at how disks are added, extended, removed, and protected using the various tools and options available by default on the Linux distributions used so far. This will include how disks are partitioned and configured for redundancy.

Creating and extending disks is the first part to managing storage on your Linux environments; once disks are added or extended, there is a requirement to extend the filesystem that is on top of these disks; the final part of this chapter will discuss the different common filesystems available and how they are managed.

Disk Management

The Linux operating system requires storage for it to be installed on just like any other operating system that is not ephemeral (not persistent through reboot basically). The storage used can be anything from local disks like solid-state drives or the older less expensive mechanical spinning disks. Linux can even be installed on a USB drive if you really wanted to.

Storage can also be added to your Linux systems from external storage arrays or storage solutions like Ceph, Gluster, or NFS. All these storage solutions are also network based and will require additional planning when using them.

One thing most of these storage options have in common is that they need to be configured on your Linux operating system to allow your Linux systems to make use of them. This typically requires the creation of disk partitions and if you wanted, a layer above the disk partitions that allows easier management of your storage.

© Kenneth Hitchcock 2023
K. Hitchcock, *The Enterprise Linux Administrator*, https://doi.org/10.1007/978-1-4842-8801-6_9

Before we continue with this chapter, it is important that you have a solid understanding of what computer disks are and how they are configured at a very basic level. In Chapter 1, it was recommended to run through some basic IT training if you were new to the industry. During your preparation studies, you should have learned about the following:

- Hard drive partitioning

- Primary vs. extended partitions.

- Boot partitions

- Filesystems

In the remainder of this chapter, we will continue to discuss these subjects as though you are familiar with them.

The goal of this chapter is to discuss the Linux utilities and methods that can be used to manage any disk attached to your environments.

Disk Layers

No matter what operating system you use for your systems, you will always need to configure some kind of disk configuration for your operating system to be installed on. For this, you need to create partitions and filesystems. Figure 9-1 shows the layers a storage device can have.

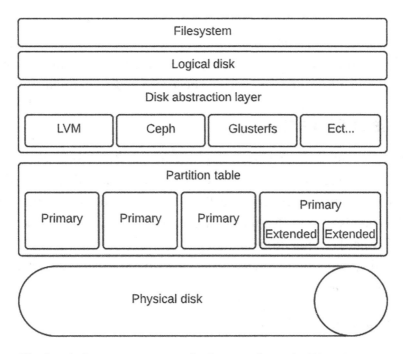

Figure 9-1. *The basic layers a storage device can have in Linux*

The base of a storage disk will always be the physical disk itself. This can be a solid-state disk or a spinning hard drive. With the physical disk, you need to create partitions. As there can only be a maximum of four primary partitions, the use of extended partitions is required if you need more physical partitions. The next layer is all about disk abstraction. This is the process of separating the filesystem from the partition table, allowing easier creation of logical disks, similar to partitioning but not quite the same. The final layer is the filesystem that will be used to install your operating system on.

Tools Available

To manage the different layers of your system disk, there are a few utilities that need to be used that are mostly available on common Linux distributions.

The next few pages will look at both command-line and graphical desktop-based tools that can be used to configure your system disk. Most enterprise Linux administrators tend to prefer the command line mostly due to the lack of Linux desktops installed. This is why it is always recommended to understand both the command-line and graphical tools available.

One important point to make that slightly contradicts what was said previously is that when something can be done in a simpler and reduced risk manner, that should always be the path to follow. We will look at both command-line utilities and graphical utilities. However, in most situations, you will be forced to use command line only.

Showing Disks Available

Before you can even think about configuring your disks in your Linux system, you need to understand how to see what disks you have available. So far in this book, we have only deployed our Linux systems with one disk. The primary operating system disk (in most cases, this disk is around 10 gigabytes large, which for any system, that will run a meaningful workload) will not be enough.

In the preceding situation, if you needed to add a new disk to your system, how could you tell what disks are available?

/proc/partitions File

There are a couple of options to do this. You could run a command that outputs the contents of the "partitions" file. Remember that everything in Linux is a file, even the disk layout.

```
# cat /proc/partitions
```

```
[root@fedora-server ~]# cat /proc/partitions
major minor  #blocks   name

  11        0     1048575 sr0
 252        0    20971520 vda
 252        1     1048576 vda1
 252        2    19921920 vda2
 253        0    15728640 dm-0
 251        0     2015232_zram0
```

Figure 9-2. *The output for the /proc/partitions*

lsblk

Another nice way to view what disks you have available on your Linux system is through the use of the "lsblk" utility.

```
# lsblk
```

```
[root@fedora-server ~]# lsblk
NAME                    MAJ:MIN RM  SIZE RO TYPE MOUNTPOINTS
sr0                      11:0    1 1024M  0 rom
zram0                   251:0    0  1.9G  0 disk [SWAP]
vda                     252:0    0   20G  0 disk
├─vda1                  252:1    0    1G  0 part /boot
└─vda2                  252:2    0   19G  0 part
  └─fedora_fedora-root  253:0    0   15G  0 lvm  /
```

Figure 9-3. *The output lsblk utility*

I personally prefer this "lsblk" command as it outputs the disk layout in a more logical way to understand.

Graphical Tools

On most Linux desktops such as GNOME or KDE, there will be a disk management utility you can use; on Fedora, the "disks" utility shown in Figure 9-4 is available.

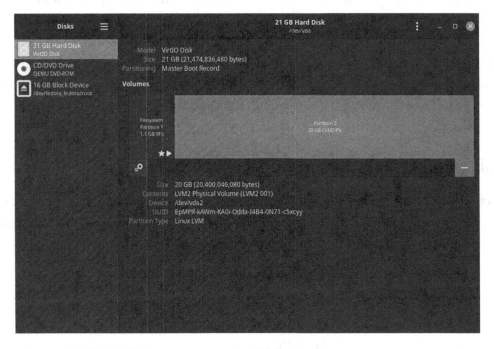

Figure 9-4. *GNOME disk management utility*

Disk Names

In the various tooling displayed earlier and their output, you would have noticed that the disks were named vda.

In the "lsblk" output shown in Figure 9-5, the "vda" disk has two child disks: vda1 and vda2.

```
[root@fedora-server ~]# lsblk
NAME                     MAJ:MIN RM  SIZE RO TYPE MOUNTPOINTS
sr0                       11:0    1 1024M  0 rom
zram0                    251:0    0  1.9G  0 disk [SWAP]
vda                      252:0    0   20G  0 disk
├─vda1                   252:1    0    1G  0 part /boot
└─vda2                   252:2    0   19G  0 part
  └─fedora_fedora-root   253:0    0   15G  0 lvm  /
```

Figure 9-5. *The lsblk utility output*

These two disks are not physical disks but are instead partitions that were created by the Linux installer. "vda1" is the partition used to store Linux system boot files and kernel files used by your Linux operating system. "vda2" is the partition used to store the rest of your operating system files and is the partition that would be used to store any files you create.

On a virtual machine, disks typically start with the letters "vd" and are your "physical" disk. These disks can also sometimes start with "sd". This will depend on your virtual machine hypervisor and the storage drive that was chosen. IE virtio will use vdx, whereas iSCSI and SATA would use sdx. The "lsblk" utility is quite nice to quickly see what disks have been presented to your Linux system.

Adding Disks

To demonstrate disk configuration in one of the Linux distributions we have been using so far, we will need to add some additional disks to our virtual machines. The following are steps on how to add a disk using "virt-manager":

1. The first step to adding a new disk to your virtual machine is to open virt-manager.

2. Open the console to the virtual machine and click the "Show virtual hardware details" button.

Figure 9-6. *The "Show virtual hardware details" button in Virtual Machine Manager*

3. Click the "Add Hardware" button.

Figure 9-7. *The Add Hardware button used to add "hardware" to a virtual machine*

4. Click the storage menu item on the left of the new window.

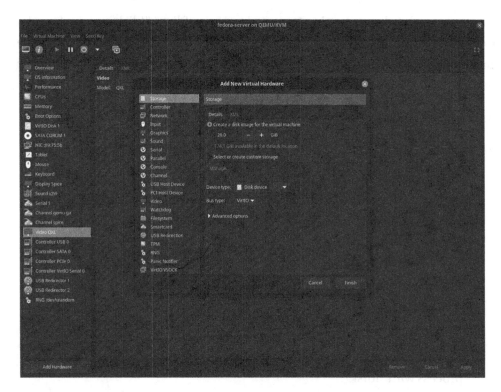

Figure 9-8. *The storage hardware options in Virtual Machine Manager*

5. Specify the size of the disk you wish to add and click "Finish". Ignore the other configuration for now. Defaults are fine for these tests.

For the testing that follows, 1–2 gigabytes of storage is more than enough.

Disk Partition Tooling

Creating partitions will be the first step when setting up a new disk on your system. The following are some of the tools and steps you can follow if a new disk is required on your system. There will be a mixture of command-line and graphical utilities used. Feel free to use whichever is easier for you.

fdisk

The most common disk partitioning tool used today is "fdisk". "fdisk" can be found on every common Linux distribution available. "fdisk" is even used for Windows and Unix disk partitioning. "fdisk" is a command-line utility that can be run with the following command:

```
# fdisk /dev/diskname
```

To configure a partition with "fdisk", the following steps can be followed:

1. To configure a partition on a new disk that has been added to your system, first, we need to know what disks are available. To do this, we run the "lsblk" command:

   ```
   # lsblk
   ```

2. From the preceding output, we can now see that a new disk "vdb" has been added to our system and that there are no partitions on the disk due to the lack of a child disk.

3. By running the following command, we start the partitioning process with "fdisk":

   ```
   # fdisk /dev/vdb
   ```

   ```
   [root@fedora-server ~]# fdisk /dev/vdb

   Welcome to fdisk (util-linux 2.38).
   Changes will remain in memory only, until you decide to write them.
   Be careful before using the write command.

   Device does not contain a recognized partition table.
   Created a new DOS disklabel with disk identifier 0xe0beaff3.

   Command (m for help): █
   ```

Figure 9-9. *The output for the fdisk command*

4. If you have never used the "fdisk" utility before, the first thing to do is to view the help. This can be done by typing "m" and pressing enter.

```
Command (m for help): m

Help:

  DOS (MBR)
   a   toggle a bootable flag
   b   edit nested BSD disklabel
   c   toggle the dos compatibility flag

  Generic
   d   delete a partition
   F   list free unpartitioned space
   l   list known partition types
   n   add a new partition
   p   print the partition table
   t   change a partition type
   v   verify the partition table
   i   print information about a partition

  Misc
   m   print this menu
   u   change display/entry units
   x   extra functionality (experts only)

  Script
   I   load disk layout from sfdisk script file
   O   dump disk layout to sfdisk script file

  Save & Exit
   w   write table to disk and exit
   q   quit without saving changes

  Create a new label
   g   create a new empty GPT partition table
   G   create a new empty SGI (IRIX) partition table
   o   create a new empty DOS partition table
   s   create a new empty Sun partition table
```

Figure 9-10. *The fdisk help menu*

5. To create a new partition on our "vdb" disk, we use the "n" option and press enter.

```
Command (m for help): n
Partition type
   p   primary (0 primary, 0 extended, 4 free)
   e   extended (container for logical partitions)
Select (default p):

Using default response p.
Partition number (1-4, default 1):
First sector (2048-2097151, default 2048):
Last sector, +/-sectors or +/-size{K,M,G,T,P} (2048-2097151, default 2097151):

Created a new partition 1 of type 'Linux' and of size 1023 MiB.
```

Figure 9-11. *Creating a new partition using fdisk*

The partition is set to primary, the partition number is set to 1, and the first and last sectors are left to the default values. This will ensure that the full capacity of the disk is used for the storage.

The disk size can also be specified if you wanted to set a different value.

6. Due to some configuration that will be done later in this chapter, we need to set the partition type. This is done by typing "t" and pressing enter.

```
Command (m for help): t
Selected partition 1
Hex code or alias (type L to list all): L

00 Empty              27 Hidden NTFS Win   82 Linux swap / So   c1 DRDOS/sec (FAT-
01 FAT12              39 Plan 9            83 Linux             c4 DRDOS/sec (FAT-
02 XENIX root         3c PartitionMagic    84 OS/2 hidden or    c6 DRDOS/sec (FAT-
03 XENIX usr          40 Venix 80286       85 Linux extended    c7 Syrinx
04 FAT16 <32M         41 PPC PReP Boot     86 NTFS volume set   da Non-FS data
05 Extended           42 SFS               87 NTFS volume set   db CP/M / CTOS / .
06 FAT16              4d QNX4.x            88 Linux plaintext   de Dell Utility
07 HPFS/NTFS/exFAT    4e QNX4.x 2nd part   8e Linux LVM         df BootIt
08 AIX                4f QNX4.x 3rd part   93 Amoeba            e1 DOS access
09 AIX bootable       50 OnTrack DM        94 Amoeba BBT        e3 DOS R/O
0a OS/2 Boot Manag    51 OnTrack DM6 Aux   9f BSD/OS            e4 SpeedStor
0b W95 FAT32          52 CP/M              a0 IBM Thinkpad hi   ea Linux extended
0c W95 FAT32 (LBA)    53 OnTrack DM6 Aux   a5 FreeBSD           eb BeOS fs
0e W95 FAT16 (LBA)    54 OnTrackDM6        a6 OpenBSD           ee GPT
0f W95 Ext'd (LBA)    55 EZ-Drive         a7 NeXTSTEP          ef EFI (FAT-12/16/
10 OPUS               56 Golden Bow        a8 Darwin UFS        f0 Linux/PA-RISC b
11 Hidden FAT12       5c Priam Edisk       a9 NetBSD            f1 SpeedStor
12 Compaq diagnost    61 SpeedStor         ab Darwin boot       f4 SpeedStor
14 Hidden FAT16 <3    63 GNU HURD or Sys   af HFS / HFS+        f2 DOS secondary
16 Hidden FAT16       64 Novell Netware    b7 BSDI fs           f8 EBBR protective
17 Hidden HPFS/NTF    65 Novell Netware    b8 BSDI swap         fb VMware VMFS
18 AST SmartSleep     70 DiskSecure Mult   bb Boot Wizard hid   fc VMware VMKCORE
1b Hidden W95 FAT3    75 PC/IX             bc Acronis FAT32 L   fd Linux raid auto
1c Hidden W95 FAT3    80 Old Minix         be Solaris boot      fe LANstep
1e Hidden W95 FAT1    81 Minix / old Lin   bf Solaris           ff BBT
24 NEC DOS

Aliases:
   linux        - 83
   swap         - 82
   extended     - 05
   uefi         - EF
   raid         - FD
   lvm          - 8E
   linuxex      - 85
Hex code or alias (type L to list all): 8e
Changed type of partition 'Linux' to 'Linux LVM'.
```

***Figure 9-12.** Setting the partition type in fdisk*

The partition type required is "8e". Type "8e" and press enter. This type is required for lvm-type partitions. It is worth noting, however, if your partition exceeds 2 terabyte, this would need to be set to "gpt".

7. The final thing to do with "fdisk" is to save the configuration. Type "w" and press enter.

```
Command (m for help): w
The partition table has been altered.
Calling ioctl() to re-read partition table.
Syncing disks.
```

Figure 9-13. *Saving any configuration changes in fdisk*

Note If you get an error about disks not being able to sync or anything similar, you may need to reboot your system or use the "partprobe" command.

---

parted

Another common disk partitioning tool used today is "parted". "parted" can be found on almost all common Linux distributions. "parted" is another command-line utility like "fdisk" that can be run with the following command:

```
# parted /dev/diskname
```

To configure a partition with "fdisk", the following steps can be followed:

1. To create a new partition on a disk added to your system, you need to identify what the name of the disk is. To do this, we run the "lsblk" command:

```
root@ubuntu-server:~# lsblk
NAME                       MAJ:MIN RM   SIZE RO TYPE MOUNTPOINTS
loop0                          7:0    0 61.9M  1 loop /snap/core20/1518
loop1                          7:1    0 79.9M  1 loop /snap/lxd/22923
loop2                          7:2    0 61.9M  1 loop /snap/core20/1405
loop3                          7:3    0   47M  1 loop /snap/snapd/16010
loop4                          7:4    0   47M  1 loop /snap/snapd/16292
sda                            8:0    0   20G  0 disk
├─sda1                         8:1    0    1M  0 part
├─sda2                         8:2    0  1.8G  0 part /boot
└─sda3                         8:3    0 18.2G  0 part
  └─ubuntu--vg-ubuntu--lv    253:0    0   10G  0 lvm  /
sdb                           8:16    0    1G  0 disk
sr0                           11:0    1 1024M  0 rom
```

Note Earlier it was mentioned that virtual machines can sometimes use different disk names. With Fedora, we saw the disks were named "vda", and now with Ubuntu, we can see the disks are called "sda" and "sdb".

---

2. With the output from "lsblk", we can see that the new disk added is called "sdb".

3. To create a new partition on disk "sdb", we run the following "parted" command:

    # parted /dev/sdb

    ```
    root@ubuntu-server:~# parted /dev/sdb
    GNU Parted 3.4
    Using /dev/sdb
    Welcome to GNU Parted! Type 'help' to view a list of commands.
    (parted)
    ```

Figure 9-14. *Using parted to configure a disk partition*

4. If you are new to "parted", the first command you should run is the "help" command within "parted". The output should be similar to that shown in Figure 9-15.

```
root@ubuntu-server:~# parted /dev/sdb
GNU Parted 3.4
Using /dev/sdb
Welcome to GNU Parted! Type 'help' to view a list of commands.
(parted) help
  align-check TYPE N                       check partition N for TYPE(min|opt) alignment
  help [COMMAND]                           print general help, or help on COMMAND
  mklabel,mktable LABEL-TYPE               create a new disklabel (partition table)
  mkpart PART-TYPE [FS-TYPE] START END     make a partition
  name NUMBER NAME                         name partition NUMBER as NAME
  print [devices|free|list,all|NUMBER]     display the partition table, available devices, free space, all found
        partitions, or a particular partition
  quit                                     exit program
  rescue START END                         rescue a lost partition near START and END
  resizepart NUMBER END                    resize partition NUMBER
  rm NUMBER                                delete partition NUMBER
  select DEVICE                            choose the device to edit
  disk_set FLAG STATE                      change the FLAG on selected device
  disk_toggle [FLAG]                       toggle the state of FLAG on selected device
  set NUMBER FLAG STATE                    change the FLAG on partition NUMBER
  toggle [NUMBER [FLAG]]                   toggle the state of FLAG on partition NUMBER
  unit UNIT                                set the default unit to UNIT
  version                                  display the version number and copyright information of GNU Parted
(parted)
```

Figure 9-15. *Parted help*

5. To get help on each subcommand, use the following format:

    # (parted) help mklabel

```
(parted) help mklabel
  mklabel,mktable LABEL-TYPE                    create a new disklabel (partition table)

    LABEL-TYPE is one of: aix, amiga, bsd, dvh, gpt, mac, msdos, pc98, sun, atari, loop
```

Figure 9-16. *Parted help on a subcommand*

6. Before you can create a partition on your new disk, you need to set a label on the disk. For a simple Linux system, the "gpt" label should be applied.

```
(parted) mklabel gpt
(parted) print
Model: ATA QEMU HARDDISK (scsi)
Disk /dev/sdb: 1074MB
Sector size (logical/physical): 512B/512B
Partition Table: gpt
Disk Flags:

Number  Start  End  Size  File system  Name  Flags
```

Figure 9-17. *Setting the gpt label on a partition*

From the output shown in Figure 9-17, you can see the command used to create the label was "`mklabel gpt`"; this was followed by the "`print`" command to display the current disk configuration.

7. With the label now created for the disk, a new partition can be created. For this, we will create a new primary partition and allocate all the space available to it. To start the partition creation process, run the following command:

```
# (parted) mkpart primary
```

```
(parted) mkpart primary
File system type?  [ext2]? ext4
Start? 0
End? 1074
Warning: The resulting partition is not properly aligned for best performance: 34s % 2048s != 0s
Ignore/Cancel? i
(parted) print
Model: ATA QEMU HARDDISK (scsi)
Disk /dev/sdb: 1074MB
Sector size (logical/physical): 512B/512B
Partition Table: gpt
Disk Flags:

Number  Start    End     Size    File system  Name     Flags
1       17.4kB   1074MB  1074MB  ext4         primary
```

Figure 9-18. *Creating a partition using parted*

The following configuration options were used:

- The filesystem type was set to ext4.

- The start size was set to 0MB

- The end size was set to 1074MB (the total disk space available). This size can be seen in the "print" command.

- The Warning message can be ignored for now.

8. The final step for the disk configuration is to quit from the "parted" utility.

```
(parted) quit
Information: You may need to update /etc/fstab.

root@ubuntu-server:~#
root@ubuntu-server:~#
root@ubuntu-server:~# lsblk
NAME                        MAJ:MIN RM   SIZE RO TYPE MOUNTPOINTS
loop0                         7:0    0 61.9M  1 loop /snap/core20/1518
loop1                         7:1    0 79.9M  1 loop /snap/lxd/22923
loop2                         7:2    0 61.9M  1 loop /snap/core20/1405
loop3                         7:3    0   47M  1 loop /snap/snapd/16010
loop4                         7:4    0   47M  1 loop /snap/snapd/16292
sda                           8:0    0   20G  0 disk
├─sda1                        8:1    0    1M  0 part
├─sda2                        8:2    0  1.8G  0 part /boot
└─sda3                        8:3    0 18.2G  0 part
  └─ubuntu--vg-ubuntu--lv   253:0    0   10G  0 lvm  /
sdb                           8:16   0    1G  0 disk
└─sdb1                        8:17   0 1024M  0 part
sr0                          11:0    1 1024M  0 rom
```

Figure 9-19. *Exiting out of parted*

Graphical

With two command-line options explained, it is also worth looking at the desktop tools that can be used for creating disk partitions.

Fedora

On the Fedora GNOME desktop, there is a utility simply called "disks."

Figure 9-20. *Opening "disks" on Fedora*

When opened, it should be similar to that shown in Figure 9-21.

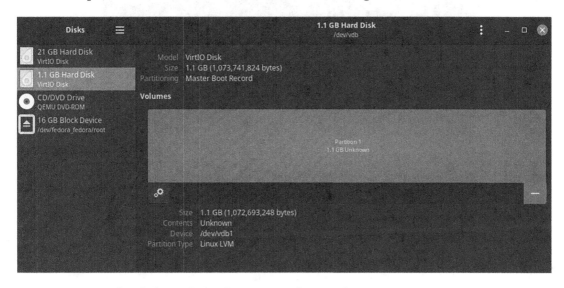

Figure 9-21. *The disks utility when opened on Fedora*

The graphical utility is quite simple to use. On the left, you have all your disks that have been assigned to your system. If you click on a disk on the left as was done in the previous image, you will see what partitions have been created. If none have been created, you can create a new partition using the "+" button. This will open a screen similar to that shown in Figure 9-22.

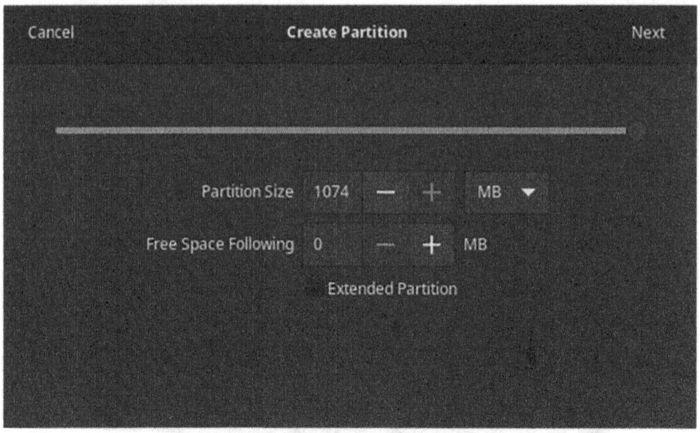

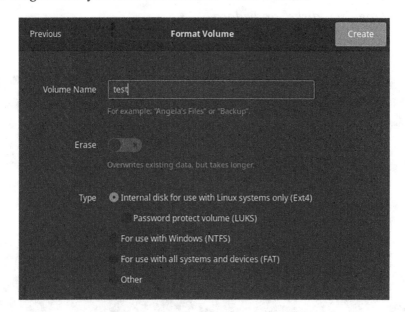

Figure 9-22. *Creating a disk partition using the disks utility*

Type or drag the size you wish and click the "Next" button.

Figure 9-23. *Giving a partition or volume a name using the disks utility*

Give your disk a name, then click the "Create" button.

Ubuntu

On Ubuntu' Unity desktop, there is also a "disks" utility almost, if not exactly, the same as what was on Fedora.

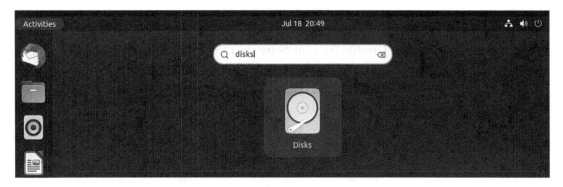

Figure 9-24. *Find the disks utility on Ubuntu*

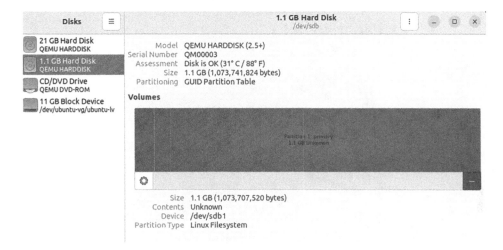

Figure 9-25. *Disks utility on an Ubuntu desktop*

Just as was done with Fedora, disks available to your system are on the left. If you click on a disk, the partition information is displayed. With the previous example, a new partition was already created. In fact, it was created using the "parted" utility.

The partition can be deleted by clicking the "-" button.

Figure 9-26. *The create new partition button*

OpenSUSE

Unlike Fedora and Ubuntu, OpenSUSE makes use of YaST for most of its system configuration. This includes the creation and management of disk partitions. To access the YaST partitioning tool on the OpenSUSE desktop (KDE), click the menu button on the desktop and type "disk".

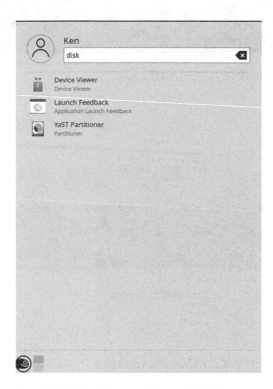

Figure 9-27. *Finding the "disks" utility on OpenSUSE*

This will list the disk utilities available, the YaST Partitioner utility is the one used for disk partition creation. You will need to authenticate your user before you can use any of the YaST utilities. Type your password and click "OK".

Figure 9-28. *The elevate permissions screen in OpenSUSE*

You will be warned that the partitioner tool can be a destructive utility, and you need to be careful when using it.

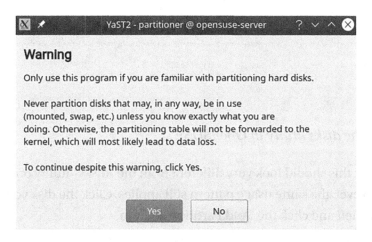

Figure 9-29. *The warning about the destructive nature of working with disk partitions*

Click "Yes" to continue.

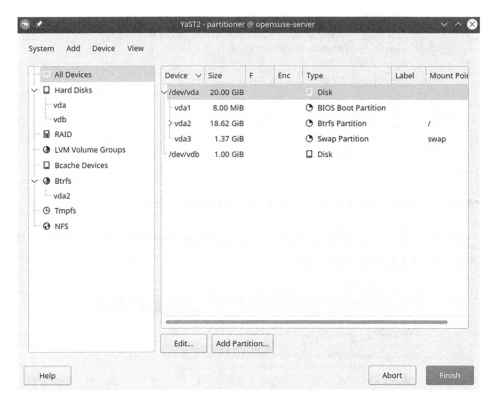

Figure 9-30. *The disks utility in OpenSUSE*

Immediately, this should look very different from the "disks" utility on Fedora or Ubuntu. However, the same usage pattern still applies. Click the disk you want to configure on the left and click the "Add Partition" button.

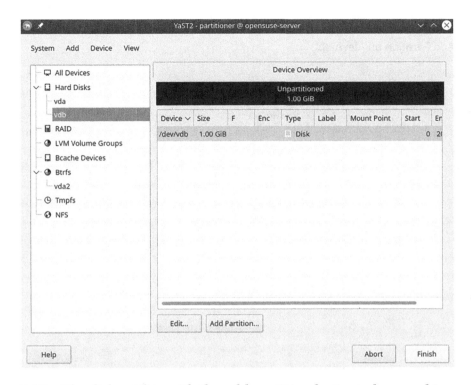

Figure 9-31. *The disks utility with the add partition button when working with a disk*

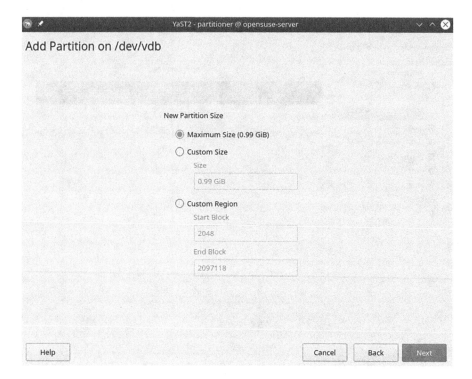

Figure 9-32. *The screen that allows you to select the size you want to use for your disk with the "Next" button to move the configuration forward*

Something that is different from the "disks" utility on Fedora and Ubuntu is that OpenSUSE YaST Partitioner will ask what you want to do with the disk partition. For this example, we will leave the defaults and click "Next".

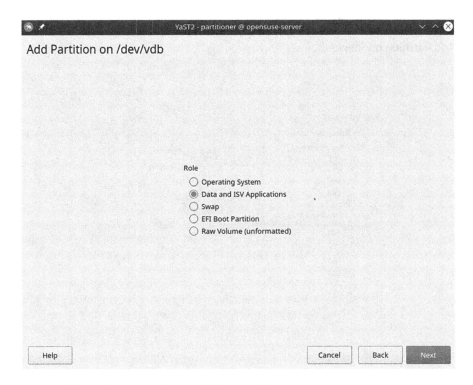

Figure 9-33. *What the partition will be used for*

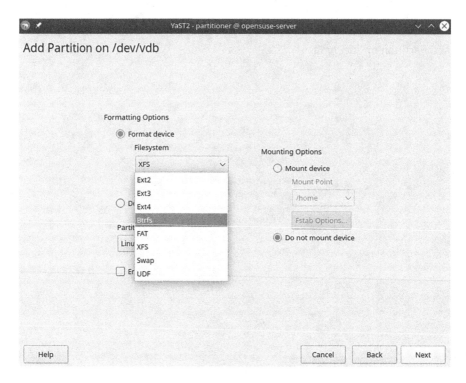

Figure 9-34. *Where the partition will be mounted*

The screen shown in Figure 9-34 allows you to select the filesystem you will use and if you want to mount the disk anywhere. For now, select ext4 as the filesystem, then click "Next".

When you return to the main YaST Partitioner screen, click the "Next" button to continue saving the partition configuration.

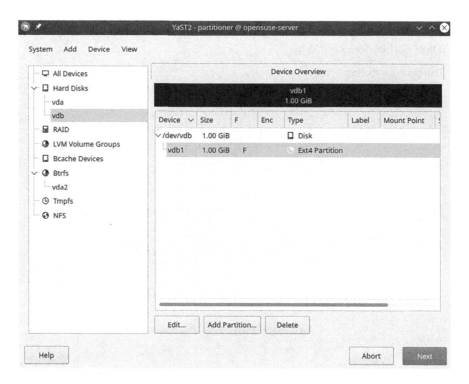

Figure 9-35. *Main partitioners screen*

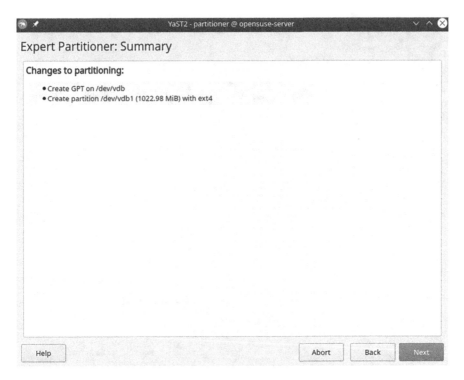

Figure 9-36. *When the "Next" button is clicked to complete your disk configuration*

Exercise

To fully understand how to create disk partitions, do the following exercises on your various Linux systems we have been using so far.

Prerequisites

With virt-manager or VirtualBox, add a 1GB disk to each of your virtual machines you have created for your Linux systems. If you have not decided to use virtual machines, you may need to see if you can install a spare hard drive to test with.

Tip   The instructions on how to add disks in virt-manager can be found near the beginning of this chapter.

Create a Partition with "fdisk"

On either your Ubuntu server or your Fedora server, create a new primary partition on the new disk added to your system using the "fdisk" utility. Use the full storage available from the disk and be sure to set the correct labels.

Create a Partition with "parted"

On either your Fedora or Ubuntu server, create a new primary partition on the new disk added using the "parted" utility. Use the full storage available and be sure to set the correct labels.

Create a Partition with "YaST Partitioner"

In your OpenSUSE environment, create a new partition using the YaST Partitioner tool that uses all the available space on your new disk. Set the filesystem to ext4 and don't mount the disk anywhere.

LVM

LVM or logical volume manager is one of the disk management systems used by many Linux distributions. LVM has also been used in one form or another on Unix platforms in the past.

LVM is an abstraction layer between storage devices and the filesystem that Linux is installed on.

LVM requires three layers of configuration. The first layer is the "physical volume." The physical volume or PV is created by setting a storage device to act as a "physical volume."

The second layer is the volume group layer or VG. Volume groups are, as the name implies, a grouping of volumes. Volume groups have physical volumes added to them and then act as the "middle person" for logical volumes to be created.

Logical volumes or LVs are the final layer used in LVM. LVs are where filesystems are configured and eventually where data is stored.

Volume groups dictate how much space is available for logical volumes. A volume group with 2 terabytes of storage can only provision logical volumes up to 2 terabytes. This could be one large volume or one thousand 2 gigabyte volumes.

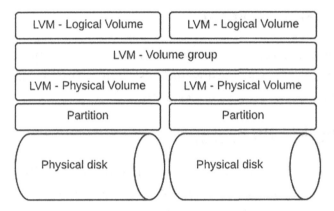

Figure 9-37. *The basic layers of logical volume manager*

Installing LVM

Not all Linux distributions support or install LVM-based utilities by default. On Red Hat-based distributions like Fedora or RHEL, LVM packages are almost always installed and used for the system installation. However, this is not the same for OpenSUSE. Ubuntu server does have LVM tools installed if you chose to do so during the installation. This is actually true for Fedora and any other Red Hat-based distributions.

Package Name

The package that is required on your system to use the LVM utilities is the "lvm2" package.

```
[root@fedora-server ~]# rpm -qf /usr/sbin/lvcreate
lvm2-2.03.11-7.fc36.x86 64
```

Figure 9-38. *The output of the RPM query to check if the LVM packages have been installed*

As mentioned with Fedora, LVM utilities are installed by default; the command shown in Figure 9-38 confirms which packages the "lvcreate" utility was installed from and confirms they are in fact installed.

To install LVM components on OpenSUSE, you can run the following command:

```
# zypper install lvm2
```

To install LVM components on Ubuntu if they are missing, you can run the following command:

```
# apt install lvm2
```

LVM Utilities

The following is a breakdown of the LVM commands that are generally used to manage storage with LVM. The commands are generally in the order in which you use them. The steps to create a logical volume will be discussed shortly, but for now, these are some basic LVM commands you will need to know when using LVM in the future. Table 9-1 lists all the basic LVM commands an Enterprise Linux administrator should know.

Table 9-1. *Basic LVM commands*

LVM Command	Description
pvcreate	Used to create a physical volume from an attached storage device.
vgcreate	Used to create a volume group.
vgextend	Used to extend a volume group.
vgdisplay	Displays details about the volume group, like free space.
lvcreate	Used to create a logical volume.
lvextend	Used to extend a logical volume.
lvdisplay	Shows information about the logical volume.

Note   The commands mentioned in Table 9-1 are not all LVM commands available. To view all the utilities available with LVM, read the man pages by running the command "man lvm".

Create

To create logical volumes with LVM, you need to check a few things.

Physical Volume

Are there any physical volumes available to use that have not been assigned to a volume group? There are a few commands you can use to interrogate what disks have been used to create "physical volumes."

```
[root@fedora-server ~]# pvscan
  PV /dev/vda2   VG fedora_fedora   lvm2 [<19.00 GiB / <4.00 GiB free]
  Total: 1 [<19.00 GiB] / in use: 1 [<19.00 GiB] / in no VG: 0 [0    ]
[root@fedora-server ~]# pvs
  PV         VG            Fmt  Attr PSize   PFree
  /dev/vda2  fedora_fedora lvm2 a--  <19.00g <4.00g
[root@fedora-server ~]# pvdisplay
  --- Physical volume ---
  PV Name               /dev/vda2
  VG Name               fedora_fedora
  PV Size               <19.00 GiB / not usable 3.00 MiB
  Allocatable           yes
  PE Size               4.00 MiB
  Total PE              4863
  Free PE               1023
  Allocated PE          3840
  PV UUID               EpMPlf-kAWm-KA0i-Odda-I4B4-0N71-c5xcyy
```

Figure 9-39. *The methods used to show physical volumes*

From the output shown in Figure 9-39, there are no free "physical volumes." The "physical volume" /dev/vda2 has been allocated to the volume group fedora_fedora.

As we have an extra disk added that we used to create a partition with, we will use this disk to create a "physical volume."

```
[root@fedora-server ~]# lsblk
NAME               MAJ:MIN RM  SIZE RO TYPE MOUNTPOINTS
sr0                  11:0   1 1024M  0 rom
zram0               251:0   0  1.9G  0 disk [SWAP]
vda                 252:0   0   20G  0 disk
├─vda1              252:1   0    1G  0 part /boot
└─vda2              252:2   0   19G  0 part
  └─fedora_fedora-root 253:0   0   15G  0 lvm  /
vdb                 252:16  0    1G  0 disk
└─vdb1              252:17  0 1023M  0 part
```

Figure 9-40. *The output of the lsblk command*

The disk we will use to create a new "physical volume" will be /dev/vdb1.

To create a physical volume on /dev/vdb1, we use the following command:

```
# pvcreate /dev/vdb1
```

```
[root@fedora-server ~]# pvcreate /dev/vdb1
WARNING: ext4 signature detected on /dev/vdb1 at offset 1080. Wipe it? [y/n]: y
  Wiping ext4 signature on /dev/vdb1.
  Physical volume "/dev/vdb1" successfully created.
```

Figure 9-41. *Creating a new physical volume*

The warning shown in Figure 9-41 is very important when you are creating physical volumes on new disks. If a disk has a filesystem signature on it like the one shown in the figure, pvcreate will warn you. Saying yes to this will wipe the signature and any data you may have had on the disk, so be 100% sure when doing this. As we know this disk was created by us and has no data, we can proceed safely.

To confirm we now have a new "physical volume" to use, run the following command:

```
# pvscan
```

```
[root@fedora-server ~]# pvscan
  PV /dev/vda2   VG fedora_fedora   lvm2 [<19.00 GiB / <4.00 GiB free]
  PV /dev/vdb1                      lvm2 [1023.00 MiB]
  Total: 2 [<20.00 GiB] / in use: 1 [<19.00 GiB] / in no VG: 1 [1023.00 MiB]
```

Figure 9-42. *The output of the pvscan utility*

From the output shown in Figure 9-42, you can now see a second "PV" has appeared with no VG next to it. You can also see the size of the new "physical volume."

Volume Group

Once you have "physical volumes" available, you are ready to create a volume group. To create a volume group, you need to know the name of the "physical volumes" you want to use.

To create a volume group by the name of vgtest, you can use the following command:

```
# vgcreate vgtest /dev/vdb1
```

```
[root@fedora-server ~]# vgcreate vgtest /dev/vdb1
  Volume group "vgtest" successfully created
```

Figure 9-43. *The creation of a new volume group*

To list what volume groups are now available, you can either run the command "vgs" or "vgscan".

```
[root@fedora-server ~]# vgs
  VG            #PV #LV #SN Attr   VSize    VFree
  fedora_fedora   1   1   0 wz--n- <19.00g  <4.00g
  vgtest          1   0   0 wz--n- 1020.00m 1020.00m
[root@fedora-server ~]# vgscan
  Found volume group "vgtest" using metadata type lvm2
  Found volume group "fedora_fedora" using metadata type lvm2
```

Figure 9-44. *The methods to show volume groups on your Linux system*

To view your volume groups' information, you can use the following command:

vgdisplay

```
[root@fedora-server ~]# vgdisplay
  --- Volume group ---
  VG Name               vgtest
  System ID
  Format                lvm2
  Metadata Areas        1
  Metadata Sequence No  1
  VG Access             read/write
  VG Status             resizable
  MAX LV                0
  Cur LV                0
  Open LV               0
  Max PV                0
  Cur PV                1
  Act PV                1
  VG Size               1020.00 MiB
  PE Size               4.00 MiB
  Total PE              255
  Alloc PE / Size       0 / 0
  Free  PE / Size       255 / 1020.00 MiB
  VG UUID               MaSETX-CEYu-ZtPI-TtK8-CLFP-lM8e-x3y1Dk

  --- Volume group ---
  VG Name               fedora_fedora
  System ID
  Format                lvm2
  Metadata Areas        1
  Metadata Sequence No  2
  VG Access             read/write
  VG Status             resizable
  MAX LV                0
  Cur LV                1
  Open LV               1
  Max PV                0
  Cur PV                1
  Act PV                1
  VG Size               <19.00 GiB
  PE Size               4.00 MiB
  Total PE              4863
  Alloc PE / Size       3840 / 15.00 GiB
  Free  PE / Size       1023 / <4.00 GiB
  VG UUID               FgZKVi-eRw2-Dhz1-u08k-6DHB-fUPG-pCPfc6
```

Figure 9-45. *The vgdisplay command output*

From the output shown in Figure 9-45, you can see the new volume group "vgtest". Within "vgtest", you can see what physical extent or disk size is available to use. This is what you would use to determine what the max amount of disk space you can use for logical volumes.

Logical Volumes

As our "vgtest" volume group has been created and the fact that there is available storage, all that is left to do is to create a logical volume to make use of the space available in the volume group.

To create a logical volume that uses all the available space in the volume group, you can use the following command:

```
# lvcreate -n lv_test -l100%FREE /dev/vgtest
```

```
[root@fedora-server ~]# lvcreate -n lv_test -l100%FREE /dev/vgtest
  Logical volume "lv test" created.
```

Figure 9-46. *The creation of a logical volume*

The command has a few important bits to understand. The "-n followed by lv_test" represents the name of the logical volume. The "-l" followed by "100%FREE" tells lvcreate to use 100% of the free extents in the volume group specified. The final parameter is the full path to the "/dev/vgtest".

Extending LVM

It is not enough to only understand how LVM components are created. Inevitably, there will always be the need to increase storage to a system. With LVM, this process is quite simple and relatively risk-free if done correctly.

Extending Physical Volumes

PVs or "physical volumes" are not extended as they use the full disk partition. In most cases, a disk partition cannot be extended without potentially destroying the data on the disk. Yes, there may be ways to extend a partition, but on a business-critical system, this should be avoided due to the risk. Instead, additional PVs should be added to your system that can be added to your volume group. By adding another disk to a virtual machine, this can be tested.

Extending Volume Groups

With an additional disk added to your system, a new PV can be created and then added to your volume group.

With the new disk and new partition, a new "physical volume" can be created with the following command:

```
# pvcreate /dev/vdc1
```

```
[root@fedora-server ~]# pvcreate /dev/vdc1
  Physical volume "/dev/vdc1" successfully created.
[root@fedora-server ~]# pvscan
  PV /dev/vdb1   VG vgtest          lvm2 [1020.00 MiB / 0     free]
  PV /dev/vda2   VG fedora_fedora   lvm2 [<19.00 GiB / <4.00 GiB free]
  PV /dev/vdc1                      lvm2 [<2.00 GiB]
  Total: 3 [21.99 GiB] / in use: 2 [19.99 GiB] / in no VG: 1 [<2.00 GiB]
```

Figure 9-47. *The creation of a new physical volume*

To extend the volume group vgtest, the following command can be used:

```
# vgextend vgtest /dev/vdc1
```

```
[root@fedora-server ~]# vgextend vgtest /dev/vdc1
  Volume group "vgtest" successfully extended
```

Figure 9-48. *The vgextend command*

The volume group will now show additional storage available.

```
# vgdisplay vgtest
```

```
[root@fedora-server ~]# vgdisplay vgtest
  --- Volume group ---
  VG Name               vgtest
  System ID
  Format                lvm2
  Metadata Areas        2
  Metadata Sequence No  5
  VG Access             read/write
  VG Status             resizable
  MAX LV                0
  Cur LV                1
  Open LV               0
  Max PV                0
  Cur PV                2
  Act PV                2
  VG Size               2.99 GiB
  PE Size               4.00 MiB
  Total PE              766
  Alloc PE / Size       255 / 1020.00 MiB
  Free  PE / Size       511 / <2.00 GiB
  VG UUID               MaSETX-CEYu-ZtPI-TtK8-CLFP-lM8e-x3y1Dk
```

Figure 9-49. *The vgdisplay command*

Extending Logical Volumes

Only with available storage in the volume group that the logical volume belongs to can the logical volume be extended.

As Figure 9-49 showed the vgdisplay output, you will notice that there is "<2.00GB" available. This means we can extend our logical volumes by a max of 2GB or we can create new logical volumes if we choose.

To extend our logical volume lv_test by 1GB, we can use the following command:

```
# lvextend /dev/vgtest/lv_test -L+1GB
```

```
[root@fedora-server ~]# lvextend /dev/vgtest/lv_test -L+1GB
  Size of logical volume vgtest/lv_test changed from 1020.00 MiB (255 extents) to <2.00 GiB (51
1 extents).
  Logical volume vgtest/lv_test successfully resized.
[root@fedora-server ~]# lvscan
  ACTIVE            '/dev/vgtest/lv_test' [<2.00 GiB] inherit
  ACTIVE            '/dev/fedora_fedora/root' [15.00 GiB] inherit
```

Figure 9-50. *The lvextend command*

The lvextend command is doing something different from the lvcreate command earlier when it comes to disk sizing. As the disk only needed to be extended by 1GB, the parameter "-L" was used followed by "+1GB". The "+" is very important as it tells the lvextend command to add an additional 1GB of storage to the logical volume.

The previous "-l100%FREE" could have been used if all the space was going to be added to the extension.

Migrate

Before looking at how to remove LVM components, it is worth mentioning one powerful feature that LVM has.

LVM has the ability to move all the data from one pv to another. This is very useful if a physical piece of hardware is starting to fail or if a physical disk needs to be replaced by a larger disk.

To move data from one pv to another, the following command can be used:

```
# pvmove /dev/vdb1 /dev/vdc1
```

```
[root@fedora-server ~]# man pvmove
[root@fedora-server ~]# pvmove /dev/vdb1 /dev/vdc1
  /dev/vdb1: Moved: 3.53%
  /dev/vdb1: Moved: 100.00%
```

Figure 9-51. *The pvmove command*

The previous command will move all data from PV /dev/vdb1 to /dev/vdc1, allowing /dev/vdb1 to be removed without losing any data.

Destroy

For each LVM component such as "physical volumes," "volume groups," and "logical volumes," there is the ability to delete them if needed.

Delete Physical Volumes

In the "Migrate" section, it was mentioned that data can be migrated when a disk needs to be replaced. To continue with this example, the "physical volume" that was migrated, "/dev/vdb1", will be deleted. To delete this "physical volume," the following command can be used:

```
# pvremove /dev/vdb1
```

```
[root@fedora-server ~]# pvremove /dev/vdb1
  PV /dev/vdb1 is used by VG vgtest so please use vgreduce first.
  (If you are certain you need pvremove, then confirm by using --force twice.)
  /dev/vdb1: physical volume label not removed.
[root@fedora-server ~]# vgreduce vgtest /dev/vdb1
  Removed "/dev/vdb1" from volume group "vgtest"
[root@fedora-server ~]# pvremove /dev/vdb1
  Labels on physical volume "/dev/vdb1" successfully wiped.
```

Figure 9-52. *The pvremove command*

By running the command, you will notice that in the output shown in Figure 9-52, this failed. Before a "physical volume" can be removed, it must be removed from a "volume group." By using the command "vgreduce vgtest /dev/vdb1", the physical volume "/dev/vdb1" was removed from the volume group "vgtest". Once the old "physical volume" was removed, the pvremove command was successful.

Delete Logical Volumes

To remove a "logical volume" is relatively simple, but it does need to be stressed that this process will lead to data being lost. To remove a logical volume, run the following command:

```
# lvremove /dev/<volume group>/<logical volume>
```

The previously created logical volume, "lv_test", can be removed with the following command:

```
# lvremove /dev/vgtest/lv_test
```

```
[root@fedora-server ~]# lvremove /dev/vgtest/lv_test
Do you really want to remove active logical volume vgtest/lv_test? [y/n]: y
  Logical volume "lv_test" successfully removed
```

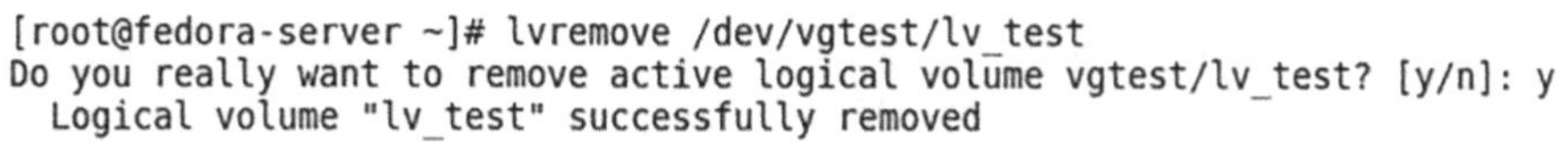

Figure 9-53. *The lvremove command*

Delete Volume Groups

As with the removal of "logical volume," "volume groups" too can be removed by a similar command. To remove the "vgtest" volume group previously created, the following command can be run:

```
# vgremove /dev/vgtest
```

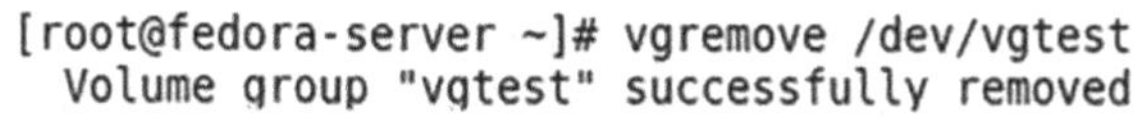

```
[root@fedora-server ~]# vgremove /dev/vgtest
  Volume group "vgtest" successfully removed
```

Figure 9-54. *The vgremove command*

Disaster Recovery

What happens when you accidentally delete a "logical volume" or "volume group"? Fortunately, another very nice feature of LVM is the ability to recover, delete, or change "logical volumes" or "volume groups."

To see what recovery options are available, the following command can be used to list all LVM backups that are made automatically:

```
# vgcfgrestore -l <volume group>
```

To see what recovery options are available for our previously deleted "volume group", "vgtest", we can run the following command:

```
# vgcfgrestore -l vgtest
```

```
[root@fedora-server ~]# vgcfgrestore -l vgtest
  File:        /etc/lvm/archive/vgtest_00000-1616409903.vg
  VG name:     vgtest
  Description: Created *before* executing 'vgcreate vgtest /dev/vdb1'
  Backup Time: Tue Jul 19 21:50:23 2022


  File:        /etc/lvm/archive/vgtest_00001-1951988390.vg
  VG name:     vgtest
  Description: Created *before* executing 'lvcreate -n lv_test -l100%FREE /dev/vgtest'
  Backup Time: Wed Jul 20 21:28:27 2022


  File:        /etc/lvm/archive/vgtest_00002-1088153377.vg
  VG name:     vgtest
  Description: Created *before* executing 'lvremove /dev/vgtest/lv_test'
  Backup Time: Wed Jul 20 21:31:41 2022


  File:        /etc/lvm/archive/vgtest_00003-194814345.vg
  VG name:     vgtest
  Description: Created *before* executing 'lvcreate -n lv_test -l100%FREE /dev/vgtest'
  Backup Time: Wed Jul 20 21:31:45 2022


  File:        /etc/lvm/archive/vgtest_00004-387653253.vg
  VG name:     vgtest
  Description: Created *before* executing 'vgextend vgtest /dev/vdc1'
  Backup Time: Wed Jul 20 21:51:59 2022



  File:        /etc/lvm/archive/vgtest_00006-974254549.vg
  VG name:     vgtest
  Description: Created *before* executing 'pvmove /dev/vdb1 /dev/vdc1'
  Backup Time: Wed Jul 20 22:09:32 2022


  File:        /etc/lvm/archive/vgtest_00007-765527098.vg
  VG name:     vgtest
  Description: Created *before* executing 'vgscan'
  Backup Time: Wed Jul 20 22:16:10 2022


  File:        /etc/lvm/archive/vgtest_00008-2000378725.vg
  VG name:     vgtest
  Description: Created *before* executing 'vgscan'
  Backup Time: Wed Jul 20 22:16:10 2022


  File:        /etc/lvm/archive/vgtest_00009-2018193218.vg
  VG name:     vgtest
  Description: Created *before* executing 'vgreduce vgtest /dev/vdb1'
  Backup Time: Wed Jul 20 22:16:23 2022


  File:        /etc/lvm/archive/vgtest_00010-413529366.vg
  VG name:     vgtest
  Description: Created *before* executing 'lvremove /dev/vgtest/lv_test'
  Backup Time: Thu Jul 21 21:44:46 2022


  File:        /etc/lvm/archive/vgtest_00011-798138348.vg
  VG name:     vgtest
  Description: Created *before* executing 'vgremove /dev/vgtest'
  Backup Time: Thu Jul 21 21:47:46 2022
```

Figure 9-55. *The vgcfgrestore command*

In the output from the "vgcfgrestore" command, there is a full listing of all the backups made before and after configuration backups are made. To restore a mistakenly deleted "volume group" and "logical" as we potentially did with "vgtest" and "lv_test", we can run the following command to restore both:

```
# vgcfgrestore -f /etc/lvm/archive/vgtest_00010-413529366.vg vgtest
```

```
[root@fedora-server ~]#
[root@fedora-server ~]# vgcfgrestore -f /etc/lvm/archive/vgtest_00010-413529366.vg vgtest
  Restored volume group vgtest.
[root@fedora-server ~]# vgs
  VG            #PV #LV #SN Attr   VSize    VFree
  fedora_fedora   1   1   0 wz--n- <19.00g <4.00g
  vgtest          1   1   0 wz--n-  <2.00g      0
[root@fedora-server ~]# lvs
  LV      VG            Attr       LSize   Pool Origin Data%  Meta%  Move Log Cpy%Sync Convert
  root    fedora_fedora -wi-ao---- 15.00g
  lv_test vgtest        -wi------- <2.00g
```

Figure 9-56. *The vgcfgrestore command restoring from a backup*

As the backup file "/etc/lvm/archive/vgtest_00010-413529366.vg" contained the "volume group" information and the "logical volume" information, the restore command recovered both the "volume group" and the "logical volume." This can be seen in the "vgs" and "lvs" commands' output.

RAID, Mirror, and HA

There are other ways to ensure that your storage is protected as much as possible through the use of "RAID." This should be something you would have read or learned about during your pre-studies for this book with physical storage.

It is also possible to do "RAID" or "mirror" configuration or even highly available storage with LVM. This is a subject best left for another time, but if you do have an interest to learn them, there is plenty of material available online. However, while you might be new to LVM, it is best to stick with the basics for now.

Exercise

For your first look into using LVM, you will need to do the following exercise.

Add Disks

On all your Linux systems, add an additional disk at least 1GB in size. Ensure that the disk has been prepared to be used. If need be, go back and look at the previous exercise in this chapter.

Install LVM

On all your Linux systems used so far, ensure that LVM utilities like "lvcreate" and "vgcreate" are installed and available.

Create LVM Components

On each of your Linux systems, create the following:

- A "volume group" named vgtest
- A "logical volume" named lv_test that is at least 1024MB in size

Delete and Recover

On your Fedora server, delete the volume group "vgtest". Then use the recovery options you have learned about so far in this book to restore your deleted "volume group."

Filesystem Management

Up till now, we have only spoken about disk creation and partition management. This is only half of the configuration required to make a disk usable, usable as in being able to mount and create files. Before a disk or "logical volume" can be mounted, you need to assign or create a "filesystem" on the disk. A filesystem is what your operating system uses to create data structure on your disk, allowing the operating system to know where files are stored.

Filesystem Types

On many of the Linux distributions today, you will find an array of filesystem types you can use.

Table 9-2 contains some of the common filesystems used today.

Table 9-2. *Common filesystem types*

Filesystem	Description
ext2	Default filesystem selected when running the mkfs command.
ext3	A journaling filesystem that was used as default on previous versions of Linux.
ext4	Developed as the successor to ext3.
xfs	High-performance 64-bit journaling filesystem.
btrfs	One of the new filesystems available today, combining the ability to do "copy on write (shadowing)" with a logical volume manager. Not the same as LVM.
ntfs	Commonly used on Windows systems.

Checking Disk Filesystem

To list disks, we previously used the utility "lsblk"; this utility listed all the disks in your system. However, this command only told us what disks were available and nothing about the disk itself.

To get more information about a particular disk, there fortunately is another utility that can be used. This utility is called "blkid".

"blkid" will return the UUID and filesystem type for a particular disk. The following is an example of a Fedora server's main disk:

```
# blkid /dev/fedora_fedora/root
```

```
[root@fedora-server ~]# blkid /dev/fedora_fedora/root
/dev/fedora_fedora/root: UUID="6c63ac69-e575-4967-895d-18d3c5978091" BLOCK_SIZE="512" TYPE="xfs
"
```

From the preceding output, you can see that the filesystem type for the main "logical volume" used to install Fedora on is "xfs".

Creating

The command to create an xfs filesystem on a disk is as follows:

```
# mkfs -t xfs /dev/path/to/disk
```

```
[root@fedora-server ~]# mkfs --help

Usage:
 mkfs [options] [-t <type>] [fs-options] <device> [<size>]

Make a Linux filesystem.

Options:
 -t, --type=<type>  filesystem type; when unspecified, ext2 is used
     fs-options     parameters for the real filesystem builder
     <device>       path to the device to be used
     <size>         number of blocks to be used on the device
 -V, --verbose      explain what is being done;
                       specifying -V more than once will cause a dry-run
 -h, --help         display this help
 -V, --version      display version

For more details see mkfs(8).
```

Figure 9-57. *The mkfs utility help menu*

The mkfs also can be used as a prefix to the filesystem you wish to create.

```
[root@fedora-server ~]# mkfs
mkfs           mkfs.cramfs  mkfs.ext2   mkfs.ext4   mkfs.minix   mkfs.ntfs   mkfs.xfs
mkfs.btrfs     mkfs.exfat   mkfs.ext3   mkfs.fat    mkfs.msdos   mkfs.vfat
```

Figure 9-58. *The various mkfs filesystem options*

To create an xfs filesystem using the variation to the first command, you could use something similar to the following:

```
# mkfs.xfs /dev/path/to/disk
```

To create a different filesystem, you can use one of the other options listed in Figure 9-58.

```
# mkfs.ext4 /dev/path/to/disk
```

or

```
# mkfs.btrfs /dev/path/to/disk
```

Mounting Filesystems

Once your disks have a filesystem created, you are ready to mount and start creating content.

The simplest method to mount a disk is with a command similar to the following:

```
# mount /path/to/disk /path/directory/to/mount
```

An example mount command is as follows:

```
# mount /dev/vgtest/lv_test /mnt
```

The preceding command will take the new logical volume we created previously in this chapter and mount it to the /mnt directory.

The mount command will attempt to work out what filesystem you are using, but if that fails, you can specify the filesystem with one of the variations to the mount command:.

```
[root@fedora-server ~]# mount
mount              mount.fuse3       mount.nfs4      mount.ntfs-fuse    mountstats
mount.cifs         mount.lowntfs-3g  mount.ntfs      mountpoint
mount.fuse         mount.nfs _       mount.ntfs-3g   mount.smb3
```

Mounts Persistent Across Reboots

The mount command will only stay mounted while the system remains turned on. If your system is rebooted or shut down, the mounted disk will disappear, and you will need to mount it manually again.

There fortunately is a way to avoid having to manually mount disks. On almost every Linux system, there is a file "/etc/fstab". This "fstab" file is what your Linux system uses to determine what filesystems (disks) should be mounted when a system boots.

```
/dev/mapper/fedora_fedora-root /                     xfs    defaults    0 0
UUID=6fac7403-3278-4ea2-ac28-f22d67ad49e1 /boot            xfs    defaults      0 0
```

A new line can be added to mount a disk if you should choose to do so. To create a new entry for the logical volume we created, we could add the following line:

```
/dev/vgtest/lv_tes   /mnt   xfs   defaults   0 0
```

For a full understanding of the fstab parameters, read the man page for fstab.

Resizing

Occasionally, there will come a need to resize a disk. The first step is to increase the disk size itself or the logical volume; previously, we discussed how a logical volume can be increased. Once your disk size has been resized, you will need to resize your filesystem.

Filesystems like ext2, ext3, and ext4 can be resized to increase capacity and shrunk to reduce capacity. This is where things can get messy if you are not careful. The general rule of thumb is to plan your disk sizing properly from the start and not resize disks. Too many times have I seen this go wrong.

If you absolutely need to resize a filesystem, the following should be done:

1. Unmount the disk:

    ```
    # umount /path/to/mount
    ```

2. Check the disk for issues:

    ```
    # e2fsck /dev/path/to/disk
    ```

3. Resize the command:

    ```
    # resize2fs </dev/path/to/disk> <size to resize to>
    ```

An example command to resize an ext4 filesystem to 2G is as follows:

```
# resize2fs /dev/vgtest/lv_test 2G
```

The preceding command will set the filesystem size to 2 gigabytes and not "reduce" or "increase" by 2 gigabytes. This is where the confusion and disaster can occur.

xfs Cannot Shrink

Some filesystems can only be increased and cannot be reduced like xfs or gfs. These filesystems also have their own commands to resize them or manage their filesystems.

```
[root@fedora-server ~]# xfs_
xfs_admin      xfs_estimate    xfs_info        xfs_metadump    xfs_repair
xfs_bmap       xfs_freeze      xfs_io          xfs_mkfile      xfs_rtcp
xfs_copy       xfs_fsr         xfs_logprint    xfs_ncheck      xfs_spaceman
xfs_db         xfs_growfs    _ xfs_mdrestore   xfs_quota
```

Directory Hierarchy

The Linux directory structure by default has many different directories and subdirectories used for different purposes. Most system administrators will be very familiar with them and will have their own opinion on what should be used for what. Fortunately, there is a standard that should be followed.

Some Linux system administrators like myself have in the past not followed the File Hierarchy Standard and may have incorrectly been configuring platforms. The FHS (www.pathname.com/fhs/) has a really good explanation of why directories are laid out as they are. If you are someone who may be looking to improve standards, I recommend reading the latest PDF document on the FHS website on what the purpose of each directory is for.

Table 9-3 is a basic breakdown of the directory structure according to the FHS.

Table 9-3. *Basic directory structure*

Linux Directory	Description
/bin	Used to store standard user binaries.
/boot	Boot-related files, kernel, initrd and grub files.
/dev	Device files.
/etc	Configuration files for the host.
/home	User home directories.
/lib	Shared library and kernel modules.
/media	Mount point for removable media.
/mnt	Mount point for temporary mounting.
/opt	Third-party vendor installation location.
/root	Home directory for the root user.
/sbin	System binaries.
/srv	Data for services provided by the system.
/tmp	Temp files that can be destroyed.

Note   Subdirectories of the aforementioned directories are quite important to know about too. If you are not familiar with them and their function, it is advisable to go and read the FHS document with a breakdown of them all.

Exercise

With disks now available for filesystem creation, the following exercise will get you to not only create a filesystem but also start using it.

Create Filesystem

With your previously created logical volumes on all your Linux systems, do the following:

1. Create an xfs filesystem on your Fedora server.

2. Create an ext4 filesystem on your Ubuntu server.

3. Create an ext3 filesystem on your OpenSUSE server.

Mount Filesystem

On all your Linux systems, do the following:

1. Create a new directory on the root filesystem called "/test".

2. Ensure that your newly created filesystems are mounted when your system reboots.

3. Reboot your system to test.

Summary

In this chapter, you were introduced to the following:

- What disk management tools are available on common Linux distributions

- How to find what disks are on your system and how to extract filesystem information

- What logical volumes are and how they are managed

- How filesystems are created and resized and most importantly why it is important to be very careful when shrinking filesystems

- How to mount your filesystem and ensure that disks are mounted when a system reboots

CHAPTER 10

Service Management

Once a Linux system has been deployed and configured, there comes the need to use the environment for its intended purpose. This could be to act as a web server or an application server or even a database server. These use cases often require packages to be installed, and with these packages, there are often services that need to be managed.

In this chapter, we will start by looking at the basic service management of a Linux system and then briefly discuss how service management has changed over the years. The final part of the chapter will look at how you can create your own service for your own custom applications or scripts.

Basic Service Management

Occasionally, when installing new packages or applications on your Linux environments, there will be the need to start and stop these applications. In today's modern Linux environments, this typically is controlled through a service.

For example, a web server could have the Apache httpd packages installed. This package has a service that needs to be managed. The service may be enabled by default, but it should never be taken for granted. Always check that your services are enabled and started when you install a new application or package.

Service Management Utilities

There are two service management utilities that can be used on a Linux system by default. The "chkconfig" utility, which was largely used before the introduction of "systemd", can still be used today if you wish but is not recommended for use anymore; instead, the "systemd" utility "systemctl" should be used.

313

© Kenneth Hitchcock 2023
K. Hitchcock, *The Enterprise Linux Administrator*, https://doi.org/10.1007/978-1-4842-8801-6_10

chkconfig

The "chkconfig" utility is generally only included by default on older versions of Linux and not used anymore by most application services. The only Linux distribution we have used so far in this book to include chkconfig by default is OpenSUSE.

The following command lists all the services managed by the "chkconfig" utility:

```
# chkconfig --list
```

For the rest of this chapter, we will not focus on the "chkconfig" utility. This was purely for information purposes only.

```
[root@localhost ~]# chkconfig --list

Note: This output shows SysV services only and does not include native
      systemd services. SysV configuration data might be overridden by native
      systemd configuration.

      If you want to list systemd services use 'systemctl list-unit-files'.
      To see services enabled on particular target use
      'systemctl list-dependencies [target]'.

ctxlogd          0:off   1:off   2:on    3:on    4:on    5:on    6:off
livesys          0:off   1:off   2:off   3:on    4:on    5:on    6:off
livesys-late     0:off   1:off   2:off   3:on    4:on    5:on    6:off
```

Figure 10-1. *The chkconfig utility*

systemctl

With the three Linux distributions we have been using so far, the utility that is responsible today for the management of services is the "systemctl" utility. You may recognize this command from previous chapters or from your preparation learning.

From the commands shown in Figure 10-2, you can see that the "systemctl" utility is part of the "systemd" package.

```
opensuse-server:~ # which systemctl
/usr/bin/systemctl
opensuse-server:~ # rpm -qf /usr/bin/systemctl
systemd-246.16-150300.7.45.1.x86_64
opensuse-server:~ # █
```

Figure 10-2. *The location fo the systemctl utility and the package that installed it*

Table 10-1 lists the very basic parameters of the systemctl command that will be used in this chapter.

Table 10-1. *Basic systemctl service options*

Systemctl Parameter	Description
`enable/disable`	Creates or deletes a symlink for the service, enabling or disabling the service on boot.
`start/stop`	Starts and stops a service. Restart will stop then start.
`status`	Will show the status of the service and if the service has been enabled or not.

Note   Further down in this chapter, we will run examples of the "systemctl" utility.

Web Console

Another quick way to manage system service on the Linux systems we have been using so far is through the web console (cockpit). If you cast your mind back to the early chapters in this book, we discussed the use of cockpit.

In Figure 10-3, you can see that the service menu item has been clicked and a list of all the system services is shown. With "cockpit," you are able to view all the services and their state with any user, but it will require admin rights to start or stop services.

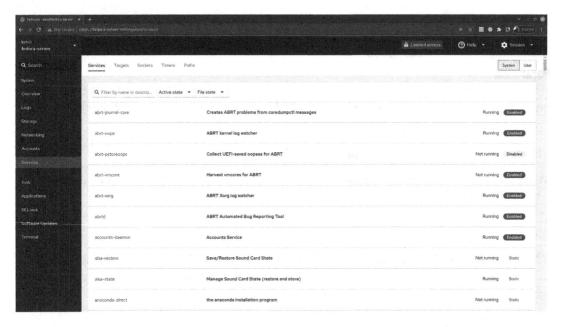

Figure 10-3. *The Cockpit web console services management*

Example Service

As an example to use in this chapter to show the starting, stopping, and viewing of services, we will install the Apache web server package: "httpd". The following are the different installation commands:

```
# dnf install httpd
# zypper install httpd
# apt install httpd
```

Starting a Service

With the "httpd" package installed, we will now learn how to start, stop, view, and enable the web server service.

Command Line

The default method many Linux system administrators use to manage services on a Linux environment is through the command line. On the command line, to start the "httpd" service of the "httpd" package, we use the following command:

```
# systemctl start httpd
```

The preceding command normally does not give an output to signal the completion or result of the command. You typically would run the status command to check.

```
[root@fedora-server ~]# systemctl start httpd
[root@fedora-server ~]# █
```

Figure 10-4. *The systemctl command to start the httpd service*

Cockpit Web Console

To start a service in the "Cockpit" web console, you would typically find and click the service name in the list and then toggle the service radio button.

Figure 10-5. *The Cockpit web console showing the service is now running and that the "blue" radio button has been toggled on*

Stopping a Service

Stopping a service on your Linux environment is as simple as starting a service. That is if the service does not fail to stop, which is something we will discuss later in this book when we look at basic troubleshooting.

Command Line

On the command line, to stop the "httpd" service of the "httpd" package, we use the following command:

```
# systemctl stop httpd
```

The preceding command normally does not give an output to signal the completion or result of the command. You typically would run the status command to check.

```
[root@fedora-server ~]# systemctl stop httpd
[root@fedora-server ~]# █
```

Figure 10-6. *The systemctl command to stop the httpd service*

Cockpit Web Console

To stop a service in the "Cockpit" web console, you would typically find and click the service name in the list of services and then toggle the service radio button.

Figure 10-7. *In the Cockpit web console, the httpd service is now stopped, and the "blue" radio button has turned to gray*

Viewing the Status of a Service

Viewing the status of a service on your Linux environment is again as simple as starting or stopping a service. The status of the service will aid in any basic troubleshooting you may need to perform.

Command Line

On the command line, to view the status of the "httpd" service, we use the following command:

```
# systemctl status httpd
```

```
[root@fedora-server ~]# systemctl status httpd
○ httpd.service - The Apache HTTP Server
     Loaded: loaded (/usr/lib/systemd/system/httpd.service; disabled; vendor pr>
     Active: inactive (dead)
       Docs: man:httpd.service(8)

Aug 02 21:28:12 fedora-server systemd[1]: Starting httpd.service - The Apache H>
Aug 02 21:28:12 fedora-server httpd[2601]: AH00558: httpd: Could not reliably d>
Aug 02 21:28:12 fedora-server httpd[2601]: Server configured, listening on: por>
Aug 02 21:28:12 fedora-server systemd[1]: Started httpd.service - The Apache HT>
Aug 02 21:51:24 fedora-server systemd[1]: Stopping httpd.service - The Apache H>
Aug 02 21:51:25 fedora-server systemd[1]: httpd.service: Deactivated successful>
Aug 02 21:51:25 fedora-server systemd[1]: Stopped httpd.service - The Apache HT>
Aug 02 21:51:25 fedora-server systemd[1]: httpd.service: Consumed 2.332s CPU ti>
lines 1-13/13 (END)
```

Figure 10-8. *The systemctl status of the httpd service*

Cockpit Web Console

The Cockpit web console is another quick way to view the status of a service.

Figure 10-9. *The Cockpit web console view of the "httpd" service status*

Enabling/Disabling a Service

The last important bit that needs to be managed for a service is to ensure that a server starts on boot. For this, you need to enable or disable a service.

Command Line

On the command line, to enable or disable a service, you use the "enable" or "disable" parameter in the "systemctl" command. To enable the "httpd" service, we use the following command:

```
# systemctl enable httpd
```

```
[root@fedora-server ~]# systemctl enable httpd
[root@fedora-server ~]# █
```

Figure 10-10. *Enabling the httpd service with the systemctl command*

To disable the "httpd" service, we use the following command:

```
# systemctl disable httpd
```

```
[root@fedora-server ~]# systemctl disable httpd
Removed /etc/systemd/system/multi-user.target.wants/httpd.service.
```

Figure 10-11. *The disabling of the httpd service using the systemctl command*

From the command shown in Figure 10-11, you can see the first bit of output from a "systemctl" command. This output indicates that the symlink that was created for the service to start on boot has now been removed.

Cockpit Web Console

The Cockpit web console automatically enables and disables services when you toggle the radio button.

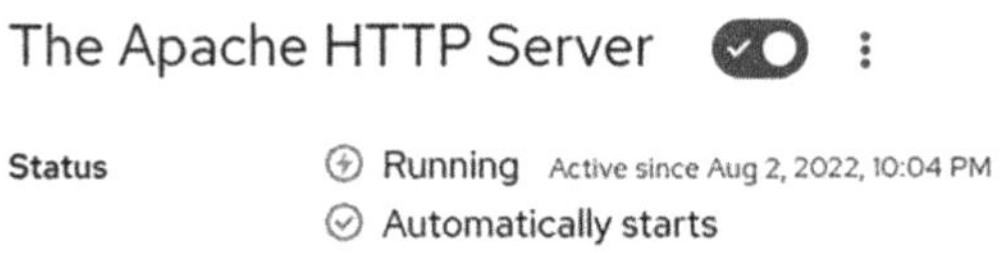

The Apache HTTP Server   ✔◯   ⋮

Status   ⊕ Running   Active since Aug 2, 2022, 10:04 PM
               ⊘ Automatically starts

Figure 10-12. *The Cockpit web console method of enabling or disabling a service*

Exercise

To test how services are managed on your Linux environments, complete the following tasks.

Prerequisites

Cockpit

Install the "Cockpit" web console on your Linux environment if you have not already. Ensure that the package is installed and that the service is started.

Apache Web Server

Install the httpd package on the Linux environment you installed your "Cockpit" web console on.

Manage httpd Service

Enable and Start

Enable and start the httpd service on your Linux environment using the command line.

Confirm Service Is Started

Using the "Cockpit" web console, confirm that the httpd service has started and is running successfully.

Stop and Disable

Stop and disable the httpd service in any way you prefer.

systemd

systemd was originally written by two engineers from Red Hat to replace the System V init system. The name "systemd" was chosen to bring the service management utilities in line with other daemon-driven utilities that end with "d".

systemd is a "suite" of utilities to manage a Linux environment. systemd manages mount points, processes, daemons, and services.

systemd provides parallelism to a Linux environment boot sequence, enabling quicker boot time due to multiple daemons, services, and utilities being able to start at the same time, making better use of resources like CPU and memory.

Configuration Files

systemd configuration files are "plain text" files with declarative syntax similar to traditional "INI" files. Systemd configuration files are typically referred to as "unit files."

Configuration File Types

There are a few types of systemd configuration files that can be used.

Table 10-2 lists the different configuration file types for systemd.

Table 10-2. *systemd configuration file types*

File Type	Description
.service	Used to create service files.
.socket	Allows the ability to manage local IPC or network sockets.
.device	Allows the exposure of kernel devices to systemd.
.mount	Controls the mounting of disks.
.automount	Allows the ability to mount on demand.
.swap	Very similar to disk mounting but for swap.
.target	Used to group units. Older versions of Linux used "run levels."
.path	Used to activate other services when filesystem objects change or are modified
.timer	Can be used in a similar way to how cron has traditionally been used.
.slice	Allows the ability to manage processes and resources.
.scope	Can be used to group worker processes but really should not be configured though unit files.

Example Configuration File

```
[Unit]
Description=OpenSSH server daemon
Documentation=man:sshd(8) man:sshd_config(5)
After=network.target sshd-keygen.target
Wants=sshd-keygen.target

[Service]
Type=notify
EnvironmentFile=-/etc/sysconfig/sshd
ExecStart=/usr/sbin/sshd -D $OPTIONS
ExecReload=/bin/kill -HUP $MAINPID
KillMode=process
Restart=on-failure
RestartSec=42s

[Install]
WantedBy=multi-user.target
~
~
~
~
```

Figure 10-13. *An example of the sshd service configuration file stored on a Fedora server*

Configuration File Locations

Many systemd configuration files can be found in the following directory:

/etc/systemd/system/

```
[root@fedora-server ~]# ls -al /etc/systemd/system
total 20
drwxr-xr-x. 22 root root 4096 Jun  3 09:23 .
drwxr-xr-x.  5 root root 4096 Jul  5 21:27 ..
drwxr-xr-x.  2 root root   64 Jun  4 22:56 basic.target.wants
drwxr-xr-x.  2 root root   31 Jun  4 22:56 bluetooth.target.wants
lrwxrwxrwx.  1 root root   37 Jun  4 22:56 ctrl-alt-del.target -> /usr/lib/systemd/system/reboot.target
lrwxrwxrwx.  1 root root   41 Jun  4 22:56 dbus-org.bluez.service -> /usr/lib/systemd/system/bluetooth.service
lrwxrwxrwx.  1 root root   41 Jun  4 22:57 dbus-org.fedoraproject.FirewallD1.service -> /usr/lib/systemd/system/firewalld.service
lrwxrwxrwx.  1 root root   44 Jun 15 20:58 dbus-org.freedesktop.Avahi.service -> /usr/lib/systemd/system/avahi-daemon.service
lrwxrwxrwx.  1 root root   44 Jun  4 22:56 dbus-org.freedesktop.ModemManager1.service -> /usr/lib/systemd/system/ModemManager.service
lrwxrwxrwx.  1 root root   57 Jun  4 22:56 dbus-org.freedesktop.nm-dispatcher.service -> /usr/lib/systemd/system/NetworkManager-dispatcher.service
lrwxrwxrwx.  1 root root   44 Jun  4 22:56 dbus-org.freedesktop.oom1.service -> /usr/lib/systemd/system/systemd-oomd.service
lrwxrwxrwx.  1 root root   48 Jun  4 22:56 dbus-org.freedesktop.resolve1.service -> /usr/lib/systemd/system/systemd-resolved.service
lrwxrwxrwx.  1 root root   43 Jun  4 22:56 dbus.service -> /usr/lib/systemd/system/dbus-broker.service
lrwxrwxrwx.  1 root root   40 Jun 15 21:06 default.target -> /usr/lib/systemd/system/graphical.target
drwxr-xr-x.  2 root root   38 Jun 15 21:02 'dev-virtio\x2dports-org.qemu.guest_agent.0.device.wants'
lrwxrwxrwx.  1 root root   39 Jun 15 21:01 display-manager.service -> /usr/lib/systemd/system/lightdm.service
drwxr-xr-x.  2 root root   32 Jun  4 22:56 getty.target.wants
drwxr-xr-x.  2 root root  110 Jun 15 21:00 graphical.target.wants
drwxr-xr-x.  2 root root   36 Jun 15 21:00 local-fs.target.wants
drwxr-xr-x.  2 root root 4096 Aug  2 22:04 multi-user.target.wants
drwxr-xr-x.  2 root root   48 Jun  4 22:56 network-online.target.wants
drwxr-xr-x.  2 root root   33 Jun  4 22:57 nfs-blkmap.service.requires
drwxr-xr-x.  2 root root   33 Jun  4 22:57 nfs-idmapd.service.requires
drwxr-xr-x.  2 root root   33 Jun  4 22:57 nfs-mountd.service.requires
drwxr-xr-x.  2 root root   33 Jun  4 22:57 nfs-server.service.requires
drwxr-xr-x.  2 root root   52 Jun  4 22:57 remote-fs.target.wants
drwxr-xr-x.  2 root root   33 Jun  4 22:57 rpc-gssd.service.requires
drwxr-xr-x.  2 root root   33 Jun  4 22:57 rpc-statd-notify.service.requires
drwxr-xr-x.  2 root root   33 Jun  4 22:57 rpc-statd.service.requires
drwxr-xr-x.  2 root root 4096 Jun 15 21:01 sockets.target.wants
drwxr-xr-x.  2 root root 4096 Jun 15 21:09 sysinit.target.wants
drwxr-xr-x.  2 root root  158 Jun 15 21:00 timers.target.wants
drwxr-xr-x.  2 root root   29 Jun 15 21:00 vmtoolsd.service.requires
```

Figure 10-14. *The location of the systemd configuration files*

Changing to and from Graphical Desktops

One important configuration file to take note of with systemd is the "default.target" symlink. From the image shown in Figure 10-14, you can see that the Fedora system has been "targeted" to "graphical.target". This will ensure that the desktop installed on your Linux system will start when your system boots.

To switch to the command line only when a system boots, you will need to remove this default.target symlink and create a new one using the following command:

```
# ln -s /usr/lib/systemd/system/multi-user.target \
/etc/systemd/system/default.target
```

Utilities

The following utilities are available to the systemd utility suite. These are the command tools you will use with systemd.

systemctl

This is used to restart and view the state of services. Systemctl was briefly discussed further up in this chapter; the following are some very simple uses of systemctl you will need to know.

To start a service, you would use a command similar to the following. In this example, we will use the sshd service that is used to control the ssh daemon.

```
# systemctl start sshd
```

To stop the sshd service, we would use the following command:

```
# systemctl stop sshd
```

If a service is not responding or you want to ensure a service is running, allow check the status of the service. The following command will output the status of the sshd service:

```
# systemctl status sshd
```

journalctl

In the inevitable situation where something goes wrong with your Linux environment, there is the journalctl utility that can help identify where the issue could be. A basic command that can always be run to see the current issues is as follows:

```
# journalctl -xe
```

The preceding command will take you into an editor that will allow you to scroll back through the output. The output is typically color coded to allow for easier identification of errors.

Another useful parameter to use when debugging an ongoing issue is the "-f" option to follow the logs as they appear.

Other Useful Utilities

A few other utilities worth exploring are as follows.

Table 10-3 lists the various systemd utilities that can be used to manage your system.

Table 10-3. *systemd utilities*

Utility	Description
hostnamectl	Allows the changing of your system hostname.
timedatectl	Allows for quick updating of time zones with date and time.
loginctl	Shows who is currently logged into your system.
bluetoothctl	Useful if you need to manage Bluetooth devices.

Exercise

To start being more familiar with system, run through the simple exercises shown as follows.

Basic Service Management

1. Install the "httpd" package.

2. Check if the httpd service has started.

3. If the service has not started, start it and enable the service to start on boot.

Check Your Default Target

Check what your system's default target has been set to. If you are set to start in graphical mode, switch to multi-user and reboot. Confirm that you are able to boot into a "command line"-only mode.

Once confirmed, switch back to graphical mode if you prefer a desktop.

Creating a New Service

The final part of this chapter is around creating a new service. The reason this could be useful is if you need to have a script or application running after a system boots. This could also be useful if you are looking to standardize your system administration to improve the ease of use for first line support employees.

Example Script

To test this process, I have created a very basic script that scans the content of a log file and then logs an error to the /var/log/messages file. The script is shown in Figure 10-15.

```
#!/bin/bash

while true
do
        GET_ERROR=`cat /var/log/example_app | tail -n 20 | grep -i "error" | wc -l`

        if [ $GET_ERROR -gt 0 ]
        then
                logger "something broke with the system at this time - `date`"
        fi

        echo "" >/var/log/example_app

        sleep 5
done
~
```

Figure 10-15. *Example script*

The script from Figure 10-15 has been saved to the following location:

/usr/bin/example_service.sh

The script has also had the following permissions applied to it.

```
# chmod 0750 /usr/bin/example_service.sh
```

To allow this script to function, a log file will also need to be created in the following location:

```
# /var/log/example_app
```

To test the script, the following command can be run to inject an error:

```
# echo "app is down - ERROR" | tee -a /var/log/example_app
```

Unit File

With systemd, configuration files are referred to as unit files. These files as mentioned follow a similar syntax to INI files. To continue with the example, a new service file is required that will be used to run the script from the preceding example.

The following command will create a service file that will be used for the content that follows:

```
# touch /usr/lib/systemd/system/example_service.service
```

Within the preceding created file, the following content can be entered:

```
[Unit]
Description=Example service
Documentation=
After=
Wants=

[Service]
Type=notify
EnvironmentFile=
ExecStart=/usr/bin/example_service.sh
ExecReload=/bin/pkill -9 example_service.sh
KillMode=process
Restart=on-failure
RestartSec=60s

[Install]
WantedBy=multi-user.target
~
```

Figure 10-16. *The content used for a basic service unit file*

As a shortcut, you can also copy the current sshd service file and edit the content for your own example. This is what I did for this example shown previously:

```
# cp /usr/lib/systemd/system/sshd.service \
/usr/lib/systemd/system/example_service.service
```

Unit File Explained

To better understand the unit file from the preceding example, we will look at each line.

Unit Section

In the [unit] section, the Description field is fairly self-explanatory, but the Documentation, After, and Wants parameters will need to be understood.

- "Documentation=" is used to reference any man pages your utility or script could have. If we look at the sshd.service files example, you will see that the various man pages are referenced.

```
[Unit]
Description=OpenSSH server daemon
Documentation=man:sshd(8) man:sshd_config(5)
After=network.target sshd-keygen.target
Wants=sshd-keygen.target
```

Figure 10-17. *The Unit section of a systemd service unit file*

- "After=" is used to establish the order in which your service will start. Useful if you have dependencies that are required to start before your script. For example, if your application or script requires network connectivity, you may need to wait for the network services to start.

- "Wants=" is used to tell your unit file that your script has a hard dependency on another service to start. If that service has failed, your service will fail to start.

Service Section

In the [Service] section, there are a number of options that can be configured. The following is an explanation of each option:

```
[Service]
Type=notify
EnvironmentFile=-/etc/sysconfig/sshd
ExecStart=/usr/sbin/sshd -D $OPTIONS
ExecReload=/bin/kill -HUP $MAINPID
KillMode=process
Restart=on-failure
RestartSec=42s
```

Figure 10-18. *The Service section of a systemd service unit file*

- "Type=" is used to determine the process startup type. There are a number of options that can be used:

  - "simple", starts the service immediately

  - "notify", only considers the service started once a special signal has been sent to systemd

  - "forking", only considers the service has started when the process forks and the parent has exited.

  - "dbus", only considers the service has started when the main process has been given a D-Bus name

  - "idle", delays the execution of the service binary till all jobs are finished

- "EnvironmentFile=" is used to reference an environment file where variables can be set.

- "ExecStart=" is used to start what command and parameters should be run for the service.

- "ExecReload=" is used to determine what command should be used to reload service configuration.

- "KillMode=" is used to determine how the processes in this unit will be killed. Options include control-group, process, mixed, and none.

- "Restart=" is used to restart the service if the process exits unexpectedly. This is ignored if the "systemctl stop" command is issued.

- "RestartSec=" is the number of seconds to wait before the process is restarted.

Install Section

In the [install] section, there really is only one parameter.

```
[Install]
WantedBy=multi-user.target
```

Figure 10-19. *The Install section of a systemd service unit file*

The "WantedBy=" is used to determine what other unit files require this service to start. In the sshd example image shown in Figure 10-19, this is set to the "multi-user. target", meaning that the "command line" mode requires sshd to start.

Enable and Start Service

To enable and start a customer service file is not much different than starting any other service file that exists on your Linux system.

The important bit to remember is that your service should be created in the following directory:

```
# /usr/lib/systemd/system/
```

Your service file should also have the extension ".service".

Provided you have saved your file in the correct location and you have a ".service" extension to your unit file, the following command will enable your system to use your new service:

```
# systemctl enable example_service.service
```

```
[root@fedora-server ~]# systemctl enable example_service.service
Created symlink /etc/systemd/system/multi-user.target.wants/example_service.service → /usr/lib/systemd/system/example_service.service.
```

Figure 10-20. *Enabling the example service*

In the command shown in Figure 10-20, the new service "example_service.service" will be enabled as this file was created in the "/usr/lib/systemd/system" directory.

To start the service, a similar command to the enable service command can be used. This can be seen as per the following:

```
# systemctl start example_service.service
```

Once the service has been started, you can check the status using the same command but replacing the start parameter with status.

```
[root@fedora-server ~]# systemctl status example_service.service
● example_service.service - Example service
     Loaded: loaded (/usr/lib/systemd/system/example_service.service; enabled; vendor preset: disabled)
     Active: activating (start) since Mon 2022-08-08 20:46:43 BST; 9s ago
   Main PID: 12387 (example_service)
      Tasks: 2 (limit: 2313)
     Memory: 640.0K
        CPU: 46ms
     CGroup: /system.slice/example_service.service
             ├─ 12387 /bin/bash /usr/bin/example_service.sh
             └─ 12417 sleep 5

Aug 08 20:46:43 fedora-server systemd[1]: Starting example service.service - Example service...
```

Figure 10-21. *Service is running its endless loop and sleeping for five seconds on each loop*

Remove a Service

To remove a custom service from your system will involve retracing your steps to remove any files created.

The first step is to stop and then disable your custom service. The following command will stop the example_service service:

```
# systemctl stop example_service.service
```

The following command will disable the example_service service:

```
# systemctl disable example_service.service
```

Finally, all service unit files and log files should be removed.

```
# rm -rf /usr/lib/systemd/system/example_service.service
```

If you choose, you can remove all the scripts you created and any log files you used.

This process would normally be handled for you by the installation package, which is something we will discuss a bit later in this book. For now, keep any scripts and files safe for later use.

Exercise

To test your newly acquired knowledge in Linux service creation, do the following exercises and see if you can build your own service.

Create a Script

Create a new script file named example_script.sh in the following location:

```
# /usr/bin/
```

Ensure that your script has sufficient privileges to run.

The script should run on an indefinite loop until the service has been stopped. What the script does is up to you. You can use it to create files, write to a log, or clear log files if you really want to. This is up to you. If you prefer, just copy what has been done in this book so far.

Create a Service

Create a service file for your script you just created. The service should then be enabled and started.

Once your service has started, check the status of your service and then test that your application is working as intended.

Remove Your Service

Finally, remove the service you just created and clean up any files that the service needed.

Summary

In this chapter, you were introduced to the following:

- What services are in a Linux system

- How to stop, start, and view services in your Linux environment

- What systemd is and what utilities are provided with systemd

- How to create a new custom service with a good explanation of the different service unit file parameters

- How a custom service can be enabled and started

- How a service can be viewed to see its status

- Finally, how a custom service can be disabled and removed

PART IV

Enterprise Linux

The first three parts of this book were focused on building your general Linux knowledge by looking at three common community Linux distributions. The three distributions we looked at were no accident either as they are the upstream or community versions of the enterprise Linux distributions we will use from this page onward.

In Part 4, we will start by learning more about the three enterprise Linux distributions that we will be using. We will look at their history, installation, and management. Once we have a solid understanding of these distributions, we will continue using them more in anger. In Chapter 12, we will start to build systems that can be used in a Linux enterprise. We will look at building a web server and a file server as some basic use case examples.

With these new systems, we will delve more into how enterprise environments are configured by understanding how security can be managed and how systems can be made highly available.

Finally, we will also look at automation techniques and how large estates should be managed and deployed at scale.

CHAPTER 11

Enterprise Linux Distributions

This chapter begins the journey into enterprise Linux environments. In this chapter, we will start by looking at some common enterprise Linux distributions. We will first look at where these distributions came from and get a good understanding of why they are the leading enterprise Linux solutions available today.

We will need to proceed to understand how these distributions are installed. Once they have been installed, we will discuss the basics around how these environments are managed, including how each distribution is supported by the vendor.

Finally, we will look at what training and certifications should be pursued for each major distribution to ensure you are not only skilled as an enterprise Linux administrator but also certified.

Red Hat

Red Hat is the largest provider of enterprise Linux and is valued around $34 billion. Red Hat has an impressive portfolio of products in almost every area of today's enterprise market.

In 2018, Red Hat was acquired by IBM to lead their hybrid cloud business, which predominately is focused around their Container Orchestration platform "OpenShift."

Brief History

The enterprise Linux distribution from Red Hat is unsurprisingly called "Red Hat Enterprise Linux" and has been around since 2003 when RHEL 2.1 was released. The latest version of "Red Hat Enterprise Linux" or RHEL is 9.0.

© Kenneth Hitchcock 2023
K. Hitchcock, *The Enterprise Linux Administrator*, https://doi.org/10.1007/978-1-4842-8801-6_11

RHEL, however, was not the first Linux distribution from Red Hat. In 1997, Red Hat released "Red Hat Linux 4.2" and continued to release versions of Red Hat Linux until the major release of 9.0. Please don't get confused with Red Hat Linux 9.0 and RHEL 9.0. There are almost 20 years between them now.

Upstream

RHEL makes use of Fedora as the community upstream product where many new features and configuration are tested by the community. The Fedora project is sponsored by Red Hat and continues to encourage contributors to add to the project.

Red Hat takes community projects and turns them into enterprise products. What this really means is that Red Hat takes community-based products, sanitizes codes, ensures features are enterprise ready, and then wraps it all in a supported package that enterprise customers can use.

The reason customers use enterprise Linux distributions like RHEL is for the support. Otherwise, everyone would just use the community products.

Important   OpenSource software is free. You should never pay for the actual software, just the support you get from the vendor. Enterprise-grade patching and security fixes are considered support.

RHEL

In Chapter 4, we first dove into how Linux can be deployed. We focused on three community-based distributions: Fedora, Ubuntu, and OpenSUSE. For this chapter, we will be doing a similar set of exercises but using enterprise Linux distributions. Instead of Fedora, we will be installing RHEL.

Red Hat Account

As Red Hat offers a supported enterprise Linux server, you will need to have an account with Red Hat. Don't worry, it is free and you can get evaluation subscriptions for you to play with.

You can get access to a free "developer" subscription, which will give you self-supported subscriptions to almost every Red Hat product:

https://developers.redhat.com/about

Once you have your Red Hat account created, you will need to request a RHEL subscription. As mentioned previously, you can sign up for an evaluation subscription or a developer subscription.

Exercise

Before going further in this chapter, you will need to create an account with each vendor.

Red Hat

For Red Hat, go to the following link and sign up for an account:

https://access.redhat.com/

Once you have an account, go to the subscriptions section and sign up for the 60-day evaluation. This will be needed later in the chapter.

Installation Media

In the downloads section of the https://access.redhat.com/ link, you can download the latest version of RHEL. For the exercises in this chapter, we will be downloading and using the RHEL 9.0.

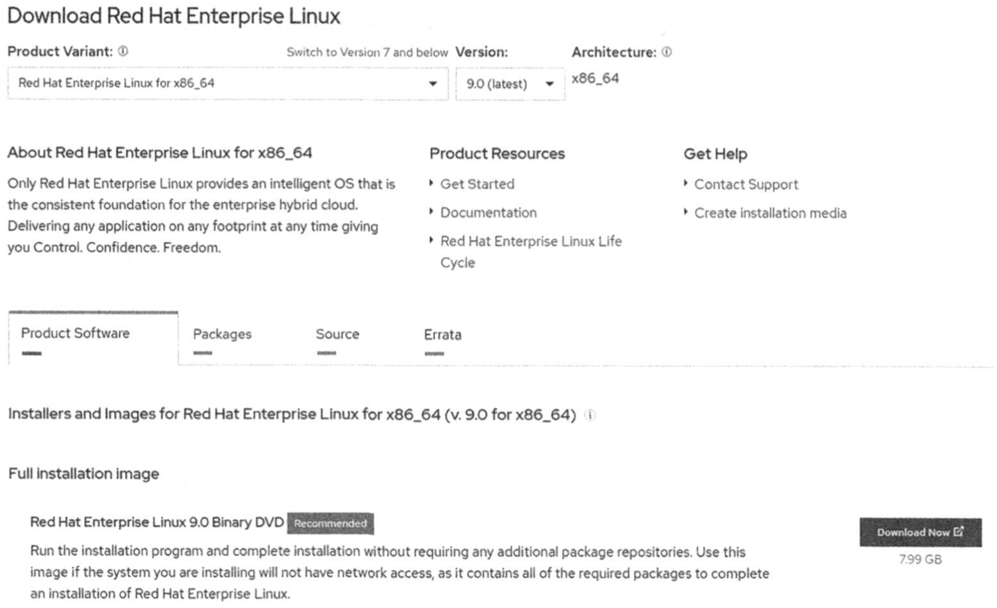

Download Red Hat Enterprise Linux

Product Variant: ⓘ		Switch to Version 7 and below	Version:	Architecture: ⓘ
Red Hat Enterprise Linux for x86_64	▼		9.0 (latest) ▼	x86_64

About Red Hat Enterprise Linux for x86_64

Only Red Hat Enterprise Linux provides an intelligent OS that is the consistent foundation for the enterprise hybrid cloud. Delivering any application on any footprint at any time giving you Control. Confidence. Freedom.

Product Resources
‣ Get Started
‣ Documentation
‣ Red Hat Enterprise Linux Life Cycle

Get Help
‣ Contact Support
‣ Create installation media

Product Software	Packages	Source	Errata

Installers and Images for Red Hat Enterprise Linux for x86_64 (v. 9.0 for x86_64) ⓘ

Full installation image

Red Hat Enterprise Linux 9.0 Binary DVD `Recommended`

Run the installation program and complete installation without requiring any additional package repositories. Use this image if the system you are installing will not have network access, as it contains all of the required packages to complete an installation of Red Hat Enterprise Linux.

Download Now ⤢
7.99 GB

Figure 11-1. *The download location for Red Hat Enterprise Linux*

Using Installation Media

In Chapter 4, we discussed how installation media can be created and used to build new Linux environments. If you have forgotten how it was done, quickly revisit the chapter and use the same methods recommended for the new images that will be downloaded.

If you are going to use a physical system instead of a virtual machine, it would be worth getting a large USB drive that can store all the images you will use. Then install and configure "Ventoy" along with all the images if you will use it.

Virtual Machine

For this book, we will continue to use virtual machines created on KVM. If you are using a physical system or virtual box, just follow what you did in Chapter 4.

Create a Virtual Machine

For the installation of RHEL, create a virtual machine with the following specifications:

- 4 vCPUS

- 4GB memory

- 20GB disk

The operating system should automatically select RHEL 9.0.

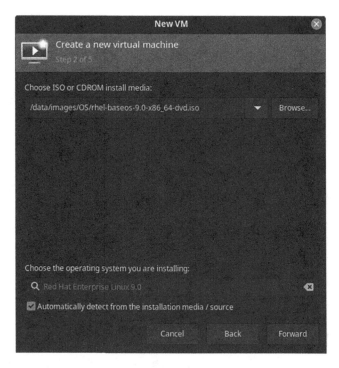

Figure 11-2. *The creation of a virtual machine with the RHEL 9.0 ISO image*

If not, ensure your ISO image is not corrupt or the wrong operating system.

When the final screen appears, stick to a similar naming convention that was used before. For the RHEL 9.0 server, the name has been set to "rhel-server".

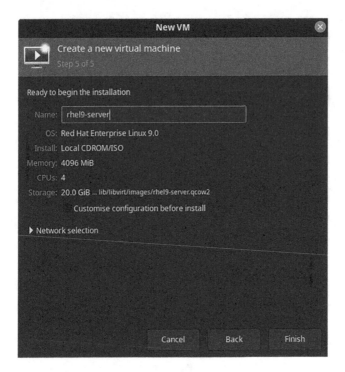

Figure 11-3. *Setting the name of the virtual machine*

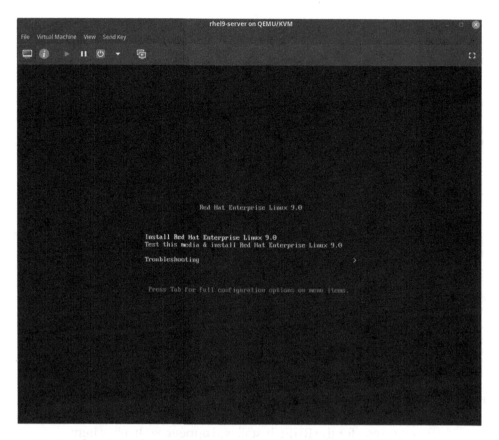

Figure 11-4. *The virtual machine manager console with RHEL 9 installation options*

Skip the media check if you are installing from a downloaded ISO. If you experience issues during the installation, then feel free to restart the installation and check the install media. For now, select the install RHEL 9.0 option.

RHEL Install

1. The first screen of the RHEL 9.0 installation is similar to Fedora; select your language options and click the "Continue" button.

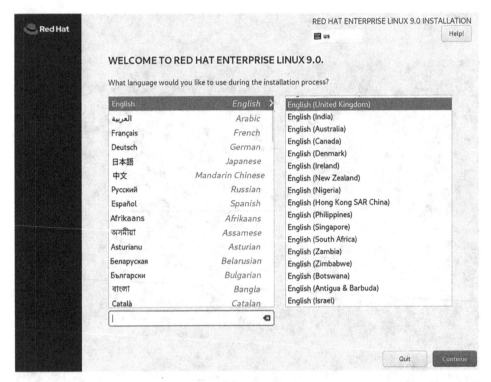

Figure 11-5. *The language selection screen for the RHEL installation*

2. The main screen for the RHEL install will appear, with a few items requiring attention.

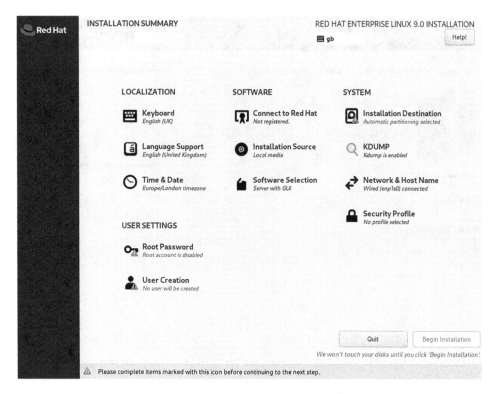

Figure 11-6. *The main menu screen for the RHEL installation*

3. The first configuration will be the installation destination. Ensure that your 20GiB disk has been selected as shown in Figure 11-7. Then click the "done" button.

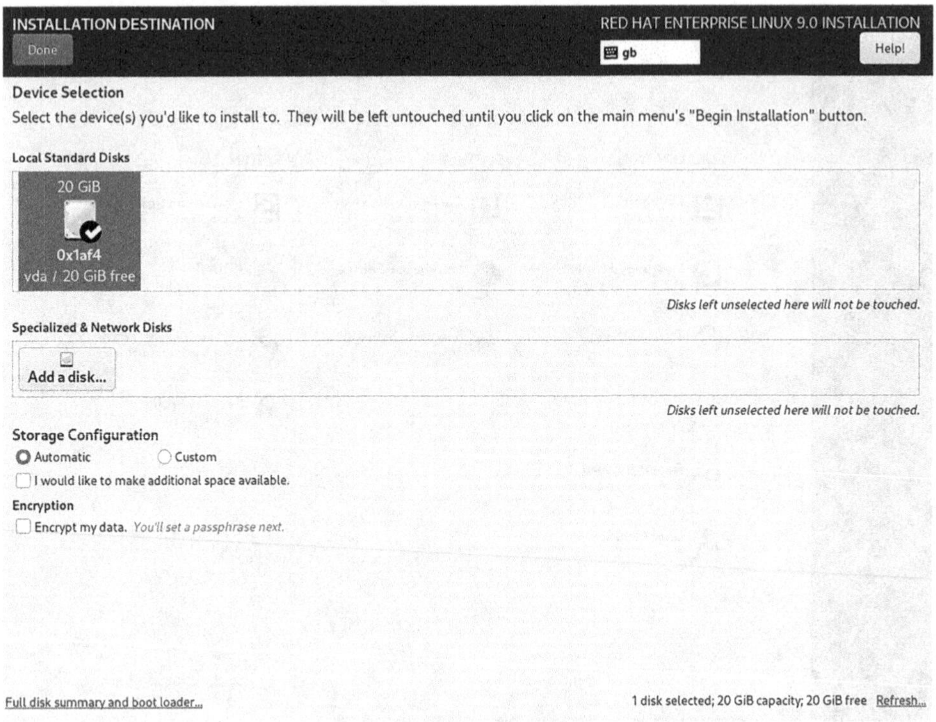

INSTALLATION DESTINATION   RED HAT ENTERPRISE LINUX 9.0 INSTALLATION

Done   ⌨ gb   Help!

Device Selection

Select the device(s) you'd like to install to. They will be left untouched until you click on the main menu's "Begin Installation" button.

Local Standard Disks

20 GiB

0x1af4
vda / 20 GiB free

Disks left unselected here will not be touched.

Specialized & Network Disks

Add a disk...

Disks left unselected here will not be touched.

Storage Configuration

⦿ Automatic   ○ Custom

☐ I would like to make additional space available.

Encryption

☐ Encrypt my data. *You'll set a passphrase next.*

Full disk summary and boot loader...   1 disk selected; 20 GiB capacity; 20 GiB free Refresh...

Figure 11-7. The disk selection screen for the RHEL installation

4. The software selection screen. Ensure the server is being installed
    with a minimal installation. This is for both speed and best
    practice purposes. To get to the screen shown in Figure 11-8, click
    the "Installation Source" button on the main installation screen.

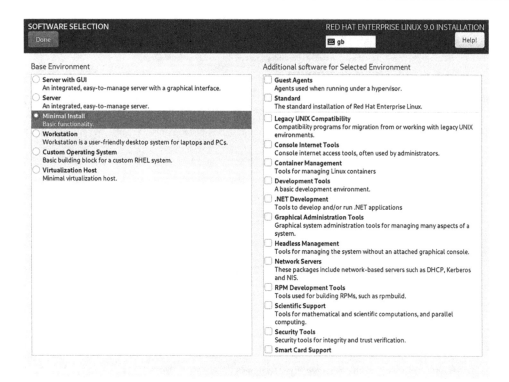

Figure 11-8. *The installation source screen*

5. Set a root password and leave all the defaults. The root account
    should not be able to ssh directly.

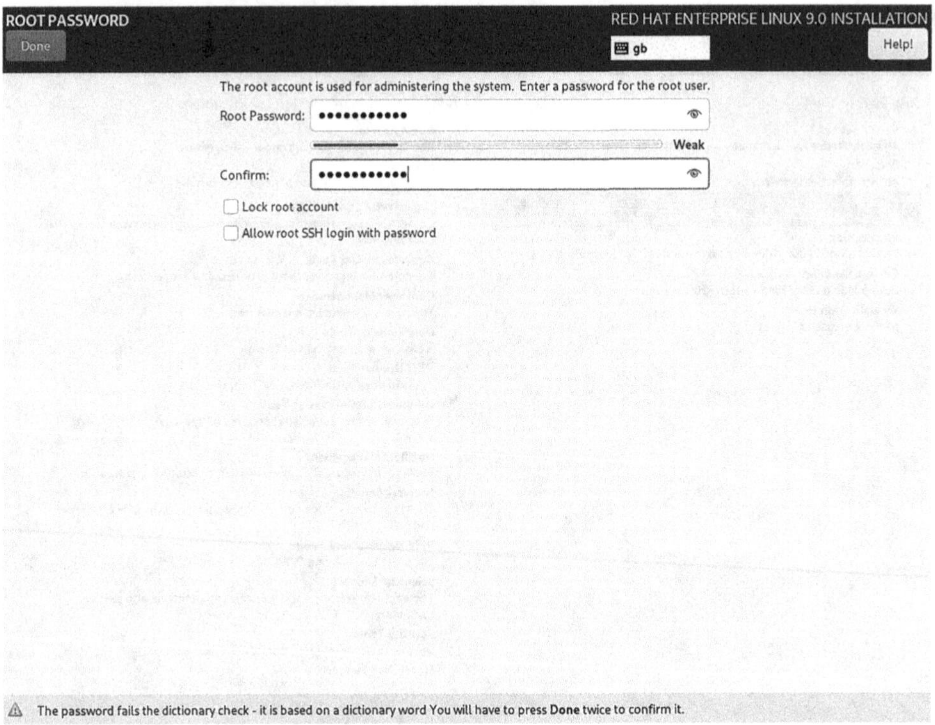

Figure 11-9. *The screen to set the root password*

6. To enable the ability to ssh to the new server, a user is required.
    Create a new user of your choosing and make sure to tick "Make
    this user administrator".

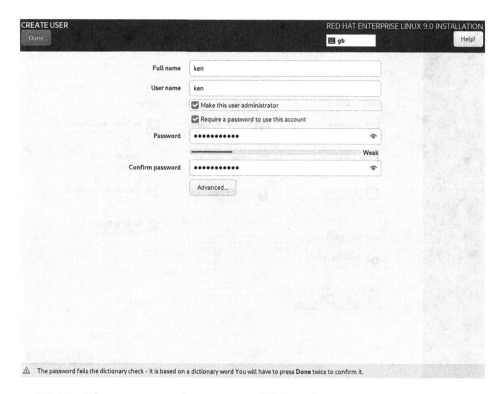

Figure 11-10. *The screen used to create additional users*

7. When all the installation configuration has been completed, click the "Begin Installation" button.

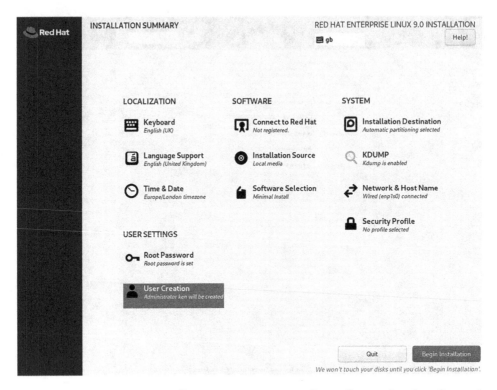

Figure 11-11. *The main installation screen once all configuration has been done*

8. Once the RHEL 9.0 installation has completed, click the "Reboot System" button.

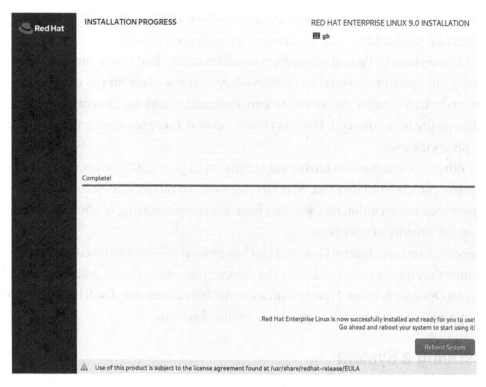

Figure 11-12. *The final screen before rebooting to complete the RHEL installation*

Subscriptions and Support

Once your first Red Hat enterprise Linux system has been installed, you will want to start using it in anger. This is where the difference between Fedora and RHEL starts to become a bit clearer. For you to configure and install packages, you will need to be able to download them. Yes, technically packages can be installed from install media, but the latest packages and errata are available immediately directly from Red Hat. You could wait for new install media to be released, but that could take time, leaving you at risk of having vulnerabilities that could leave you exposed.

These packages and updates are not freely available once you install RHEL. You will need to subscribe your system to Red Hat. With a valid subscription, you will then have access to all the packages the subscription allows.

With Fedora being based on community packages and updates, there is no need to have any subscriptions to access them. However, updates and general package releases are only available when the community has managed to provide them. There is no agreed release date or time, and there are no promises. In the end, Fedora is not meant for production workloads where uptime and support are a priority.

RHEL compared to Fedora is another product entirely. Red Hat is committed to pushing out updates and errata as soon as they become ready for the enterprise market, and when security vulnerabilities are detected, errata are generally released as the vulnerability is announced. For this kind of service, there is a cost, and that is the subscriptions they sell.

The other major benefit to having subscriptions to your RHEL environment is the support you can get from Red Hat. Support cases can be raised, and based on the level of support your subscription has, you can have someone speaking to you within an hour based on the severity of your issue.

There are even incidents where Red Hat has proactively contacted customers to let them know they have a problem before they knew there was even an issue. Technically, this was an OpenShift-related query with a connected cluster, but it still highlights the value support you can have when you have a critical system.

Subscribing a System

With being convinced that having a subscription is vital. You will now need to understand how to subscribe a system.

Verify Subscriptions

In the beginning of this chapter, there was an exercise for you to create a Red Hat account. With that account, you needed to add a 60-day subscription to even be allowed to download RHEL. To verify that you have a subscription, open your subscriptions section in your Red Hat account at the following URL:

`https://access.redhat.com/management/`

In Figure 11-13, you will see that there are two active subscriptions with one of them being the 60-day trial. The steps that follow will use this subscription to register a RHEL server, which will allow the RHEL to download packages.

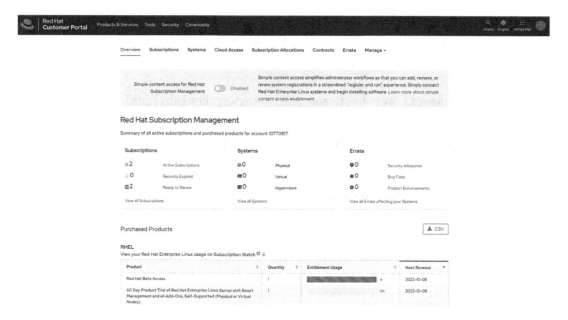

Figure 11-13. The Red Hat portal where subscriptions can be viewed

Register with Red Hat

The first step to subscribing your system with Red Hat is to register the system with your Red Hat account. This step will only register the system with Red Hat and not make packages available. For that, we need to attach a subscription. This basically means you can register as many systems as you like, but if you do not have subscriptions, they still won't be able to download packages. We will cover linking subscriptions to registered systems next.

To register a system, you need to do the following:

1. Log in to your RHEL system.

```
[ken@localhost ~]$ ssh ken@rhel9-server
ken@rhel9-server's password:
Last login: Sun Aug 14 20:23:01 2022 from 192.168.122.1
[ken@rhel9-server ~]$ 
```

Tip Use your console to check your IP address if you did not configure a static address during the installation.

---

2. Make sure your RHEL system has a hostname configured with a fully qualified domain name. This is just good practice and will help identify your systems when you need them.

```
# hostnamectl set-hostname rhel9-server.kenlab.local
```

3. To register your system with Red Hat, you run the following command:

```
# sudo subscription-manager register
```

4. Enter the username and password you created when you created your Red Hat account.

```
[ken@rhel9-server ~]$ sudo subscription-manager register
[sudo] password for ken:
Registering to: subscription.rhsm.redhat.com:443/subscription
Username: ▮▮▮▮▮
Password:
The system has been registered with ID: ▮▮▮▮▮▮▮▮▮▮▮▮▮▮▮▮▮▮▮▮▮▮▮▮▮▮
The registered system name is: rhel9-server.kenlab.local
[ken@rhel9-server ~]$ ▮
```

Figure 11-14. *The subscription-manager command to register a system*

5. In your Red Hat account on the Red Hat portal, you will also be able to see what systems have been registered.

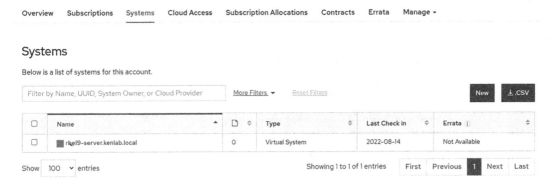

Figure 11-15. *The Red Hat web portal showing the registered system*

Attaching Subscriptions

Once your system has been registered with Red Hat, you can attach any subscriptions you may have.

1. Check what subscriptions are available.

    ```
    # sudo subscription-manager list --available
    ```

```
[ken@rhel9-server ~]$ sudo subscription-manager list --available
+-------------------------------------------+
      Available Subscriptions
+-------------------------------------------+
Subscription Name:  Red Hat Beta Access
Provides:           Red Hat CodeReady Linux Builder for x86_64 Beta
                    Red Hat Enterprise Linux for IBM z Systems Beta
                    Red Hat Enterprise Linux Fast Datapath Beta for Power, little endian
                    Red Hat Enterprise Linux Resilient Storage Beta
                    Red Hat Enterprise Linux for x86_64 Beta
                    Red Hat Enterprise Linux for Real Time for NFV Beta
                    Red Hat Enterprise Linux for Real Time Beta
                    Red Hat Enterprise Linux for SAP HANA for x86_64 Beta
                    Red Hat Directory Server Beta
                    Red Hat Enterprise Linux Advanced Virtualization Beta (for RHEL Server for IBM System Z)
                    Red Hat Enterprise Linux for SAP Applications for x86_64 Beta
                    Red Hat Enterprise Linux for SAP Applications for IBM z Systems Beta
                    Red Hat CodeReady Linux Builder for ARM 64 Beta
                    Red Hat Enterprise Linux for SAP Applications for Power, little endian Beta
                    Red Hat Enterprise Linux Fast Datapath Beta for x86_64
                    Red Hat CodeReady Linux Builder for Power, little endian Beta
                    Red Hat CodeReady Linux Builder for IBM z Systems Beta
                    Red Hat Enterprise Linux High Availability Beta
                    Red Hat Certificate System Beta
                    Red Hat Enterprise Linux for Power, little endian Beta
                    Red Hat Enterprise Linux for ARM 64 Beta
                    Red Hat Enterprise Linux for SAP HANA for Power, little endian Beta
SKU:                RH00069
```

Figure 11-16. *Subscription-manager command listing available subscriptions*

2. From the available subscription output, you should see the Pool ID. This is what is used when you attach to a specific subscription.

```
SKU:                    RH00066
Contract:               ▓▓▓▓▓▓
Pool ID:                2c94d4b4828▓▓▓▓▓▓▓▓▓▓▓▓▓
Provides Management:    Yes
Available:              2
Suggested:              1
Service Type:
Roles:                  Red Hat Enterprise Linux Server
Service Level:          Self-Support
Usage:                  Development/Test
Add-ons:
Subscription Type:      Instance Based
Starts:                 09/08/22
Ends:                   08/10/22
Entitlement Type:       Physical
```

Figure 11-17. *Details of the available subscription*

3. To attach a registered system to the Pool ID shown in Figure 11-17, we would use a command similar to the following:

```
# sudo subscription-manager attach --pool 2x94d4b82xxxxx
```

4. If you did not care what subscription you attached to your system, you could replace the "--pool" parameter with "--auto". This approach is not advised in a production environment as you will not always know quickly what system is linked to what subscription when raising support cases.

5. With a successful attachment of a subscription, you will now be able to download and install packages.

```
[ken@rhel9-server ~]$ sudo dnf install tmux
Updating Subscription Management repositories.
Red Hat Enterprise Linux 9 for x86_64 - AppStream (RPMs)                          4.6 MB/s | 9.2 MB    00:02
Red Hat Enterprise Linux 9 for x86_64 - BaseOS (RPMs)                             2.1 MB/s | 3.6 MB    00:01
Dependencies resolved.
================================================================================================================
 Package            Architecture      Version           Repository                                       Size
================================================================================================================
Installing:
 tmux               x86_64            3.2a-4.el9         rhel-9-for-x86_64-baseos-rpms                   476 k
Installing dependencies:
 libevent           x86_64            2.1.12-6.el9       rhel-9-for-x86_64-baseos-rpms                   268 k

Transaction Summary
================================================================================================================
Install  2 Packages

Total download size: 744 k
Installed size: 2.0 M
Is this ok [y/N]: y
```

Figure 11-18. *Example of a package installation after a successful subscription attachment*

6. As with your system being shown on the Red Hat portal as being registered, you can also see what subscriptions your system has.

Overview   Subscriptions   Systems   Cloud Access   Subscription Allocations   Contracts   Errata   Manage ▾

rhel9–server.kenlab.local

● Virtual System, Last checked in August 14, 2022 19:44

Details	Subscriptions	Errata	Enabled Modules	Installed Packages	System Facts

Subscriptions attached to this system

1 subscription attached

[Download Certificates] [Attach Subscriptions] [Run Auto-Attach]

60 Day Product Trial of Red Hat Enterprise Linux Server with Smart Management and all Add-Ons, Self-Supported (Physical or Virtual Nodes)

Service Level	Self-Support	[REMOVE]
SKU	RH00066	
Contract Number	████████	
Start Date	August 09, 2022	
End Date	October 08, 2022	
Entitlements Consumed	1	

Figure 11-19. *Red Hat web portal showing system subscriptions attached*

Unregister with Red Hat

When a system is no longer required to be subscribed, it is possible to unregister and free up subscriptions. This is another good practice to stick to when managing your enterprise Linux estate.

To unregister a system, you need to run the following command:

```
# sudo subscription-manager unregister
```

```
[ken@rhel9-server ~]$ sudo subscription-manager unregister
[sudo] password for ken:
Unregistering from: subscription.rhsm.redhat.com:443/subscription
System has been unregistered.
```

Figure 11-20. *Subscription-manager command to unregister a system*

Estate Management Basics

The management of large Linux estates can quickly spiral out of control if you do not have any decent management basics and tools.

Estate Management Tools

Red Hat provides very good management tools to manage Red Hat enterprise Linux. There are two main areas you will need to manage in a large Linux estate:

1. Package management and system deployment

2. Automation and configuration management

Red Hat has a brilliant tool for both 1 and 2 called Red Hat Satellite Server; however, it is recommended to separate 1 from 2 depending on your estate size and complexity.

Red Hat Satellite Server

This is used for managing system updates by syncing content from Red Hat's main repositories to your local environment. Red Hat Satellite Server has the ability to version control these packages and sort them into your different environments, allowing you to manage what packages go into what environment and to test updates before pushing them into production.

Red Hat Satellite Server does not just do package updates, and it is well advised for you to look into Red Hat Satellite Server when you start managing large Red Hat enterprise Linux server estates. We will briefly discuss Red Hat Satellite Server a bit more in a later chapter.

Red Hat Automation Platform

Previously known as Ansible Tower, Red Hat automation platform is now a full collection of Ansible tools to help you automate and manage your estate. Ansible will also be discussed a bit more in detail in a later chapter.

For now, it is important for you to associate Ansible as a potential tool to use when managing your RHEL systems.

Training and Certifications

To become a Linux administrator is as simple as getting to know Linux and understanding how to resolve issues and manage user configuration. This much will get you an interview and if you are lucky, a job to start gaining experience.

If you, however, wish to be taken seriously and gain some very good knowledge around Red Hat products, it is highly recommended to get started with some certifications and training. These certifications can be difficult to achieve as the exams are all hands-on practical exams. No multiple choice and no easy braindumps to follow. You either know how to use the platform you are looking to be certified in or you fail. In most cases, even if you know the product, you can still fail. These exams are notoriously difficult. The two main certifications you should have as an enterprise Linux system administrator are as follows.

RHCSA

The Red Hat Certified System Administrator is the entry-level certification you need to start with. This exam will challenge your ability to manage basic Linux configuration. For you to move on to the RHCE certification, you will need to pass this exam first.

RHCE

The Red Hat Certified Engineer certification is what most experienced enterprise Linux system administrators should have. The RHCE exam challenges you to configure your Linux systems in line with today's best practices by using the latest configuration and automation tooling.

Expertise Exams

Once you have achieved your RHCSA and RHCE, the next logical step is to work on expertise exams. Once you have passed five different exams, you will be awarded the Red Hat Certified Architect certification. There are many expertise exams to choose from, and with each expertise exam passed, you will refresh your RHCE for another three years.

Exercise

To get started using an enterprise Linux server, this exercise will require that you install Red Hat enterprise Linux.

Your RHEL server must be built with the following configuration.

Virtual Machine

Create a virtual machine in KVM or VirtualBox with the following specifications:

- 4096MB of memory

- 4 vCPUs

- 20GB disk

- Default network

RHEL Server

Your RHEL server must be installed with the following configuration options:

- The server name must be "rhel9-server".

- Your network must use DHCP; if you do not have DHCP, set a static address.

- Your server will need its hostname set to rhel9-server.

- The packages installed should be the absolute minimum with no desktop or GUI installed.

- Use the default disk layout from the installer.

Important   Do not delete this virtual machine; it will be used in future exercises.

Register to Red Hat

Once your RHEL server has been built, register and subscribe your system to your Red Hat account. To validate that this has worked, install the "tmux" package.

SUSE Linux Enterprise Server

SUSE is a German-based company that started circa 1992. SUSE has been through a few acquisitions over the years with the latest being in 2019 where SUSE was sold to EQT Partners for $2.5 billion.

Brief History

Early versions of SUSE Linux were based on both Slackware and Jurix up until around 1998. Between 1998 and 2003, SUSE Linux was released with versions 6.0 through to 8.2. Version 9.0 of SUSE Linux was the first distribution to be labelled as enterprise, with the

SUSE Linux Enterprise Server (SLES) being released. The current version of SLES being used is 15 with service pack 4. This will be the version used in this book.

Upstream

As RHEL has its upstream based on Fedora, SUSE bases their SLES server on OpenSUSE. Both products are managed by SUSE with much of the community supporting the evolution of OpenSUSE and SLES.

SLES

For the OpenSUSE equivalent in this book, we will be installing SUSE Linux Enterprise Server distribution, which can be downloaded from the SUSE website.

SUSE Account

As with Red Hat, SUSE also offers a supported enterprise Linux server; you will need to have an account with SUSE, just as with Red Hat. The account like with Red Hat won't cost you anything either, and you will also be able to request a 60-day evaluation that you can use for your learning.

Exercise

Before going further in this chapter, you will need to create an account with SUSE.

SUSE

For SUSE, go to the following link to create an account:

   `www.suse.com/account/create/`

   Once your account is created, go to the following link to request a free evaluation subscription. You will need to scroll down and look for the "Activation trial code" button.

   `www.suse.com/download/sles/`

Installation Media

To download the installation media for SLES, you can use the following link:

   `www.suse.com/download/sles/`

The downloads are available with a few different options. The first downloads are quite large and meant for environments where Internet access might not be available.

Figure 11-21. *Download location for SLES installation media*

The online options are smaller but require an Internet connection.

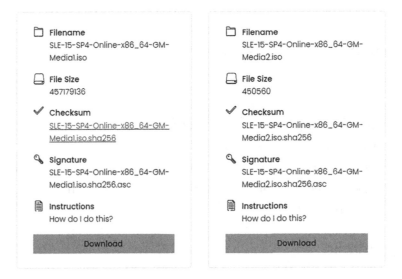

Figure 11-22. *Online SLES installation ISO downloads*

For the exercise in this book, download these online options if you can; otherwise, if Internet is an issue, use the larger options.

Using Installation Media

As mentioned with the RHEL installation media, in Chapter 4, we discussed how installation media can be created and used to build new Linux environments. Revisit Chapter 4 for a quick refresher if need be.

If you prefer a physical system, it is still recommended to use "Ventoy" and copy all the images you will use in this book to it.

Virtual Machine

Our SLES server will be installed in a virtual machine and will be created on KVM. If you are using a physical system or virtual box, just follow what you did in Chapter 4.

Create a Virtual Machine

For the installation of SLES, create a virtual machine with the following specifications:

- 4 vCPUS

- 4GB memory

- 20GB disk

The operating system should be set to Generic OS as SLES 15 is not available in the list.

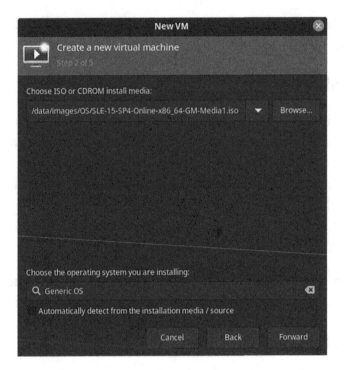

Figure 11-23. *Create a virtual machine for SLES using the SLES ISO image*

When the final screen appears, stick to a similar naming convention that was used before. For the SLES 15 server, the name has been set to "sles15-server".

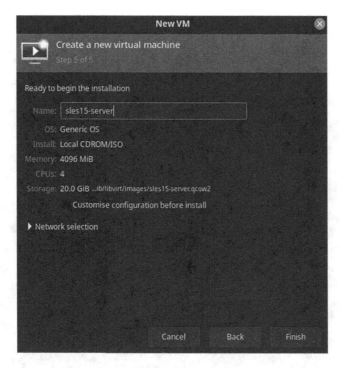

Figure 11-24. *Giving the virtual machine a name for the SLES installation*

When you click Finish, the console should appear with the SLES 15 installation starting.

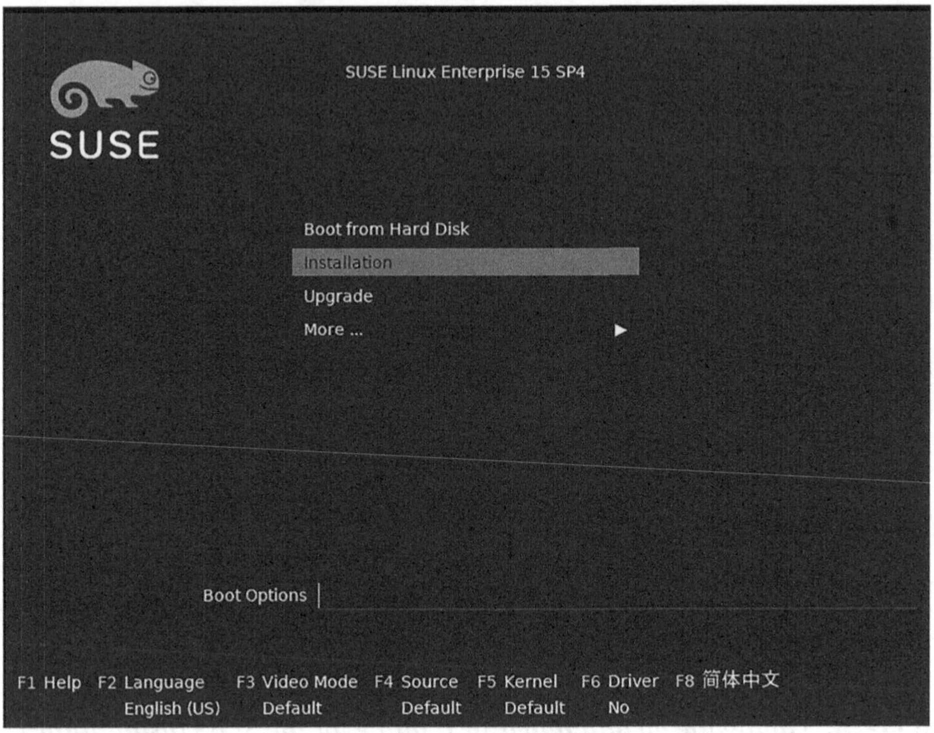

Figure 11-25. *SLES installation options when installation media boots*

Installing SLES

1. Once your system has booted into the SLES installation, select the Installation option and press enter.

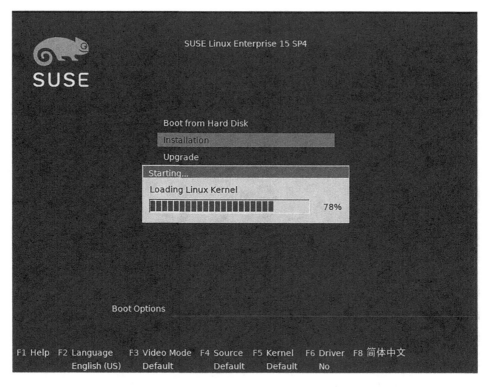

Figure 11-26. *Starting the SLES installation*

2.   Let the boot process continue through the initial screens.

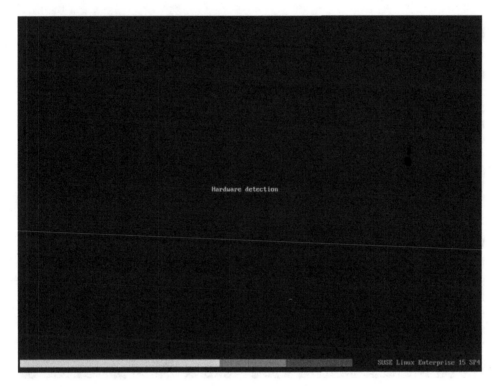

Figure 11-27. *Initial boot process screen*

3.   You are almost ready to install once the network configuration has
     finished initializing.

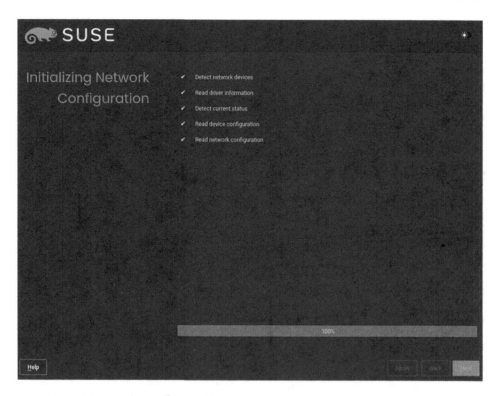

Figure 11-28. *Network configuration screen*

4. Select SUSE Linux Enterprise Server 15 SP4 when the options
    appear to begin the installation. Then click the Next button.

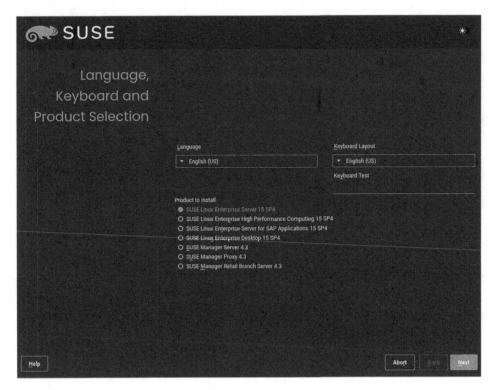

Figure 11-29. *Language and keyboard selection screen*

5.   Accept the licensing agreement and click the Next button.

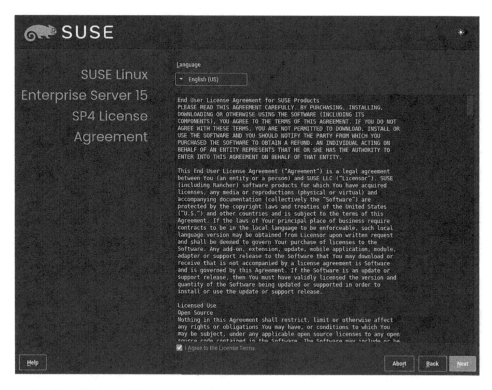

Figure 11-30. *License agreement screen*

6. As the installation media for this SLES install is the online
    variant, the registration details will need to be entered during
    the installation. If you don't want to do this, you will need
    to download the full ISO that does not require an Internet
    connection.

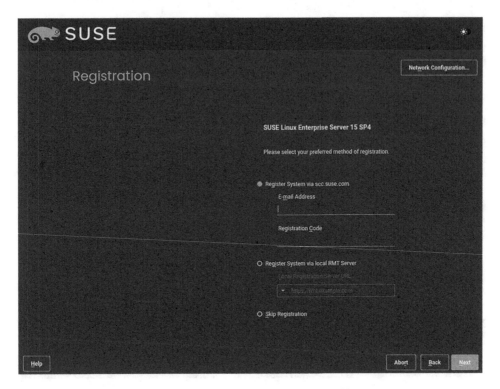

Figure 11-31. *SUSE registration screen for online installations*

7.   Enable any updated repositories so you can get all the latest
     packages.

Figure 11-32. *Option to enable updated repositories*

8.   Leave the default options selected for extensions and modules.
     These are the basics for now.

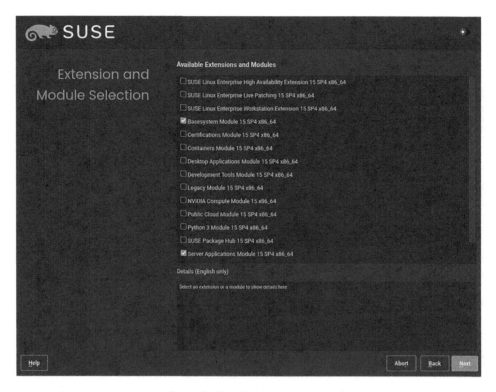

Figure 11-33. *Extension and module selection screen*

9.   Click Next and let the registries update.

10.   Leave all add-on products to default and click Next.

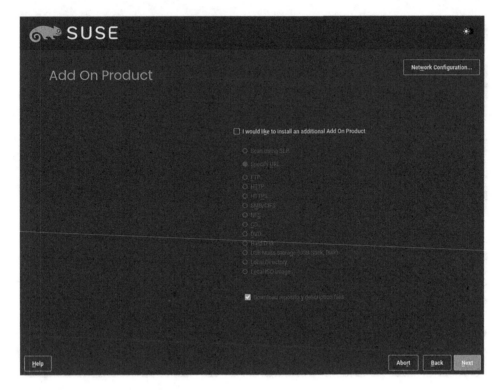

Figure 11-34. *Product add-ons*

11.   Select the minimal option for system roles. This is to ensure the
       minimal packages are installed. Then click Next.

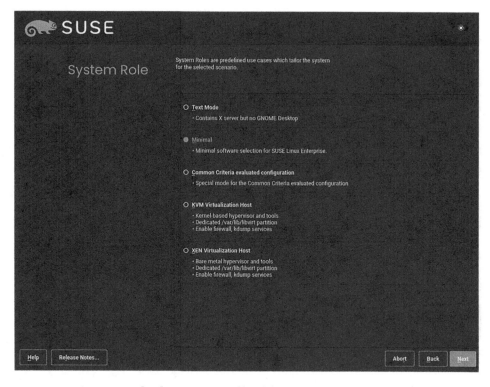

Figure 11-35. *System role the server will take on*

12.   Leave the disk layout to defaults and click Next.

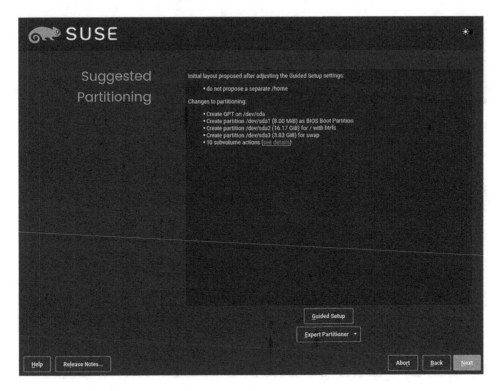

Figure 11-36. *Disk layout configuration screen*

13.   Set your time zone and click Next.

Figure 11-37. *Time zone selection screen*

14.   Create a local user and tick the box for the password to be set for
your system administrator. Once done, click the Next button.

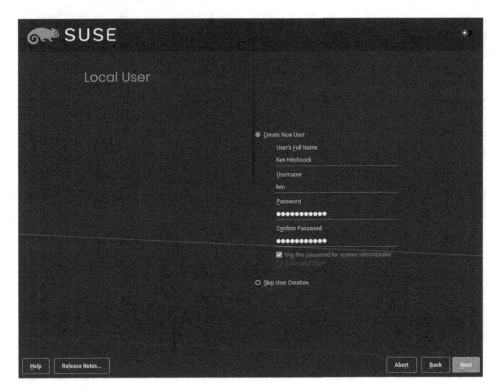

Figure 11-38.   *Create additional local users.*

15.   Review your installation options and click the Install button.

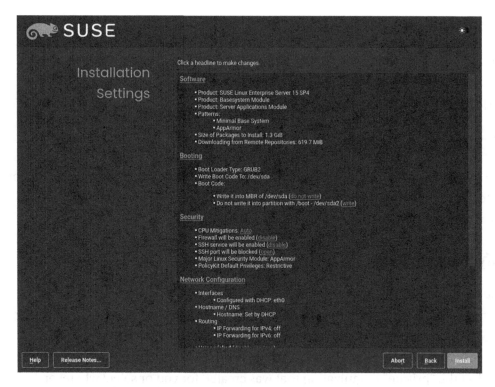

Figure 11-39. *Final installation settings review screen*

16.   Once the installation has completed, the system will reboot and
      you will be presented with a login prompt.

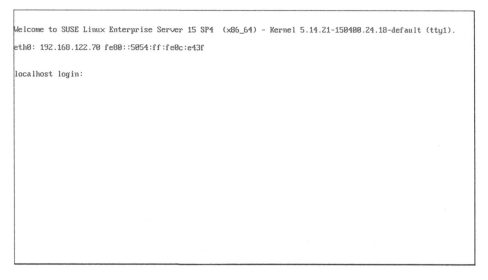

Figure 11-40. *SLES login prompt on the virtual machine manager console*

Subscriptions and Support

Support and subscriptions are part of using enterprise Linux or enterprise products. SUSE is not different from Red Hat, they too require that you have subscriptions for your enterprise products.

Subscribing a System

If you decided to install your SLES server using the full installation media and did not register your SLES server, you will need to understand how to add your newly built SLES server to your SUSE account.

Verify Subscriptions

In the same process that was required for your Red Hat account, a SUSE account is required. At the beginning of the SUSE in this chapter, you were tasked with creating your SUSE account. You should be able to log in to the following URL:

`https://scc.suse.com/organizations/`

Select the "private" organization that was created for you or select whatever organization you may have created for your subscriptions.

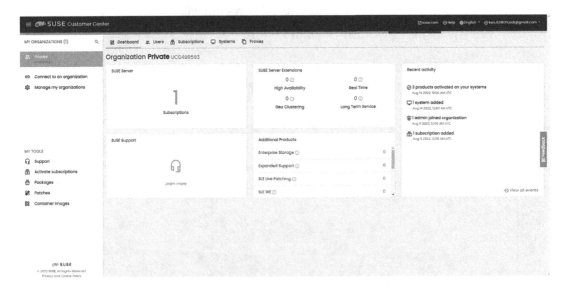

Figure 11-41. *SUSE dashboard to manage systems and subscriptions*

Your dashboard should look similar to Figure 11-41. From here, you can check what systems are registered and what subscriptions are available.

Register with SUSE

There are two things you need to do when registering a system with your SUSE account:

1. Open your SUSE web portal and get the registration code for the subscription you wish to attach your system to.

Figure 11-42. *Retrieving registration codes from the SUSE web portal*

From the image shown in Figure 11-42, you can see that the 60-day trial subscription has been opened. In the details section, you can see the registration code. You will need to take a note of this code for the next step.

2. Log in to your SLES system and su to your root user or any other administrator-level user.

Once you are logged in, you can register your system with your SUSE account. The following command will register your system. Be sure to replace the registration code with your own:

```
# suseconnect -r 49Dxxxxxxxxxxxxxxx
```

```
localhost:~ # suseconnect -r 49D█████████████
Registering system to SUSE Customer Center

Announcing system to https://scc.suse.com ...

Activating SLES 15.4 x86_64 ...
-> Adding service to system ...

Activating sle-module-basesystem 15.4 x86_64 ...
-> Adding service to system ...
-> Installing release package ...

Activating sle-module-server-applications 15.4 x86_64 ...
-> Adding service to system ...
-> Installing release package ...

Successfully registered system
localhost:~ # █
```

Figure 11-43. *The suseconnect command*

Verify the System Registered with SUSE

To check that your system has been registered with your SUSE account, you can either run the following command:

suseconnect -s

or you can check the SUSE web portal in the systems section.

Figure 11-44. *Checking system subscription status in the SUSE web portal*

Deregister with SUSE

To deregister your system from your SUSE account, you simply need to run the following command from the root user or administrator user of your choice:

suseconnect -d

```
localhost:~ # suseconnect -d
Deregistering system from SUSE Customer Center

Deactivating sle-module-server-applications 15.4 x86_64 ...
-> Removing service from system ...
-> Removing release package ...

Deactivating sle-module-basesystem 15.4 x86_64 ...
-> Removing service from system ...
-> Removing release package ...
-> Removing service from system ...

Cleaning up ...
Successfully deregistered system
```

Figure 11-45. *suseconnect deregister command*

Estate Management Basics

As mentioned in the "Red Hat" section of this chapter, the management of large Linux estates can quickly spiral out of control if you do not have good management tools.

Estate Management Tools

Like Red Hat, SUSE provides very good management tools to manage SLES. The main management tool provided by SUSE is called SUSE Manager. SUSE Manager provides the following:

- Package management
- System deployment
- Configuration management

SUSE Manager

Originally based on the Spacewalk upstream project, SUSE Manager has evolved quite a bit since then. As Spacewalk is no longer being developed, SUSE has opted to base newer versions of SUSE Manager on Uyuni. Uyuni too was forked from Spacewalk but has continued to develop the product.

We will briefly discuss SUSE Manager a bit more in a later chapter.

SaltStack

Spacewalk traditionally has not been a great platform for configuration management or automation. It worked well enough if you were not using Puppet but could easily become a massive pile of confusion.

With Uyuni and SUSE continuing the use of Spacewalk, newer versions have completely ripped out the configuration management system and replaced it with SaltStack, a system that is very similar to Puppet but instead makes use of YAML syntax. SaltStack has a number of very nice features and is definitely worth investing some time into when learning platform configuration management.

Training and Certifications

Like Red Hat, SUSE has their own certifications that are worth doing if you want to be taken seriously as an enterprise Linux system administrator.

The two main SUSE certifications you should consider are as follows.

SCA

The SUSE Certified System Administrator is the entry-level certification you need to start with, which is very similar to the RHCSA certification from Red Hat. This exam will also challenge your ability to manage basic Linux configuration on a SUSE environment using both graphical-based tools and command-line utilities.

SCE

The SUSE Certified Engineer certification is the equivalent to the RHCE certification and is highly recommended for experienced enterprise Linux system administrators. The SCE, very much like the RHCE exam, challenges you to configure your Linux systems in line with today's best practices. The SCE exam will also test your ability to install and configure the SaltStack environment that can be used for platform configuration management.

Speciality Exams

Unlike Red Hat, SUSE does not have an enormous portfolio of other certifications. There are a few, mostly around the products that SUSE provides outside of SLES. SUSE Manager and Rancher are some examples. For a career working with SUSE products, these certifications are well recommended.

Exercise

To continue using enterprise Linux systems, we now need to install and configure our second enterprise Linux server. This exercise will require that you install SUSE Linux Enterprise Server.

Your SLES server must be built with the following configuration.

Virtual Machine

Create a virtual machine in KVM or VirtualBox with the following specifications:

- 4096MB of memory
- 4 vCPUs
- 20GB disk
- Default network

SLES Server

Your SLES server must be installed with the following configuration options:

- The server name must be "sles15-server".
- Your network must use DHCP; if you do not have DHCP, set a static address.
- Register your system during the installation.
- Your server will need its hostname set to sles15-server.
- The packages installed should be the absolute minimum with no desktop or GUI installed.
- Use the default disk layout from the installer.

Important   Do not delete this virtual machine; it will be used in future exercises.

Ubuntu

Finally, we come to Canonical and Ubuntu. Canonical is a UK-based company that was started in 2004 by a South African entrepreneur named Mark Shuttleworth.

Canonical, unlike Red Hat and SUSE, does not have their own separate enterprise Linux product that they develop from upstream communities. Instead, we will explore how Canonical turns Ubuntu upstream into an enterprise product.

Brief History

The first ever release of Ubuntu was 4.10 and comically code named the "Warty Warthog" and was released in 2004. The latest version of Ubuntu and the version used in this book is 22.04, which too has the interesting name of "Jammy Jellyfish."

Upstream Is Enterprise

The upstream and the enterprise versions of Ubuntu are the same, except for one feature. Canonical provides support for Ubuntu by using a subscription service to provide enterprise updates like security fixes and errata. This is a paid-for service and is used for customers to subscribe systems they require enterprise support for.

Ubuntu

The Ubuntu section will be a lot shorter than the Red Hat and SUSE sections for one important reason. The installation won't be any different than what was done in Chapter **4**. In the interest of not just repeating exactly what was done, go back to Chapter **4** if you need to know how the Ubuntu server is installed.

Training and Certifications

Unlike Red Hat and SUSE, Canonical does not have any certification exams anymore as they were discontinued a number of years back. The recommendation is to either do the Red Hat or SUSE certifications if you wish to build your credentials.

Ubuntu Account

As with Red Hat and SUSE, Ubuntu also offers a subscription service for their Linux servers. To make use of these, you will need to have an account with Ubuntu. The account is free to use and has the added bonus of already having three subscriptions you can use that won't expire, which means you will not need any 60-day trials.

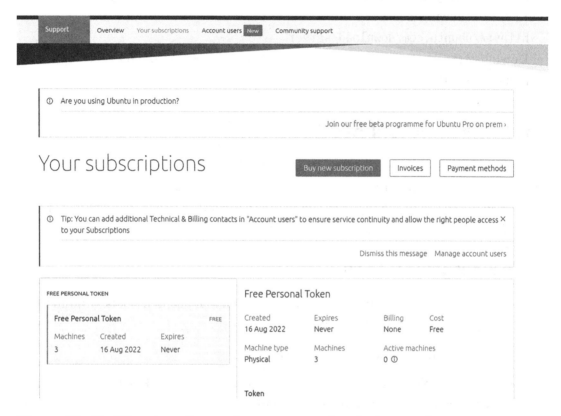

Figure 11-46. *Ubuntu web portal to manage subscriptions and systems*

Exercise

Before going further in this section, you will need to create an account with Ubuntu.

Ubuntu

For Ubuntu, go to the following link to create an account:

```
https://login.ubuntu.com/
```

Once your account is created, log in and look at your subscriptions. There will be a unique code you will need to subscribe your systems.

Ubuntu Installation

To install Ubuntu, you will need to download the Ubuntu server ISO image. This can be found at the following location:

`https://ubuntu.com/download/server`

Download the image now if you have not already done so in Chapter 4 and follow the instructions already discussed in the said chapter.

Estate Management Basics

Estate management tools for Ubuntu are just as vital as they are for Red Hat and SUSE. The same concepts are important for an Ubuntu estate as a RHEL or SUSE. There will need to be a package management tool and a configuration management tool. These are important to avoid your estate from spinning out of control.

Estate Management Tools

Like Red Hat and SUSE, Ubuntu too provides their own management tools. Ubuntu has the following management tools that can be used:

- Package management with Landscape.

- System deployment can be done with building your own PXE boot server and using the auto install options.

- Juju for service and utility management.

- Configuration management provided by Ansible, Puppet, Chef, or any other tools that will manage a Linux environment.

Landscape

Similar in nature to Spacewalk and Red Hat Satellite Server. Landscape provides the ability to patch systems with the latest security updates. Not as rich in features but a good alternative. Ubuntu can also be managed via the web portal "Advantage" to register and provide updates.

Subscriptions and Support

As with Red Hat and SUSE, support and subscriptions are part of using their enterprise Linux products. Ubuntu as mentioned also has a subscriptions-based support offering.

Subscribing a System

When using Ubuntu in an enterprise environment, it is highly recommended to have an active subscription. This will allow the raising of support cases and the ability to update systems with the latest security updates.

Verify Subscriptions

Before attempting to subscribe to any of your Ubuntu servers, you should verify you have available subscriptions. You will also need to get the subscription token for you to register your system. You should be able to log in to the following URL:

```
https://ubuntu.com/advantage
```

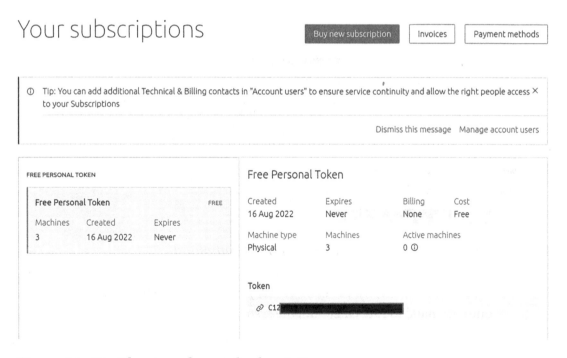

Figure 11-47. *Ubuntu web portal subscriptions screen*

Under the subscriptions link, you will find your free personal token. Make a note of the token as you will need it shortly.

Register with Ubuntu

There are two things you need to do to register your Ubuntu with your subscriptions available.

1. Get the subscription token from the subscriptions link in the https://ubuntu.com/advantage portal.

2. Log in to your Ubuntu system as your own user.

   Once you are logged in, you can run the following command to register your system. Be sure to replace the token with your own.

   ```
   # sudo ua attach C1xxxxxxxxxxxxxxxxxxxxx
   ```

Figure 11-48. *Ubuntu subscription attachment command*

From the image shown in Figure 11-48, you can see that there is only one command to run. Once run, the system is now registered in the Ubuntu portal.

Machine type	Machines	Active machines
Physical	3	1 ⓘ

Figure 11-49. *Ubuntu web portal subscription availability status*

Verify the System Registered with SUSE

To check that your system has been registered with your Ubuntu account, you can run the following command:

```
# sudo ua status
```

```
ken@ubuntu-server:~$ sudo ua status
SERVICE         ENTITLED  STATUS    DESCRIPTION
cc-eal          yes       n/a       Common Criteria EAL2 Provisioning Packages
esm-infra       yes       enabled   UA Infra: Extended Security Maintenance (ESM)
fips            yes       n/a       NIST-certified core packages
fips-updates    yes       n/a       NIST-certified core packages with priority security updates
livepatch       yes       enabled   Canonical Livepatch service
usg             yes       n/a       Security compliance and audit tools

Enable services with: ua enable <service>
```

Figure 11-50. *Ubuntu subscription status using the ua command*

Detach from the Ubuntu Account

To remove your system from your Ubuntu account, you can run the following command:

```
# sudo ua detach
```

```
ken@ubuntu-server:~$ sudo ua detach
Detach will disable the following services:
    livepatch
    esm-infra
Are you sure? (y/N) y
Updating package lists
This machine is now detached.
```

Figure 11-51. *Ubuntu ua command to detach subscriptions from a system*

Summary

In this chapter, you were introduced to the following:

- The three common enterprise Linux distributions used today

- How RHEL is installed and managed in an enterprise estate

- How SLES is installed and managed in an enterprise estate

- How Ubuntu is managed in an enterprise estate

- What subscription services are provided by each enterprise Linux vendor and how to subscribe a Linux system to their respective subscription

- What training and certifications are available for each of the Linux distributions discussed in this chapter

## CHAPTER 12

Example Use Cases for Linux

This chapter is the first chapter where we will start using our Linux servers to provide a service. There are many different uses of Linux, but for this chapter, we will focus on how to build a Linux web server and how to build a Linux file server.

During the building process of each use case, we will discuss configuration files, firewall and SELinux configuration, custom configuration, and finally how to automate the configuration for each use case type.

As with other chapters, there will be exercises for you to follow and practice with.

Building a Web Server

The first use case commonly used for enterprise Linux systems is to configure the server as a web server. There are a number of options that can be used, and they vary in complexity. For this book and as this may be still very new to many who read this book, the methods that will be used will be the least complex as possible.

Web Server Options

There are a few web server options to use on a Linux server. All worth discussing are OpenSource and free to use. There are enterprise products that can be used where required, but as we are only starting to understand these simple use cases, we will stick to the commonly used options.

© Kenneth Hitchcock 2023
K. Hitchcock, *The Enterprise Linux Administrator*, https://doi.org/10.1007/978-1-4842-8801-6_12

Apache httpd

Apache httpd is one of the more popular and common web server platforms to use. It is relatively simple to install and configure and has a rich feature set to suit most platform requirements.

Apache httpd is modular, which means modules can be added and removed to add functionality. Apache httpd can be used as a web server, load balancer, reverse proxy, and loads of other interesting things where modules are added.

Nginx

An alternative to Apache httpd for one very important reason. Nginx is fast and has the ability to handle a massive amount of concurrent connections. Apache httpd has improved over the years, but Nginx became popular because of how much more performant it is. This was reinforced by the fact that Nginx was bought into the F5 Inc. family in 2019.

Nginx, very much like Apache httpd, can be used as a web server, load balancer, reverse proxy, and many more including the ability to act as a proxy in front of an email server.

Web Server Configuration Overview

Before we begin configuring our web server, it is worth going over what will be done and what the use case requirement is. This is to mimic a similar request you may have when working as an enterprise Linux administrator.

Use Case Overview

It has been requested that a new web server is built to host your organization's internal intranet site. Previously Windows IIS was used, but as the organization is looking to be more OpenSource oriented, you have been tasked with building and configuring a web server on the Linux distribution of your choice.

The server must have the following requirements met:

- HTTP and HTTPS traffic must be accepted.

- Two different sites need to be configured. Both sites are plain static HTML sites.

- The web server should be locked down to only allow ports 80, 443, and 22.

- All other possible security measures must be taken.

Design Decision

The design decision has been to use Apache httpd server as this was recommended by an experienced Linux administrator. This has also been discussed and learned in vendor certification training in the past.

Due to the fact that the installation needs to be very simple and not very reliant on performance, Apache httpd seemed to be the logical choice. At a later stage, a Nginx server could be built to compare features, but for now, Apache httpd will be used.

Linux Distribution

As the budget was limited for this project, the Ubuntu distribution would be used as there are three subscriptions available that can be used. The eventual goal is to purchase more subscriptions once more OpenSource adoption has occurred in the organization.

Linux Installation and Configuration

For the Linux distribution, a new Ubuntu 22.04 server was already built called "ubuntu-server", very unimaginative and not very well thought through. However, the server was already available, and to save time, this server was to be used.

User Account

The new Ubuntu "ubuntu-server" has had an administrator account created with sudo permissions. The user that will be used is called "ken".

```
ken@ubuntu-server:~$ whoami
ken

ken@ubuntu-server:~$ id
uid=1000(ken) gid=1000(ken) groups=1000(ken),4(adm),24(cdrom),27(sudo),30(dip),46(plugdev),110(lxd)
```

Figure 12-1. *User information for the currently logged-in user*

From the image shown in Figure 12-1, you can see that the "ken" user is part of the sudo group and the adm groups, allowing this user to have enough permissions to configure the system as a web server.

Subscribe to an Ubuntu Account

The new Ubuntu "ubuntu-server" was subscribed to the available subscription in the organization's Ubuntu account.

Figure 12-2. *Subscribe an Ubuntu server to a subscription*

This was previously done in Chapter 11. Sensitive information was redacted as this document is being made public.

Web Server Package Installation

There are a couple packages that will need to be installed for a fully compliant and functional web server.

Firewalld

The first package that needs to be installed to meet security requirements is the "firewalld" package. The package can be installed on the Ubuntu server using the following command:

```
# sudo apt install firewalld -y
```

```
ken@ubuntu-server:~$ sudo apt install firewalld
Reading package lists... Done
Building dependency tree... Done
Reading state information... Done
The following packages were automatically installed and are no longer required:
  pastebinit python3-newt run-one
Use 'sudo apt autoremove' to remove them.
The following additional packages will be installed:
  ipset libipset13 python3-cap-ng python3-firewall python3-nftables
The following NEW packages will be installed:
  firewalld ipset libipset13 python3-cap-ng python3-firewall python3-nftables
0 upgraded, 6 newly installed, 0 to remove and 122 not upgraded.
Need to get 648 kB of archives.
After this operation, 4,290 kB of additional disk space will be used.
Do you want to continue? [Y/n] y
Get:1 http://gb.archive.ubuntu.com/ubuntu jammy/universe amd64 python3-nftables amd64 1.0.2-1ubuntu2 [11.5 kB]
Get:2 http://gb.archive.ubuntu.com/ubuntu jammy/universe amd64 python3-firewall all 1.1.1-1ubuntu1 [130 kB]
Get:3 http://gb.archive.ubuntu.com/ubuntu jammy/universe amd64 firewalld all 1.1.1-1ubuntu1 [394 kB]
Get:4 http://gb.archive.ubuntu.com/ubuntu jammy/main amd64 libipset13 amd64 7.15-1build1 [63.4 kB]
Get:5 http://gb.archive.ubuntu.com/ubuntu jammy/universe amd64 python3-cap-ng amd64 0.7.9-2.2build3 [17.1 kB]
Get:6 http://gb.archive.ubuntu.com/ubuntu jammy/main amd64 ipset amd64 7.15-1build1 [32.8 kB]
Fetched 648 kB in 0s (1,676 kB/s)
```

Figure 12-3. *Firewalld package installation*

The image shown in Figure 12-3 has had its output reduced to save space. The package can be verified by running the following command:

sudo firewall-cmd --list-all

```
ken@ubuntu-server:~$ sudo firewall-cmd --list-all
public (active)
  target: default
  icmp-block-inversion: no
  interfaces: ens3
  sources:
  services: dhcpv6-client ssh
  ports:
  protocols:
  forward: yes
  masquerade: no
  forward-ports:
  source-ports:
  icmp-blocks:
  rich rules:
```

Figure 12-4. *Firewall current configuration*

Apache2

The main package required for the httpd web server is the "apache2" package. This package can be installed using the following command:

sudo apt install apache2 -y

```
ken@ubuntu-server:~$ sudo apt install apache2 -y
Reading package lists... Done
Building dependency tree... Done
Reading state information... Done
The following packages were automatically installed and are no longer required:
  pastebinit python3-newt run-one
Use 'sudo apt autoremove' to remove them.
The following additional packages will be installed:
  apache2-bin apache2-data apache2-utils libapr1 libaprutil1 libaprutil1-dbd-sqlite3 libaprutil1-ldap
Suggested packages:
  apache2-doc apache2-suexec-pristine | apache2-suexec-custom www-browser
The following NEW packages will be installed:
  apache2 apache2-bin apache2-data apache2-utils libapr1 libaprutil1 libaprutil1-dbd-sqlite3 libaprutil1-ldap
0 upgraded, 8 newly installed, 0 to remove and 122 not upgraded.
Need to get 1,918 kB of archives.
After this operation, 7,702 kB of additional disk space will be used.
Get:1 http://gb.archive.ubuntu.com/ubuntu jammy/main amd64 libapr1 amd64 1.7.0-8build1 [107 kB]
Get:2 http://gb.archive.ubuntu.com/ubuntu jammy/main amd64 libaprutil1 amd64 1.6.1-5ubuntu4 [92.4 kB]
Get:3 http://gb.archive.ubuntu.com/ubuntu jammy/main amd64 libaprutil1-dbd-sqlite3 amd64 1.6.1-5ubuntu4 [11.3 kB]
Get:4 http://gb.archive.ubuntu.com/ubuntu jammy/main amd64 libaprutil1-ldap amd64 1.6.1-5ubuntu4 [9,162 B]
Get:5 http://gb.archive.ubuntu.com/ubuntu jammy-updates/main amd64 apache2-bin amd64 2.4.52-1ubuntu4.1 [1,347 kB]
Get:6 http://gb.archive.ubuntu.com/ubuntu jammy-updates/main amd64 apache2-data all 2.4.52-1ubuntu4.1 [165 kB]
Get:7 http://gb.archive.ubuntu.com/ubuntu jammy-updates/main amd64 apache2-utils amd64 2.4.52-1ubuntu4.1 [89.1 kB]
Get:8 http://gb.archive.ubuntu.com/ubuntu jammy-updates/main amd64 apache2 amd64 2.4.52-1ubuntu4.1 [97.8 kB]
```

Figure 12-5. *Apache2 package installation*

The image shown in Figure 12-5 shows a reduced output of the package installation.

To verify that the "apache2" package has installed correctly, check that the "apache2" service has started.

sudo systemctl status apache2

```
ken@ubuntu-server:~$ systemctl status apache2
● apache2.service - The Apache HTTP Server
     Loaded: loaded (/lib/systemd/system/apache2.service; enabled; vendor preset: enabled)
     Active: active (running) since Wed 2022-08-17 20:24:12 UTC; 1min 8s ago
       Docs: https://httpd.apache.org/docs/2.4/
   Main PID: 7813 (apache2)
      Tasks: 55 (limit: 4568)
     Memory: 5.1M
        CPU: 122ms
     CGroup: /system.slice/apache2.service
             ├─7813 /usr/sbin/apache2 -k start
             ├─7814 /usr/sbin/apache2 -k start
             └─7815 /usr/sbin/apache2 -k start
```

Figure 12-6. *apache2 server is active and running*

If your service is not running, do not start it yet. This will be done shortly.

Configuration Files

The configuration required for this web server is going to be relatively simple as all that will be required is to configure two virtual hosts for the two different websites the web server will host.

apache2.conf

The main configuration file that is used by the Apache httpd server is the apache2.conf file and can be found in the following location:

```
# ls -al /etc/apache2/
```

```
ken@ubuntu-server:~$ sudo ls -al /etc/apache2/
[sudo] password for ken:
total 96
drwxr-xr-x.   8 root root  4096 Aug 17 20:24 .
drwxr-xr-x. 147 root root 12288 Aug 17 20:44 ..
-rw-r--r--.   1 root root  7224 Jun 14 12:30 apache2.conf
drwxr-xr-x.   2 root root  4096 Aug 17 20:24 conf-available
drwxr-xr-x.   2 root root  4096 Aug 17 20:24 conf-enabled
-rw-r--r--.   1 root root  1782 Mar 23 02:00 envvars
-rw-r--r--.   1 root root 31063 Mar 23 02:00 magic
drwxr-xr-x.   2 root root 12288 Aug 17 20:24 mods-available
drwxr-xr-x.   2 root root  4096 Aug 17 20:24 mods-enabled
-rw-r--r--.   1 root root   320 Mar 23 02:00 ports.conf
drwxr-xr-x.   2 root root  4096 Aug 17 20:24 sites-available
drwxr-xr-x.   2 root root  4096 Aug 17 20:24 sites-enabled
```

Figure 12-7. *Apache configuration file location*

Within the location, which can be seen in the image shown in Figure 12-7, is the file apache2.conf.

In the apache2.conf file are the main configuration parameters used by the Apache httpd web server, everything from which configuration files to include through to what users should be used to run the web server processes.

```
MaxKeepAliveRequests 100

#
# KeepAliveTimeout: Number of seconds to wait for the next request
# same client on the same connection.
#
KeepAliveTimeout 5


# These need to be set in /etc/apache2/envvars
User ${APACHE_RUN_USER}
Group ${APACHE_RUN_GROUP}
```

Figure 12-8. *apache2.conf main configuration lines*

Included Configuration

Within the apache2.conf file, there is configuration that includes further configuration files. These include the ones shown in Figure 12-9.

```
# Include generic snippets of statements
IncludeOptional conf-enabled/*.conf

# Include the virtual host configurations:
IncludeOptional sites-enabled/*.conf
```

Figure 12-9. *Apache2 configuration files included in the main configuration file*

The configuration shown in Figure 12-9 will include all files that end with a ".conf" extension. The configuration that is most important for this use case will be a new file that will be created in the "sites-enabled" directory.

Website Configuration

There are two websites that need to be hosted on this web server. They are as follows:

– site1.example.com

– site2.example.com

For each site, there will be a new directory created, a new website file (index.html), and a new configuration file.

Create Directories

For each site, there needs to be a new directory. As the current location for the web server to host website files is /var/www/html, we will use the same location and add a couple new directories:

```
# sudo mkdir /var/www/html/site1
# sudo mkdir /var/www/html/site2
```

Create Website Files

Within each of the preceding directories, a simple file with some basic text needs to be created and saved as index.html.

Site Configuration Files

For each site, a new configuration file is required to be created. For this book, the default configuration file has been copied and edited for each site.

sudo cp /etc/apache2/sites-enabled/000-default.conf /etc/apache2/sites-enabled/001-site1.conf

sudo cp /etc/apache2/sites-enabled/000-default.conf /etc/apache2/sites-enabled/001-site2.conf

```
ken@ubuntu-server:~$ sudo cp /etc/apache2/sites-enabled/000-default.conf /etc/apache2/sites-enabled/001-site1.conf
ken@ubuntu-server:~$ sudo cp /etc/apache2/sites-enabled/000-default.conf /etc/apache2/sites-enabled/002-site2.conf
```

Within each file, a basic bit of configuration needs to be added to ensure that web traffic flows to the correct site.

Site 1 configuration file

```
<VirtualHost site1.example.com:80>
        ServerName site1.example.com

        ServerAdmin webmaster@localhost
        DocumentRoot /var/www/html/site1

        ErrorLog ${APACHE_LOG_DIR}/error.log
        CustomLog ${APACHE_LOG_DIR}/access.log combined

</VirtualHost>
```

Site2 configuration file

```
<VirtualHost site2.example.com:80>
        ServerName site2.example.com

        ServerAdmin webmaster@localhost
        DocumentRoot /var/www/html/site2

        ErrorLog ${APACHE_LOG_DIR}/error.log
        CustomLog ${APACHE_LOG_DIR}/access.log combined

</VirtualHost>
```

Figure 12-10. *Two example virtual host configuration files*

Important   To test this configuration you will either need to update DNS or your local /etc/hosts file; in Windows, it's in the c:\windows folder. For this book, /etc/hosts was updated to resolve site1.example.com and site2.example.com to the same IP address as the Ubuntu server.

Firewall Configuration

The first major bit of security that needs to be applied to your Ubuntu server for your web server to be functional is to configure the local firewall.

Firewall Status

To check what ports and services are currently configured in the local firewall, run the following command:

```
# sudo firewall-cmd --list-all
```

```
ken@ubuntu-server:~$ sudo firewall-cmd --list-all
public (active)
  target: default
  icmp-block-inversion: no
  interfaces: ens3
  sources:
  services: dhcpv6-client ssh
  ports:
  protocols:
  forward: yes
  masquerade: no
  forward-ports:
  source-ports:
  icmp-blocks:
  rich rules:
```

Figure 12-11. *Firewall current configuration*

From the image shown in Figure 12-11, you can see only the dhcpv6-client and ssh services are allowed through the firewall. As our web server relies on TCP ports 80 and 443, there is no conventional way a user could open any content on this web server with the current configuration.

Opening Ports

To allow ports 80 and 443, we need to run the following command:

```
# sudo firewall-cmd --add-port=80/tcp --permanent
# sudo firewall-cmd --add-port=443/tcp --permanent
```

```
ken@ubuntu-server:~$ sudo firewall-cmd --add-port=80/tcp --permanent
success
ken@ubuntu-server:~$ sudo firewall-cmd --add-port=443/tcp --permanent
success
```

Figure 12-12. *Commands to open TCP ports 80 and 443*

Reload Firewall Configuration

It is very important to reload the firewall configuration once you are finished adding ports or services. If you fail to do this, it will appear as though you have not added the ports or services to the firewall configuration. To reload the firewall configuration, run the following command:

```
# sudo firewall-cmd --reload
```

```
ken@ubuntu-server:~$ sudo firewall-cmd --reload
success
```

Figure 12-13. *Command to reload the firewall*

Verify Configuration

To verify that all the ports are open, run the following command once again:

```
# sudo firewall-cmd --list-all
```

```
ken@ubuntu-server:~$ sudo firewall-cmd --list-all
public (active)
  target: default
  icmp-block-inversion: no
  interfaces: ens3
  sources:
  services: dhcpv6-client ssh
  ports: 80/tcp 443/tcp
  protocols:
  forward: yes
  masquerade: no
  forward-ports:
  source-ports:
  icmp-blocks:
  rich rules:
```

Figure 12-14. *Firewall configuration with newly added ports*

In Figure 12-14, we can see that TCP ports 80 and 443 have been added to the list of ports. Users should now be able to open content from the web server.

SELinux Configuration

To comply with the organization's security requirements, SELinux should be configured for your web server.

No SELinux on Ubuntu

As the chosen Linux distribution for this use case is Ubuntu, there is no SELinux installed by default. Due to the security requirements of your organization, SELinux is an absolute must and should be installed if the web server is to be allowed on the network.

AppArmor

Ubuntu uses a product called AppArmor as a SELinux alternative, but due to AppArmor not being as secure as SELinux, it needs to be removed.

To remove AppArmor, run the following commands:

```
# sudo systemctl stop apparmor
# sudo apt-get remove apparmor -y
# sudo reboot
```

Install SELinux

Once the Ubuntu server has restarted, the SELinux packages can be installed, and any SELinux configuration can be done. To install SELinux, use the following command:

```
# sudo apt install policycoreutils selinux-utils selinux-basics -y
```

```
ken@ubuntu-server:~$ sudo apt install policycoreutils selinux-utils selinux-basics -y
[sudo] password for ken:
Reading package lists... Done
Building dependency tree... Done
Reading state information... Done
The following packages were automatically installed and are no longer required:
  pastebinit python3-newt run-one
Use 'sudo apt autoremove' to remove them.
The following additional packages will be installed:
```

Figure 12-15. *Ubuntu package installation for SELinux*

Activate SELinux

Once SELinux has been installed, it will need to be activated. To activate SELinux, you will need to run the following command:

```
# sudo selinux-activate
```

```
ken@ubuntu-server:~$ sudo selinux-activate
Activating SE Linux
Sourcing file `/etc/default/grub'
Sourcing file `/etc/default/grub.d/init-select.cfg'
Generating grub configuration file ...
Found linux image: /boot/vmlinuz-5.15.0-46-generic
Found initrd image: /boot/initrd.img-5.15.0-46-generic
Found linux image: /boot/vmlinuz-5.15.0-41-generic
Found initrd image: /boot/initrd.img-5.15.0-41-generic
Found memtest86+ image: /memtest86+.elf
Found memtest86+ image: /memtest86+.bin
Warning: os-prober will not be executed to detect other bootable partitions.
Systems on them will not be added to the GRUB boot configuration.
Check GRUB_DISABLE_OS_PROBER documentation entry.
done
SE Linux is activated.  You may need to reboot now.
```

Figure 12-16. *Command to activate SELinux*

Once activated, your Ubuntu server will need to be restarted.

sudo reboot

SELinux Permissive First

Once your system has rebooted again, the SELinux configuration needs to be confirmed that it has been set to permissive. This will ensure that all SELinux relabelling is done during the boot without breaking your system. To configure permissive mode, update the /etc/selinux/config file. Reboot your system when done.

```
ken@ubuntu-server:~$ cat /etc/selinux/config
# This file controls the state of SELinux on the system.
# SELINUX= can take one of these three values:
# enforcing - SELinux security policy is enforced.
# permissive - SELinux prints warnings instead of enforcing.
# disabled - No SELinux policy is loaded.
SELINUX=permissive
# SELINUXTYPE= can take one of these two values:
# default - equivalent to the old strict and targeted policies
# mls     - Multi-Level Security (for military and educational use)
# src     - Custom policy built from source
SELINUXTYPE=default

# SETLOCALDEFS= Check local definition changes
SETLOCALDEFS=0
```

Figure 12-17. */etc/selinux/config file set to permissive*

Important   If you set enforcing and reboot, your system will most likely break.

SELinux Relabel

Before you can enable enforcing mode in SELinux, you will need to relabel the file system with SELinux labels. This is the configuration SELinux uses to manage its policies.

To relabel your filesystem, you need to create a "/.autorelabel" file.

```
# touch /.autorelabel
```

```
ken@ubuntu-server:~$ sudo touch /.autorelabel
ken@ubuntu-server:~$ ls -al /
total 12952
drwxr-xr-x.  19 root root     4096 Aug 21 19:22 .
drwxr-xr-x.  19 root root     4096 Aug 21 19:22 ..
-rw-r--r--.   1 root root        0 Aug 21 19:22 .autorelabel
lrwxrwxrwx.   1 root root        7 Apr 21 00:57 bin -> usr/bin
drwxr-xr-x.   4 root root     4096 Aug 12 20:40 boot
-rw-------.   1 root root 30879744 Aug 17 21:30 core.913
drwxr-xr-x.  21 root root     4160 Aug 17 21:50 dev
drwxr-xr-x. 147 root root    12288 Aug 17 20:44 etc
drwxr-xr-x.   3 root root     4096 Jun  3 22:13 home
lrwxrwxrwx.   1 root root        7 Apr 21 00:57 lib -> usr/lib
lrwxrwxrwx.   1 root root        9 Apr 21 00:57 lib32 -> usr/lib32
lrwxrwxrwx.   1 root root        9 Apr 21 00:57 lib64 -> usr/lib64
lrwxrwxrwx.   1 root root       10 Apr 21 00:57 libx32 -> usr/libx32
drwx------.   2 root root    16384 Jun  3 22:00 lost+found
drwxr-xr-x.   2 root root     4096 Apr 21 00:57 media
drwxr-xr-x.   2 root root     4096 Apr 21 00:57 mnt
drwxr-xr-x.   2 root root     4096 Apr 21 00:57 opt
dr-xr-xr-x. 265 root root        0 Aug 17 21:50 proc
drwx------.   5 root root     4096 Aug 17 21:47 root
drwxr-xr-x.  39 root root     1060 Aug 21 19:20 run
lrwxrwxrwx.   1 root root        8 Apr 21 00:57 sbin -> usr/sbin
drwxr-xr-x.   8 root root     4096 Aug 16 21:31 snap
drwxr-xr-x.   2 root root     4096 Apr 21 00:57 srv
dr-xr-xr-x.  13 root root        0 Aug 17 21:50 sys
drwxrwxrwt.  20 root root     4096 Aug 21 19:20 tmp
drwxr-xr-x.  14 root root     4096 Apr 21 00:57 usr
drwxr-xr-x.  15 root root     4096 Aug 17 20:24 var
```

Figure 12-18. *Creating the .autorelabel file to force SELinux to relabel on reboot*

Once you have created the .autorelabel file, reboot your system. You will see your system relabel during the boot process.

```
*** Warning -- SELinux default policy relabel is required.
*** Relabeling could take a very long time, depending on file
*** system size and speed of hard drives.
[  OK  ] Started Network Manager.
[  OK  ] Reached target Network.
         Starting Network Manager Wait Online...
         Starting Hostname Service...
[  OK  ] Started Hostname Service.
         Starting Network Manager Script Dispatcher Service...
[  OK  ] Started Network Manager Script Dispatcher Service.
         Starting Network Name Resolution...
[  OK  ] Finished Network Manager Wait Online.
[  OK  ] Reached target Network is Online.
[  OK  ] Reached target Preparation for Remote File Systems.
[  OK  ] Finished Availability of block devices.
[  OK  ] Started Network Name Resolution.
[  OK  ] Reached target Host and Network Name Lookups.
libsemanage.get_home_dirs: Error while fetching users.  Returning list so far.
libsemanage.add_user: user sddm not in password file
Relabeling / /boot
9.1%
```

Figure 12-19. *SELinux relabeling system on reboot*

SELinux Enforcing (Optional)

Once your system has rebooted for the last time and you saw the relabelling appear during the reboot, you can now proceed to set SELinux to enforcing. This will ensure that all SELinux configuration is strictly adhered to. To configure Enforcing mode, either run the following command or update the /etc/selinux/config file. Reboot your system when done.

```
# sudo selinux-config-enforcing
```

```
ken@ubuntu-server:~$ sudo selinux-config-enforcing
[sudo] password for ken:
Configured enforcing mode in /etc/selinux/config for the next boot.
This can be overridden by "enforcing=0" on the kernel command line.
ken@ubuntu-server:~$ cat /etc/selinux/config
# This file controls the state of SELinux on the system.
# SELINUX= can take one of these three values:
# enforcing - SELinux security policy is enforced.
# permissive - SELinux prints warnings instead of enforcing.
# disabled - No SELinux policy is loaded.
SELINUX=enforcing
# SELINUXTYPE= can take one of these two values:
# default - equivalent to the old strict and targeted policies
# mls     - Multi-Level Security (for military and educational use)
# src     - Custom policy built from source
SELINUXTYPE=default

# SETLOCALDEFS= Check local definition changes
SETLOCALDEFS=0
```

***Figure 12-20.** Setting SELinux to enforcing in the /etc/selinux/config file*

Important   At the time of writing, SELinux in enforcing the environment used for this book kept breaking. As this use case relies on a secure environment, the use of Ubuntu may not have been the best choice. Feel free to switch to Fedora or SLES.

Set SELinux Labels

Previously in the "Configuration Files" section, a couple new directories and files were created for the web server. If the new files have not inherited the correct labels, the web server will be unable to access the files and serve the content to the users. To resolve this, we need to run the following command:

```
# sudo restorecon -Rv /var/www/html
```

Exercise

As a simple exercise, take the lessons learned from the first use case and attempt to do the following exercise.

Prerequisites

Build and prepare a Linux server of your choosing. Potentially avoid Ubuntu due to complications around SELinux, but feel free to challenge yourself if you wish.

Troubleshooting techniques are discussed in a later chapter if you run into issues. Use the troubleshooting steps as a guide if you encounter a system that will not boot.

Build a Web Server

Configure a web server that will host two different websites. The sites can be anything you wish. The use case discussed in this chapter has some examples you can use. Try to be more creative than site1 and site2.

The web server must be able to serve two different websites when someone puts the different URLs in their browser.

The following security considerations should also be taken into account:

- The local firewall must be enabled and configured.

- SELinux should be set to Enforcing mode.

Success Criteria

Your web server services should be started on boot, and users should be able to open two different websites from the same server.

Building a File Server

Another use case that does sometimes occur in the industry is that Linux systems sometimes can provide storage solutions to other systems. For this second use case, we will explore building a Linux environment that will provide storage to the web server from the previous use case.

NFS vs. Samba

In today's Linux world, there are many options available that can serve files to users. Most enterprise Linux vendors have storage solutions such as Ceph or Gluster. However, these solutions are more for enterprise solution requirements, or to provide storage on a larger scale. These solutions do require more hardware and tend to have a larger subscription cost involved.

All Linux distributions do have the ability to provide storage to other Linux or Windows systems relatively simply. It will be these methods we will explore for now.

The two main basic options that can be used are NFS and Samba. NFS traditionally was only used on Linux but now can be mounted in Windows environments. Creating an interesting conundrum on which to choose. To make the choice clear, Table 12-1 lists the differences between NFS and Samba.

Table 12-1. *NFS vs. Samba*

NFS	Samba
Traditionally used on Linux systems for Linux systems.	Commonly used to provide Linux storage to Windows systems.
Commonly used for server to server storage.	Used for end users to share files. Commonly used on Windows systems.
No support for ACL files to be transferred.	Can use ACL files.
Quicker at writing larger quantities of smaller files.	Performance is not as good with smaller files but on par with NFS for larger files.
Security can be a concern and should only be used on a secured network.	Files and directories can be locked down to specific users or groups.

File Server Configuration Overview

The following is the use case requirement for the file server.

Use Case Overview

After the introduction of the organization's new web server, it has been discovered that storage is becoming an issue. New content on the web server has given users the ability to upload files; this new functionality is vital to the organization, and as a result, it is now causing the web server to run out of disk space.

NFS Solution

To resolve this issue, the architecture team has decided that a new NFS server should be built with a large amount of storage to provide storage to web and application servers in the future.

The NFS server must have the following requirements met:

- Two exports need to be configured.

- The NFS file server should be locked down to only allow required ports.

- All other possible security measures must be taken.

- There is no need to have individual user permissions.

Linux Distribution

Due to complications with the Ubuntu web server, the organization has decided that spending some money on a Red Hat Enterprise Linux subscription is the way to go. For the new NFS server, a new RHEL server will need to be built, and a large disk should be attached.

Linux Installation and Configuration

For the new NFS server, a RHEL 9.0 server has been commissioned. This server will have the following configured:

   –   No desktop to be installed.

   –   Built using minimal packages.

   –   An administrative user will need to be created called "ken".

   –   The server must be connected to a Red Hat subscription to install packages and provide support if required.

User Account

An administrator account should always be created that is not root to configure your system. This use case is no different; this administrative account allows the organization to trace who did what in the audit logs.

To keep in this best practice configuration, a new user with root-level privileges should be created called "ken". This is done during the RHEL installation.

```
[ken@rhel9-server ~]$ id
uid=1000(ken) gid=1000(ken) groups=1000(ken),10(wheel)
```

Figure 12-21. *Details about the currently logged-in user*

From the image shown in Figure 12-21, you can see that the "ken" user is part of the wheel group, allowing this user to have enough permissions to configure the system as an administrator.

Subscribe to a Red Hat Account

From the image shown in Figure 12-22, you can see that the new RHEL "rhel9.0-server" was subscribed to the available subscription in the organization's Red Hat account.

```
[ken@rhel9-server ~]$ sudo subscription-manager register
Registering to: subscription.rhsm.redhat.com:443/subscription
Username: ▬▬▬▬▬
Password:
The system has been registered with ID: 7(▬▬▬▬▬▬▬▬▬▬▬▬▬▬▬
The registered system name is: rhel9-server.kenlab.local
[ken@rhel9-server ~]$ sudo subscription-manager attach --auto
Installed Product Current Status:
Product Name: Red Hat Enterprise Linux for x86_64
Status:       Subscribed
```

Figure 12-22. *Registering and attaching the system to a subscription with Red Hat*

NFS Server Package Installation

There are a couple packages that will need to be installed for a fully compliant and functional NFS file server.

Firewalld

The first package that needs to be installed if it is not already available is the "firewalld" package. The package can be installed on the RHEL 9.0 server using the following command:

```
# sudo dnf install firewalld -y
```

As this package was already installed by default, there is nothing further to add.

```
[ken@rhel9-server ~]$ sudo dnf install firewalld
Updating Subscription Management repositories.
Red Hat Enterprise Linux 9 for x86_64 - AppStream (RPMs)
Last metadata expiration check: 0:00:01 ago on Mon 22 Aug 2022 18:06:48 BST.
Package firewalld-1.0.0-4.el9.noarch is already installed.
Dependencies resolved.
Nothing to do.
Complete!
```

***Figure 12-23.** Firewall package installation on RHEL*

The firewall configuration can be checked by running the following command:

```
# sudo firewall-cmd --list-all
```

```
[ken@rhel9-server ~]$ sudo firewall-cmd --list-all
public (active)
  target: default
  icmp-block-inversion: no
  interfaces: enp1s0
  sources:
  services: cockpit dhcpv6-client ssh
  ports:
  protocols:
  forward: yes
  masquerade: no
  forward-ports:
  source-ports:
  icmp-blocks:
  rich rules:
```

***Figure 12-24.** Current firewall configuration*

nfs-utils

The only real package that is required to configure an NFS server is the nfs-utils package. This package can be installed using the following command:

```
# sudo dnf install nfs-utils -y
```

```
[ken@rhel9-server ~]$ sudo dnf install nfs-utils
[sudo] password for ken:
Updating Subscription Management repositories.
Last metadata expiration check: 2:59:10 ago on Mon 22 Aug 2022 18:36:38 BST.
Dependencies resolved.
================================================================================================
 Package              Architecture    Version             Repository                       Size
================================================================================================
Installing:
 nfs-utils            x86_64          1:2.5.4-10.el9      rhel-9-for-x86_64-baseos-rpms   454 k
Installing dependencies:
 gssproxy             x86_64          0.8.4-4.el9         rhel-9-for-x86_64-baseos-rpms   114 k
 keyutils             x86_64          1.6.1-4.el9         rhel-9-for-x86_64-baseos-rpms    68 k
 libev                x86_64          4.33-5.el9          rhel-9-for-x86_64-baseos-rpms    56 k
 libnfsidmap          x86_64          1:2.5.4-10.el9      rhel-9-for-x86_64-baseos-rpms    67 k
 libtirpc             x86_64          1.3.2-1.el9         rhel-9-for-x86_64-baseos-rpms    96 k
 libverto-libev       x86_64          0.3.2-3.el9         rhel-9-for-x86_64-baseos-rpms    15 k
 python3-pyyaml       x86_64          5.4.1-6.el9         rhel-9-for-x86_64-baseos-rpms   209 k
 quota                x86_64          1:4.06-6.el9        rhel-9-for-x86_64-baseos-rpms   202 k
 quota-nls            noarch          1:4.06-6.el9        rhel-9-for-x86_64-baseos-rpms    81 k
 rpcbind              x86_64          1.2.6-2.el9         rhel-9-for-x86_64-baseos-rpms    62 k
 sssd-nfs-idmap       x86_64          2.6.2-2.el9         rhel-9-for-x86_64-baseos-rpms    41 k

Transaction Summary
================================================================================================
Install  12 Packages

Total download size: 1.4 M
Installed size: 3.9 M
Is this ok [y/N]: y
Downloading Packages:
(1/12): rpcbind-1.2.6-2.el9.x86_64.rpm                        79 kB/s |  62 kB     00:00
(2/12): python3-pyyaml-5.4.1-6.el9.x86_64.rpm                230 kB/s | 209 kB     00:00
(3/12): nfs-utils-2.5.4-10.el9.x86_64.rpm                    421 kB/s | 454 kB     00:01
(4/12): quota-nls-4.06-6.el9.noarch.rpm                      240 kB/s |  81 kB     00:00
(5/12): libverto-libev-0.3.2-3.el9.x86_64.rpm                 54 kB/s |  15 kB     00:00
(6/12): sssd-nfs-idmap-2.6.2-2.el9.x86_64.rpm                132 kB/s |  41 kB     00:00
(7/12): keyutils-1.6.1-4.el9.x86_64.rpm                      173 kB/s |  68 kB     00:00
(8/12): libev-4.33-5.el9.x86_64.rpm                          108 kB/s |  56 kB     00:00
(9/12): libtirpc-1.3.2-1.el9.x86_64.rpm                      331 kB/s |  96 kB     00:00
(10/12): gssproxy-0.8.4-4.el9.x86_64.rpm                     343 kB/s | 114 kB     00:00
```

***Figure 12-25.** Reduced output of the nfs-utils package installation*

To see the status of your NFS service, run the following command:

```
# sudo systemctl status nfs
```

```
[ken@rhel9-server ~]$ sudo systemctl status nfs-server
○ nfs-server.service - NFS server and services
     Loaded: loaded (/usr/lib/systemd/system/nfs-server.service; disabled; vendor preset: disabled)
     Active: inactive (dead)
```

***Figure 12-26.** Status of the nfs service*

In Figure 12-26, you can see the nfs-server service is not currently active and not started. Do not start the service yet. This will be done shortly.

Firewall Configuration

As with the web server use, the local firewall does also need to be configured to provide access to your NFS server. The firewall configuration is vital in ensuring that only the ports required for your server are allowed. It adds that extra layer of security in case there is ever a network breach.

Firewall Status

To check what ports and services are currently configured in the local firewall, run the following command:

```
# sudo firewall-cmd --list-all
```

```
[ken@rhel9-server ~]$ sudo firewall-cmd --list-all
public (active)
  target: default
  icmp-block-inversion: no
  interfaces: enp1s0
  sources:
  services: cockpit dhcpv6-client ssh
  ports:
  protocols:
  forward: yes
  masquerade: no
  forward-ports:
  source-ports:
  icmp-blocks:
  rich rules:
```

Figure 12-27.   *Current firewall configuration*

In Figure 12-27, you can see only the dhcpv6-client and ssh services are allowed through the firewall.

Opening NFS Ports

To allow the ports for NFS, you can either enable TCP and UDP port 111 or you can use the service option. To enable the NFS service, run the following command:

```
# sudo firewall-cmd --add-service=nfs --permanent
```

```
[ken@rhel9-server ~]$ sudo firewall-cmd --add-service=nfs --permanent
[sudo] password for ken:
success
```

Figure 12-28.   *Adding the NFS service to the firewall configuration*

Reload Firewall Configuration

Do not forget to reload the firewall configuration once you are finished adding ports or services. To reload the firewall configuration, run the following command:

```
# sudo firewall-cmd --reload
```

```
[ken@rhel9-server ~]$ sudo firewall-cmd --reload
success                        _
```

Figure 12-29. *Reloading the firewall configuration*

Verify Configuration

To verify that all the ports are open, run the following command once again:

sudo firewall-cmd --list-all

```
[ken@rhel9-server ~]$ sudo firewall-cmd --list-all
public (active)
  target: default
  icmp-block-inversion: no
  interfaces: enp1s0
  sources:
  services: cockpit dhcpv6-client nfs ssh
  ports:
  protocols:
  forward: yes
  masquerade: no
  forward-ports:
  source-ports:
  icmp-blocks:
  rich rules:
```

Figure 12-30. *Updated firewall configuration*

In Figure 12-30, you can now see that the NFS service has been added to the list of services. Users should now be able to mount NFS mounts from this server.

SELinux Configuration

To comply with the organization's security requirements, SELinux should be configured for your NFS server.

SELinux Enforcing

SELinux should be configured to be in enforcing mode. If Enforcing mode is not configured, update the /etc/selinux/config file and then reboot your system when done.

sudo vim /etc/selinux/config

```
# This file controls the state of SELinux on the system.
# SELINUX= can take one of these three values:
#     enforcing - SELinux security policy is enforced.
#     permissive - SELinux prints warnings instead of enforcing.
#     disabled - No SELinux policy is loaded.
# See also:
# https://docs.fedoraproject.org/en-US/quick-docs/getting-started-with-selinux/#getting-started-with-selinux-selinux-states-and-modes
#
# NOTE: In earlier Fedora kernel builds, SELINUX=disabled would also
# fully disable SELinux during boot. If you need a system with SELinux
# fully disabled instead of SELinux running with no policy loaded, you
# need to pass selinux=0 to the kernel command line. You can use grubby
# to persistently set the bootloader to boot with selinux=0:
#
#     grubby --update-kernel ALL --args selinux=0
#
# To revert back to SELinux enabled:
#
#     grubby --update-kernel ALL --remove-args selinux
#
SELINUX=enforcing
# SELINUXTYPE= can take one of these three values:
#     targeted - Targeted processes are protected,
#     minimum - Modification of targeted policy. Only selected processes are protected.
#     mls - Multi Level Security protection.
SELINUXTYPE=targeted
```

Figure 12-31. *Setting SELinux to enforcing mode in the /etc/selinux/config file*

The SELinux boolean "http_use_nfs" will also need to be set to on if you want to use an NFS mount with your httpd server.

```
# sudo setsebool httpd_use_nfs on
```

```
[ken@rhel9-server ~]$ sudo setsebool httpd_use_nfs on
[sudo] password for ken:
[ken@rhel9-server ~]$
[ken@rhel9-server ~]$
[ken@rhel9-server ~]$ sudo getsebool -a | grep httpd_use_nfs
httpd_use_nfs --> on
```

Figure 12-32. *Setting the httpd_use_nfs SELinux boolean to on*

Disk to Share

As the main function of an NFS server is to share disk with other systems, it is important for your NFS server to have disk available to use. Dedicated disk for the NFS sharing is the better option, but for this use case, we will use the local disk of the RHEL 9.0 server.

Disk

As the local disk of the RHEL 9.0 server is going to be used, all that is required is to create a couple directories:

```
# mkdir -p /nfs_shares/site1
# mkdir -p /nfs_shares/site2
```

414

```
ken@rhel9-server ~]$ sudo mkdir -p /nfs_shares/site1
sudo] password for ken:
ken@rhel9-server ~]$ sudo mkdir -p /nfs_shares/site2
ken@rhel9-server ~]$ ls -alrt /
:otal 24
lrwxr-xr-x.    2 root root      6 Aug  9  2021 srv
.rwxrwxrwx.    1 root root      8 Aug  9  2021 sbin -> usr/sbin
lrwxr-xr-x.    2 root root      6 Aug  9  2021 opt
lrwxr-xr-x.    2 root root      6 Aug  9  2021 mnt
lrwxr-xr-x.    2 root root      6 Aug  9  2021 media
.rwxrwxrwx.    1 root root      9 Aug  9  2021 lib64 -> usr/lib64
.rwxrwxrwx.    1 root root      7 Aug  9  2021 lib -> usr/lib
.rwxrwxrwx.    1 root root      7 Aug  9  2021 bin -> usr/bin
lr-xr-xr-x.    2 root root      6 Aug  9  2021 afs
lrwxr-xr-x.   12 root root    144 Aug 12 22:26 usr
lrwxr-xr-x.    3 root root     17 Aug 12 22:29 home
lr-xr-xr-x.  201 root root      0 Aug 12 22:32 proc
lr-xr-xr-x.   13 root root      0 Aug 12 22:32 sys
lrwxr-xr-x.   19 root root   4096 Aug 12 22:32 var
lrwxr-xr-x.   21 root root   3300 Aug 12 22:32 dev
lr-xr-xr-x.    5 root root   4096 Aug 12 22:32 boot
lrwxr-xr-x.   30 root root    940 Aug 22 21:35 run
lrwxr-xr-x.   83 root root   8192 Aug 22 21:43 etc
lr-xr-x---.    2 root root    167 Aug 22 21:43 root
lrwxrwxrwt.    9 root root   4096 Aug 22 21:43 tmp
lr-xr-xr-x.   19 root root    253 Aug 22 22:02 ..
lr-xr-xr-x.   19 root root    253 Aug 22 22:02 .
lrwxr-xr-x.    4 root root     32 Aug 22 22:02 nfs_shares
ken@rhel9-server ~]$ ls -alrt /nfs_shares/
:otal 0
lrwxr-xr-x.    2 root root      6 Aug 22 22:02 site1
lr-xr-xr-x.   19 root root    253 Aug 22 22:02 ..
lrwxr-xr-x.    2 root root      6 Aug 22 22:02 site2
lrwxr-xr-x.    4 root root     32 Aug 22 22:02 .
```

Figure 12-33. *Creating directories for NFS mount points*

NFS Server Configuration

Once the directories have been created or the disks configured that will be used to share storage, the NFS configuration can be done.

Configuration File

There is only one configuration file that is normally configured on an NFS server. This is the /etc/exports file. In recent versions of RHEL, the introduction of the /etc/exports.d directory has been added so custom configuration files can be added to the directory for the NFS server to use. For this use case, we will ignore the exports.d directory.

/etc/exports

For this use case, we will add the following lines to the /etc/exports configuration:

```
/nfs_shares/site1 *(rw,sync,no_root_squash)
/nfs_shares/site2 *(rw,sync,no_root_squash)
~
```

Figure 12-34. *Creating NFS exports in the /etc/exports file*

nfs-server Service

To start using the NFS server, the nfs-server service needs to be enabled and started.

To enable the nfs-server service, run the following command:

```
# sudo systemctl enable nfs-server
```

To start the nfs-server service, run the following command:

```
# sudo systemctl start nfs-server
```

```
[ken@rhel9-server ~]$ sudo systemctl enable nfs-server
Created symlink /etc/systemd/system/multi-user.target.wants/nfs-server.service → /usr/lib/systemd/system/nfs-server.service.
[ken@rhel9-server ~]$ sudo systemctl start nfs-server


[ken@rhel9-server ~]$ sudo systemctl status nfs-server
● nfs-server.service - NFS server and services
     Loaded: loaded (/usr/lib/systemd/system/nfs-server.service; enabled; vendor preset: disabled)
     Active: active (exited) since Mon 2022-08-22 22:18:18 BST; 35s ago
    Process: 25668 ExecStartPre=/usr/sbin/exportfs -r (code=exited, status=0/SUCCESS)
    Process: 25669 ExecStart=/usr/sbin/rpc.nfsd (code=exited, status=0/SUCCESS)
    Process: 25689 ExecStart=/bin/sh -c if systemctl -q is-active gssproxy; then systemctl reload gssproxy ; fi (code=exited, status=0/SUCCESS)
   Main PID: 25689 (code=exited, status=0/SUCCESS)
        CPU: 57ms
```

Figure 12-35. *The status of the nfs.server*

Validate Configuration

To confirm that your NFS server configuration is correct, run the following command:

```
# sudo exportfs -rv
```

The output of the command should be similar to that shown in Figure 12-36. This will indicate what directories are being exported by the NFS server.

```
[ken@rhel9-server ~]$ sudo exportfs -rv
exporting *:/nfs_shares/site2
exporting *:/nfs_shares/site1
```

Figure 12-36. *Listing NFS exports after NFS service restart*

Test NFS Mounts

To test that your NFS server is working, attempt to mount the disk on your web server.

NFS Server

On your NFS server, get the IP address of your NFS server so that you can use the IP address to mount the NFS shares.

```
# ip a
```

```
[ken@rhel9-server ~]$ ip a
1: lo: <LOOPBACK,UP,LOWER_UP> mtu 65536 qdisc noqueue state UNKNOWN group default qlen 1000
    link/loopback 00:00:00:00:00:00 brd 00:00:00:00:00:00
    inet 127.0.0.1/8 scope host lo
       valid_lft forever preferred_lft forever
    inet6 ::1/128 scope host
       valid_lft forever preferred_lft forever
2: enp1s0: <BROADCAST,MULTICAST,UP,LOWER_UP> mtu 1500 qdisc fq_codel state UP group default qlen 1000
    link/ether 52:54:00:16:0d:64 brd ff:ff:ff:ff:ff:ff
    inet 192.168.122.237/24 brd 192.168.122.255 scope global dynamic noprefixroute enp1s0
       valid_lft 3354sec preferred_lft 3354sec
    inet6 fe80::5054:ff:fe16:d64/64 scope link noprefixroute
       valid_lft forever preferred_lft forever
```

Figure 12-37. *Listing all the network interfaces and their IP addressing*

Web Server

On your web server, there are a few things that need to be done. First, you need to install the nfs-common package and then attempt to mount an NFS share.

To install the required packages, run the following command:

```
# sudo apt install nfs-common
```

```
ken@ubuntu-server:~$ sudo apt install nfs-common
Reading package lists... Done
Building dependency tree... Done
Reading state information... Done
The following packages were automatically installed and are no longer required:
  pastebinit python3-newt run-one
Use 'sudo apt autoremove' to remove them.
The following additional packages will be installed:
  keyutils rpcbind
Suggested packages:
  watchdog
The following NEW packages will be installed:
  keyutils nfs-common rpcbind
0 upgraded, 3 newly installed, 0 to remove and 118 not upgraded.
Need to get 338 kB of archives.
After this operation, 1,229 kB of additional disk space will be used.
```

Figure 12-38. *nfs-common package installation on the Ubuntu web server*

Provided the packages from the output shown in Figure 12-38 are installed on your web server, you will be able to mount the NFS export on your web server.

To test, we will only attempt to mount to the /mnt location:

```
# sudo mount.nfs 192.168.122.237:/nfs_shares/site1 /mnt
```

Provided that all the configuration has been done correctly and you do not have a security issue, the previous command should complete without error. To confirm that your disk has mounted, run the command and checks shown in Figure 12-39.

```
ken@ubuntu-server:~$ sudo mount 192.168.122.237:/nfs_shares/site1 /mnt
ken@ubuntu-server:~$ df -h
Filesystem                        Size  Used Avail Use% Mounted on
tmpfs                             393M  1.3M  392M   1% /run
/dev/mapper/ubuntu--vg-ubuntu--lv 9.8G  6.6G  2.7G  72% /
tmpfs                             2.0G     0  2.0G   0% /dev/shm
tmpfs                             5.0M  4.0K  5.0M   1% /run/lock
/dev/sda2                         1.8G  256M  1.4G  16% /boot
tmpfs                             393M   68K  393M   1% /run/user/1000
192.168.122.237:/nfs_shares/site1  17G  1.1G   16G   7% /mnt
```

Figure 12-39. *Disks mounted on the Ubuntu web server*

In Figure 12-39, you can see that the /mnt directory has been successfully mounted to the NFS share on the NFS server.

Exercise

To test your new NFS server skills, attempt to complete the following exercise.

Prerequisites

Build and prepare a RHEL 9.0 server with an administrator user that can be used for system configuration.

NFS Server

On your new RHEL 9.0 server, configure the following:

- NFS exports site1 and site2.

- The local firewall must be enabled and configured.

- SELinux should be set to Enforcing mode.

Web Server

On the web server from the previous exercise, mount the new NFS exports to host the two different websites' content, thus allowing users to add content without filling the local disk of the web server.

Success Criteria

Your web server services should be started, and the NFS exports should be mounted in the locations where the web server content is stored.

Tip   This exercise, and chapter, has purposely left out configuration to some required steps. If you have any major problems, set SELinux to permissive and try again. Otherwise, read the "SELinux Configuration" chapter and the troubleshooting chapter to further assist.

Summary

In this chapter, you were introduced to the following:

- Two use cases that a Linux server can be used for

- How a Linux server can be configured as a web server

- How a Linux server can be configured as a file server

- What security considerations should be taken when building Linux systems

CHAPTER 13

Security

As an enterprise Linux administrator, security is of the utmost importance. System or security breaches can spell financial doom for any organization with customer data or financial services.

In this chapter, we will look at the basic security requirements you as an enterprise Linux administrator should know. We will start by looking at the local firewall and SELinux configuration; we will explore what they are and how they should be configured.

The next vital bit of knowledge this chapter looks to impart is around system and Linux hardening; we will look at hardening standards, how systems are checked, what tools are used, and finally how remediation can be done for vulnerable systems.

The last major section this chapter will tackle will be encryption. We will explore what encryption is and how it is configured both at a system and a network level.

Firewall

The Linux firewall is the Netfilter toolset that allows access to the network stack at the Linux kernel level.

To configure the firewall and in turn the network stack in the Linux kernel, a ruleset tool is required. By default, all enterprise Linux systems have a firewall ruleset tool installed (with the exception of some cloud image versions, due to being cutdown versions).

The ruleset tools available are either iptables or firewalld. Both options are very feature rich and can be used to secure your Linux system at the network layer.

© Kenneth Hitchcock 2023
K. Hitchcock, *The Enterprise Linux Administrator*, https://doi.org/10.1007/978-1-4842-8801-6_13

Command-Line Configuration

To configure these ruleset tools, you can use either the command-line utilities, desktop, or web console. As mentioned many times before, the command line will most likely be the only method available to you, and so it is important to understand the command-line utilities before looking for any graphical alternatives.

Iptables

In previous Linux distros and in a few that have decided to not move forward with systemd still use the firewall ruleset configuration tool known as iptables. Iptables can get complex, but if you have a basic understanding and know how to check if a rule has been enabled, you are well on your way.

For this book, we will mainly focus on Firewalld, but just for completeness, we will briefly look at iptables.

In the following is a breakdown of the basic iptables commands. The two important ones to take note of is how to see what ports are open and how to add a new rule.

Hint   While learning, just flush out your ruleset and test adding and testing rules one by one. A good example that should not cause you too much pain is to deploy a web server on your Linux system and try to open port 80.

Table 13-1 lists all the basic iptables commands that can be used.

Table 13-1. *Basic iptables commands*

LVM command	Description
`iptables -L -n`	List all rules in all chains in numerical format.
`iptables --help`	Help on what parameters are available.
`iptables -A INPUT -p tcp --dport 22 -j ACCEPT`	Example of adding TCP port 22.
`iptables -F`	Flush all rules from the iptable configuration.
`iptables-save > /etc/iptables/rules.v4`	Save iptables configuration on Debian/Ubuntu.
`iptables-save > /etc/sysconfig/iptables`	Save iptables configuration on RHEL.

Firewalld

If you are using an enterprise Linux distribution, chances are you most likely will be using systemd. With system, you will be using firewalld as the ruleset configuration tool. You also have noticed we have used it a fair bit already in this book and in particular in the previous chapter.

Firewalld was designed to be simpler and easier to use than iptables. Firewalld like iptables has a few commands all Linux system administrators should know. The following are the basics you will need to know to get started. From these commands, you can later expand into more advanced configuration.

Service

Before your firewall can be configured, you will need to ensure that it has been installed and that the firewalld service has been started.

To check that your firewall has been installed, you can run the following command:

```
# sudo rpm -qa | grep firewall
```

```
[ken@rhel9-server ~]$ sudo rpm -qa | grep firewall
[sudo] password for ken:
firewalld-filesystem-1.0.0-4.el9.noarch
python3-firewall-1.0.0-4.el9.noarch
firewalld-1.0.0-4.el9.noarch
```

Figure 13-1. *Determining the package that installs the firewall utility*

From the rpm query output shown in Figure 13-1, you will notice that there are a couple firewalld packages installed. There is no need to install anything. If your output is not similar to Figure 13-1, you may need to install the firewalld packages, which can be done with the following command:

```
# sudo dnf install firewalld -y
```

Status

Assuming firewalld has been installed. It is worth always checking that the firewalld service has been started and what configuration has been performed on the firewall since the last reload or restart.

To check the firewalld service, run the following command:

```
# sudo systemctl status firewalld
```

```
firewalld-1.0.0-4.el9.noarch
[ken@rhel9-server ~]$ sudo systemctl status firewalld
● firewalld.service - firewalld - dynamic firewall daemon
    Loaded: loaded (/usr/lib/systemd/system/firewalld.service; enabled; vendor preset: enabled)
    Active: active (running) since Fri 2022-08-12 22:32:27 BST; 1 week 4 days ago
      Docs: man:firewalld(1)
  Main PID: 721 (firewalld)
     Tasks: 4 (limit: 23572)
    Memory: 40.0M
       CPU: 2.959s
    CGroup: /system.slice/firewalld.service
            └─721 /usr/bin/python3 -s /usr/sbin/firewalld --nofork --nopid

Aug 12 22:32:26 localhost systemd[1]: Starting firewalld - dynamic firewall daemon...
Aug 12 22:32:27 localhost systemd[1]: Started firewalld - dynamic firewall daemon.
```

Figure 13-2. *Firewalld service has been started and is currently active*

To check what configuration has been applied to the firewall since the last reload or restart, we run the following command:

```
# sudo firewall-cmd --list-all
```

```
[ken@rhel9-server ~]$ sudo firewall-cmd --list-all
public (active)
  target: default
  icmp-block-inversion: no
  interfaces: enp1s0
  sources:
  services: cockpit dhcpv6-client nfs samba ssh
  ports:
  protocols:
  forward: yes
  masquerade: no
  forward-ports:
  source-ports:
  icmp-blocks:
  rich rules:          _
```

Figure 13-3. *Firewall current configuration*

In Figure 13-3, you will notice that there are a few services that have been added. As an enterprise Linux administrator, you need to ensure only the minimal ports or services are configured on your systems.

Adding Ports and Services

With the status of your firewall determined, you are now in a position to add ports and services.

To add a simple port like TCP port 111, you can use the following command:

```
# sudo firewall-cmd --add-port=111/tcp --permanent
```

```
[ken@rhel9-server ~]$ sudo firewall-cmd --add-port=111/tcp --permanent
success
[ken@rhel9-server ~]$ sudo firewall-cmd --list-all
public (active)
  target: default
  icmp-block-inversion: no
  interfaces: enp1s0
  sources:
  services: cockpit dhcpv6-client nfs samba ssh
  ports:
  protocols:
  forward: yes
  masquerade: no
  forward-ports:
  source-ports:
  icmp-blocks:
  rich rules:
```

Figure 13-4. *Firewall configuration after adding TCP port 111 without reloading*

Did you notice in the output shown in Figure 13-4 the new port did not appear in the list of ports when the "firewall-cmd --list-all" command was run?

If you do not reload the firewall after adding configuration, the new configuration will not be applied until the firewalld service is restarted or the system is rebooted.

If we reload the firewall configuration with the following command, you will now notice the port has appeared:

```
# sudo firewall-cmd --reload
```

```
[ken@rhel9-server ~]$ sudo firewall-cmd --list-all
public (active)
  target: default
  icmp-block-inversion: no
  interfaces: enp1s0
  sources:
  services: cockpit dhcpv6-client nfs samba ssh
  ports: 111/tcp 53/tcp
  protocols:
  forward: yes
  masquerade: no
  forward-ports:
  source-ports:
  icmp-blocks:
  rich rules:
```

Figure 13-5. *Firewall configuration after reloading firewall configuration*

Removing Ports and Services

Looking at the image shown in Figure 13-5, you can see that another port, 53/TCP, has found its way in the firewall configuration. Obviously someone added the port and did not reload. As we reloaded the firewall configuration, the new port has now appeared.

This can be a problem if you are not paying attention and accidentally add unwanted access to your system. If this happens, you need to know how to remove ports and services. The following command will remove the unwanted TCP port 53:

```
# sudo firewall-cmd --remove-port=53/tcp --permanent
```

```
[ken@rhel9-server ~]$ sudo firewall-cmd --remove-port=53/tcp --permanent
success
[ken@rhel9-server ~]$ sudo firewall-cmd --reload
success
[ken@rhel9-server ~]$ sudo firewall-cmd --list-all
public (active)
  target: default
  icmp-block-inversion: no
  interfaces: enp1s0
  sources:
  services: cockpit dhcpv6-client nfs samba ssh
  ports: 111/tcp
  protocols:
  forward: yes
  masquerade: no
  forward-ports:
  source-ports:
  icmp-blocks:
  rich rules:
```

Figure 13-6. *Firewall configuration after removing ports no longer required*

Important   Always remember to reload the firewall when making changes. This will uncover any issues before they can become a bigger problem later.

Cheatsheet

Table 13-2 lists some basic firewall-cmd commands to remember.

Table 13-2. *Simple firewall-cmd cheat sheet*

LVM command	Description
`firewall-cmd --list-all`	Lists all rules currently configured.
`firewall-cmd --add-port=80/ tcp -permanent`	Opens TCP port 80.
`firewall-cmd --remove-port=80/ tcp -permanent`	Removes TCP port 80.
`firewall-cmd --add-service= samba -permanent`	Opens the ports required for Samba by referencing the service name.
`firewall-cmd --remove- service=samba -permanent`	Removes the samba service and the ports associated with it.
`firewall-cmd -help`	Help.
`firewall-cmd -reload`	Reload firewall to enable the new rules.

Web UI Configuration

Another quick way to configure your local firewall is through the web console, also known as Cockpit. If you cast your mind back to Chapter 5, we discussed the installation and usage of Cockpit. If you have forgotten or skipped the chapter, it is advisable to give it another quick read.

Using Cockpit

To configure your local firewall using Cockpit, first open a web browser and navigate to the following URL. Adjust the ip address to match your system:

`https://192.168.122.237:9090/network`

Log in with a root level account to be able to update the firewall configuration.

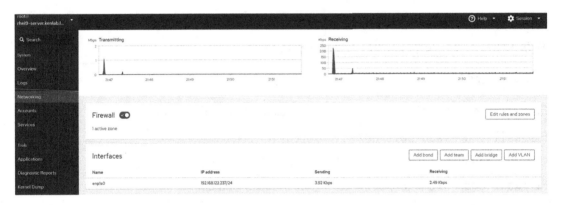

Figure 13-7. *Firewall management in the Cockpit web console*

In the image shown in Figure 13-7, you can see that the Network menu has been clicked on the left. The firewall has been enabled and is running. This can be seen with the "Firewall" radio button being turned on.

Figure 13-8. *Firewall status in the Cockpit web console*

To add or remove ports and services from the firewall in the web console, click the "Edit rules and zones" button.

> Edit rules and zones

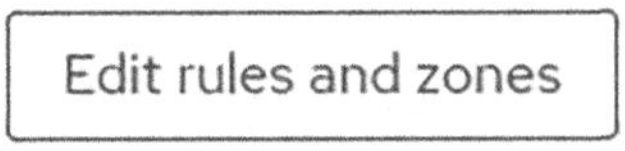

Figure 13-9. *Firewall editing can be done using the Edit rules and zones button*

This will open the main page that can be used to add or remove services.

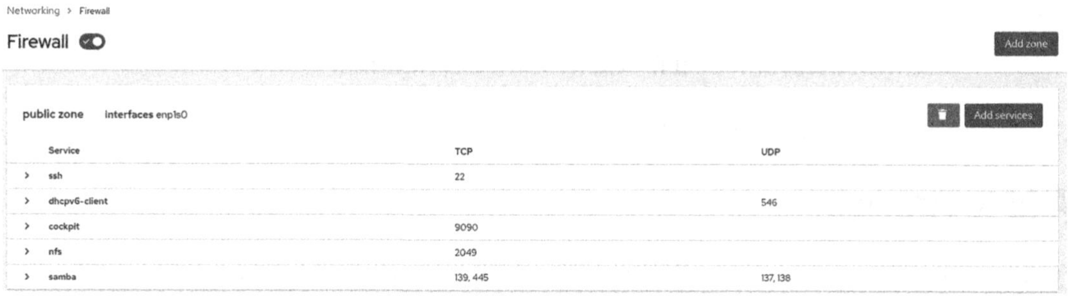

Figure 13-10. *Firewall rules list in the Cockpit web console*

To add a service, click the "Add services" button. When the new screen opens, add the custom port or service you want and click the "Add service" button.

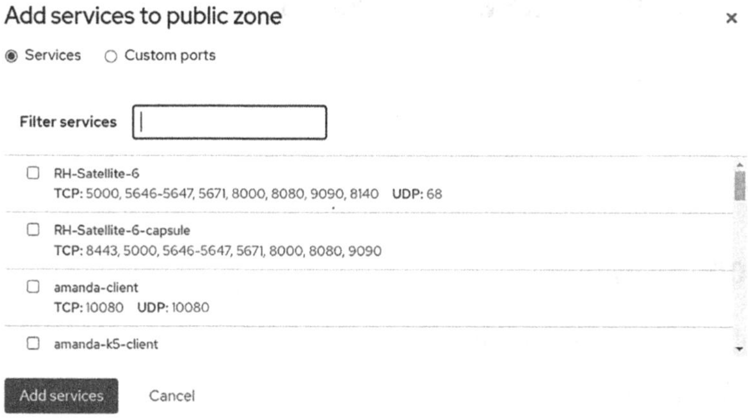

Figure 13-11. *Firewall services list when adding a firewall rule*

Exercise

Being familiar with the Linux firewall ruleset tools is vital for all enterprise Linux administrators, and to test what you now have learned, run through the following quick exercises to test your knowledge retention.

Firewall Status

Check the following on your RHEL server:

- Confirm that your local firewalld service is running.

- Confirm only required ports are open.

Add to Firewall

Add the following to your firewall. Once added, confirm the ports or services are actually being enforced:

- TCP and UDP ports 53

- Samba service

Learning More About Firewall Services

See ports that the following services use:

- ssh

- Samba service

Remove from Firewall

Remove the following to your firewall:

- TCP and UDP ports 53

- Samba service

SELinux

Another measure of security used on most enterprise Linux distributions is SELinux, originally conceptualized and worked on by the United States National Security Agency.

To explain SELinux in a single sentence, it would be that SELinux is a Linux kernel security module that allows access to parts of the Linux operating system.

A longer explanation in the form of an analogy is if you imagine your Linux system being a secure building. The outside fencing, walls, doors, and windows act as your firewall. The inside rooms, doors, cupboards, and general facilities are governed by the on-duty security personnel. It is the job of the security personnel to check who has access to what room and what facilities. The security team would in this case be acting as SELinux.

Just as you need to understand the basics of your Linux firewall, you too need to understand the basics of SELinux. For now, all you need to know is how to enable, disable, and restore basic configuration. The more complicated configuration will come with experience.

SELinux Modes

Table 13-3 lists the three SELinux modes.

Table 13-3. *SELinux modes*

Mode	Description
Disabled	SELinux is disabled.
Permissive	Logs violations to SELinux but still allows the action to continue.
Enforcing	Enforces all SELinux violations.

Command-Line Configuration

Being familiar with SELinux configuration through the command line is vital, largely due to the fact that you won't have access to anything in most circumstances.

SELinux Mode

To set the different SELinux modes, you will need to edit one important file:

```
# /etc/selinux/config
```

```
# This file controls the state of SELinux on the system.
# SELINUX= can take one of these three values:
#     enforcing - SELinux security policy is enforced.
#     permissive - SELinux prints warnings instead of enforcing.
#     disabled - No SELinux policy is loaded.
# See also:
# https://docs.fedoraproject.org/en-US/quick-docs/getting-started-with-selinux/#getting-started-with-selinux-selinux-states-and-modes
#
# NOTE: In earlier Fedora kernel builds, SELINUX=disabled would also
# fully disable SELinux during boot. If you need a system with SELinux
# fully disabled instead of SELinux running with no policy loaded, you
# need to pass selinux=0 to the kernel command line. You can use grubby
# to persistently set the bootloader to boot with selinux=0:
#
#     grubby --update-kernel ALL --args selinux=0
#
# To revert back to SELinux enabled:
#
#     grubby --update-kernel ALL --remove-args selinux
#
SELINUX=enforcing
# SELINUXTYPE= can take one of these three values:
#     targeted - Targeted processes are protected,
#     minimum - Modification of targeted policy. Only selected processes are protected.
#     mls - Multi Level Security protection.
SELINUXTYPE=targeted
```

Figure 13-12.   *The contents of the /etc/selinux/config file*

There are two parameters in this file that can be changed.

SELINUX

The SELINUX parameter is used to change the SELinux modes. Always have when possible SELinux in Enforcing mode.

SELINUXTYPE

The SELINUXTYPE parameter should be left to targeted and only changed if absolutely required.

SELinux Commands

There are a few commands that can help with quick SELinux information, configuration, and status. These commands are typically used to quickly identify the state of SELinux or to set SELinux to permissive mode for testing.

getenforce

getenforce will output the current applied configuration for SELinux.

```
[ken@rhel9-server ~]$ getenforce
Enforcing
```

Figure 13-13.   *The output of the getenforce command*

setenforce

If you wanted to set SELinux to a different mode to test a configuration, you can use the setenforce command.

```
[ken@rhel9-server ~]$ sudo setenforce 0
[ken@rhel9-server ~]$ getenforce
Permissive
```

Figure 13-14. *The setting of SELinux to permissive mode temporarily*

Figure 13-14 shows that SELinux is now running in permissive mode due to the "setenforce 0" command being run. If the system is rebooted, the SELinux mode will revert to the configuration in the /etc/selinux/config file.

setenforce only supports two parameters: 1 and 0.

```
usage:  setenforce [ Enforcing | Permissive | 1 | 0 ]
```

Figure 13-15. *The setenforce command only supports parameters 1 and 0*

Listing SELinux Labels

ls -alZ

```
[ken@rhel9-server ~]$ ls -alZ
total 24
drwx------. 2 ken  ken  unconfined_u:object_r:user_home_dir_t:s0  115 Aug 28 15:57 .
drwxr-xr-x. 3 root root system_u:object_r:home_root_t:s0          17 Aug 12 22:29 ..
-rw-------. 1 ken  ken  unconfined_u:object_r:user_home_t:s0     2034 Aug 22 22:40 .bash_history
-rw-r--r--. 1 ken  ken  unconfined_u:object_r:user_home_t:s0       18 Nov  5  2021 .bash_logout
-rw-r--r--. 1 ken  ken  unconfined_u:object_r:user_home_t:s0      141 Nov  5  2021 .bash_profile
-rw-r--r--. 1 ken  ken  unconfined_u:object_r:user_home_t:s0      492 Nov  5  2021 .bashrc
-rw-------. 1 ken  ken  unconfined_u:object_r:user_home_t:s0       37 Aug 24 21:45 .lesshst
-rw-------. 1 ken  ken  unconfined_u:object_r:user_home_t:s0     1877 Aug 28 15:57 .viminfo
```

Figure 13-16. *Command to view the SELinux labels assigned to files and directories*

SELinux Context Labels

It was mentioned earlier that SELinux labels can be listed in a directory listing. As SELinux needs to understand what files and directories are used for, there is a labeling mechanism that SELinux uses. These labels are then associated with users and processes. It is these labels that are listed with the directory listing.

Listing Context Labels

As an example, the httpd or Apache process would only be allowed to access the files and directories that have the SELinux context labels configured for it.

In the image shown in Figure 13-17, you will see that the /var/www/html files are configured with an http_sys_content_t label. Without this label set on the directories or files. The web server will not be allowed to serve the content. Users will be denied access.

```
[ken@rhel9-server ~]$ ls -alZ /var/www/html/
total 0
drwxr-xr-x. 2 root root system_u:object_r:httpd_sys_content_t:s0  6 Mar 21 15:47 .
drwxr-xr-x. 4 root root system_u:object_r:httpd_sys_content_t:s0 33 Aug 28 16:09 ..
```

***Figure 13-17.** The current SELinux context labels*

Where the labelling becomes very important is when you want to adjust where content is stored. If you do not add the correct labels, the process or application that wishes to use the content will be blocked by SELinux.

Setting Context Labels

With the previous example, we mentioned that content would be blocked if SELinux labels are not set correctly. To prevent SELinux blocking content, you can set SELinux labels on new directories and files.

Taking the previous example of the web server configuration, if the web server for some reason needed to host its content in a different location than the default /var/www/html directory, new context labels would need to be applied as you can see in Figure 13-18.

```
[ken@rhel9-server ~]$ ls -alZ /webserver/
total 0
drwxr-xr-x.  4 root root unconfined_u:object_r:default_t:s0  32 Aug 28 16:28 .
dr-xr-xr-x. 20 root root system_u:object_r:root_t:s0        270 Aug 28 16:27 ..
drwxr-xr-x.  2 root root unconfined_u:object_r:default_t:s0   6 Aug 28 16:28 site1
drwxr-xr-x.  2 root root unconfined_u:object_r:default_t:s0   6 Aug 28 16:28 site2
```

***Figure 13-18.** SELinux context labels for the /webserver directory*

With this configuration, the users would not be able to access the websites.

To resolve the new directory configuration issue for the Apache web server, you can do either of the following.

chcon

Chcon allows you to set a SELinux context label on a file or directory. The command shown in Figure 13-19 will change the new directory, and all child directories including their files to have the httpd_sys_content_t SELinux label:

```
# sudo chcon -R -t httpd_sys_content_t /webserver
```

```
[ken@rhel9-server ~]$ sudo chcon -R -t httpd_sys_content_t /webserver
[sudo] password for ken:
[ken@rhel9-server ~]$ ls -alZ /webserver/
total 0
drwxr-xr-x.  4 root root unconfined_u:object_r:httpd_sys_content_t:s0  32 Aug 28 16:28 .
dr-xr-xr-x. 20 root root system_u:object_r:root_t:s0                  270 Aug 28 16:27 ..
drwxr-xr-x.  2 root root unconfined_u:object_r:httpd_sys_content_t:s0   6 Aug 28 16:28 site1
drwxr-xr-x.  2 root root unconfined_u:object_r:httpd_sys_content_t:s0   6 Aug 28 16:28 site2
```

Figure 13-19. *Updated SELinux context labels now applied*

In Figure 13-19, you can see that the command completes silently. The ls -alZ command, however, shows the labels have now changed to the correct label. This configuration would now allow users to access the content.

semanage

An alternative to changing the files or directory SELinux label is to add an entry to SELinux configuration that adds SELinux mappings to the directory. This where you could use the semanage command.

```
[ken@rhel9-server ~]$ sudo semanage fcontext -at httpd_sys_content_t "/webserver(/.*)?"
[ken@rhel9-server ~]$
[ken@rhel9-server ~]$
[ken@rhel9-server ~]$ sudo semanage fcontext -l | grep httpd_sys_content
/etc/htdig(/.*)?                          all files      system_u:object_r:httpd_sys_content_t:s0
/srv/([^/]*/)?www(/.*)?                   all files      system_u:object_r:httpd_sys_content_t:s0
/srv/gallery2(/.*)?                       all files      system_u:object_r:httpd_sys_content_t:s0
/usr/share/doc/ghc/html(/.*)?             all files      system_u:object_r:httpd_sys_content_t:s0
/usr/share/drupal.*                       all files      system_u:object_r:httpd_sys_content_t:s0
/usr/share/glpi(/.*)?                     all files      system_u:object_r:httpd_sys_content_t:s0
/usr/share/htdig(/.*)?                    all files      system_u:object_r:httpd_sys_content_t:s0
/usr/share/icecast(/.*)?                  all files      system_u:object_r:httpd_sys_content_t:s0
/usr/share/nginx/html(/.*)?               all files      system_u:object_r:httpd_sys_content_t:s0
/usr/share/ntop/html(/.*)?                all files      system_u:object_r:httpd_sys_content_t:s0
/usr/share/openca/htdocs(/.*)?            all files      system_u:object_r:httpd_sys_content_t:s0
/usr/share/selinux-policy[^/]*/html(/.*)? all files      system_u:object_r:httpd_sys_content_t:s0
/usr/share/z-push(/.*)?                   all files      system_u:object_r:httpd_sys_content_t:s0
/var/lib/cacti/rra(/.*)?                  all files      system_u:object_r:httpd_sys_content_t:s0
/var/lib/htdig(/.*)?                      all files      system_u:object_r:httpd_sys_content_t:s0
/var/lib/trac(/.*)?                       all files      system_u:object_r:httpd_sys_content_t:s0
/var/www(/.*)?                            all files      system_u:object_r:httpd_sys_content_t:s0
/var/www/icons(/.*)?                      all files      system_u:object_r:httpd_sys_content_t:s0
/var/www/svn/conf(/.*)?                   all files      system_u:object_r:httpd_sys_content_t:s0
/webserver(/.*)?                          all files      system_u:object_r:httpd_sys_content_t:s0
```

Figure 13-20. *Setting new SELinux context labels to new directories*

In Figure 13-20, the following command was run to map the httpd_sys_content SELinux label to the /webserver directory:

```
# sudo semanage fcontext -t httpd_sys_content_t "/webserver(/.*)?"
```

To list all the SELinux label mappings, you can run the following command:

```
# sudo semanage fcontext --list
```

To filter the list to only httpd_sys_content labelled directories, run the following command:

```
# sudo semanage fcontext --list |  grep httpd_sys_content
```

SELinux Booleans

File and directory protection is one form of SELinux protection. Another is the ability to restrict processes and some of their functionality. For this, there are SELinux boolean values that can be set or unset.

getsebool

To list all the SELinux boolean values that are available, run the following command:

```
# sudo getsebool -a
```

```
[ken@rhel9-server ~]$ sudo getsebool -a
abrt_anon_write --> off
abrt_handle_event --> off
abrt_upload_watch_anon_write --> on
antivirus_can_scan_system --> off
antivirus_use_jit --> off
auditadm_exec_content --> on
authlogin_nsswitch_use_ldap --> off
authlogin_radius --> off
authlogin_yubikey --> off
awstats_purge_apache_log_files --> off
boinc_execmem --> on
cdrecord_read_content --> off
cluster_can_network_connect --> off
cluster_manage_all_files --> off
cluster_use_execmem --> off
```

Figure 13-21. *Reduced output of the getsebool -a command*

The list has over three hundred entries; for this reason, the image has been cropped to only list the first few.

setsebool

To set a value to a boolean list in the getsebool command, you can use the setsebool command. With the previous image, there was an entry called antivirus_can_scan_ system that was set to off. If you needed your antivirus system to scan your environment, this entry would need to be set to on. The following command would do this for you:

```
# sudo setsebool antivirus_can_scan_system on
```

```
[ken@rhel9-server ~]$ sudo setsebool antivirus_can_scan_system on
[ken@rhel9-server ~]$ sudo getsebool -a | grep antivirus_can
antivirus_can_scan_system --> on
```

Figure 13-22. *Using the setsebool command to set a SELinux boolean value*

In Figure 13-22, you can see that the setsebool command completes silently. To check if the value has been changed for the antivirus_can_scan_system entry, run the getsebool command again but grep for the antivirus entry to reduce your output.

SELinux Debugging

When SELinux has not been configured correctly, troubleshooting the cause can be tricky if you do not know where to look.

Journalctl

```
AnalyzeThread.run(): Cancel pending alarm
failed to retrieve rpm info for /webserver2
SELinux is preventing /usr/sbin/httpd from read access on the directory webserver2. For complete
SELinux is preventing /usr/sbin/httpd from read access on the directory webserver2.

*****  Plugin catchall_labels (83.8 confidence) suggests   ********************

If you want to allow httpd to have read access on the webserver2 directory
Then you need to change the label on webserver2
Do
# semanage fcontext -a -t FILE_TYPE 'webserver2'
where FILE_TYPE is one of the following: NetworkManager_unit_file_t, abrt_retrace_spool_t, abrt_u
Then execute:
restorecon -v 'webserver2'


*****  Plugin catchall (17.1 confidence) suggests   ***************************

If you believe that httpd should be allowed read access on the webserver2 directory by default.
Then you should report this as a bug.
You can generate a local policy module to allow this access.
Do
allow this access for now by executing:
# ausearch -c 'httpd' --raw | audit2allow -M my-httpd
# semodule -X 300 -i my-httpd.pp
```

Figure 13-23. *Command used to troubleshoot SELinux issues*

```
# sudo journalctl -t setroubleshoot
```

Below the preceding journalctl command is the output of the journalctl command indicating that there are SELinux issues. The command output is generally quite useful in that it will suggest possible fixes to the issue. In this case, the problem was that the web server was improperly configured with a new directory that would serve website content.

Ausearch

Another command that can be run to show SELinux denials is the following ausearch command:

```
# sudo ausearch -m AVC,USER_AVC -ts recent
```

```
[ken@rhel9-server ~]$ sudo ausearch -m AVC,USER_AVC -ts recent
[sudo] password for ken:
----
time->Sun Aug 28 22:08:02 2022
type=PROCTITLE msg=audit(1661720882.078:5362): proctitle=2F7573722F7362696E2F6874747064002D44464F524547524F554E44
type=SYSCALL msg=audit(1661720882.078:5362): arch=c000003e syscall=257 success=no exit=-13 a0=ffffff9c a1=7f6414004978
=48 tty=(none) ses=4294967295 comm="httpd" exe="/usr/sbin/httpd" subj=system_u:system_r:httpd_t:s0 key=(null)
type=AVC msg=audit(1661720882.078:5362): avc:  denied  { read } for  pid=46332 comm="httpd" name="webserver2" dev="dm-0
----
time->Sun Aug 28 22:08:04 2022
type=PROCTITLE msg=audit(1661720884.090:5364): proctitle=2F7573722F7362696E2F6874747064002D44464F524547524F554E44
type=SYSCALL msg=audit(1661720884.090:5364): arch=c000003e syscall=257 success=no exit=-13 a0=ffffff9c a1=7f64140089b0
=48 tty=(none) ses=4294967295 comm="httpd" exe="/usr/sbin/httpd" subj=system_u:system_r:httpd_t:s0 key=(null)
type=AVC msg=audit(1661720884.090:5364): avc:  denied  { read } for  pid=46332 comm="httpd" name="webserver2" dev="dm-0
```

Figure 13-24. *Output from the ausearch command*

/var/log/messages

Instead, another option would be to look at the /var/log/messages file. This should give you a better idea of what is going wrong.

```
Aug 28 22:07:55 rhel9-server systemd[1]: Stopped The Apache HTTP Server.
Aug 28 22:07:55 rhel9-server systemd[1]: Starting The Apache HTTP Server...
Aug 28 22:07:55 rhel9-server systemd[1]: Started The Apache HTTP Server.
Aug 28 22:07:55 rhel9-server httpd[46330]: Server configured, listening on: port 80
Aug 28 22:08:02 rhel9-server setroubleshoot[29232]: failed to retrieve rpm info for /webserver2
Aug 28 22:08:02 rhel9-server systemd[1]: Created slice Slice /system/dbus-:1.2-org.fedoraproject.SetroubleshootPrivileged.
Aug 28 22:08:02 rhel9-server systemd[1]: Started dbus-:1.2-org.fedoraproject.SetroubleshootPrivileged@0.service.
Aug 28 22:08:04 rhel9-server setroubleshoot[29232]: SELinux is preventing /usr/sbin/httpd from read access on the directory webserver2.
Aug 28 22:08:04 rhel9-server setroubleshoot[29232]: SELinux is preventing /usr/sbin/httpd from read access on the directory webserver2.#
nt to allow httpd to have read access on the webserver2 directory#012Then you need to change the label on webserver2#012Do#012# semanage
 file t, abrt retrace spool t, abrt unit file t, accountsd unit file t, alsa unit file t, amanda unit file t, antivirus unit file t, apc
```

Figure 13-25. *The /var/log/message file*

From Figure 13-25, you can see that the /var/log/messages file is reporting that there is a problem with the httpd process reading the webserver2 directory.

Cheatsheet

Table 13-4 lists a few basic commands to remember for SELinux configuration.

Table 13-4. *SELinux cheatsheet*

LVM command	Description
Getenforce	Displays current SELinux state.
setenforce 0	Temporarily disables SELinux.
setenforce 1	Temporarily enables SELinux.
/etc/selinux/config	Configures permanent state of SELinux.
semanage fcontext -t <type> "/<directory>(/.*)?"	Sets SELinux directory mapping.
chcon -t label <file or dir>	Sets the SELinux label to a file or directory.
journalctl -t setroubleshoot	Output any SELinux issues on the system.
restorecon -Rvv /path/to/file	Restores the SELinux configuration set by current labels on the directory.

Exercise

To understand more about SELinux, run through the following exercise.

Setting SELinux Modes

Set SELinux to permissive mode without having to reboot your system. Check that permissive mode is the current SELinux mode.

Once done, set SELinux back to Enforcing mode.

List SELinux Booleans

List all the SELinux booleans that are currently set to on.

Web Server and SELinux

Install the Apache httpd server on your RHEL 9 server and change the default website to point to a new directory on the root filesystem called "webserver."

You will need to read Chapter 12 again with the web server use case if you have forgotten what to do.

Hint: You will need to edit the httpd.conf file and adjust the parameter that is responsible for where the web content is stored.

Hardening

The Linux firewall and SELinux are important parts to keeping your system secure. However, there is more you can do to reduce the security holes your system could potentially have. This is the process of hardening your system. This typically involves removing services or functionality that is not required.

Hardening Standards

As the process of hardening a Linux system with hundreds if not thousands of configurable options can be daunting, remembering them is even worse, which is one reason why hardening standards and their guides is a major benefit to enterprise Linux engineers. These standards typically are written by security authorities who take the time to document all the security configuration required to achieve a certain security level. They provide guides with a full explanation of the issue and how to remediate them.

There are two main security standards that are used today, one slightly more stringent than the other. Some organizations will harden their systems for compliance reasons and will follow further hardening procedures to achieve accreditations such as PCI DSS.

Center for Internet Security (CIS)

The commonly used hardening standard is the CIS or the Center for Internet Security standard:

`www.cisecurity.org/`

On the preceding link, you will find guides freely available for almost all enterprise platforms and operating systems. This includes the enterprise Linux hardening guides for RHEL, Ubuntu, and SUSE.

In the guides available, all the hardening points are mentioned along with how to check if they are set or not. Even the remediation is given, allowing you to copy and paste the commands to rectify any issues.

Security Technical Implementation Guide (STIG)

The other major security guide that is used is the STIG standard. The STIG standard is commonly used within government departments and other similar agencies.

To download or view the STIG guides for Linux systems, have a look at the following URL:

```
https://public.cyber.mil/stigs/downloads/?_dl_facet_stigs=unix-linux
```

The downloads from STIG are not formatted like the CIS guides and do require some work to convert them to html files.

Compliance Scanning

How would you know if your system was not compliant with any of the previous standards mentioned? The answer is to scan the system with a scanning tool that has the various standards configured.

There are many different security scanning tools that are used today. Some OpenSource and some not. Some OpenSource enterprise tooling such as Red Hat Satellite Server does include the ability in its dashboard to check system compliance based on different standards.

A few scanning tools you may hear of in the industry as of 2022 will include some of the following:

- Rapid7 Nexpose

- Qualys

- Nessus

There are many more that will scan everything from on-premise environments through to cloud infrastructure. The main points to look for when selecting a scanning tool are as follows:

- Definitions are updated regularly.

- They are accurate and reliable.

- Useful reporting.

- Remediation advice or commands ideally. (This one is nice to have to be honest.)

OpenSCAP

To keep this section as short as possible and to not turn this chapter into a full-blown security scanning tool discussion, we will only discuss the OpenSCAP tool as this is a commonly available tool on most Linux distributions.

Installation

To install OpenSCAP, run the following install command on a RHEL 9 system:

```
# sudo dnf install openscap-scanner openscap-utils scap-security-
guide wget -y
```

Running Vulnerability Scans

To run an OpenSCAP vulnerability scan on a system, follow the following steps:

1. SSH on to the system that needs to be scanned.

2. Download the required RHEL 9 file using the following command:

    ```
    # wget -O - https://www.redhat.com/security/data/oval/v2/RHEL9/
    rhel-9.oval.xml.bz2 | bzip2 --decompress > rhel-9.oval.xml
    ```

    If you prefer to manually download and copy to your system, open the following URL and download the rhel-9.oval.xml.bz2 file:

    ```
    www.redhat.com/security/data/oval/v2/RHEL9/
    ```

3. Run an initial evaluation (scan) of your system using a command similar to the following:

    ```
    # oscap oval eval --report vulnerability.html rhel-9.oval.xml
    ```

4. Once the scan has completed, copy the vulnerability.html file to your desktop and open the file in a web browser to see the results:

    ```
    # scp ken@rhel9-server:vulnerability.html .
    ```

The results of the scan run in step 3 can be seen in Figure 13-26.

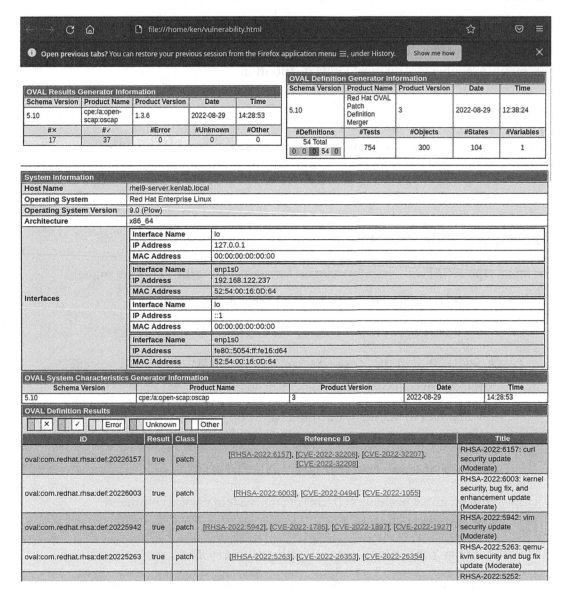

Figure 13-26. OpenSCAP report

In Figure 13-26, you can see that there are 17 items that need to be corrected. This is more than likely due to the system not being updated for a couple weeks. To remediate this is relatively simple and can be resolved by running a system update.

OpenSCAP Profiles

All compliance profiles are stored in files located in the following path:

sudo ls -al /usr/share/sml/scap/ssg/content/

```
[ken@rhel9-server ~]$ sudo ls -al /usr/share/xml/scap/ssg/content/
total 19676
drwxr-xr-x. 2 root root       30 Aug 29 14:12 .
drwxr-xr-x. 3 root root       21 Aug 29 14:12 ..
-rw-r--r--. 1 root root 20145599 Mar 28 14:05 ssg-rhel9-ds.xml
```

Figure 13-27. *OpenSCAP profiles file location*

Available Profiles

To view what profiles are available, run the following command:

sudo oscap info /usr/share/xml/scap/ssg/content/ssg-rhel9-ds.xml

```
[ken@rhel9-server ~]$ sudo oscap info /usr/share/xml/scap/ssg/content/ssg-rhel9-ds.xml
Document type: Source Data Stream
Imported: 2022-03-28T14:05:12

Stream: scap_org.open-scap_datastream_from_xccdf_ssg-rhel9-xccdf-1.2.xml
Generated: (null)
Version: 1.3
Checklists:
        Ref-Id: scap_org.open-scap_cref_ssg-rhel9-xccdf-1.2.xml
WARNING: Datastream component 'scap_org.open-scap_cref_security-data-oval-com.redhat.rhsa-RHEL9.xml.bz2' points out to
the remote 'https://access.redhat.com/security/data/oval/com.redhat.rhsa-RHEL9.xml.bz2'. Use '--fetch-remote-resources'
 option to download it.
WARNING: Skipping 'https://access.redhat.com/security/data/oval/com.redhat.rhsa-RHEL9.xml.bz2' file which is referenced
 from datastream
                Status: draft
                Generated: 2022-03-28
                Resolved: true
                Profiles:
                        Title: ANSSI-BP-028 (enhanced)
                                Id: xccdf_org.ssgproject.content_profile_anssi_bp28_enhanced
                        Title: ANSSI-BP-028 (high)
                                Id: xccdf_org.ssgproject.content_profile_anssi_bp28_high
                        Title: ANSSI-BP-028 (intermediary)
                                Id: xccdf_org.ssgproject.content_profile_anssi_bp28_intermediary
                        Title: ANSSI-BP-028 (minimal)
                                Id: xccdf_org.ssgproject.content_profile_anssi_bp28_minimal
                        Title: [DRAFT] CIS Red Hat Enterprise Linux 9 Benchmark for Level 2 - Server
                                Id: xccdf_org.ssgproject.content_profile_cis
                        Title: [DRAFT] CIS Red Hat Enterprise Linux 9 Benchmark for Level 1 - Server
                                Id: xccdf_org.ssgproject.content_profile_cis_server_l1
                        Title: [DRAFT] CIS Red Hat Enterprise Linux 9 Benchmark for Level 1 - Workstation
                                Id: xccdf_org.ssgproject.content_profile_cis_workstation_l1
                        Title: [DRAFT] CIS Red Hat Enterprise Linux 9 Benchmark for Level 2 - Workstation
                                Id: xccdf_org.ssgproject.content_profile_cis_workstation_l2
                        Title: [DRAFT] Unclassified Information in Non-federal Information Systems and Organizations (N
IST 800-171)
                                Id: xccdf_org.ssgproject.content_profile_cui
                        Title: Australian Cyber Security Centre (ACSC) Essential Eight
                                Id: xccdf_org.ssgproject.content_profile_e8
                        Title: Health Insurance Portability and Accountability Act (HIPAA)
                                Id: xccdf_org.ssgproject.content_profile_hipaa
                        Title: Australian Cyber Security Centre (ACSC) ISM Official
                                Id: xccdf_org.ssgproject.content_profile_ism_o
```

Figure 13-28. *OpenSCAP profiles available in profile file*

From the outputted list, you will see the id of each profile. This id is used to tell the OpenSCAP scanning tool what profile should be used.

Profile Information

To get more information on a particular profile, run the following command:

```
# oscap info --profile cis /usr/share/xml/scap/ssg/content/ssg-rhel9-ds.xml
```

```
[ken@rhel9-server ~]$ oscap info --profile xccdf_org.ssgproject.content_profile_cis_server_l1 /usr/share/xml/scap/ssg/c
ontent/ssg-rhel9-ds.xml
Document type: Source Data Stream
Imported: 2022-03-28T14:05:12

Stream: scap_org.open-scap_datastream_from_xccdf_ssg-rhel9-xccdf-1.2.xml
Generated: (null)
Version: 1.3
WARNING: Datastream component 'scap_org.open-scap_cref_security-data-oval-com.redhat.rhsa-RHEL9.xml.bz2' points out to
the remote 'https://access.redhat.com/security/data/oval/com.redhat.rhsa-RHEL9.xml.bz2'. Use '--fetch-remote-resources'
 option to download it.
WARNING: Skipping 'https://access.redhat.com/security/data/oval/com.redhat.rhsa-RHEL9.xml.bz2' file which is referenced
 from datastream
Profile
        Title: [DRAFT] CIS Red Hat Enterprise Linux 9 Benchmark for Level 1 - Server
        Id: xccdf_org.ssgproject.content_profile_cis_server_l1

        Description: This is a draft profile based on its RHEL8 version for experimental purposes. It is not based on t
he CIS benchmark for RHEL9, because this one was not available at time of the release.
```

Figure 13-29. *OpenSCAP profile information*

In Figure 13-29, you can see that this is the CIS profile that has been adapted for RHEL 9 from RHEL 8. Technically this is still a draft profile and should not be considered the final profile to use.

Running a Scan with a Profile

To scan a system with a compliance profile, use a command similar to the following:

```
# sudo oscap xccdf eval --report report.html --profile cis /usr/share/xml/
scap/ssg/content/ssg-rhel9-ds.xml
```

To view the report from the preceding command, copy the report.html file to your local system and open in a web browser for easier viewing

The report of the previous command scan can be seen in Figure 13-30.

Compliance and Scoring

The target system did not satisfy the conditions of **141 rules!** Please review rule results and consider applying remediation.

Rule results

121 passed	141 failed

Severity of failed rules

6	12 low	121 medium	2

Score

Scoring system	Score	Maximum	Percent
urn:xccdf:scoring:default	66.993042	100.000000	66.99%

Rule Overview

☑ pass   ☑ fail   ☑ notchecked
☑ fixed   ☑ error   ☑ notapplicable
☑ informational ☑ unknown

Search through XCCDF rules   Search

Group rules by:
Default

Title	Severity	Result
▼ Guide to the Secure Configuration of Red Hat Enterprise Linux 9 (141x fail)		
▼ System Settings (122x fail)		
▼ Installing and Maintaining Software (11x fail)		
▼ System and Software Integrity (3x fail)		
▼ Software Integrity Checking (2x fail)		
▼ Verify Integrity with AIDE (2x fail)		
Install AIDE	medium	fail

Figure 13-30. *OpenSCAP report from a CIS profile scan*

In Figure 13-30, you will see that 141 items have failed compliance. To bring this system in line with CIS compliance, these items need to be corrected.

Remediation

To resolve any issues found in the compliance scan report, all you need to do is click on each item and follow the instructions provided.

Figure 13-31. *OpenSCAP remediation advice*

Simple enough, but there are 141 items to fix. To do this with hundreds if not thousands of systems will be a nightmare beyond measure.

Automated Remediation

When stuck with many systems to remediate, automation is going to be a massive requirement. Either that or the systems need to be rebuilt from a more secure base.

Fortunately with OpenSCAP, there is a very nice feature to generate a script to fix it all for you.

First, you need to generate a results xml file:

```
# sudo oscap xccdf eval --results results-cis.xml --profile cis /usr/share/
xml/scap/ssg/content/ssg-rhel9-ds.xml
```

From the results-cis.xml file, a remediated script can be generated:

```
# sudo oscap xccdf generate fix --fix-type ansible --profile cis /usr/
share/xml/scap/ssg/content/ssg-rhel9-ds.xml --result-id "results-cis.xml"
report.xml > remediation-playbook.yml
```

The output of this command will be an Ansible playbook that could be run against the vulnerable system.

Within the remediation Ansible playbook, tasks like in Figure 13-32 can be found that will correct any missing system configuration.

```
tasks:
  - name: Ensure aide is installed
    package:
      name: aide
      state: present
    when: ansible_virtualization_type not in ["docker", "lxc", "openvz", "podman", "container"]
    tags:
    - CCE-90843-4
    - CJIS-5.10.1.3
    - NIST-800-53-CM-6(a)
    - PCI-DSS-Req-11.5
    - enable_strategy
    - low_complexity
    - low_disruption
    - medium_severity
    - no_reboot_needed
    - package_aide_installed
```

Figure 13-32. *OpenSCAP-generated Ansible that can be used for remediation*

Exercise

To experience your first compliance scanning activity, run through the following exercise based on what you have learned so far in this chapter.

Prerequisites

Build a new RHEL 9 system and subscribe it to a subscription. You may need to unregister your previous system to do this. Either that or get yourself a Red Hat developer subscription. They too are free of charge.

Compliance Scans

Install and configure your new RHEL 9 system with the ability to scan for vulnerabilities.

Use the CIS profile and output your results to an html file. Review the results in a web browser.

Remediate

Based on the results of the CIS report, remediate as much of the issues as possible. Attempt to do this in an automated manner.

Encryption

To explain encryption in the simplest way is to describe it as follows:

"Encryption is the process in which plain text is converted into a scrambled unreadable format called ciphertext."

Encryption is required when you wish to move or store sensitive information that you wish to protect.

How Does Encryption Work

To encrypt data, you need three things:

1. The data that needs to be encrypted

2. A private key to encrypt the data with

3. A public key to decrypt the received data

The public and private keys are generated where the encryption needs to occur. It goes without saying that the system needs to be secure and trusted.

The public key then needs to be sent to where the data needs to be unencrypted. Once both sides are confirmed to be secure, the keys can be used to encrypt and decrypt data between these locations.

Figure 13-33. *Basic encryption flow*

In Figure 13-33, plain text is encrypted using a private key. The scrambled data is then transferred to the destination and unencrypted with the public key. This process would prevent any plain text data from being viewed in transit between locations.

Linux Encryption

There are a number of places where encryption can be used within an enterprise Linux environment. They range from how you would log in securely to how data is transmitted over the network.

SSH Keys

The first use of encryption most Linux administrators experience is with the use of public and private ssh keys.

Ssh keys are mostly used because administrators want a "passwordless" login process. However, by using ssh keys with no password configured on an account, the security is further enhanced by not having a password to worry about that could possibly become compromised. Cannot guess a password if there is none configured.

Asymmetric Encryption

Ssh keys make use of asymmetric encryption. What this basically means is that the private key of the ssh key set can be used to derive the public key but not the other way around.

There are three classes of asymmetric encryption algorithms used today; they are as follows:

- RSA

- DSA

- Elliptic curve-based algorithms

These algorithms are what the ssh keys are generated with. RSA is the most commonly used today, where DSA is not really used anymore as it is regarded as less secure. The two other elliptic curve-based algorithms that can be used are ECDSA and EDDSA, with EDDSA being regarded as the more secure and better performing algorithm of them all.

Generate ssh Keys

To generate ssh keys on a Linux system is a relatively simple task. The command shown in Figure 13-34 will generate a default RSA ssh key set for the currently logged in user:

```
# ssh-keygen
```

```
[ken@rhel9-server ~]$ ssh-keygen
Generating public/private rsa key pair.
Enter file in which to save the key (/home/ken/.ssh/id_rsa):
Created directory '/home/ken/.ssh'.
Enter passphrase (empty for no passphrase):
Enter same passphrase again:
Your identification has been saved in /home/ken/.ssh/id_rsa
Your public key has been saved in /home/ken/.ssh/id_rsa.pub
The key fingerprint is:
SHA256:VhTRBIHRaC5WCtpOTzd1cUO4N0erys8b67K2xJ7xjOM ken@rhel9-server.kenlab.local
The key's randomart image is:
+---[RSA 3072]----+
|        .=*Bo++  |
|    .   =.o +. ..|
|   o . = ... . ..|
|  . o = +.  . o..|
|   o + oS.   ..o |
|    . ..   .  .  |
|         .+..    |
|         o*B o   |
|         oEBO.   |
+----[SHA256]-----+   _
```

Figure 13-34. *ssh keys generated*

In the output shown in Figure 13-34, you can see that the default location was left for the logged in use and that no passphrase was entered.

Different Algorithm

To generate an ssh key set based on a different algorithm, the "-t" parameter can be used with the ssh-keygen command, followed by the algorithm you wish to use.

```
[ken@rhel9-server ~]$ ssh-keygen --help
unknown option -- -
usage: ssh-keygen [-q] [-a rounds] [-b bits] [-C comment] [-f output_keyfile]
                  [-m format] [-N new_passphrase] [-O option]
                  [-t dsa | ecdsa | ecdsa-sk | ed25519 | ed25519-sk | rsa]
                  [-w provider] [-Z cipher]
```

Figure 13-35. *ssh-keygen help*

Figure 13-35 shows the first few lines of the ssh-keygen help. From the "-t" row, you can see the different algorithms that can be used to generate ssh keys.

Using ssh Keys

To use your ssh key set, you will need to copy the public key to your destination system. With most Linux systems that use ssh, there will be a utility called ssh-copy-id.

The command to set up a passwordless login between the RHEL 9 system and the SUSE 15 system that were built in a previous chapter can be seen as follows:

```
# ssh-copy-id -i ~/.ssh/id_rsa.pub ken@192.168.122.70
```

```
[ken@rhel9-server ~]$ ssh-copy-id -i ~/.ssh/id_rsa.pub ken@192.168.122.70
/usr/bin/ssh-copy-id: INFO: Source of key(s) to be installed: "/home/ken/.ssh/id_rsa.pub"
The authenticity of host '192.168.122.70 (192.168.122.70)' can't be established.
ED25519 key fingerprint is SHA256:ru81jaDYTw4F7ypsvJLz90RChaBC6Wkzm7vZ8pnP370.
This key is not known by any other names
Are you sure you want to continue connecting (yes/no/[fingerprint])? yes
/usr/bin/ssh-copy-id: INFO: attempting to log in with the new key(s), to filter out any that are already installed
/usr/bin/ssh-copy-id: INFO: 1 key(s) remain to be installed -- if you are prompted now it is to install the new keys
(ken@192.168.122.70) Password:
client_global_hostkeys_private_confirm: server gave bad signature for RSA key 0: error in libcrypto

Number of key(s) added: 1

Now try logging into the machine, with:   "ssh 'ken@192.168.122.70'"
and check to make sure that only the key(s) you wanted were added.
```

Figure 13-36. *Copying ssh keys to other Linux systems*

In Figure 13-36, you can see that the command prompted for the password of the user that was being used to log in the SUSE 15 server. Once the correct password was passed, the ssh key configuration was done on the remote system. Now a new login can be done to the remote system with no password being requested.

```
[ken@rhel9-server ~]$ ssh ken@192.168.122.70
client_global_hostkeys_private_confirm: server gave bad signature for RSA key 0: error in libcrypto
Last login: Mon Aug 15 21:32:35 2022 from 192.168.122.1
ken@sles15-server:~>
```

Figure 13-37. *ssh now works without a password*

Manual Configuration

If you wanted to manually setup the ssh key pairing on the remote system, you could also inject the public key information into the authorized_keys file.

```
ken@sles15-server:~> cat ~/.ssh/authorized_keys
ssh-rsa AAAAB3NzaC1yc2EAAAADAQABAAABgQCPtcYDre0i30qZ28y6Xli9fjJ3enFX18qaTDcNKWlXd1VpWdP9nN1zo2FgYaUdnJ8u8rql
3i91UwhWOrQ5V15A3Ne0ywhJ0eA6KDPT0+s+TeM318718jyy85ZfZr0Vr+UdNJwkmScbZBubH5P76VA3+P3P5uLZt+sCT8RpTytwWDSNBFl
4CXskrHAoWMsQjuvJMnBltA17YrOWbHSzqmIJSPOb9qgxduTQetVgCqdwu9izXKdTGeQ78Q4du8= ken@rhel9-server.kenlab.local
```

Figure 13-38. *The reduced output of the authorized_keys file*

Disk Encryption

Once logged into your system with your encrypted ssh keys, you may be on a drive to encrypt as much as you can. One further bit of encryption you can do is to encrypt any data sensitive drives or disks you may have. This is known as data at rest encryption. This means that files and sensitive data on a disk are stored in an encrypted form until required to be read; only then would the data be decrypted, provided the correct security and trusted configuration is in place.

Cryptsetup

On enterprise Linux distributions such as Red Hat enterprise Linux, the disk encryption tool cryptsetup is generally used to encrypt disks. Cryptsetup is based on the DMCrypt kernel module with an emphasis on the LUKS design.

LUKS or Linux Unified Key Setup has become the standard for Linux disk encryption, largely due to its ability to allow compatibility with multiple Linux distributions.

Create a LUKS Encrypted Disk

To encrypt a disk using the cryptsetup tool, you will need to install the following package:

```
# sudo dnf install cryptsetup -y
```

```
[ken@rhel9-server ~]$ sudo dnf install cryptsetup -y
Updating Subscription Management repositories.
Last metadata expiration check: 2:38:35 ago on Mon 29 Aug 2022 19:33:32 BST.
Dependencies resolved.
================================================================================
 Package            Architecture    Version        Repository              Size
================================================================================
Installing:
 cryptsetup         x86_64          2.4.3-4.el9     rhel-9-for-x86_64-baseos-rpms    213 k

Transaction Summary
================================================================================
Install  1 Package
```

Figure 13-39. *The package installation of cryptsetup*

A disk will also need to be added to the system that will be encrypted.

To encrypt the new 2GB disk /dev/vdb, the following command can be used for a basic configuration:

```
# sudo cryptsetup luksFormat /dev/vdb
```

```
[ken@rhel9-server ~]$ sudo cryptsetup luksFormat /dev/vdb

WARNING!
========
This will overwrite data on /dev/vdb irrevocably.

Are you sure? (Type 'yes' in capital letters): YES
Enter passphrase for /dev/vdb:
Verify passphrase:      _
```

Figure 13-40. *The cryptsetup command to encrypt the /dev/vdb disk*

The passphrase needs to be a strong password with a combination of numbers, letters, and uppercase characters for the best results.

Decrypting a LUKS Disk

To use an encrypted disk, first you need to open it. To open the previous encrypted disk, you can use a command similar to the following:

```
# sudo cryptsetup luksOpen /dev/vdb encrypteddata
```

```
[ken@rhel9-server ~]$ sudo cryptsetup luksOpen /dev/vdb encrypteddata
Enter passphrase for /dev/vdb:
[ken@rhel9-server ~]$ ls -al /dev/mapper/
total 0
drwxr-xr-x.  2 root root    120 Aug 29 22:24 .
drwxr-xr-x. 21 root root   3340 Aug 29 22:24 ..
crw-------.  1 root root 10, 236 Aug 29 22:10 control
lrwxrwxrwx.  1 root root      7 Aug 29 22:24 encrypteddata -> ../dm-2
lrwxrwxrwx.  1 root root      7 Aug 29 22:10 rhel-root -> ../dm-0
lrwxrwxrwx.  1 root root      7 Aug 29 22:10 rhel-swap -> ../dm-1
```

Figure 13-41. *The device files created for new disk*

In Figure 13-41, you can see that the decryption was successful and a new disk device file was created in the /dev/mapper location. The name of the device file is determined by the name that is given when the "cryptsetup luksOpen" command is run.

Encrypted Disk Status

To view the status of an encrypted disk, you can run a command similar to the following:

```
# sudo cryptsetup -v status encrypteddata
```

```
[ken@rhel9-server ~]$ sudo cryptsetup -v status encrypteddata
/dev/mapper/encrypteddata is active.
  type:    LUKS2
  cipher:  aes-xts-plain64
  keysize: 512 bits
  key location: keyring
  device:  /dev/vdb
  sector size:  512
  offset:  32768 sectors
  size:    4161536 sectors
  mode:    read/write
Command successful.
```

Figure 13-42. *The encrypted disk status*

In Figure 13-42, you can see that the encrypteddata disk is currently active.

Formatting an Encrypted Disk

With the newly encrypted disk open and available to use, the disk will need to be prepared like any other disk. However, one step is generally recommended for an encrypted disk. The disk should be zeroed first; the command to do this can be seen as follows:

```
# sudo dd if=/dev/zero of=/dev/mapper/encrypteddata status=progress
```

```
[ken@rhel9-server ~]$ sudo dd if=/dev/zero of=/dev/mapper/encrypteddata status=progress
2121740800 bytes (2.1 GB, 2.0 GiB) copied, 60 s, 35.4 MB/s
dd: writing to '/dev/mapper/encrypteddata': No space left on device
4161537+0 records in
4161536+0 records out
2130706432 bytes (2.1 GB, 2.0 GiB) copied, 61.0455 s, 34.9 MB/s
```

Figure 13-43. *dd command to zero encrypted disk*

This command can take a while with larger disks; it is recommended to use the status=progress parameter to judge how long it will take.

Once you have zeroed the disk, you will need to create a filesystem on the disk:

```
# sudo mkfs.ext4 /dev/mapper/encrypteddata
```

```
[ken@rhel9-server ~]$ sudo mkfs.ext4 /dev/mapper/encrypteddata
mke2fs 1.46.5 (30-Dec-2021)
Creating filesystem with 520192 4k blocks and 130048 inodes
Filesystem UUID: ea67aa3d-528f-499f-94ee-82f0a18563e3
Superblock backups stored on blocks:
        32768, 98304, 163840, 229376, 294912

Allocating group tables: done
Writing inode tables: done
Creating journal (8192 blocks): done
Writing superblocks and filesystem accounting information: done
```

Figure 13-44. *Create a filesystem on the encrypted disk*

Mounting an Encrypted Disk

To mount the encrypted disk is not much different than mounting a normal disk. First, create a directory to mount to:

```
# sudo mkdir /encrypteddata
```

```
[ken@rhel9-server ~]$ sudo mkdir /encrypteddata
[ken@rhel9-server ~]$ ls -al /encrypteddata/
total 4
drwxr-xr-x.  2 root root    6 Aug 29 22:42 .
dr-xr-xr-x. 22 root root 4096 Aug 29 22:42 ..
```

Once the directory has been created, mount the encrypteddata device to the newly created directory:

```
# sudo mount /dev/mapper/encrypteddata /encrypteddata
```

```
[ken@rhel9-server ~]$ sudo mount /dev/mapper/encrypteddata /encrypteddata
[ken@rhel9-server ~]$ df -h
Filesystem                Size  Used Avail Use% Mounted on
devtmpfs                  1.8G     0  1.8G   0% /dev
tmpfs                     1.9G     0  1.9G   0% /dev/shm
tmpfs                     745M  8.7M  736M   2% /run
/dev/mapper/rhel-root      17G  1.5G   16G   9% /
/dev/vda1                1014M  197M  818M  20% /boot
tmpfs                     373M     0  373M   0% /run/user/1000
/dev/mapper/encrypteddata 2.0G   24K  1.9G   1% /encrypteddata
```

Figure 13-45. *Create directory and mount encrypted disk*

Files and directories can now be created in the new encrypted disk.

Persistent Mounting

Encrypted disk can be mounted persistently through reboots by configuring the following file:

/etc/crypttab

Read the man pages and further online configuration for this process. It is recommended to encrypt any data disks on a data sensitive laptop. For that you may wish to enable persistent mounting.

Network Encryption

To encrypt traffic between Linux systems or any system that is capable of transmitting data is known as encryption in transit. This is very similar to how ssh keys encrypt and decrypt data when logging into a Linux system.

There are many ways to do this, but as a simple example, we will only discuss the use of VPNs.

VPN

A VPN allows two private networks to communicate with each other over a public network using an encrypted tunnel.

Figure 13-46. *How a VPN works at its basic level*

In the image shown in Figure 13-46, traffic from Network 1 is "tunneled" through the Internet to Network 2. All traffic from Network 1 to Network 2 is passed through the VPN software that encrypts traffic, allowing secure communication and reducing the possibility of anyone reading any unencrypted data that is being transmitted.

Create a VPN Connection

To create a VPN connection from a Linux system to another would involve having an endpoint configured to connect to; for the explanation on how to do this would go well beyond the scope of this book and would be something you would need to read further on your own.

To connect to a VPN that is already configured, you can use the openvpn utility. The configuration for this too is quite complex and would require a chapter of its own to explain. Again this is something you will need to read further on your own.

Hint   The simplest method would be to do this through a Linux desktop like Gnome.

Certificates

To briefly put what a certificate is into a sentence, it would be described as a digital document that is used to identify an organization or individual.

What Are Certificates Used For

Certificates are used to encrypt content from a source system to the intended recipient and vice versa. For example when you log in to your online banking, all the information passed from your system to the banking site and back again needs to be encrypted so no one can intercept the plain text data you work with. Important information like passwords, bank account numbers, and credit card numbers need to be protected.

SSL and TLS

The protocols SSL (secure socket layer) and TLS (transport layer security) along with certificates are what provides data encryption, data integrity, and authentication. SSL is no longer used due to vulnerabilities discovered in SSLv3. Since then, TLS has been the main protocol to use.

Certificate Authority

TLS or SSL makes use of a set of keys similar to your ssh keys, a public and private key. However, as anyone can generate these keys, how do end users know the keys provided are secure and are from your secured environment? To resolve this issue, digital certificates are generated from the public key when the CA has verified the information about you and validated that the keys belong to you. This certificate then becomes a convenient way to distribute the public key to any who wishes to use your secure environment.

This is known as certificate signing. Self-signed certificates can also be generated but are not regarded as secure as a certificate generated by a CA.

Manual Certificate Generation

To generate a set of keys that will be used for a certificate is quite simple. The following are the general steps for certificate generation:

1. Log in to the system that will require the certificate.

2. Install the openssl packages required for certificate generation:

   ```
   # sudo dnf install openssl
   ```

3. Run the following command or similar based on your requirements:

   ```
   # openssl req -new -newkey rsa:2048 -nodes -keyout
   securesite.com.key -out securesite.com.csr
   ```

```
[ken@rhel9-server ~]$
[ken@rhel9-server ~]$ openssl req -new -newkey rsa:2048 -nodes -keyout securesite.com.key -out securesite.com.csr
...+......+.+++++++++++++++++++++++++++++++++++++++++++++++++++++++*...........+.....+++++++++++++++++++++++
+++++++++++++++++++++++++++++++++++*.+.+..+.+......+........+.+.....+......+...+.......+......+.........+....
...+...+...+..+.+..+...+........+.....+.+..+.+..+........+++++++++++++++++++++++++++++++++++++++++++++++++++++
+++++++++++++++
.....+..+...............+.....+.+..+..+..+..........+......++++++++++++++++++++++++++++++++++++++++++++++++++
*...+.....+++++++++++++++++++++++++++++++++++++++++++++++++++*.+...+......+.............+...+.+.......+...+
...........+..+......+.....+....+.+..+.+........+.....++++++++++++++++++++++++++++++++++++++++++++++++++++++
++++++++++++++
-----
You are about to be asked to enter information that will be incorporated
into your certificate request.
What you are about to enter is what is called a Distinguished Name or a DN.
There are quite a few fields but you can leave some blank
For some fields there will be a default value,
If you enter '.', the field will be left blank.
-----
Country Name (2 letter code) [XX]:gb
State or Province Name (full name) []:▮▮▮▮▮▮▮
Locality Name (eg, city) [Default City]:▮▮▮▮▮▮
Organization Name (eg, company) [Default Company Ltd]:
Organizational Unit Name (eg, section) []:Private company
Common Name (eg, your name or your server's hostname) []:rhel9-server.securesite.com
Email Address []:admin@securesite.com

Please enter the following 'extra' attributes
to be sent with your certificate request
A challenge password []:password123
An optional company name []:private company
```

Figure 13-47. *Using openssl to generate csr file for certificate signing*

4. Using the content from the csr file generated, you can now go
    to the CA of your choice to have your certificate signed and
    generated.

```
[ken@rhel9-server ~]$ cat securesite.com.csr
-----BEGIN CERTIFICATE REQUEST-----
MIIDODCCAiACAQAwgbYxCzAJBgNVBAYTAmdiMRIwEAYDVQQIDAlIYW1wc2hpcmUx
EDAOBgNVBAcMB0FuZG92ZXIxHDAaBgNVBAoME0RlZmF1bHQgQ29tcGFueSBMdGQx
GDAWBgNVBAsMD1ByaXZhdGUgY29tcGFueTEkMCIGA1UEAwwbcmhlbDktc2VydmVy
LnNlY3VyZXNpdGUuY29tMSMwIQYJKoZIhvcNAQkBFhRhZG1pbkBzZWN1cmVzaXRl
LmNvbTCCASIwDQYJKoZIhvcNAQEBBQADggEPADCCAQoCggEBALY4s6AN4QzCCyQ9
ITGP/LhVYeo+nCYCFCQCs9EUeYmMHUNLZ8BmAAyJiGUp3OqD5zoT8VK8oDdihh6O
6dFS8hBCGJQZDD8xl8tgIfaq7hVQXmTi0gmDdzPrbWIKOq9b33cClc43TIJloQo+
CRNGTt5Zxyw8tFzxXz+zuzYUw7iIFwmTfsDotbjIaa5TNSF3bVVQxDs57Jz2Gtj5
HOIkARXLDIv7nd6ta27iUBtsJGPObJyeL6HjVTcO1DCiFT99lKjPJdYmSgIV+Vex
WAlw98d0lFJIJARgfh8/CY4ZfQXZREeQQ4grb9ERZm0rbyBLEr9bKrrDuw6Cbpuy
L+yKD1ECAwEAAaA8MBoGCSqGSIb3DQEJBzENDAtwYXNzd29yZDEyMzAeBgkqhkiG
9w0BCQIxEQwPcHJpdmF0ZSBjb21wYW55MA0GCSqGSIb3DQEBCwUAA4IBAQBMo+On
hQdDwLc0R/ICZxhFmbpyqlG133R1Mm9HREUZnZuJShBEVrkx46fYXFgxzxeE4PYz
ulZyOJC7awm3u0tokzG7r8sUvn3ZN0ovV/aQgIE25LKBYgZ/fPk22+wBRcxOhfzS
H4Ij8RFrd6CjEirkgTbXHbg6X7lhbsgPnb5T1IPz53tU4S7Q0dhn2C9LwYcYgSIV
LOTxmPyazcoYXWAB0x8ZfUz8e4++unYHbbgLG5QfbjBEqSKFgMLuyk6OrStUPSiL
R0oFutWZ991q5j5yTr7HXrVWxH8F+P3n/ZYf5vILsmyywzyHUXliA285M3bUqOl0
8aTAm84hQJa53tgG
-----END CERTIFICATE REQUEST-----
```

Figure 13-48. *Output of the csr file*

Automated Certificate Generation

There are options today for automated certificate management. Companies like Let's Encrypt have tools that will automatically generate csr, sign them, and configure the platform you wish to use. They will even manage the renewals for you so you never have the misfortune of having an expired certificate.

Have a look at the following link on how letsencrypt works:

`https://letsencrypt.org/`

Exercise

To get some experience with encryption, run through the following exercises and see how much you are able to do.

SSH Keys

Generate a set of ssh keys and configure passwordless login between two Linux systems of your choice.

Encrypted Disk

Add a new disk to a Linux system and then configure the disk so that any data stored on it is encrypted. The disk does not need to be mounted persistently across reboots, but if you choose to work it out on your own, feel free.

Generate a csr

Run through the steps to generate csr.

Note   If you want to generate a 60-day certificate for free, you can use sites similar to the following:

`https://getacert.com/signacert.html`

Summary

In this chapter, you were introduced to the following:

- What the Linux firewall is and how it can be configured

- How the Linux firewall can be checked to see what is allowed through

- What SELinux is and the basic configuration that can be done to ensure your system remains as secure as possible

- System hardening and how you as an enterprise Linux administrator can scan systems for compliance

- Different encryption methods used on a Linux system

- How encryption is used to ensure a network, disk, and system remain as secure as possible

- What certificates are and how they are generated

CHAPTER 14

High Availability

So far in your journey to becoming an enterprise Linux administrator, you have been mostly working with single systems. In this chapter, we will start looking at how individual Linux systems can be brought together to provide a highly available service through the use of clustering.

We will look at the basic concepts that you will need to know when discussing or planning a cluster. We will explore how a cluster can be built on RHEL, SUSE, and Ubuntu. We will run through the process of creating a very basic cluster with some basic cluster resources.

This chapter, however, will not be an exhaustive explanation of all the clustering configuration available. That would require an entire new book to explain. Instead, this chapter is only here to give you your first experience with clustering enterprise Linux systems.

Clustering

In computer terminology, a cluster is a group of systems that work together to provide a service in a highly available or distributed manner.

Types

Clusters can be configured in a number of ways depending on the requirement of the environment.

© Kenneth Hitchcock 2023
K. Hitchcock, *The Enterprise Linux Administrator*, https://doi.org/10.1007/978-1-4842-8801-6_14

High Availability

The first and often the most common configuration for Linux clustering is in a highly available configuration. In this configuration, a minimum of two nodes are configured to act as a cluster with only one node being active at a time. In the event of the primary node failing, the secondary node would continue to serve requests. This is known as an "Active/Passive" configuration.

Load Balancing

Another type of cluster that can be configured is a "load balancing" cluster. With this configuration, the services provided by the cluster are balanced across all nodes. This is more commonly known as an "Active/Active" cluster.

Distributed

A distributed cluster is very similar to a load balancing cluster in that workload is spread across nodes. The only difference is around the workload, as the different nodes could be serving different workloads or applications.

For example, if a two-node cluster was built to be distributed, node 1 could potentially be hosting a website, and node 2 could be hosting a database server. Both nodes are capable of hosting either workload but prefer to be separated. In the event of a node failure, the workload from the failed node would move over to the running node. The nodes are both being used and are not configured purely for failover. Failover is an added benefit in case one node fails. This would generally not be a two-node cluster as you would want to plan for better resource usage and not overload one node.

High Performance

The final kind of cluster you may come across is a cluster built for high performance. This kind of cluster runs workloads in parallel across all nodes, enabling a workload to leverage all the resources of all the nodes potentially at the same time. These kinds of clusters are known as "Beowulf" clusters.

Cluster Concepts

Once you start working with computer clusters, you will be introduced to some of the following terms. There are a few more that may not be mentioned, but to get you started, these are some of the basic concepts you should know.

Table 14-1 lists a few of the basic clustering concepts used today.

Table 14-1. *Basic clustering concepts*

Name	Description
Node	The system that will be part of the cluster. A node usually represents a single Linux server.
Quorum	Used to determine if a cluster has the required number of nodes.
Split brain	When cluster nodes are disconnected from each other, forcing each node to form its own cluster.
Heartbeat	The connection between cluster nodes. When the heartbeat dies, a split brain can occur.
Fencing	The process where nodes attempt to correct a failed node.

Enterprise Linux Clustering

The three major enterprise Linux distributions (RHEL, SUSE, and Ubuntu) have all based their cluster suite on the same community cluster projects. The installation and configuration of the clusters are mostly the same across all of these distributions. For this reason, we will only focus on the RHEL cluster installation and configuration. For the SUSE and Ubuntu variations, it is recommended to read the official documentation and follow the steps there. In fact, this is highly recommended if you have the time to build separate clusters.

Projects

Red Hat Enterprise Linux, SUSE, and Ubuntu clustering components are built using the following tools.

Corosync

Corosync is the component that allows servers to communicate as a cluster. Corosync is part of the high availability suite provided by most enterprise Linux distributions.

If you are interested to understand more about Corosync, have a look at the community documentation:

```
http://corosync.github.io/corosync/
```

Pacemaker

Where Corosync enables servers to communicate as a cluster, Pacemaker in turn manages the resources that run on the cluster, the services, the applications, and how the cluster behaves.

As with Corosync, Pacemaker has community documentation you can read if you want to familiarize yourself more with how Pacemaker works:

```
https://clusterlabs.org/pacemaker/
```

RHEL Cluster Example

To build a Red Hat Enterprise Linux cluster, there are a number of configuration steps that will need to be followed including a few prerequisites.

Prerequisites

For this example, we will need to have two RHEL systems built. These two nodes will form a special case cluster:

- rhel9-node1.kenlab.local

- rhel9-node2.kenlab.local

For this chapter, we will install both RHEL 9 environments using the same steps we used in Chapter 11. The minimal packages will be installed, and the network configuration will be done during the installation.

Node 1

```
[root@rhel9-node1 ~]# ip a
1: lo: <LOOPBACK,UP,LOWER_UP> mtu 65536 qdisc noqueue state UNKNOWN group default qlen 1000
    link/loopback 00:00:00:00:00:00 brd 00:00:00:00:00:00
    inet 127.0.0.1/8 scope host lo
       valid_lft forever preferred_lft forever
    inet6 ::1/128 scope host
       valid_lft forever preferred_lft forever
2: enp1s0: <BROADCAST,MULTICAST,UP,LOWER_UP> mtu 1500 qdisc fq_codel state UP group default qlen 1000
    link/ether 52:54:00:91:f0:e8 brd ff:ff:ff:ff:ff:ff
    inet 192.168.122.110/24 brd 192.168.122.255 scope global noprefixroute enp1s0
       valid_lft forever preferred_lft forever
    inet6 fe80::5054:ff:fe91:f0e8/64 scope link noprefixroute
       valid_lft forever preferred_lft forever
```

Node 2

```
[root@rhel9-node2 ~]# ip a
1: lo: <LOOPBACK,UP,LOWER_UP> mtu 65536 qdisc noqueue state UNKNOWN group default qlen 1000
    link/loopback 00:00:00:00:00:00 brd 00:00:00:00:00:00
    inet 127.0.0.1/8 scope host lo
       valid_lft forever preferred_lft forever
    inet6 ::1/128 scope host
       valid_lft forever preferred_lft forever
2: enp1s0: <BROADCAST,MULTICAST,UP,LOWER_UP> mtu 1500 qdisc fq_codel state UP group default qlen 1000
    link/ether 52:54:00:a0:57:c1 brd ff:ff:ff:ff:ff:ff
    inet 192.168.122.111/24 brd 192.168.122.255 scope global noprefixroute enp1s0
       valid_lft forever preferred_lft forever
    inet6 fe80::5054:ff:fea0:57c1/64 scope link noprefixroute
       valid_lft forever preferred_lft forever
```

Figure 14-1. *Network information on the two nodes used for this chapter*

In Figure 14-1, you can see that both nodes rhel9-node1 and rhel9-node2 are installed and configured with network addresses 192.168.122.110 and 192.168.122.111, respectively.

Configuration Requirements

The following configuration is required on each node:

- – Static IP address configured.

- – Hostnames need to be resolvable from both systems.

- – NTP needs to be configured with the time in sync on both systems.

- – Both systems need to be able to communicate with each other.

- – Both systems will need to be registered to a valid high availability subscription.

Static IP Addresses

In Figure 14-1, you can see that both nodes have static IP addresses assigned. Node 1 with the hostname rhel9-node1 was assigned the IP address 192.168.122.110. Node 2 with the hostname rhel9-node2 was assigned the IP address 192.168.122.111.

Hostname Resolution

As no DNS server is being used for this environment, both rhel9-node1 and rhel9-node2 have had their /etc/hosts file configured with entries shown in Figure 14-2 to allow hostname resolution.

```
127.0.0.1    localhost localhost.localdomain localhost4 localhost4.localdomain4
::1          localhost localhost.localdomain localhost6 localhost6.localdomain6

192.168.122.110 rhel9-node1 rhel9-node1.kenlab.local
192.168.122.111 rhel9-node2 rhel9-node2.kenlab.local
~
~
```

Figure 14-2. */etc/hosts file configuration for the two nodes*

NTP

Both RHEL 9 nodes have the default NTP configuration provided during the installation, and both systems have their date and time in sync with each other.

rhel9-node1

```
[root@rhel9-node1 ~]# date
Mon  5 Sep 22:31:31 BST 2022
```

rhel9-node2

```
[root@rhel9-node2 ~]# date
Mon  5 Sep 22:31:35 BST 2022
```

Communication Between Nodes

Both rhel9-node1 and rhel9-node2 can communicate with each other.

```
[root@rhel9-node1 ~]# ping rhel9-node2
PING rhel9-node2 (192.168.122.111) 56(84) bytes of data.
64 bytes from rhel9-node2 (192.168.122.111): icmp_seq=1 ttl=64 time=1.23 ms
64 bytes from rhel9-node2 (192.168.122.111): icmp_seq=2 ttl=64 time=0.769 ms
64 bytes from rhel9-node2 (192.168.122.111): icmp_seq=3 ttl=64 time=0.946 ms
64 bytes from rhel9-node2 (192.168.122.111): icmp_seq=4 ttl=64 time=0.683 ms

[root@rhel9-node2 ~]# ping rhel9-node1
PING rhel9-node1 (192.168.122.110) 56(84) bytes of data.
64 bytes from rhel9-node1 (192.168.122.110): icmp_seq=1 ttl=64 time=0.760 ms
64 bytes from rhel9-node1 (192.168.122.110): icmp_seq=2 ttl=64 time=0.908 ms
64 bytes from rhel9-node1 (192.168.122.110): icmp_seq=3 ttl=64 time=0.930 ms
64 bytes from rhel9-node1 (192.168.122.110): icmp_seq=4 ttl=64 time=0.720 ms
```

Figure 14-3. *Network connectivity between both nodes confirmed*

In Figure 14-3, you can see that rhel9-node1 can ping rhel9-node2 and vice versa. Both nodes are also pinging using hostnames, and as you can see, the hostnames are being resolved into IP addresses.

Subscribe to Subscription

Both nodes have been registered with Red Hat using the following commands:

```
# sudo subscription-manager register
# sudo subscription-manager attach --auto
```

The --auto option was used as there is only one subscription in the account I am using. With accounts that have multiple subscriptions, you will want to use the --pool option and specify the subscription you wish to use.

```
The registered system name is: rhel9-node1
[root@rhel9-node1 ~]# subscription-manager attach --auto
Installed Product Current Status:
Product Name: Red Hat Enterprise Linux for x86_64
Status:        Subscribed

The registered system name is: rhel9-node2
[root@rhel9-node2 ~]# subscription-manager attach --auto
Installed Product Current Status:
Product Name: Red Hat Enterprise Linux for x86_64
Status:        Subscribed
```

Figure 14-4. *Subscription status of both RHEL nodes*

In Figure 14-4, you can see that both rhel9-node1 and rhel9-node2 have been registered and subscribed to a valid Red Hat subscription.

Cluster Installation

To configure two or more RHEL nodes into a cluster, the following steps will need to be followed.

Install Packages

Before any clustering packages can be installed on RHEL, you need to enable the correct repositories. This can be done with the following command:

```
# sudo subscription-manager repos --enable=rhel-9-for-x86_64-
highavailability-rpms
```

```
[root@rhel9-node1 ~]# subscription-manager repos --enable=rhel-9-for-x86_64-highavailability-rpms
Repository 'rhel-9-for-x86_64-highavailability-rpms' is enabled for this system.

[root@rhel9-node2 ~]# subscription-manager repos --enable=rhel-9-for-x86_64-highavailability-rpms
Repository 'rhel-9-for-x86_64-highavailability-rpms' is enabled for this system.
```

Figure 14-5. *Subscription-manager command to enable repositories*

From the figures, you can see that both rhel9-node1 and rhel9-node2 have their repositories enabled.

With the repositories now enabled, you can install the required packages using the following command:

```
# sudo dnf install pcs fence-agents-all -y
```

```
[root@rhel9-node1 ~]# sudo dnf install pcs fence-agents-all -y
Updating Subscription Management repositories.
Red Hat Enterprise Linux 9 for x86_64 - High Availability (RPMs)         218 kB/s | 447 kB      00:02
Dependencies resolved.
=================================================================================================
 Package                      Arch      Version                 Repository                           Size
=================================================================================================
Installing:
 fence-agents-all             x86_64    4.10.0-20.el9_0.2       rhel-9-for-x86_64-highavailability-rpms    11 k
 pcs                          x86_64    0.11.1-10.el9_0.2       rhel-9-for-x86_64-highavailability-rpms   8.6 M
Installing dependencies:
 avahi-libs                   x86_64    0.8-12.el9              rhel-9-for-x86_64-baseos-rpms          71 k
 bzip2                        x86_64    1.0.8-8.el9             rhel-9-for-x86_64-baseos-rpms          60 k
 corosync                     x86_64    3.1.5-3.el9             rhel-9-for-x86_64-highavailability-rpms   275 k
 corosynclib                  x86_64    3.1.5-3.el9             rhel-9-for-x86_64-appstream-rpms       60 k
 cups-libs                    x86_64    1:2.3.3op2-13.el9_0.1   rhel-9-for-x86_64-baseos-rpms         267 k
 device-mapper-multipath      x86_64    0.8.7-7.el9             rhel-9-for-x86_64-baseos-rpms         151 k
 device-mapper-multipath-libs x86_64    0.8.7-7.el9             rhel-9-for-x86_64-baseos-rpms         287 k
 fence-agents-amt-ws          noarch    4.10.0-20.el9_0.2       rhel-9-for-x86_64-highavailability-rpms    16 k
 fence-agents-apc             noarch    4.10.0-20.el9_0.2       rhel-9-for-x86_64-highavailability-rpms    16 k
 fence-agents-apc-snmp        noarch    4.10.0-20.el9_0.2       rhel-9-for-x86_64-highavailability-rpms    19 k
```

Figure 14-6. *Package installation for cluster components*

Your install should look similar to the reduced output shown in Figure 14-6. There will be a number of packages that will be installed that will be used to create the cluster.

Firewall Rules

Before the cluster can be configured or started, both nodes will need to speak to each other on the high availability ports. To enable this, the following firewall rule needs to be added:

```
# sudo firewall-cmd --permanent --add-service=high-availability
# sudo firewall-cmd --reload
```

```
[root@rhel9-node1 ~]# firewall-cmd --permanent --add-service=high-availability
success
[root@rhel9-node1 ~]# firewall-cmd --reload
success

[root@rhel9-node2 ~]# firewall-cmd --permanent --add-service=high-availability
success
[root@rhel9-node2 ~]# firewall-cmd --reload
success
```

Figure 14-7. *Firewall configuration updated to allow cluster communication between nodes*

Warning   If you do not configure your firewall and the firewall is enabled, you will fail to form a cluster in the next steps.

Cluster User Account

For cluster nodes to communicate with each other, they need to use a user account. The account hacluster is used on all nodes. This account is created when the pcs packages are installed. However, the hacluster account needs to have its password set. On all nodes, set the same password for the hacluster account.

```
# sudo passwd hacluster
```

```
[root@rhel9-node1 ~]# passwd hacluster
Changing password for user hacluster.
New password:
BAD PASSWORD: The password fails the dictionary check - it is based on a dictionary word
Retype new password:
passwd: all authentication tokens updated successfully.



[root@rhel9-node2 ~]# passwd hacluster
Changing password for user hacluster.
New password:
BAD PASSWORD: The password fails the dictionary check - it is based on a dictionary word
Retype new password:
passwd: all authentication tokens updated successfully.
```

Figure 14-8. *Password updated for the hacluster user on both nodes*

Warning   In a production environment, be sure to use a strong password.
The example here is using a weak password of password123, hence the BAD
PASSWORD warning.

Cluster Services

Start and enable the cluster services using the following commands:

sudo systemctl start pcsd.service
sudo systemctl enable pcsd.service

```
[root@rhel9-node1 ~]# systemctl start pcsd.service
[root@rhel9-node1 ~]# systemctl enable pcsd.service
Created symlink /etc/systemd/system/multi-user.target.wants/pcsd.service → /usr/lib/systemd/system/pcsd.service.
[root@rhel9-node2 ~]# systemctl start pcsd.service
[root@rhel9-node2 ~]# systemctl enable pcsd.service
Created symlink /etc/systemd/system/multi-user.target.wants/pcsd.service → /usr/lib/systemd/system/pcsd.service.
```

Figure 14-9. *pscd service started and enabled*

It is vital that all nodes have the pcsd service started. Without the service started, the
next steps will fail.

Cluster Setup

With all the prerequisites now in place and all packages installed, the cluster can finally
be configured. On one node only, run the following commands to create a cluster.

Authorize Nodes

```
# pcs host auth rhel9-node1.kenlab.local rhel9-node2.kenlab.local
```

```
[root@rhel9-node1 ~]# pcs host auth rhel9-node1.kenlab.local rhel9-node2.kenlab.local
Username: hacluster
Password:
rhel9-node2.kenlab.local: Authorized
rhel9-node1.kenlab.local: Authorized
```

Figure 14-10.   *pcs host auth command*

For the username, use the hacluster account and the password that was configured.

Form the Cluster

Once your nodes have been authorized successfully from the previous command, run
the following command or similar to create the cluster:

```
# pcs cluster setup ken_cluster --start rhel9-node1.kenlab.local rhel9-
node2.kenlab.local
```

```
[root@rhel9-node1 ~]# pcs cluster setup ken_cluster --start rhel9-node1.kenlab.local rhel9-node2.kenlab.local
No addresses specified for host 'rhel9-node1.kenlab.local', using 'rhel9-node1.kenlab.local'
No addresses specified for host 'rhel9-node2.kenlab.local', using 'rhel9-node2.kenlab.local'
Destroying cluster on hosts: 'rhel9-node1.kenlab.local', 'rhel9-node2.kenlab.local'...
rhel9-node1.kenlab.local: Successfully destroyed cluster
rhel9-node2.kenlab.local: Successfully destroyed cluster
Requesting remove 'pcsd settings' from 'rhel9-node1.kenlab.local', 'rhel9-node2.kenlab.local'
rhel9-node1.kenlab.local: successful removal of the file 'pcsd settings'
rhel9-node2.kenlab.local: successful removal of the file 'pcsd settings'
Sending 'corosync authkey', 'pacemaker authkey' to 'rhel9-node1.kenlab.local', 'rhel9-node2.kenlab.local'
rhel9-node1.kenlab.local: successful distribution of the file 'corosync authkey'
rhel9-node1.kenlab.local: successful distribution of the file 'pacemaker authkey'
rhel9-node2.kenlab.local: successful distribution of the file 'corosync authkey'
rhel9-node2.kenlab.local: successful distribution of the file 'pacemaker authkey'
Sending 'corosync.conf' to 'rhel9-node1.kenlab.local', 'rhel9-node2.kenlab.local'
rhel9-node1.kenlab.local: successful distribution of the file 'corosync.conf'
rhel9-node2.kenlab.local: successful distribution of the file 'corosync.conf'
Cluster has been successfully set up.
Starting cluster on hosts: 'rhel9-node1.kenlab.local', 'rhel9-node2.kenlab.local'...
```

Figure 14-11.   *pcs cluster setup command*

The cluster command shown in Figure 14-11 has succeeded in creating the new
cluster called ken_cluster.

The final bit to the cluster creation is to enable the remaining cluster services on
all nodes. The following command should be run on the same nodes the previous
commands were run:

```
# sudo pcs cluster enable --all
```

```
[root@rhel9-node1 ~]# pcs cluster enable --all
rhel9-node1.kenlab.local: Cluster Enabled
rhel9-node2.kenlab.local: Cluster Enabled
```

Figure 14-12. *pcs cluster enable command for all nodes*

In Figure 14-12, you can see that all nodes are configured using the --all switch. For this reason, it is not required to run the command on each node individually.

Cluster Quorum

If there are only two nodes in the cluster, ensure that the two_node and wait_for_all options are enabled in the quorum section of /etc/corosync/corosync.conf. Once you have updated the configuration file, run the following commands:

```
# sudo pcs cluster sync
# sudo pcs cluster stop --all
# sudo pcs cluster start --all
```

Cluster Status

To view the status of the newly created cluster, you can run the following command:

```
# sudo pcs status
```

Two nodes have been added to the cluster and can be seen in Figure 14-13 as being online.

```
[root@rhel9-node1 ~]# pcs status
Cluster name: ken_cluster

WARNINGS:
No stonith devices and stonith-enabled is not false

Cluster Summary:
  * Stack: corosync
  * Current DC: rhel9-node2.kenlab.local (version 2.1.2-4.el9-ada5c3b36e2) - partition with quorum
  * Last updated: Tue Sep  6 21:55:12 2022
  * Last change:  Tue Sep  6 21:41:56 2022 by hacluster via crmd on rhel9-node2.kenlab.local
  * 2 nodes configured
  * 0 resource instances configured

Node List:
  * Online: [ rhel9-node1.kenlab.local rhel9-node2.kenlab.local ]

Full List of Resources:
  * No resources

Daemon Status:
  corosync: active/enabled
  pacemaker: active/enabled
  pcsd: active/enabled
```

Figure 14-13. *pcs status command*

A slightly different way to view the cluster status is to run the following command:

pcs cluster status

```
[root@rhel9-node1 ~]# pcs cluster status
Cluster Status:
 Cluster Summary:
   * Stack: corosync
   * Current DC: rhel9-node2.kenlab.local (version 2.1.2-4.el9-ada5c3b36e2) - partition with quorum
   * Last updated: Tue Sep  6 21:59:00 2022
   * Last change:  Tue Sep  6 21:41:56 2022 by hacluster via crmd on rhel9-node2.kenlab.local
   * 2 nodes configured
   * 0 resource instances configured
 Node List:
   * Online: [ rhel9-node1.kenlab.local rhel9-node2.kenlab.local ]

PCSD Status:
  rhel9-node1.kenlab.local: Online
  rhel9-node2.kenlab.local: Online
```

Figure 14-14. *pcs cluster status command*

Note   Not much has been explained about quorum in this book and other
clustering concepts. For this, it is best to do further reading on this subject before
building any production clusters.

Fencing

In the cluster concepts table at the beginning of this chapter, we spoke about fencing and how fencing is the process of dealing with nodes that have failed. To deal with the failed node, a fence device is required. This fence device is usually a device that has the ability to physically restart a node. A physical server, for instance, would be configured with the ILO or DRAC or similar; this would then allow the remaining cluster nodes to physically turn off the failed node and turn it back on again.

KVM Fencing

For the example in this chapter, the cluster nodes have been built and configured using KVM virtual machines. For the fencing to work for these nodes, the KVM host needs to be configured to allow fencing. To configure a KVM hypervisor to allow fencing, the following needs to be done:

1. Install the fencing packages using the following command:

   ```
   # sudo dnf -y install fence-virtd fence-virtd-libvirt
   fence-virtd-multicast
   ```

2. Create the /etc/cluster directory and generate a fence_xvm. key file:

   ```
   # sudo mkdir -p /etc/cluster
   # sudo dd if=/dev/urandom of=/etc/cluster/fence_xvm.key
   bs=1k count=4
   ```

3. Create the fencing configuration by running the following command and accepting all the defaults:

   ```
   # sudo fence_virtd -c
   ```

4. Start and enable the fence_virtd service:

   ```
   # systemctl enable fence_virtd
   # systemctl start fence_virtd
   ```

5. Open the TCP and udp 1229 port on the KVM hypervisor:

```
# sudo firewall-cmd --permanent --add-port=1229/
tcp --zone=libvirt
# sudo firewall-cmd --permanent --add-port=1229/
udp --zone=libvirt
# sudo firewall-cmd --reload
```

Node Fencing

To use the fence_xvm fencing device on the nodes in this chapter's cluster example, the following needs to be done on each node:

1. On each node, open the TCP port 1229 to allow fencing:

```
# sudo firewall-cmd --permanent --add-port=1229/tcp
# sudo firewall-cmd --reload
```

2. On each node, create the following directory:

```
# sudo mkdir /etc/cluster
```

3. Copy the /etc/cluster/fence_xvm.key file from the KVM hypervisor that was configured earlier to the directory that was just created in step 2:

```
# scp /etc/cluster/fence_xvm.key root@rhel9-node1:/etc/cluster/
# scp /etc/cluster/fence_xvm.key root@rhel9-node2:/etc/cluster/
```

```
[ken@localhost ~]$ scp /etc/cluster/fence_xvm.key root@rhel9-node1:/etc/cluster/
root@rhel9-node1's password:
fence_xvm.key                                                  100% 4096     5.7MB/s   00:00
[ken@localhost ~]$ scp /etc/cluster/fence_xvm.key root@rhel9-node2:/etc/cluster/
root@rhel9-node2's password:
fence_xvm.key           _                                     100% 4096     6.8MB/s   00:00
```

Figure 14-15. *fence_xvm.key file copied to both nodes*

4. Before adding the fence device to the cluster, confirm that the following command succeeds on both cluster nodes first:

```
# fence_xvm -o list
```

```
[root@rhel9-node1 ~]# fence_xvm -o list
fedora-server                   be49f0db-2edb-4a85-b4dc-ed855ddf32e5 off
opensuse-server                 5c3e14c6-f1e6-439e-b35d-94418f23d3a7 off
rhel9-node1                     ad111fec-08d4-400d-9307-cfcc3dce10f1 on
rhel9-node2                     bc24d3e3-023c-450b-9b19-4d84a531731d on
rhel9-server                    1ef05bb7-e790-4a95-82b2-07708a8393ce off
sles15-server                   61674fa9-a3d2-42bd-9b15-1776d5735f32 off
Ubuntu-Server             _     71dc68c8-44c2-419a-94a4-156124cd5d76 off
```

Figure 14-16. *Fence_xvm -o list command*

Warning   This command will not work if your firewalls are not configured successfully. If you get timeout errors, turn off the firewall on your hypervisor and test again. If it works, you most likely have not configured the correct zone in your firewall.

---

5.   Finally, create the fencing device in the cluster using the following command or similar:

pcs stonith create xvmfence fence_xvm pcmk_host_map="rhel9-node1.kenlab.local:rhel9-node1 rhel9-node2.kenlab.local:rhel9-node2" key_file=/etc/cluster/fence_xvm.key

The pcmk_host_map parameter is used to match the hostname of the virtual machine with the actual virtual machine name.

The command "pcs status" should look very similar to that shown in Figure 14-17.

```
[root@rhel9-node1 ~]# pcs status
Cluster name: ken_cluster
Cluster Summary:
  * Stack: corosync
  * Current DC: rhel9-node2.kenlab.local (version 2.1.2-4.el9-ada5c3b36e2) - partition with quorum
  * Last updated: Wed Sep  7 22:31:06 2022
  * Last change:  Wed Sep  7 22:24:18 2022 by root via cibadmin on rhel9-node1.kenlab.local
  * 2 nodes configured
  * 1 resource instance configured

Node List:
  * Online: [ rhel9-node1.kenlab.local rhel9-node2.kenlab.local ]

Full List of Resources:
  * xvmfence     (stonith:fence_xvm):     Started rhel9-node1.kenlab.local

Daemon Status:
  corosync: active/enabled
  pacemaker: active/enabled
  pcsd: active/enabled
```

Figure 14-17. *pcs status after fence devices were created*

If the fence device configured has not started, there is most likely an issue communicating with the fence device on the hypervisor or remote system. Check firewalls and check that network communication is working.

Note   This example in this chapter relies on multicast traffic; if there is anything blocking multicast traffic on your network, this example will not work for you.

Cluster Resources

Once your cluster has been configured and fencing is in place, you are ready to start adding services on your cluster.

Depending how you want to use the cluster will determine how you configure the services. In the cluster example of this chapter, we will configure the following services.

Virtual IP Address

Adding a virtual IP address to the cluster can be done using a command similar to the following:

```
# pcs resource create webip ocf:heartbeat:IPaddr2 ip=192.168.122.115 cidr_
netmask=24
```

The service can be seen running using the command "pcs status".

```
[root@rhel9-node1 ~]# pcs status
Cluster name: ken_cluster
Cluster Summary:
  * Stack: corosync
  * Current DC: rhel9-node2.kenlab.local (version 2.1.2-4.el9-ada5c3b36e2) - partition with quorum
  * Last updated: Wed Sep  7 22:41:55 2022
  * Last change:  Wed Sep  7 22:41:01 2022 by root via cibadmin on rhel9-node1.kenlab.local
  * 2 nodes configured
  * 2 resource instances configured

Node List:
  * Online: [ rhel9-node1.kenlab.local rhel9-node2.kenlab.local ]

Full List of Resources:
  * xvmfence    (stonith:fence_xvm):     Started rhel9-node1.kenlab.local
  * webip       (ocf:heartbeat:IPaddr2):         Started rhel9-node2.kenlab.local

Daemon Status:
  corosync: active/enabled
  pacemaker: active/enabled
  pcsd: active/enabled_
```

Figure 14-18. *pcs cluster status*

In Figure 14-18, you can now see that the new "webip" service has started on rhel9-node2.kenlab.local.

On node rhel9-node2.kenlab.local, you will also see that the new IP address has been added to the interface.

```
[root@rhel9-node2 ~]# ip a
1: lo: <LOOPBACK,UP,LOWER_UP> mtu 65536 qdisc noqueue state UNKNOWN group default qlen 1000
    link/loopback 00:00:00:00:00:00 brd 00:00:00:00:00:00
    inet 127.0.0.1/8 scope host lo
       valid_lft forever preferred_lft forever
    inet6 ::1/128 scope host
       valid_lft forever preferred_lft forever
2: enp1s0: <BROADCAST,MULTICAST,UP,LOWER_UP> mtu 1500 qdisc fq_codel state UP group default qlen 1000
    link/ether 52:54:00:a0:57:c1 brd ff:ff:ff:ff:ff:ff
    inet 192.168.122.111/24 brd 192.168.122.255 scope global noprefixroute enp1s0
       valid_lft forever preferred_lft forever
    inet 192.168.122.115/24 brd 192.168.122.255 scope global secondary enp1s0
       valid_lft forever preferred_lft forever
    inet6 fe80::5054:ff:fea0:57c1/64 scope link noprefixroute
       valid_lft forever preferred_lft forever
```

Figure 14-19. *Additional IP address now attached to the network interface on rhel9-node2*

Web Server

The final service that will be added to this cluster is a web server. This web server will be able to run on either node in an active-passive configuration, meaning that only one node will be active at a time.

Before adding the service to the cluster, each node will need to have the Apache web server packages installed.

```
# sudo dnf install httpd -y
```

You will also need to open the firewall on each node for the web server.

```
# sudo firewall-cmd --add-port=80/tcp --permanent
# sudo firewall-cmd --reload
```

Once the packages are installed and the firewall opened, you can add the web server to the cluster as a service.

```
# pcs resource create webserver ocf:heartbeat:apache
```

```
[root@rhel9-node1 ~]# pcs status
Cluster name: ken_cluster
Cluster Summary:
  * Stack: corosync
  * Current DC: rhel9-node2.kenlab.local (version 2.1.2-4.el9-ada5c3b36e2) - partition with quorum
  * Last updated: Wed Sep  7 22:50:23 2022
  * Last change:  Wed Sep  7 22:50:20 2022 by root via cibadmin on rhel9-node1.kenlab.local
  * 2 nodes configured
  * 3 resource instances configured

Node List:
  * Online: [ rhel9-node1.kenlab.local rhel9-node2.kenlab.local ]

Full List of Resources:
  * xvmfence    (stonith:fence_xvm):     Started rhel9-node1.kenlab.local
  * webip       (ocf:heartbeat:IPaddr2):      Started rhel9-node2.kenlab.local
  * webserver   (ocf:heartbeat:apache):  Started rhel9-node1.kenlab.local

Daemon Status:
  corosync: active/enabled
  pacemaker: active/enabled
  pcsd: active/enabled
```

Figure 14-20. *pcs cluster status after the webserver cluster resource was added*

Note   Do you notice the problem with configuration in Figure 14-20?

Fixing the Cluster

In Figure 14-20, the output of the cluster configuration shows that the "webip" and "webserver" have started on separate nodes. This would mean that when browsing to the "webserver" on the "webip" would not work, the "webserver" starts the "httpd" service on the node, and the "webip" provides the IP address. If both are not on the same node, the overall solution would not work.

To resolve the cluster issue above, the following will need to be done.

Removing resource

The first thing to do would be to remove the two resources created. This is simply done by running the following commands:

```
# pcs resource delete webserver
# pcs resource delete webip
```

```
[root@rhel9-node1 ~]# pcs resource delete webserver
Attempting to stop: webserver... Stopped
[root@rhel9-node1 ~]# pcs resource delete webip
Attempting to stop: webip... Stopped
```

Figure 14-21. *The removal of cluster resources*

In Figure 14-21, you can see that the service attempts to stop first and then deletes. If you delete resources in the wrong order, this can sometimes hang as the resource is being used elsewhere. In the figure, the "webserver" is deleted first as it uses the "webip"; this way, the "webip" can be deleted without being held by the "webserver".

Group Resources

Once the "incorrect" configuration has been removed, we recreate each and include the --group parameter to add both resources to a single group.

```
# pcs resource create webip ocf:heartbeat:IPaddr2 ip=192.168.122.115
cidr_netmask=24 --group webconfig
# pcs resource create webserver ocf:heartbeat:apache --group webconfig
```

Cluster Status

As mentioned previously, to view the status of your cluster, you can run the following command:

```
# pcs status
```

```
[root@rhel9-node1 ~]# pcs status
Cluster name: ken_cluster
Cluster Summary:
  * Stack: corosync
  * Current DC: rhel9-node2.kenlab.local (version 2.1.2-4.el9-ada5c3b36e2) - partition with quorum
  * Last updated: Thu Sep  8 22:08:00 2022
  * Last change:  Thu Sep  8 22:07:54 2022 by root via cibadmin on rhel9-node1.kenlab.local
  * 2 nodes configured
  * 3 resource instances configured

Node List:
  * Online: [ rhel9-node1.kenlab.local rhel9-node2.kenlab.local ]

Full List of Resources:
  * xvmfence     (stonith:fence_xvm):      Started rhel9-node2.kenlab.local
  * Resource Group: webconfig:
    * webip      (ocf:heartbeat:IPaddr2):       Started rhel9-node1.kenlab.local
    * webserver (ocf:heartbeat:apache):  Started rhel9-node1.kenlab.local

Daemon Status:
  corosync: active/enabled
  pacemaker: active/enabled
  pcsd: active/enabled_
```

Figure 14-22. *pcs cluster status command after correcting the cluster issue*

In Figure 14-22, you can see the updated status after fixing the cluster resources. In this figure, it now shows that both "webip" and "webserver" are running on the same node. If the resource group "webconfig" fails to start on rhel9-node1, it will attempt to start on rhel9-node2.

Cluster Troubleshooting

There may be times when a cluster will misbehave or not function as you were intending. This can be down to many things, and to explain them all would extend this chapter far beyond the scope of this book. As an absolute minimum, the following should help with most issues.

Logs

The logs on your cluster nodes will give you a wealth of information that could help pinpoint your issue. The logs are generally located in the following locations:

```
# /var/log/messages
# /var/log/pacemaker/pacemaker.log
# /var/log/cluster/corosync.log
```

These logs should always be your first port of call when hunting down a cluster issue. Everything from resources failing to start or nodes being fenced can be found in them.

Official Documentation

There is no replacement for official documentation. Always read and follow the documentation when building your environments. The latest documentation will include known bugs, workarounds, warnings, and fully tested steps. Even the most seasoned enterprise Linux administrators follow the documentation.

```
https://access.redhat.com/documentation/en-us/red_hat_enterprise_
linux/9/pdf/configuring_and_managing_high_availability_clusters/red_hat_
enterprise_linux-9-configuring_and_managing_high_availability_clusters-
en-us.pdf
```

If the URL is too long, just google Red Hat clustering installation guide.

Official Training

Enterprise Linux companies like Red Hat also have training available on RHEL clustering if you want to extend your knowledge through a structured training course.

Exercise

To gain some experience around building clusters, run through the following exercise and see how far you are able to get based on what you have learned so far.

Prerequisites

To build a cluster, you will need to create and configure two new RHEL 9 servers. The servers will need at least 2 CPUs and 4GB of memory with no more than 20GB of disk.

The reason for two RHEL 9 systems is because the 60-day subscription will only allow a maximum of two entitlements. You could unregister one and register a third system, but it is up to you if you want to build a three-node cluster.

Build a Cluster

With your newly built RHEL 9 systems, do the following:

- Create a new cluster named "test_cluster".

- Do not add any fencing devices but ensure that you do not get any errors.

- Add a virtual IP address to your cluster and configure a highly available web server.

- Add a custom HTML page for each node.

Success Criteria

To determine if you have successfully built a working web server in a highly available cluster, run through the following steps:

1. Ensure that your web server is running on node 1.

2. Open a browser and connect to the virtual IP address to confirm you can see your custom HTML page for node 1.

3. Shutdown node 1 and confirm that your cluster has failed over to node 2.

4. Refresh your web browser and confirm that the custom HTML page for node 2 is now showing.

5. Turn node 1 back on and confirm that the cluster has failed back over to node 1.

Summary

In this chapter, you were introduced to the following:

- What enterprise Linux clustering is and what the different types of clusters there are available

- How RHEL, SUSE, and Ubuntu all use the same cluster technologies provided by the Pacemaker and Corosync communities

- What are some of the basic terms that are used in clustering such as Quorum, heartbeat, and fencing

- How to build and configure a RHEL cluster

## CHAPTER 15

Scripting and Automation

There comes a time when tasks need to be performed more than once as an enterprise Linux administrator. In this chapter, we will start exploring how this can be done and what tools are available to you to use.

This chapter will be the introduction to automation that all enterprise Linux administrators should have when starting their career. It will give you the basic foundation to get started and allow you to expand into more advanced scripting.

In this chapter, we will look at traditional shell scripting and the different shell scripting languages that can be used. We will explore some examples and some basic syntax that can be used in your own scripts in the future.

We will continue with automation in the chapter by looking at Ansible and how Ansible can be used in a more enterprise manner than traditional shell scripts. We will explore the tools that can be used with Ansible and how Ansible can be used in different use cases. Finally we will run through a few basic Ansible examples to give you an idea of how Ansible can be used.

Shell Scripting

Shell scripting is the process of automating tasks that are normally run manually on a Linux shell environment. Often certain tasks need to be repeated as an administrator; to run these tasks manually would be a very inefficient use of time when dealing with many systems. To speed up system configuration, shell scripts have traditionally been used.

Linux Shell

When you log in to a Linux system through the command line, you are logging into a shell. The shell is where your different utilities can be used and the system can be configured. This is often referred to as the command-line interface or CLI.

© Kenneth Hitchcock 2023
K. Hitchcock, *The Enterprise Linux Administrator*, https://doi.org/10.1007/978-1-4842-8801-6_15

There are numerous shells available today, with each having their own features and syntax.

A user-friendly Linux shell typically has the following:

- Command autocomplete

- Command history

- Command history search capabilities

- Simple to use syntax

The most commonly used shell today is bash, which includes all of the aforementioned. There are a number of other shell options available, which are listed in the following.

Shell Environments

There are many different shell environments that can be used today; the common shell environment most enterprise Linux system administrators use is the "Bourne again shell" or bash as it is more commonly known.

In the following are a few examples of different Linux and Unix shell environments that can be used.

Table 15-1 lists a few of the common shells used today.

Table 15-1. *Shell environments*

Shell	Description
sh	Bourne shell (sh) was the original shell used by most on Unix and later Linux.
bash	Bourne again shell. Created as a replacement for the Bourne shell and is most commonly used today.
ksh	Used mostly by administrators with a HP-UX or AIX background.
zsh	Another shell that is an extension of the Bourne shell boasting improved variable and array handling as one of the improved features.
csh	C shell was written to keep the shell's syntax in-line with the C programming language used to write Linux code.
tcsh	Its effectivity is the same as csh with extra functionality such as command-line completion.

Check Your Shell Environment

A quick method to check the shell environment you are using is through the $SHELL environmental variable. Run the following command to show your current shell environment configured for your account:

```
# echo  $SHELL
```

Change Shell Environments

When a user account is created on a Linux system, a shell is typically automatically assigned. The default shell for most enterprise Linux distributions is normally bash, but if you wanted to use a different shell, you can use the following command to change it:

```
# sudo usermod -s <path to shell> <user account>
# sudo usermod -s /bin/ksh ken
```

To take effect, you will need to log out and back in again.

```
[ken@rhel9-server ~]$ sudo usermod -s /bin/ksh ken
[sudo] password for ken:
[ken@rhel9-server ~]$ echo $SHELL
/bin/bash
[ken@rhel9-server ~]$ exit
logout
Connection to rhel9-server closed.
[ken@localhost ~]$ ssh rhel9-server
ken@rhel9-server's password:
Activate the web console with: systemctl enable --now cockpit.socket

Last login: Sat Sep 10 16:06:35 2022 from 192.168.122.1
$ echo $SHELL
/bin/ksh
$ sudo usermod -s /bin/bash ken
[sudo] password for ken:
$ echo $SHELL
/bin/ksh
$ exit
Connection to rhel9-server closed.
[ken@localhost ~]$ ssh rhel9-server
ken@rhel9-server's password:
Activate the web console with: systemctl enable --now cockpit.socket

Last login: Sat Sep 10 16:11:35 2022 from 192.168.122.1
[ken@rhel9-server ~]$ echo $SHELL
/bin/bash
[ken@rhel9-server ~]$ ▮
```

Figure 15-1. *Setting different shell environments for a user*

In the example shown in Figure 15-1, the shell for the user account ken was changed to /bin/ksh and then changed back to /bin/bash.

> **Note**   To use another shell environment, you will need to install the shell packages. For the previous example, the "ksh" package was installed.

Shell Scripting Basics

Now with the understanding that there are different shell environments and with each environment there will be differences in how they are used, we can begin by looking at how to build a shell script.

For the purpose of this book, we will stick to bash shell scripting as this will most likely be what you would be using as an enterprise Linux administrator. However, feel free to research and try other shells to find what suits you best.

Before Writing a Script

Writing Linux shell scripts is definitely a good way to automate tasks that need to be repeated, but there are a few things you should always ask before starting any automation tasks.

Is a Script Needed?

Does this task really need to be automated? Sometimes a task only ever needs to be run once or once every few years. Automating for the sake of automation is not always a good idea as the process of writing a script or automation will take time. The command or process could have changed the next time the script needs to run and could require a rewrite. Only write scripts that will save time.

Does This Already Exist?

Is there a script on the Internet you could download and use? Why reinvent the wheel if someone has already done the work for you. By all means, read the code and sanitize it for your organization but do not rewrite some time for the sake of writing a script.

Check if any utilities available will do the same thing you want to do. That is, don't write an email replay application if you can just install one already available.

Keep It Simple

Do not overcomplicate your script. You do not have to add every check and function to every script. Remember this script is supposed to save you time. If you want to write an overly complicated script, write a Python application or similar.

Script Structure

A typical shell script has the following structure. This is typically how most scripts will start and then evolve into a massively overcomplicated bit of over-engineering if you are not careful. Remember to keep your scripts as simple as possible:

```
<The interpreter>
#!/bin/bash
<Variables>
VAR1=1
<Script body>
echo $VAR1
```

Interpreters

The interpreter is what scripting language or shell scripts will use. There are numerous shell environments that can be used, some of which have already been explained on previous pages of this book.

However, there are also other options that can be used. Programming languages such as Python and Perl can also be specified as an interpreter. This would then allow the script to be used in conjunction with the corresponding compiler or runtime to execute your code.

For this chapter, we will continue to use the /bin/bash shell interpreter with all our examples. For all our examples, our scripts will all start with the following line:

```
#!/bin/bash
```

The "#!" in front of the "/bin/bash" is known as a "shebang" and effectively tells the operating system what interpreter or programming language to use when the script is executed. It does exactly the same as the following command, which uses the "/bin/bash" executable to run the script:

```
# /bin/bash <nameofscript>.sh
```

Variables

Once you have set your interpreter, the next bit of a script focuses on your variables.

Variables do not need to be declared; you only need to set a value to it. Shell scripting variables do not have a data type set to them; just set the value, and if you need to do any mathematical calculations, you will need to do something a bit different, which will get explained further down in the succeeding text.

Setting Variables

Variables are set by typing the name you wish to use for your variable followed by the "=" character, followed by the value you wish to store in the variable:

```
MYVAR="myvalue"
```

Note   Variables are case sensitive. I typically type my variables in uppercase so it is easy for me to find. However, this might not always be the best thing to do. The general rule of thumb is if the variables are only used within your script, feel free to do what you want. If you export the variables outside of your script, be very careful as you could inadvertently change an environmental variable as they are all capitalized.

Variable Names

The golden rule with variables is to make sure they make sense to you and to anyone else that will read your code. Always try to use names that make sense to what you will be doing with the variable:

```
#!/bin/bash
TODAYS_DATE=`date`
```

With the previous example, the variable "TODAYS_DATE" is very clear to what it will store.

Special Variables

There are a few special variables you can use within your scripts. The $1 or $2 or $3, etc. are variables that are set based on the parameters you pass after your script when you execute it. The following command will show the value for a $1 variable, assuming the script name is test.sh:

```
# ./test.sh testvalue
```

The value of the $1 variable will be "testvalue".

Table 15-2 lists a few other special variables.

Table 15-2. *Special variables*

Variable	Description
$0	File name of the script being executed.
$#	The number of arguments being passed with the script.
$*	All the arguments will be wrapped with double quotes and combined. The values of $1 and $2 will appear as $1 $2.
$@	Each argument is wrapped individually with double quotes.
$?	Will display the exit code of the last executed command.
$$	Will display the process number of the current running shell.
$!	Will display the process number of the last task set to run in the background. Useful when you need to find and kill the task.

Variable Arithmetic

When you have to do some mathematical calculations with variables, you will need to use different syntax to set a normal variable. This is due to the fact that all values are interpreted as string values.

Take the following variable as an example:

```
x=1
```

With the previous variable, the value of 1 will be interpreted as a string with the character 1.

The example in Figure 15-2 shows that if we try to add 1 to the variable's value, the value returned is not as expected.

```
[ken@rhel9-server ~]$ x=1
[ken@rhel9-server ~]$ x=$x+1
[ken@rhel9-server ~]$ echo $x
1+1                          _
```

Figure 15-2. *Code that does not compute*

To make the example work, we need to change how our variable is stored and used. One option is to use the declare method.

```
[ken@rhel9-server ~]$ declare -i x=1
[ken@rhel9-server ~]$ echo $x
1
[ken@rhel9-server ~]$ declare -i x=$x+1
[ken@rhel9-server ~]$ echo $x
2
```

Figure 15-3. *Declare variable option*

You can also use the let command similar to the one shown in Figure 15-4.

```
[ken@rhel9-server ~]$ let x=1
[ken@rhel9-server ~]$ echo $x
1
[ken@rhel9-server ~]$ let x=$x+1
[ken@rhel9-server ~]$ echo $x
2
```

Figure 15-4. *Let variable option*

Both of the options are not the best to use as they can complicate your scripts slightly when reading them. Both work, but there is a better way of setting your variables that can make readability a bit easier and is also the recommended way for setting and calculating numerical values.

The best method for calculating numerical values in bash is through the use of bash arithmetic expansion. This is a built-in functionality that can be used with bash shell scripting that makes use of double round brackets "((..))". Anything within the double brackets will apply mathematical calculations if requested. Figure 15-5 is an example in action.

```
[ken@rhel9-server ~]$ echo $x
1
[ken@rhel9-server ~]$ x=$((x + 1))
[ken@rhel9-server ~]$ echo $x
2
```

Figure 15-5. *Bracket option*

Script Body

With variables set, you are finally ready to get to the heart of your script. This is the part that actually matters.

Conditionals

Conditionals are the decisions you want your script to make based on the information that has been passed. These can include the use of variables with "if-else" or "case" statements. An example of this could be a script that needs to execute something when a variable value is set to a specific value. The following is an example using the if-else conditional:

```
x=$1
if [ $x -eq 1 ]
 then
    echo "Passed"
 else
    echo "Failed"
fi
```

The preceding example has a condition based on the value of the variable x. The variable x has been set by the first parameter passed when the script is executed. If the user passed the value of 1, the code in the success part of the script is executed, or else the code in the failed part of the script is executed.

A similar example to the if-else statement is the use of the case statement. The following case statement is prepared to accept different values from the x variable:

```
x=$1
case $x in
  1)
    echo -n "The value is 1"
    ;;
  2)
    echo -n "The value is 2"
    ;;
  3)
    echo -n "The value is 3"
    ;;
  *)
    echo -n "The value is unknown"
    ;;
esac
```

The previous case example will accept values 1, 2, and 3 and execute an action based on the value passed. Any value that is not expected would be handed by the "*" parameter.

Conditional Operands

With conditional statements like if-else and case statements, there will become a time when you need to compare or check values. For that, there are a number of operands you can use.

Table 15-3 lists the various variable operands that can be used.

Table 15-3. *Variable operands*

Variable	Description
-eq	Determines if two numbers are equal.
-lt	Determines if one number is less than another.
-gt	Determines if one number is greater than another.
==	Returns true if two string values are the same.
=!	Returns true if two string values are not the same.
!	Returns true if the statement is false.
-d	Checks if a directory exists.
-e	Checks if a file exists.
-r or -w or -x	Checks if a file exists and if the permission of the file is either read, write, or executed.

Loops

Occasionally in a script, you may need to run a task a few times or wait for something to become available. To do this, you may need to use a loop construct. The following examples demonstrate looping.

The first loop you can use is the while loop. This will execute in a loop while a specific condition is value:

```
x=1
while [ x -lt 10 ]
do
  x=$((x+1))
done
```

The previous example will loop nine times before the value of x has increased to ten. At that point, the while loop will exit and continue with the rest of the script.

The same example can be done with an until statement, which is similar to the while loop except that the commands will execute until a condition has been met:

```
x=1
until [ x -gt 9 ]
do
  x=$((x+1))
done
```

But what happens when you want to loop through a list of string values? Say you have a list of server names and you want to run an action on each of them.

The following example could do something similar:

```
SERVER_LIST="server1 server2 server3"
for server in $SERVER_LIST
do
  ssh $server "ls -al"
done
```

The previous example will loop through the values in the variable SERVER_LIST and run a ssh command with each value.

The final loop structure that can be used is to loop through a set value list:

```
for x in {1..5}
do
    echo $value
done
```

In the previous example, the script will loop five times, one through to five, and display the value of each iteration.

Examples

The following are a few simple examples of scripts.

Create Directory

Create a directory if it doesn't exit:

```
#!/bin/bash
dir="/testdir"
if [[ ! -d $dir ]]; then
    mkdir $dir
else
    echo "$dir already exists"
fi
```

Package Installation

Install packages using a loop:

```
#!/bin/bash
packages="vim tmux wget"
for package in $packages
do
  sudo dnf install $package -y
done
```

Exercise

Create the following shell scripts that can be used to configure a new system. The new system will be one of many that will need to be configured the same.

Create Users

All systems are using local system accounts. These accounts are for Linux system administrators and need to have the further configuration done to allow them to do their normal day jobs.

The list of user accounts are John, Mary, Sue, Bob, Mo, Xua, and Simon. Each account will need the following:

- Be added to the wheel group

- A home directory created in the "/home" directory with the correct permissions

Packages Managed

All new systems will need to be checked if they do not have certain packages installed and checked that certain packages are installed.

No system should have the telnet package installed. Before executing any commands to remove packages, you need to check if the package was installed.

All systems should have the vim, wget, and tmux packages installed. They do not need to be checked if installed. Just make sure when the script has completed that they are installed.

Ansible

Prior to 2012, everything that needed to be automated was written in either shell scripts or using tools like Puppet. Today, one of the more powerful automation tools available is Ansible.

For this part of the chapter, we will briefly look at Ansible and its components with a few examples. Ansible is a big subject and deserves its own book, but to get you familiar with the tool is the first step. From here, it is recommended to do further reading and get used to the tool.

Explained

Ansible today is a suite of OpenSource tools that allows system administrators to automate the configuration of many different systems, from Unix servers through to network switches. If you are able to either run ssh, use APIs, or connect to a system using WinRM, Ansible will be able to configure it.

Ansible is a modular-based tool that can be extended through the development of Ansible modules. Modules are written using Python and typically communicate with the system that it will configure through the use of its APIs.

The Ansible community and vendors are constantly producing modules for you to use; the growth of Ansible over the last ten years has been explosive. This combined with a much smaller learning curve has made Ansible the automation tool of choice when it comes to automated system configuration.

Control Node

When using the command-line version of Ansible, you will need a host or system that will be used as the central command center. On this system, you will need to install Ansible. This system will be used to execute Ansible playbooks, and this system will communicate with all the managed nodes. This system will also need to have access to all the systems, preferably through the use of public and private ssh keys, meaning that the control node needs to be secured and locked down to only those who need it.

Managed Nodes

Managed nodes are the systems that will be configured by the control node. These systems will require that Python is installed and/or has the capabilities for the control node to connect to it. Managed nodes are also referred to as hosts.

Inventory

The inventory in Ansible is the list of all the managed nodes or hosts that will be configured using Ansible. Hosts can also be grouped into groups within the inventories, or you can have separate inventories for different systems.

Playbooks

The tasks that are created to complete a system configuration are executed from a playbook. A playbook can include roles, tasks, and handlers, which in turn are written to perform certain actions such as installing packages or updating configuration files.

Roles

Ansible roles are reusable code that can be used by different playbooks, reducing the need to write new Ansible code each time you want to repeat a task. Ansible role can be as simple as installing a package or as complicated as deploying an entire provisioning environment.

Modules

How a system can be configured and managed is done through a module. To connect to Amazon web services and configure a new instance, for example, is done using the AWS modules. The same is done when managing Cisco devices. Special modules are written by these vendors to provide an "Infrastructure as Code" approach to configuring their services and systems.

Plug-ins

To expand core functionality of Ansible, plug-ins are developed. These plug-ins add additional features that users can make use of. This could include how information is outputted or how a managed node is contacted.

Collections

Ansible is OpenSource, which means there are many developers writing their own modules, plug-ins, playbooks, etc. To share their work, Ansible provides a way to package everything up. This is where collections are used. Collections can easily be installed and are often required for certain modules to work.

Ansible Configuration

To get a working ansible example, you will need to do the following.

Control Node

To start using Ansible, we need to configure a control node. On a RHEL 9 node, run the following command to install the Ansible core packages:

```
# sudo dnf install ansible-core -y
```

```
[ken@rhel9-server ~]$ sudo dnf install ansible-core
Updating Subscription Management repositories.
Last metadata expiration check: 20:56:19 ago on Sat 10 Sep 2022 16:02:03 BST.
Dependencies resolved.
========================================================================================================
 Package                 Architecture   Version                 Repository                          Size
========================================================================================================
Installing:
 ansible-core            x86_64         2.12.2-2.el9_0          rhel-9-for-x86_64-appstream-rpms   2.4 M
Installing dependencies:
 git                     x86_64         2.31.1-2.el9.2          rhel-9-for-x86_64-appstream-rpms   128 k
 git-core                x86_64         2.31.1-2.el9.2          rhel-9-for-x86_64-appstream-rpms   3.6 M
 git-core-doc            noarch         2.31.1-2.el9.2          rhel-9-for-x86_64-appstream-rpms   2.5 M
 perl-DynaLoader         x86_64         1.47-479.el9            rhel-9-for-x86_64-appstream-rpms    36 k
 perl-Error              noarch         1:0.17029-7.el9         rhel-9-for-x86_64-appstream-rpms    46 k
 perl-File-Find          noarch         1.37-479.el9            rhel-9-for-x86_64-appstream-rpms    36 k
 perl-Git                noarch         2.31.1-2.el9.2          rhel-9-for-x86_64-appstream-rpms    45 k
 perl-TermReadKey        x86_64         2.38-11.el9             rhel-9-for-x86_64-appstream-rpms    40 k
 perl-lib                x86_64         0.65-479.el9            rhel-9-for-x86_64-appstream-rpms    25 k
 python3-babel           noarch         2.9.1-2.el9             rhel-9-for-x86_64-appstream-rpms   6.0 M
 python3-cffi            x86_64         1.14.5-5.el9            rhel-9-for-x86_64-appstream-rpms   257 k
 python3-cryptography    x86_64         36.0.1-1.el9_0          rhel-9-for-x86_64-appstream-rpms   1.2 M
 python3-jinja2          noarch         2.11.3-4.el9            rhel-9-for-x86_64-appstream-rpms   253 k
 python3-markupsafe      x86_64         1.1.1-12.el9            rhel-9-for-x86_64-appstream-rpms    39 k
 python3-packaging       noarch         20.9-5.el9             rhel-9-for-x86_64-appstream-rpms    81 k
 python3-ply             noarch         3.11-14.el9            rhel-9-for-x86_64-appstream-rpms   111 k
 python3-pycparser       noarch         2.20-6.el9             rhel-9-for-x86_64-appstream-rpms   139 k
 python3-pyparsing       noarch         2.4.7-9.el9            rhel-9-for-x86_64-baseos-rpms      154 k
 python3-pytz            noarch         2021.1-4.el9           rhel-9-for-x86_64-appstream-rpms    56 k
 python3-resolvelib      noarch         0.5.4-5.el9            rhel-9-for-x86_64-appstream-rpms    38 k
 sshpass                 x86_64         1.09-4.el9             rhel-9-for-x86_64-appstream-rpms    30 k

Transaction Summary
========================================================================================================
Install  22 Packages

Total download size: 17 M
Installed size: 77 M
Is this ok [y/N]: █
```

Figure 15-6. *Package installation for Ansible*

Once Ansible is installed, you can verify the version with the following command:

```
# sudo ansible --version
```

```
[ken@rhel9-server ~]$ sudo ansible --version
[sudo] password for ken:
ansible [core 2.12.2]
  config file = /etc/ansible/ansible.cfg
  configured module search path = ['/root/.ansible/plugins/modules', '/usr/share/ansible/plugins/modules']
  ansible python module location = /usr/lib/python3.9/site-packages/ansible
  ansible collection location = /root/.ansible/collections:/usr/share/ansible/collections
  executable location = /bin/ansible
  python version = 3.9.10 (main, Feb  9 2022, 00:00:00) [GCC 11.2.1 20220127 (Red Hat 11.2.1-9)]
  jinja version = 2.11.3
  libyaml = True
```

Figure 15-7. *The Ansible version on the system*

Setup ssh Keys

Configure your control node to have passwordless ssh access to the nodes that will be managed. Ensure that you have the same user created on all your nodes that will be used for any Ansible playbooks. Your Ansible code can always include configuration to elevate permissions.

```
[ken@rhel9-server ~]$ sudo vim /etc/hosts
[ken@rhel9-server ~]$
[ken@rhel9-server ~]$ ssh-copy-id -i ~/.ssh/id_rsa.pub root@rhel9-node1
/usr/bin/ssh-copy-id: INFO: Source of key(s) to be installed: "/home/ken/.ssh/id_rsa.pub"
The authenticity of host 'rhel9-node1 (192.168.122.110)' can't be established.
ED25519 key fingerprint is SHA256:RKlkPliw7drBktqss2/BSmsrJilCwkpaR4UvexycGZU.
This key is not known by any other names
Are you sure you want to continue connecting (yes/no/[fingerprint])? yes
/usr/bin/ssh-copy-id: INFO: attempting to log in with the new key(s), to filter out any that are already installed
/usr/bin/ssh-copy-id: INFO: 1 key(s) remain to be installed -- if you are prompted now it is to install the new keys
root@rhel9-node1's password:

Number of key(s) added: 1

Now try logging into the machine, with:   "ssh 'root@rhel9-node1'"
and check to make sure that only the key(s) you wanted were added.
```

Figure 15-8. *ssh key generation to be used with Ansible*

For the example shown in Figure 15-8, we set up passwordless ssh to the two RHEL 9 cluster nodes used in the last chapter. Also as no DNS server was available, the /etc/hosts file was configured with the different managed nodes, host names, and IP addresses.

Ansible Configuration Files

When Ansible is installed from an installation package or from a package management tool such as "dnf," configuration files are created for you. In the command that we ran earlier to show the Ansible version, you would have noticed the path to the Ansible configuration file was listed.

Hierarchy

The default configuration file for Ansible is "/etc/ansible/ansible.cfg". However, there can exist multiple ansible.cfg files on your system. For this reason, it is important to understand the hierarchy.

The following hierarchy is used by Ansible when deciding which ansible.cfg to use:

1. The config file is in the current directory: "./ansible.cfg"

2. The config file is in the home directory of the current user: "~/.ansible.cfg"

3. Finally, the config file is set in the /etc/ansible directory: "/etc/ansible/ansible.cfg"

$ANSIBLE_CONFIG variable can also be used to define where the config is located. The first configuration file found will only be used, and all other files will be ignored.

Creating Ansible Content

To create Ansible content, you first need to create a workable Ansible directory structure. An example of how your Ansible working directory should be set up can be seen in Figure 15-9.

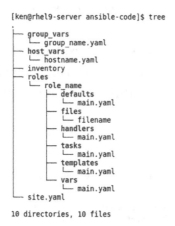

Figure 15-9. *Basic Ansible directory structure*

The image directory structure can be simplified to only an inventory file and a playbook if you really wanted to have a very basic structure to work with.

The following link has a Python application, which can generate a playbook structure for you. It's very basic and only really creates the bare minimum:

https://pypi.org/project/ansible-generator/

Inventory File

Figure 15-10 is an example of an inventory file.

```
[ken@rhel9-server ansible-code]$ cat inventory

[haservers]
rhel9-node1
rhel9-node2

[primary]
rhel9-node1                        _
```

Figure 15-10. *Ansible inventory file example*

The "[ ]" entries are the group names. This is used later when you want to target specific managed nodes or hosts. In the example, there are two groups:

– [haservers]

– [primary]

If you only wanted to target the primary cluster node "rhel9-node1", you would use the "[primary]" group name.

The ansible documentation is amazing at explaining how the full inventory works. It is highly recommended to have a look when you are building your Ansible inventories:

https://docs.ansible.com/ansible/latest/user_guide/intro_inventory.html

Playbook

```
[ken@rhel9-server ansible-code]$ cat site.yaml
---

- name: "Install tmux"
  hosts: haservers
  become: true

  tasks:
    - name: "Use package module to install tmux"
      ansible.builtin.package:
        name: tmux
        state: present
```

Figure 15-11. *A basic example of a playbook that will target one of the groups in the inventory. On all the nodes in the group, the playbook will execute the tasks*

Execute Playbook

To execute the playbook shown in Figure 15-11 and install the "tmux" package on all the hosts in the haservers group, run the following command:

```
# ansible-playbook site.yaml -i inventory
```

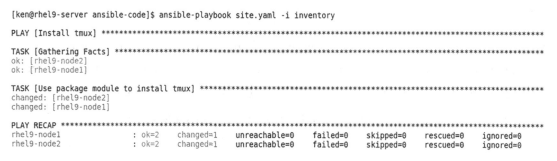

Figure 15-12. *Output of the Ansible playbook being run*

In Figure 15-12, you can see that the task "[Use package module to install tmux]" was successful on both nodes.

If the same playbook is run again, you will see that the status of each node just returns ok and node changed.

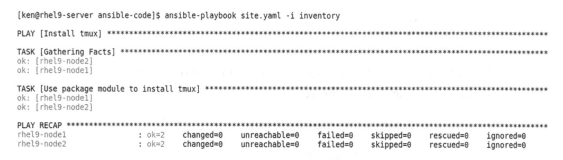

Figure 15-13. *The same playbook from Figure 15-12 but this time no changes made*

The reason for this is because Ansible is idempotent, which means Ansible will only maintain the state of a configuration and only change the configuration if the desired state does not match. This kind of management is vital when working with systems that require reboots when configuration changes. If nothing changes, then a reboot is not required, allowing you to run the playbooks as many times as you wish.

> **Warning**   Not all Ansible code is written to be idempotent. Always read the code and test on a system that is not in use. Using modules like "shell" and "command" is not idempotent.

Role

With the example in the preceding playbook section, the package module was used in the playbooks' tasks section. If you wanted to create a role (reusable code) to install the packages instead, you could do something very similar to the following:

1. Create a new role in the roles directory with a file called main.yaml:

   ```
   # mkdir -p roles/install_tmux/tasks
   # touch roles/install_tmux/tasks/main.yaml
   ```

2. Update the previous main.yaml file with the task from the old playbook:

   ```
   [ken@rhel9-server ansible-code]$ cat roles/install_tmux/tasks/main.yaml
   ---
   - name: "Use package module to install tmux"
     ansible.builtin.package:
       name: tmux
       state: present
   ```

3. Update the site.yaml to include the role instead of running the task directly from the playbook.

   ```
   [ken@rhel9-server ansible-code]$ cat site.yaml
   ---

   - name: "Install tmux"
     hosts: haservers
     become: true

     tasks:
       - name: "Include role to run tasks"
         include_role:
           name: ../roles/install_tmux
   ```

Figure 15-14. *A playbook now using a role instead of tasks*

Ansible Galaxy

As Ansible has been around for a while, many people have already been in your situation where they are wanting to write Ansible roles and code. Fortunately, there is an online repository that contains a library of this code. Before you start writing any new Ansible roles or code, search the following location or do a Google search to see what is available to use:

`https://galaxy.ansible.com/`

Ansible also has the ability for you to install the Ansible Galaxy content from the command line using the "ansible-galaxy" utility.

Variable Files

Variable files are files that contain variables that your Ansible playbooks or roles can use. You can create the following variable files.

Custom Variables

Custom variable files can be included within playbooks that contain variables that all systems will use that the Ansible playbook is being executed on.

Group_vars

Group variable files are files that are named after the group name in the inventory. When tasks are executed against a group, if a group variable file exists, the variables from that group variable file are applied to the hosts that the playbook or task is being executed against.

For example, if a file called "haservers" was created in the group_vars directory, all the variables stored in that file would only be used for servers that exist in that group. If a file called "primary" was created in the group_vars directory, then only the server "rhel9-node1" would have the variables stored in that file applied to it. This is a useful way to apply certain variables to certain systems.

Host_vars

Host variable files are files that are named after the host in the inventory. This is very similar to the group_vars but at an individual host level.

Using Variables

To continue with the previous package installation example, if your new "install_tmux" role was meant to be more flexible, you could replace the package name with a variable. This would then allow you to adjust what package you could install. To configure this using group_vars, you would need to do the following:

1. Create a new file in the group_vars directory called "haservers.yaml".

2. Add the content shown in Figure 15-15 to the previous file.

```
[ken@rhel9-server ansible-code]$ cat group_vars/haservers.yaml
---
package_name: wget
```

Figure 15-15. A variable file created with a single variable called package_name

3. Update the main.yaml file in the install_tmux role.

```
[ken@rhel9-server ansible-code]$ cat roles/install_tmux/tasks/main.yaml
---
- name: "Use package module to install {{ package_name }}"
  ansible.builtin.package:
    name: "{{ package_name }}"
    state: present
```

Figure 15-16. Ansible task updated to use variables

In the code shown in Figure 15-16, the original "tmux" package name has been replaced with the "{{ package_name }}" variable name. The name text has also been updated to use the variable.

Now when the playbook is executed, the tmux package is no longer being installed. Instead the content of the "package_name" variable in the groups_vars/haservers.yaml file is being used. In the previous case, this is now the "wget" package.

Figure 15-17. *A playbook running tasks that use variables*

Ansible Documentation

To explain all the variations you can use, Ansible would take an entire book by itself. For this reason, it is highly recommended to read more about Ansible from the official documentation. Everything from code examples to how Ansible should be configured can be found there. The following is the link to the Ansible official documentation:

https://docs.ansible.com/ansible/latest/

The best way to find what you are looking for is to use a similar Google search:

"Ansible install package"

This tends to take you directly to the module and code examples for what you want to do.

Exercise

As your first time with Ansible, attempt to do the following.

Ansible Environment

Set up a new control host that is able to communicate with at least one other system. The Ansible control node should have an Ansible directory structure setup that could be used by anyone with some basic Ansible knowledge.

Create a Playbook

Create an Ansible playbook that will install the "vim" package on the systems in your inventory. Your playbook should have no direct tasks in the playbook but should instead be calling an Ansible role. The Ansible code should also be idempotent and should not change anything if the package is already installed.

Create a Variable File

Create a variable file that contains the name of the package you want to install from the previously created roles. Update any of the Ansible you have already written to accomplish this.

Bonus Task

After reading the official Ansible documentation, attempt to update your variable file to contain a dictionary. With this new dictionary variable, update your Ansible role to install all the packages that exist in the dictionary.

The results of this task should allow you to specify a list of packages that will be installed.

Summary

In this chapter, you were introduced to the following:

- What Linux shell scripting is and how it can still be used today

- What the different shell scripting interpreters are and how a basic shell script can be written

- What bash scripting variables are and how arithmetic calculation can be done

- What Ansible is and how Ansible is different from traditional shell scripting

- What the various Ansible components are and how to write your first Ansible tasks

- How to use variables with Ansible and how the various variable files can be used

## CHAPTER 16

Deployment at Scale

Being this far into this book, you are now reaching the point where you can work in an enterprise Linux environment. You now have a solid foundation of the Linux basics and how to manage basic Linux systems.

This chapter will now start to explore how you can deploy systems at scale and how you can speed up your deployment process, what tooling you have available, and what you still need to learn.

In this chapter, we will discuss the methods that can be used for mass system deployment and look at what the best approach should be. We will then continue to explore the tooling that can make the mass deployment easier, including the different automation tools available today and how they differ from each other.

Finally, we will look at the certifications and training you should consider doing to expand your career options in the future.

Deployment Methods

So far in this book, the only deployment method that has been used for Linux systems has been to manually install them, which is fine if all you are doing is installing one or two systems every now and again. It, however, is not fine when you need to build multiple hardware or virtual machine-based systems on a regular basis. For that, there needs to be a streamlined approach.

Kickstart

The first and simplest method of speeding up your deployments is through the use of an answer file or, as we refer to it in the Linux world, a kickstart file.

© Kenneth Hitchcock 2023
K. Hitchcock, *The Enterprise Linux Administrator*, https://doi.org/10.1007/978-1-4842-8801-6_16

Create Kickstart File

To use a kickstart file with a RHEL 9 installation, you will first need to generate or create a kickstart file. On the Red Hat website, there is a generator tool that can be used:

    https://access.redhat.com/labs/kickstartconfig/

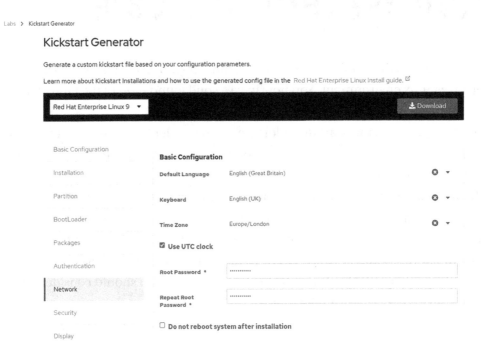

Figure 16-1. *Kickstart generator on the Red Hat portal*

Using the generator on the Red Hat site, you can select all the options you wish your kickstart file to have. Once you have selected all the options, you can click the "Download" button to save the file.

The contents of the file should look similar if you are using the basic configuration options.

```
lang en_GB
keyboard --xlayouts='gb'
timezone Europe/London --isUtc
rootpw $2b$10$5y.Wh9ij8D2CO1vrJfZG8euRWDFcnN9U8cSC4djxB0Qw8WxwGxJZa --iscrypted
reboot
text
cdrom
bootloader --append="rhgb quiet crashkernel=1G-4G:192M,4G-64G:256M,64G-:512M"
zerombr
clearpart --all --initlabel
autopart
auth --passalgo=sha512 --useshadow
skipx
firstboot --disable
selinux --enforcing
firewall --enabled
%packages
@^minimal-environment
kexec-tools
%end
```

Figure 16-2. *Kickstart example*

Copy Kickstart File to Web Server

To use this kickstart file during a RHEL 9 installation, you will need to copy this file to a web server, NFS server, file server, or any other location you will be able to download the file from over the network. You could rebuild the RHEL 9 ISO file for your RHEL installation and bake the kickstart file within it, but that could take a bit of tweaking to get right. For this example, we will just copy the kickstart file to a web server that was created before. This was another RHEL 9 server built previously.

Copy the kickstart file to the "/var/www/html" directory of your web server on your network. If you do not have one, start one of your previous built systems, install, and configure the httpd or Apache package:

```
[ken@rhel9-server ~]$ ls -al /var/www/html/
total 8
drwxr-xr-x. 2 root root  45 Sep 11 21:40 .
drwxr-xr-x. 4 root root  33 Aug 28 16:09 ..
-rw-r--r--. 1 root root   9 Sep 11 20:38 index.html
-rw-r--r--. 1 root root 437 Sep 11 21:28 kickstart.cfg
```

Figure 16-3. *Kickstart files can be copied to web servers to use for installs*

Build a New System

To build a new system with your new kickstart file, create a virtual machine or start up a new installation on a system with your previously downloaded ISO or installation media.

When the screen shown in Figure 16-4 appears, press the tab key.

517

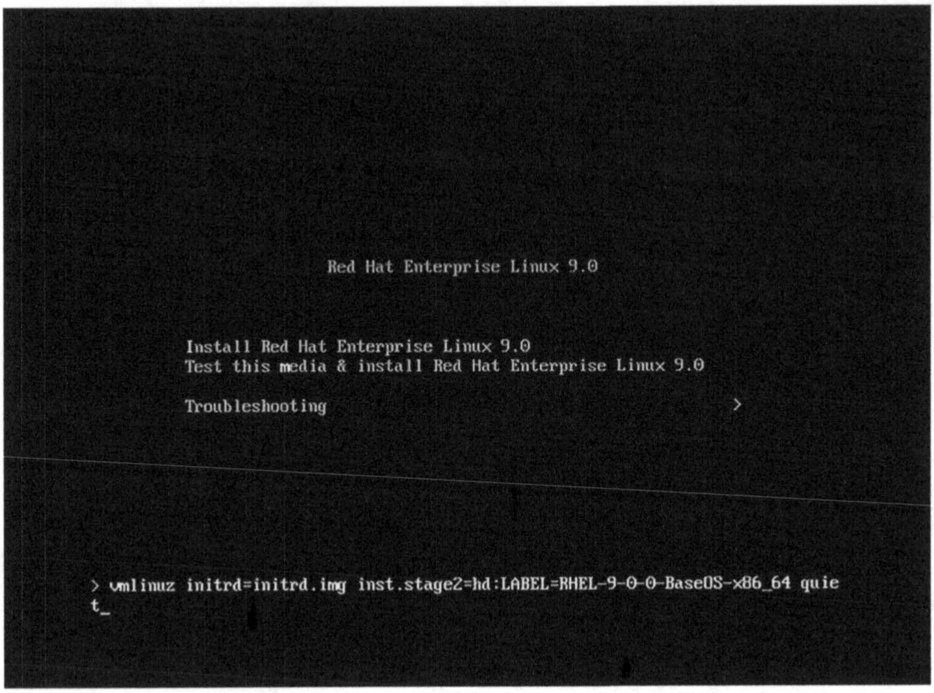

Figure 16-4. *Using a kickstart file during the installation of RHEL*

Once the tab key has been pressed, you will notice a new line at the bottom of the screen appears; this is the area we will use to tell the installer to use a kickstart file. At the end of the text, add similar to what is shown here, adjusting for your web server address and kickstart file names:

```
inst.ks=http://192.168.122.237/kickstart.cfg
```

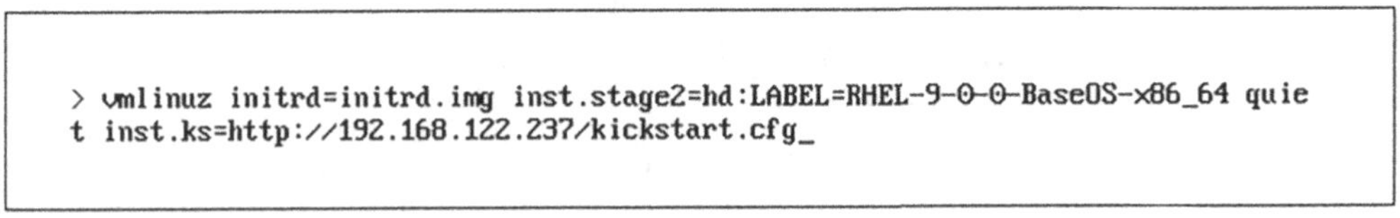

Figure 16-5. *Kickstart configuration expanded*

Press enter once you have typed in the line.

The installation will now begin and complete without you needing to do anything further.

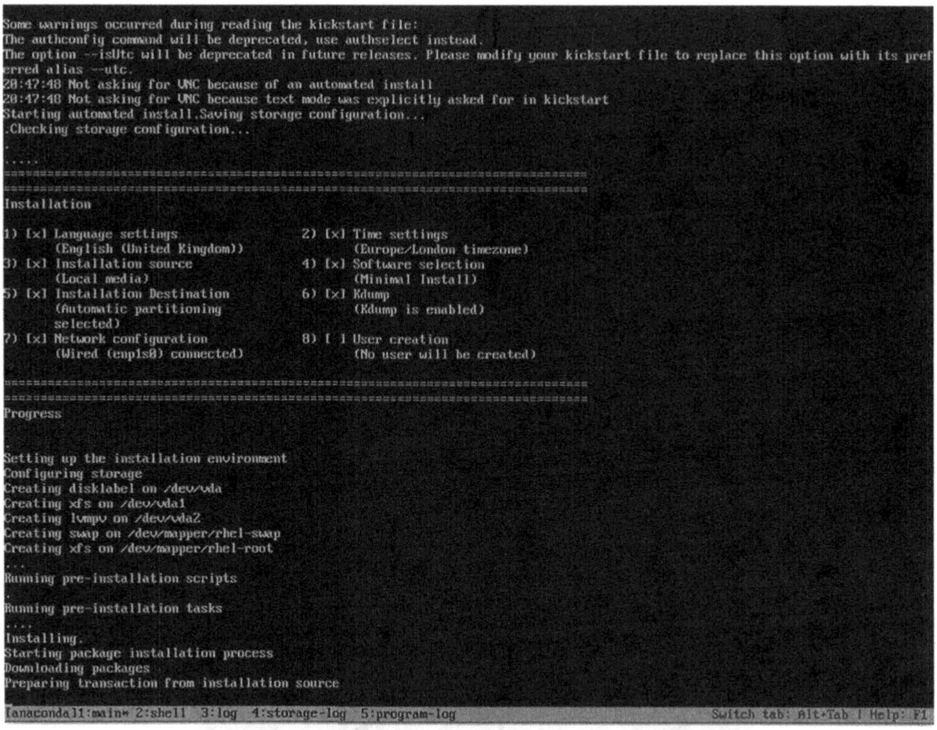

Figure 16-6. *RHEL installation running with kickstart file*

Once completed, you will be presented with the login prompt for your new system.

This example is a very basic kickstart file with minimal configuration. Kickstart files can include network configuration, package installation, post- and prescripts, and much more. Depending on the complexity of your system, you can configure your kickstart to do almost anything.

Official Documentation

As always, it is important to read the official documentation when configuring and building systems. For kickstart files and more information on how to configure them, read the Red Hat documentation as follows:

https://access.redhat.com/documentation/en-us/red_hat_enterprise_linux/9/html-single/performing_an_advanced_rhel_9_installation/index

Image Cloning

Another quick and useful way to build systems is through virtualization cloning. This does require that you already have an operating system deployed on a virtual machine that can be cloned.

With the previous deployed system using kickstart, the following are the steps to create a clone of that virtual machine:

1. Open virt-manager.

2. Right-click on the virtual machine you wish to clone and click the clone button.

3. Give your new cloned virtual machine a new name.

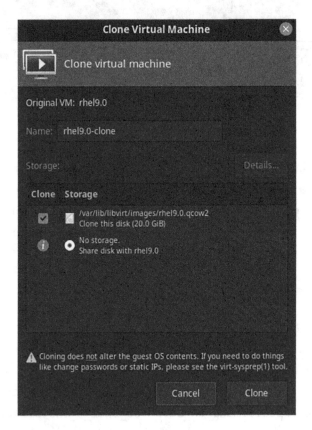

Figure 16-7. *Virtual machine manager clone screen*

4. Click the clone button.

Kickstart vs. Cloning

The downside to cloning virtual machines is that you need to do the following:

- Configure a new hostname and network address.

- Register the system to a subscription.

- Update and configure the system for the purpose it will serve.

- The original image will need to be maintained and updated on a regular basis.

Kickstart files can do a few of the previously mentioned for you but will require you to build and maintain the kickstart files, which can quickly become a laborious task when dealing with multiple systems.

Kickstarting and cloning are both very good and quick ways to build systems quickly, but they are by no means an enterprise solution to building systems. For that, you need to make use of enterprise deployment tools, which we will discuss shortly.

Exercise

For you to gain some experience with automated RHEL 9 installations, attempt to do the following tasks.

Prerequisite

Build a web server and ensure that you can access the web server content on your network.

Create a Kickstart File

Create a basic kickstart file that has your time zone and keyboard layout. Packages should be minimal but feel free to install what you like.

Copy the kickstart file to your web server created in the prerequisite task.

Build RHEL 9 Using Kickstart

Build a new RHEL 9 server using the kickstart from the previous task. Take a note of how much quicker the installation is compared to doing it manually.

Clone a VM

If you are using a hypervisor like Libvirt/KVM, clone the new RHEL 9 system just built. Log in to the new VM and update any configuration you like. Finally, delete the VM if you have no use for it. The process to create a new VM is much quicker now, and any new servers can be created within a few minutes.

Deployment Tools

So far in this book and chapter, we have discussed how to install Linux systems using manual installation methods, through the use of kickstart files and through the use of virtual machine cloning.

All these methods work well on their own and do offer some improvements on each other. Kickstarting and cloning are definitely much quicker than manual installations and can speed up the process, but they too have their own setbacks.

For an enterprise Linux deployment solution, you will need to use a combination of different systems.

Figure 16-8 is a rough diagram that shows how each system would be responsible for different parts of the system deployment, configuration, and management.

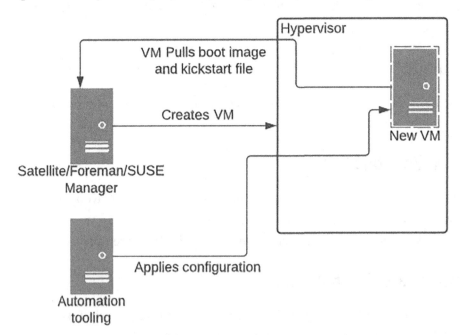

Figure 16-8. *Basic automated build and configuration flow*

Enterprise Deployment Tools

For system deployment in an enterprise environment, you have a few options. Some are community based for organizations that are not reliant on enterprise support, and then there are the supported platforms.

Each of these tools is quite feature rich and would require their own chapters to explain them. For now, it is important that you are aware of these tools and where you can get more information about them. It is also recommended that once you are done with this book, you start to familiarize yourself with these tools, build your own systems, and follow the installation guides for each of them.

Foreman

The Foreman project is one of the projects that provides the upstream to Red Hat Satellite Server. Foreman provides lifecycle management, provisioning, configuration management, and monitoring to name some of the functionality.

Foreman's provisioning capabilities allow the user to provision new virtual machines in different hypervisors and even have the ability to provision hypervisors themselves and allow you to build the platform that you will build your environments on.

You can read more about the Foreman project on their website. You can also get involved with the project if you wish to contribute:

`https://theforeman.org/`

The Foreman project is OpenSource and can be installed free of charge. The official Foreman documentation explains how to install and use Foreman:

`https://theforeman.org/manuals/3.4/quickstart_guide.html`

With the preceding link, choose the operations you will install Foreman on and the installation instructions will update for you.

Red Hat Satellite Server

As mentioned previously, Foreman is one of the upstream projects for Red Hat Satellite Server. Red Hat Satellite Server as of the time of writing was still at version 6. Red Hat Satellite Server is built on the following community projects:

- Foreman
- Katello
- Pulp

- Hammer

- Candlepin

Each component plays a vital role in allowing Red Hat Satellite Server to be one of the best Linux management tools available today.

Subscription Required

Red Hat Satellite Server does require a subscription for you to download and install the platform. There however is a subscription that Red Hat makes available for people who are learning and generally building test environments to play with. For more information, either Google "Red Hat developer subscription" or go to the following link:

```
https://developers.redhat.com/articles/faqs-no-cost-red-hat-
enterprise-linux
```

Installing Red Hat Satellite Server

To install your own Red Hat Satellite Server, you will need to have a system with a fair bit of CPU and memory. Read the official documentation before you begin. Follow the steps as closely as possible to avoid any issues:

```
https://access.redhat.com/documentation/en-us/red_hat_satellite/6.11/
html-single/installing_satellite_server_in_a_connected_network_
environment/index
```

To configure your Red Hat Satellite Server as a provisioning system, you will need to add additional functionality. More can be found in the Red Hat documentation:

```
https://access.redhat.com/documentation/en-us/red_hat_satellite/6.11/
html-single/provisioning_hosts/index
```

Uyuni

The first versions of Red Hat Satellite Server were built on the upstream community project called Spacewalk:

```
https://spacewalkproject.github.io/
```

In 2020, the Spacewalk project was discontinued by the community and was left for anyone who wished to fork and maintain it. This is what the Uyuni (ya - uni) project did. They took the old Spacewalk and ripped out the parts that were not so great, particularly the configuration management system, which was just awful, and replaced it with SaltStack, a much more robust and performance configuration management tool.

With the good work the Uyuni team was doing, SUSE decided to base their own Linux system management tool, SUSE Manager, on it:

`www.uyuni-project.org/`

Uyuni is community based and does not require a subscription to install; very much like Foreman, it is recommended that you install and get familiar with the tool.

SUSE Manager

As Red Hat has a tool for their enterprise Linux distribution, SUSE has also got theirs. Where you would use Red Hat Satellite Server for RHEL systems, you would typically use SUSE Manager for SLES systems.

At the time of writing, SUSE Manager 4 was the latest SUSE Linux platform management tool. SUSE Manager 4 as mentioned previously is based on the community product Uyuni. It has all the functionality of the community project along with the enterprise updates expected from an enterprise vendor.

SUSE Manager not only supports the provisioning of new systems but also allows the configuration management through SaltStack and the system patching capabilities required to manage a large Linux estate.

To install and configure your own SUSE Manager, read the official documentation as always:

`www.suse.com/download/suse-manager/`

Automation

Once you have your Linux system deployed using your enterprise Linux deployment tool, you will need to configure and build an automation platform. With your automation platform, you will need to develop code that will configure systems according to your requirements.

Ansible

Ansible is the Red Hat recommended automation tool. Ansible is available in both enterprise and community versions. Both enterprise and community products have two "types" of Ansible that can be installed. There is the graphical tool that can be used and the command-line version.

Red Hat Enterprise Version

Red Hat recently changed their Ansible offering into a bundle called Ansible Automation Platform, which includes the enterprise graphical tool that used to be called Ansible Tower and their command-line Ansible tools called Ansible Core.

A subscription is required for AAP and a license to manage the systems that will be configured by AAP. Read the official documentation for more help on the installation:

```
https://access.redhat.com/documentation/en-us/red_hat_ansible_
automation_platform/2.0-ea/html/red_hat_ansible_automation_platform_
installation_guide/index
```

Community Ansible

For the community version of Ansible, you will need to install using the community documentation:

```
https://docs.ansible.com/ansible/latest/installation_guide/intro_
installation.html
```

If you want to install and use the community graphical Ansible tool, you will need to install AWX. Unfortunately, the documentation is not as easy to find as you would like. There are many blogs and forums with the steps you can follow if you want to install your own copy of AWX. Most of the installations require you to install AWX as a container, which means you will need to configure a system with a container runtime to use.

SaltStack

SaltStack manages Linux configuration in a very traditional way; configuration is managed on the SaltStack master and pushed to systems that have changed or require updated configuration. The SaltStack master system controls the state of its clients (minions) that it manages through understanding both the state the system needs to be and the events that have been triggered on the minion system that the master is watching. If anything changes that should not, the SaltStack master reverts the unauthorized changes.

One major difference with SaltStack is that Salt uses a message bus ZeroMQ for its task management and execution. When a client system or minion triggers an event, a message is created on the message bus for the master server to act on when it is ready. This method of using a message bus allows a vast number of systems to be managed by one master, increasing the overall performance of the tool over its competitors.

You can read more about SaltStack in their official documentation as follows:
`https://docs.saltproject.io/en/latest/topics/`

Puppet

Very much like SaltStack, Puppet requires a Puppet master to manage the state of all the systems it manages. All clients are also required to have an agent running to check in with the Puppet master.

Puppet has both community and enterprise versions available to accommodate users across the board.

Puppet is less used today than other tooling such as Ansible and Terraform, but that is not to say it is not used by anyone. There are still many organizations that use Puppet to manage their entire estate, and if you are fortunate enough to be employed by such an organization, it is advisable to be familiar with Puppet as best as you can.

You can read more about Puppet in their official documentation:
`https://puppet.com/docs/puppet/7/puppet_index.html`

Terraform

Provided by HashiCorp, Terraform is an OpenSource infrastructure as code solution that has the ability to provision across multiple cloud environments such as AWS or Azure. Terraform can be used for on-premise system configuration but is generally regarded as a cloud provisioning tool. The general idea is that Terraform would be used to spin up your environment and then you run automation tooling against the new environment.

Note   Ansible can also be used in a similar manner, but generally it is common for Terraform to be used for cloud provisioning and then Ansible being used for configuration changes. This subject is quite debatable based on who you speak to. For now, learn both methods and then later make up your own mind which you prefer.

How to Get Terraform

Terraform has both a paid for and free version that can be used. The free version can be accessed through the "free" tier option of the Terraform cloud solution.

You can read more about Terraform on their official documentation as follows: `https://learn.hashicorp.com/search?query=Terraform`

Training and Certifications

The use of the systems mentioned in this chapter can be quite complex and sometimes outright confusing; this is why each vendor has training available. These training courses and certifications can be quite expensive if you are paying for them yourself, but they do carry their weight in gold, in the value they can bring to you. If it is possible for you to do them, it is highly recommended.

Red Hat

For Red Hat-related training, have a look at the training courses and exams available in the link as follows:

`www.redhat.com/en/services/training-and-certification`

SUSE

For SUSE-related training, have a look at their catalog in the link as follows:

`www.suse.com/training/course/`

Summary

In this chapter, you were introduced to the following:

- How Linux systems can be deployed using kickstart files and how systems can be cloned

- Why kickstart and cloning by itself should not be classified as an enterprise solution

- How enterprise tools like Red Hat Satellite Server and SUSE Manager can improve on the basic kickstarting approach

- What automation tools are available for you to use and learn

- Why automation tools and configuration management tools are vital to configuring a basic Linux system into something that can be used in production

- What training courses you can do to further expand your knowledge in enterprise Linux administration

PART V

Troubleshooting and Recovery

The final part of your journey to becoming an enterprise Linux administrator is to understand some of the basic troubleshooting and recovery options that are required to solve the inevitable problem you will experience.

In the final chapters of this book, we will look at how system logs can be used to help you find where your problem could be and how to track down any potential problems that have yet to show up. We will also look at how you can use the different Linux monitoring tools to help you with your debugging process. We will look at local tools and remote systems that can be used for monitoring.

We will discuss what you should do when you become stuck and need further help. We will discuss how you should ask for help and where you should go when all options have been exhausted.

With the final chapters, we will look at when the right time is to reinstall and when you should attempt to recover a system. We will look at all the various rescue options and how to gain access to them.

Finally, we will discuss backups and how important they are. We will discuss different backup methods and why it is important to test backups.

## CHAPTER 17

Troubleshooting Linux

As an enterprise Linux administrator, you will have times when systems do not behave as expected. The best approach to resolving Linux issues or system issues is to rebuild from code, but this is not always possible. Some systems just need to be fixed no matter how much time it can take. For this reason, it is important you understand the troubleshooting techniques and understand where to look for errors.

In this chapter, we will focus on troubleshooting and finding where errors or messages are stored that can help diagnose the root cause of the issue. We will start by looking at the Linux logging system, where logs are stored, and understand what is stored in them and how to understand the content to best serve you while troubleshooting.

Later in the chapter, we will look at monitoring tools and how monitoring can be used both locally and remotely on your systems.

Finally, we will revisit how to find help when you encounter an issue you are not able to resolve on your own.

Logging

Debugging in production is never a good idea; this is why logs are vital when trying to find the source of a problem. Ideally production environments should run with no issue as proper testing has been done, but in the real world, this is not always the case. When the inevitable issue happens, logs are what will help find the problem.

When you start working as an enterprise Linux system administrator, your first job should always be to check that logging is working and that logs are being forwarded to a remote logging system.

© Kenneth Hitchcock 2023
K. Hitchcock, *The Enterprise Linux Administrator*, https://doi.org/10.1007/978-1-4842-8801-6_17

Logs

There are a few things that you need to understand about Linux logging: how logs are created, what manages the logs on a Linux system, how to increase the detail in log files, how to read log files, and most importantly where logs are stored.

Where Logs Are Located

On most Linux environments, logs will be stored in the "/var/log/" directory. It is good practice for this directory to be mounted using its own separate disk. This is to avoid the main root disk from filling up if there are any runaway logging issues.

```
[root@rhel9-server ~]# ls -al /var/log/
total 548
drwxr-xr-x. 10 root    root      4096 Sep 13 20:26 .
drwxr-xr-x. 20 root    root      4096 Aug 28 16:09 ..
drwxr-xr-x.  2 root    root      4096 Aug 12 22:29 anaconda
drwx------.  2 root    root        23 Aug 28 22:20 audit
-rw-rw----.  1 root    utmp         0 Sep  1 00:01 btmp
drwxr-x---.  2 chrony  chrony       6 Aug 17  2021 chrony
-rw-------.  1 root    root      4430 Sep 13 20:01 cron
-rw-r--r--.  1 root    root     69324 Sep 13 19:56 dnf.librepo.log
-rw-r--r--.  1 root    root    309810 Sep 13 19:56 dnf.log
-rw-r--r--.  1 root    root     24710 Sep 13 19:56 dnf.rpm.log
-rw-r-----.  1 root    root       156 Aug 24 21:37 firewalld
-rw-r--r--.  1 root    root      1320 Sep 11 15:39 hawkey.log
drwx------.  2 root    root       147 Sep 12 21:21 httpd
-rw-r--r--.  1 root    root      3064 Sep 10 15:08 kdump.log
-rw-rw-r--.  1 root    utmp    292292 Sep 11 20:43 lastlog
-rw-------.  1 root    root         0 Sep 11 12:21 maillog
-rw-------.  1 root    root     46490 Sep 13 20:24 messages
drwx------.  2 root    root         6 Aug 12 22:27 private
drwxr-xr-x.  2 root    root         6 Mar 22 13:34 qemu-ga
lrwxrwxrwx.  1 root    root        39 Aug 12 22:27 README -> ../../usr/share/doc/systemd/README.logs
drwxr-xr-x.  2 root    root      4096 Sep 11 12:21 rhsm
-rw-------.  1 root    root     10643 Sep 13 20:23 secure
-rw-------.  1 root    root         0 Sep 11 12:21 spooler
drwxr-x---.  2 sssd    sssd        26 Sep 11 13:17 sssd
-rw-------.  1 root    root         0 Aug 12 22:27 tallylog
-rw-rw-r--.  1 root    utmp     23808 Sep 11 20:43 wtmp
```

Figure 17-1. *Where logs are kept on most Linux systems*

Table 17-1 lists a few important log files you should be aware of.

Table 17-1. *Important log files*

Log file	Description
cron	Log for all cron jobs that have been run on your system.
dnf	Stores all the systems dnf transactions. All the package installations, updates, and removals.
firewalld	Used for firewalld debug messages.
lastlog	Slightly different from other log files. lastlog stores the times users last logged in. Run the command "lastlog" to see an output.
maillog	Records when system mails are sent and received.
messages	The central log for your Linux system. On some distributions, this file is called syslog. This should be the first log file you check when debugging any issue.
secure	Used to track security-related messages on your system.

Most systems or applications that are installed typically send their log files to the "/var/log" directory. You may have noticed this in the "High Availability" chapter when we discussed where cluster logs could be found.

Rsyslog

The system responsible for logging information to the log files in the "/var/log" directory is the utility "Rsyslog." Rsyslog catches input from different sources and allows you to transform the input and then output the results to where you want them to be stored.

Rsyslog has been designed in a modular way, allowing users to choose what they want to use with Rsyslog. There are a number of modules currently available that range from snmp trap configuration through to kernel logging.

Installation

Rsyslog is installed on most if not all Linux systems by default today. If by some reason Rsyslog is not installed, it can be installed either from source or from package installation files using your package management system.

Configuration File

The configuration for Rsyslog can be found in the configuration file:

```
# /etc/rsyslog.conf
```

Within the Rsyslog configuration file, there are three main sections you need to be familiar with.

Global Directives

They are used to enable and disable additional modules and configure library locations.

Templates

They are used to help format how you want logs to be recorded and used to create dynamic file names. It is a useful configuration if you are building a central Rsyslog system and want to record the hostname of the system sending logs.

Rules

Rules consist of selectors and actions. These are the fields that set what will be logged and where the logs will be sent.

Verbosity

The detail that is found in a log is based on the verbosity level configured for the system that the logs are coming from. Normally log verbosity is set to Error or Warn in production systems as you do not want your logs filling up.

Log Detail Levels

The following log levels are typically available for users to use when setting logging levels:

- Fatal
- Error
- Warn

- Info

- Debug

- Trace

Set Log Level

Log level is normally set at an application level, or if you are debugging system configuration, the log level needs to be set at the system you are debugging. Remember that Rsyslog only receives and redirects messages. However, if you wanted to have a separate file for errors, you could configure Rsyslog to do this with something similar to the cron.err in Figure 17-2.

```
#### RULES ####

# Log all kernel messages to the console.
# Logging much else clutters up the screen.
#kern.*                                          /dev/console

# Log anything (except mail) of level info or higher.
# Don't log private authentication messages!
*.info;mail.none;authpriv.none;cron.none         /var/log/messages

# The authpriv file has restricted access.
authpriv.*                                       /var/log/secure

# Log all the mail messages in one place.
mail.*                                           -/var/log/maillog


# Log cron stuff
cron.*                                           /var/log/cron

cron.err                                         █/var/log/cron.errors
```

Figure 17-2. *rsyslog.conf*

Don't Leave Debugging On

It is not a good idea to enable anything more than Error or Warn in a production environment, but when you have no choice, always remember to revert logging back to Error or Warn.

Understanding Errors

The entries in the standard Linux log files are relatively simple enough to understand. The language used is fairly clear in most cases. Typically you would look for any Errors or Warn messages for a clue as to what is going wrong. These Errors normally have an error code you can use to Google with and 9 times out of 10 you will get a result with someone experiencing a similar issue.

```
Sep 11 12:21:55 rhel9-server systemd[1]: Finished Rotate log files.
Sep 11 12:21:56 rhel9-server dnf[13220]: Updating Subscription Management repositories.
Sep 11 12:21:56 rhel9-server dnf[13220]: Red Hat Enterprise Linux 9 for x86 64 - BaseOS  0.0  B/s |   0 B     00:00
Sep 11 12:21:56 rhel9-server dnf[13220]: Errors during downloading metadata for repository 'rhel-9-for-x86 64-baseos-rp
ms":
Sep 11 12:21:56 rhel9-server dnf[13220]:  - Curl error (6): Couldn't resolve host name for https://cdn.redhat.com/conte
nt/dist/rhel9/9/x86 64/baseos/os/repodata/repomd.xml [Could not resolve host: cdn.redhat.com]
Sep 11 12:21:56 rhel9-server dnf[13220]: Error: Failed to download metadata for repo 'rhel-9-for-x86 64-baseos-rpms': C
annot download repomd.xml: Curl error (6): Couldn't resolve host name for https://cdn.redhat.com/content/dist/rhel9/9/x
86 64/baseos/os/repodata/repomd.xml [Could not resolve host: cdn.redhat.com]
Sep 11 12:21:56 rhel9-server systemd[1]: dnf-makecache.service: Main process exited, code=exited, status=1/FAILURE
Sep 11 12:21:56 rhel9-server systemd[1]: dnf-makecache.service: Failed with result 'exit-code'.
Sep 11 12:21:56 rhel9-server systemd[1]: Failed to start dnf makecache.
Sep 11 12:21:57 rhel9-server chronyd[756]: Forward time jump detected!
Sep 11 12:21:57 rhel9-server chronyd[756]: Can't synchronise: no selectable sources
```

Figure 17-3. *An example of an error in the /var/log/message file*

In the errors in Figure 17-3, it is clear that there was some kind of name resolution issue. Possibly a network issue or the Internet was not working. As this was a virtual machine installed on a laptop that got shutdown each evening, it was most likely the network configuration encountered an issue on startup. After a system reboot, the system recovered.

Warning   Rebooting a system should never be your first action to resolve an issue. In some cases, logs can be cleaned out or deleted if rebooted. Always backup the logs first or offload the logs to a remote logging system if you need to reboot.

Tail Logs as You Work

Log files can grow quite large and have thousands of entries; this can be problematic when you need to find the exact message when an issue occurred. For this, it is recommended that you open a separate shell session when you test the system for issues. In the separate shell session, run a tail command that follows any new entries being added to a log. Figure 17-4 is an example of tailing the /var/log/messages file.

```
# tail -f /varlog/messages
```

```
[root@rhel9-server ~]# tail -f /var/log/messages
Sep 13 21:48:12 rhel9-server NetworkManager[799]: <info>  [1663102092.1658] dhcp4 (enp1s0): state changed new lease, ad
dress=192.168.122.237
Sep 13 21:52:51 rhel9-server systemd[1]: Stopping System Logging Service...
Sep 13 21:52:51 rhel9-server rsyslogd[763]: [origin software="rsyslogd" swVersion="8.2102.0-101.el9" x-pid="763" x-info
="https://www.rsyslog.com"] exiting on signal 15.
Sep 13 21:52:51 rhel9-server systemd[1]: rsyslog.service: Deactivated successfully.
Sep 13 21:52:51 rhel9-server systemd[1]: Stopped System Logging Service.
Sep 13 21:52:51 rhel9-server systemd[1]: rsyslog.service: Consumed 4.393s CPU time.
Sep 13 21:52:51 rhel9-server systemd[1]: Starting System Logging Service...
Sep 13 21:52:51 rhel9-server rsyslogd[19067]: [origin software="rsyslogd" swVersion="8.2102.0-101.el9" x-pid="19067" x-
info="https://www.rsyslog.com"] start
Sep 13 21:52:51 rhel9-server systemd[1]: Started System Logging Service.
Sep 13 21:52:51 rhel9-server rsyslogd[19067]: imjournal: journal files changed, reloading... [v8.2102.0-101.el9 try ht
tps://www.rsyslog.com/e/0 ]
```

Figure 17-4. *Tailing log files*

All new messages will appear on the screen as they are written to the log.

Figure 17-5. *Two screens side by side can speed up the debugging process*

Journalctl

Another important location to find information about your system is by using the journalctl utility. Journalctl is used to look at the logs generated from systemd's logging service journald.

Traditionally and it was previously mentioned, the /var/log/messages file should be the first place to look, but looking at journalctl outputs is not a bad idea either.

To get a quick view of the current state of your Linux system, with the added ability to scroll pages, run the following command:

```
# journalctl -xe
```

```
Subject: A start job for unit systemd-udevd.service has begun execution
Defined-By: systemd
Support: https://access.redhat.com/support

A start job for unit systemd-udevd.service has begun execution.

The job identifier is 6597.
Sep 14 21:38:52 rhel9-server.kenlab.local systemd[1]: Started Rule-based Manager for Device Events and Files.
Subject: A start job for unit systemd-udevd.service has finished successfully
Defined-By: systemd
Support: https://access.redhat.com/support

A start job for unit systemd-udevd.service has finished successfully.

The job identifier is 6597.
Sep 14 21:38:53 rhel9-server.kenlab.local dnf[19161]: Updating Subscription Management repositories.
Sep 14 21:38:53 rhel9-server.kenlab.local dnf[19161]: Unable to read consumer identity
Sep 14 21:38:53 rhel9-server.kenlab.local dnf[19161]: This system is not registered with an entitlement server
Sep 14 21:38:53 rhel9-server.kenlab.local dnf[19161]: There are no enabled repositories in "/etc/yum.repos.d",
Sep 14 21:38:53 rhel9-server.kenlab.local systemd[1]: dnf-makecache.service: Deactivated successfully.
Subject: Unit succeeded
Defined-By: systemd
Support: https://access.redhat.com/support

The unit dnf-makecache.service has successfully entered the 'dead' state.
Sep 14 21:38:53 rhel9-server.kenlab.local systemd[1]: Finished dnf makecache.
Subject: A start job for unit dnf-makecache.service has finished successfully
Defined-By: systemd
Support: https://access.redhat.com/support

A start job for unit dnf-makecache.service has finished successfully.

The job identifier is 6421.
Sep 14 21:38:55 rhel9-server.kenlab.local NetworkManager[799]: <info>  [1663187935.2367] dhcp4 (enp1s0): state
Sep 14 21:42:05 rhel9-server.kenlab.local chronyd[756]: Selected source 93.93.131.118 (2.rhel.pool.ntp.org)
Sep 14 21:42:05 rhel9-server.kenlab.local chronyd[756]: System clock wrong by -1.545388 seconds
Sep 14 21:44:14 rhel9-server.kenlab.local chronyd[756]: Selected source 212.71.253.212 (2.rhel.pool.ntp.org)
Sep 14 21:46:25 rhel9-server.kenlab.local chronyd[756]: Selected source 103.214.44.30 (2.rhel.pool.ntp.org)
lines 3989-4026/4026 (END)
```

Figure 17-6. *Journalctl -xe output*

If you have any issues with your system, this command will give you some clue as to what is happening.

Real-Time Messages

As we did with tailing logs, you can do something very similar with journalctl. By using the "-f" switch, you can follow the logs as they enter journald:

```
# journalctl -xf
```

Figure 17-7. *Journalctl outputting messages as they appear*

In Figure 17-7, you can see that the "logger error" command generates a log entry in the journald logs. This is immediately displayed in the tailing command.

This is another useful way to debug a system that is experiencing issues.

Useful journalctl Commands

Table 17-2 lists useful journalctl commands you can use as an enterprise Linux administrator.

Table 17-2. *Journalctl commands*

Log file	Description
journalctl -xe	Basic journalctl command that should be used. The "x" gives a further explanation, and the "e" jumps to the end of the pager.
journalctl -f	Follows the logs from journald and outputs real time.
journalctl -u name. service	Lists all the logs for a particular unit. In this case a service.
journalctl -p "crit"	Shows all critical messages. Crit can be replaced by any other priority such as "emerg" (0), "alert" (1), "crit" (2), "err" (3), "warning" (4), "notice" (5), "info" (6), debug" (7).
journalctl _UID	Records when system mails are sent and received.
journalctl -e --since "10 minutes ago"	Restricts logs to a time period since they were logged. This command will list logs from the last 10 minutes.
journalctl --list-boots	Lists all the recorded system boots.

For more interesting ways to use journalctl, have a look at the man pages and the help provided:

```
# journalctl --help
```

```
journalctl [OPTIONS...] [MATCHES...]

Query the journal.

Options:
       --system              Show the system journal
       --user                Show the user journal for the current user
  -M --machine=CONTAINER     Operate on local container
  -S --since=DATE            Show entries not older than the specified date
  -U --until=DATE            Show entries not newer than the specified date
  -c --cursor=CURSOR         Show entries starting at the specified cursor
       --after-cursor=CURSOR Show entries after the specified cursor
       --show-cursor         Print the cursor after all the entries
       --cursor-file=FILE    Show entries after cursor in FILE and update FILE
  -b --boot[=ID]             Show current boot or the specified boot
       --list-boots          Show terse information about recorded boots
  -k --dmesg                 Show kernel message log from the current boot
  -u --unit=UNIT             Show logs from the specified unit
       --user-unit=UNIT      Show logs from the specified user unit
  -t --identifier=STRING     Show entries with the specified syslog identifier
  -p --priority=RANGE        Show entries with the specified priority
       --facility=FACILITY...Show entries with the specified facilities
  -g --grep=PATTERN          Show entries with MESSAGE matching PATTERN
       --case-sensitive[=BOOL] Force case sensitive or insensitive matching
  -e --pager-end             Immediately jump to the end in the pager
  -f --follow                Follow the journal
  -n --lines[=INTEGER]       Number of journal entries to show
       --no-tail             Show all lines, even in follow mode
  -r --reverse               Show the newest entries first
```

Figure 17-8. *Journalctl help menu*

...

output reduced

Remote Logging

Log forwarding to a remote system is the preferred option for most organizations today. Enterprise tooling like Splunk or Fluentd is a great way to off-load local logs to a central location. It removes the need for local systems to retain logs for extended periods and reduces the disk footprint.

Rsyslog can also act as a remote log system if you do not have an enterprise solution. Rsyslog can be configured to receive logs over either TCP or udp and can also be configured to send and receive logs securely using certificates.

Rsyslog as a Central Logging System

To configure Rsyslog as a central logging system, you need to ensure the following are in place.

Firewall

The firewall was configured to allow either TCP/udp port 514 depending on what protocol you are choosing to use or TCP/udp port 6514 depending if you are using a more secure method involving certificates.

SELinux

If SELinux is enabled, you will need to enable the following booleans:

```
# sudo semanage -a -t syslogd_port_t -p tcp 514
# sudo semanage -a -t syslogd_port_t -p udp 514
```

rsyslog.conf

Configure rsyslog.conf to enable modules to the following receive logs:

```
$ModLoad imtcp
$InputTCPServerRun 514
```

Restart Service

Restart the Rsyslog service:

```
# sudo systemctl restart rsyslog
```

Forward Logs to Rsyslog server

To configure all the systems that will forward logs to the central Rsyslog server, you will need to make one simple configuration change. All that is required is a simple configuration line in the rsyslog.conf file:

```
*.*   @@<central logging server address>:514
```

"*.*" means that all the systems with all their messages will be forwarded.

"@@" means that the TCP protocol will be used to communicate with the central logging server.

"<central logging server address>" is the IP address or hostname of your central logging Rsyslog server.

Note   A single @ is used for udp where two @@ are used to send via TCP.

Restart Service

As with the central Rsyslog server, once the configuration file rsyslog.conf has been updated, the Rsyslog service will need to be restarted:

```
# sudo systemctl restart rsyslog
```

Exercise

For a simple exercise around logs, run through the following tasks on a Linux system with systemd installed.

Journalctl

Using journalctl, do the following:

- Output all critical logs that have occurred within the last two days.

- Open a new terminal to your system and tail the journalctl logs. On the current terminal you have opened, run the command "logger testerror". Observe that the log appears in the other window.

- Output all the logs for your logged in user. To get your UID, you can run the command "id".

Logs

Open and view the various logs in the /var/log directory. Once done, open a new terminal and tail the /var/log/messages file. In the other terminal you have opened, run the logger command again and observe logs being entered into the messages' log.

Remote Logging

As an added bonus exercise, attempt to build a remote logging server. Configure a "client" server to forward all logs to the remote server using TCP.

Monitoring

When it comes to Linux system monitoring, there are many tools and utilities that can give you metrics about your system. Some keep historical data and others do not. For troubleshooting and attempting to find root causes of issues, it is important to know what these tools are.

Process-Related Tools

The following are the standard tools most enterprise Linux administrators use to show process-related information.

ps and top

Two very basic tools found on every Linux distribution are the tools "ps" and "top".

top

```
# top
```

```
top - 22:32:53 up 4 days,  7:24,  2 users,  load average: 0.00, 0.00, 0.00
Tasks: 176 total,   1 running, 175 sleeping,   0 stopped,   0 zombie
%Cpu(s):  0.1 us,  0.1 sy,  0.0 ni, 99.8 id,  0.0 wa,  0.1 hi,  0.0 si,  0.0 st
MiB Mem :   3722.6 total,   2510.5 free,    337.2 used,    874.9 buff/cache
MiB Swap:   2048.0 total,   2048.0 free,      0.0 used.   3118.6 avail Mem

  PID USER      PR  NI    VIRT    RES    SHR S  %CPU  %MEM     TIME+ COMMAND
19164 root      20   0       0      0      0 I   0.3   0.0   0:05.17 kworker/1:0-events
19261 root      20   0   10684   4308   3476 R   0.3   0.1   0:00.04 top
    1 root      20   0  179672  15808  10340 S   0.0   0.4   0:05.63 systemd
    2 root      20   0       0      0      0 S   0.0   0.0   0:00.07 kthreadd
    3 root       0 -20       0      0      0 I   0.0   0.0   0:00.00 rcu_gp
    4 root       0 -20       0      0      0 I   0.0   0.0   0:00.00 rcu_par_gp
    6 root       0 -20       0      0      0 I   0.0   0.0   0:00.00 kworker/0:0H-events_highpri
    9 root       0 -20       0      0      0 I   0.0   0.0   0:00.00 mm_percpu_wq
   10 root      20   0       0      0      0 S   0.0   0.0   0:00.00 rcu_tasks_kthre
   11 root      20   0       0      0      0 S   0.0   0.0   0:00.00 rcu_tasks_rude_
   12 root      20   0       0      0      0 S   0.0   0.0   0:00.00 rcu_tasks_trace
   13 root      20   0       0      0      0 S   0.0   0.0   0:00.01 ksoftirqd/0
   14 root      20   0       0      0      0 I   0.0   0.0   0:06.99 rcu_preempt
   15 root      rt   0       0      0      0 S   0.0   0.0   0:00.13 migration/0
   16 root      20   0       0      0      0 S   0.0   0.0   0:00.00 cpuhp/0
   17 root      20   0       0      0      0 S   0.0   0.0   0:00.00 cpuhp/1
   18 root      rt   0       0      0      0 S   0.0   0.0   0:00.20 migration/1
   19 root      20   0       0      0      0 S   0.0   0.0   0:00.02 ksoftirqd/1
   21 root       0 -20       0      0      0 I   0.0   0.0   0:00.00 kworker/1:0H-events_highpri
   22 root      20   0       0      0      0 S   0.0   0.0   0:00.00 cpuhp/2
   23 root      rt   0       0      0      0 S   0.0   0.0   0:00.20 migration/2
```

Figure 17-9. *top command*

Figure 17-9 shows the top command output. top runs until killed or stopped. top displays the current memory usage, load average, number of running processes including zombie processes, and a list of processes currently running. There are "live" commands you can give top while it is running, like pressing the "1" key to list all the cpus.

For more information about top, read the help and man pages.

ps

To search for processes and to list only processes, you can use the "ps" command:

ps -ef

```
[root@rhel9-server ~]# ps -ef
UID          PID    PPID  C STIME TTY          TIME CMD
root           1       0  0 Sep10 ?        00:00:05 /usr/lib/systemd/systemd --switched-root --system --deseria
root           2       0  0 Sep10 ?        00:00:00 [kthreadd]
root           3       2  0 Sep10 ?        00:00:00 [rcu_gp]
root           4       2  0 Sep10 ?        00:00:00 [rcu_par_gp]
root           6       2  0 Sep10 ?        00:00:00 [kworker/0:0H-events_highpri]
root           9       2  0 Sep10 ?        00:00:00 [mm_percpu_wq]
root          10       2  0 Sep10 ?        00:00:00 [rcu_tasks_kthre]
root          11       2  0 Sep10 ?        00:00:00 [rcu_tasks_rude_]
root          12       2  0 Sep10 ?        00:00:00 [rcu_tasks_trace]
root          13       2  0 Sep10 ?        00:00:00 [ksoftirqd/0]
root          14       2  0 Sep10 ?        00:00:07 [rcu_preempt]
root          15       2  0 Sep10 ?        00:00:00 [migration/0]
root          16       2  0 Sep10 ?        00:00:00 [cpuhp/0]
```

Figure 17-10. *A reduced output of the ps -ef command.*

There are a few useful commands that can help diagnose process issues you can use. Search for a specific process:

```
# ps -ef | grep <process name>
# ps -ef | grep httpd
```

Memory-intensive processes:

```
# ps -auxf | sort -nr -k 4 | head -5
```

CPU-intensive processes:

```
# ps -auxf | sort -nr -k 3 | head -5
```

pstree

A simple tool to see all the processes and the parents of each process is the "pstree" command:

```
# pstree
```

```
[root@rhel9-server ~]# pstree
systemd─┬─NetworkManager───2*[{NetworkManager}]
        ├─agetty
        ├─auditd─┬─sedispatch
        │        └─2*[{auditd}]
        ├─chronyd
        ├─crond
        ├─dbus-broker-lau───dbus-broker
        ├─firewalld───{firewalld}
        ├─gssproxy───5*[{gssproxy}]
        ├─httpd─┬─httpd
        │       ├─2*[httpd───64*[{httpd}]]
        │       └─httpd───80*[{httpd}]
        ├─irqbalance───{irqbalance}
        ├─nfsdcld
        ├─polkitd───7*[{polkitd}]
        ├─qemu-ga───{qemu-ga}
        ├─rhsmcertd
        ├─rpc.idmapd
        ├─rpc.mountd
        ├─rpc.statd
        ├─rpcbind
        ├─rsyslogd───2*[{rsyslogd}]
        ├─sshd─┬─sshd───sshd───bash───sudo───bash
        │      └─sshd───sshd───bash───sudo───bash───pstree
        ├─systemd───(sd-pam)
        ├─systemd-journal
        ├─systemd-logind
        └─systemd-udevd
```

Figure 17-11. *An output of the pstree command run as root*

Disk-Related Tools

The following are the standard tools most enterprise Linux administrators use to show disk information.

lsblk

To list all the disks attached to your system, you can use the command shown in Figure 17-12.

```
# lsblk
```

```
NAME            MAJ:MIN RM  SIZE RO TYPE MOUNTPOINTS
sr0              11:0    1 1024M  0 rom
vda             252:0    0   20G  0 disk
├─vda1          252:1    0    1G  0 part /boot
└─vda2          252:2    0   19G  0 part
  ├─rhel-root   253:0    0   17G  0 lvm  /
  └─rhel-swap   253:1    0    2G  0 lvm  [SWAP]
vdb             252:16   0    2G  0 disk
```

Figure 17-12. *lsblk output*

blkid

To display information about a disk or filesystem, you can use the command shown in Figure 17-13.

```
# blkid /dev/diskname
```

```
[root@rhel9-server ~]# blkid /dev/vda2
/dev/vda2: UUID="ILDQXA-5eva-YMid-EH0x-OB0h-z6Wr-bEtC6w" TYPE="LVM2_member" PARTUUID="b2032c19-02"
[root@rhel9-server ~]# blkid /dev/rhel/root
/dev/rhel/root: UUID="b47db0bd-f185-4860-8267-f7d58f36fdd0" BLOCK_SIZE="512" TYPE="xfs"
```

Figure 17-13. *blkid output*

In Figure 17-13, you can see the disk information for the main disk being used in the system and the disk information for the logical volume that was created on the disk.

du

To view the disk usage in your system, you can use the du command:

du -hs /home

```
[root@rhel9-server ~]# du -hs /home/
25M     /home/
```

Figure 17-14. *du output on the /home directory*

The output in Figure 17-14 gives a summary of all parent directories and the disk space being used by each. The "-h" gives a human readable output in megabytes, gigabytes, etc.

df

The df command will give you a listing of all disks and partitions currently mounted:

df -h

```
[root@rhel9-server ~]# df -h
Filesystem             Size  Used Avail Use% Mounted on
devtmpfs               1.8G     0  1.8G   0% /dev
tmpfs                  1.9G     0  1.9G   0% /dev/shm
tmpfs                  745M  8.7M  736M   2% /run
/dev/mapper/rhel-root   17G  2.0G   16G  12% /
/dev/vda1             1014M  197M  818M  20% /boot
tmpfs                  373M     0  373M   0% /run/user/1000
```

Figure 17-15. *df -h output showing all mounted filesystems*

Network-Related Tools

The following are a few useful network tools you can use to help with your administration tasks.

ss

As the netstat command has been deprecated, the ss command is a very useful replacement. To get quick information about your system's network socket, you can use the "ss" command.

To view all TCP and udp sockets on a Linux system with ss, you can use the following command:

ss -t -a

```
[root@rhel9-server ~]# ss -t -a
State      Recv-Q   Send-Q            Local Address:Port          Peer Address:Port        Process
LISTEN     0        64                   0.0.0.0:nfs                   0.0.0.0:*
LISTEN     0        64                   0.0.0.0:33097                 0.0.0.0:*
LISTEN     0        4096                 0.0.0.0:sunrpc                0.0.0.0:*
LISTEN     0        4096                 0.0.0.0:mountd                0.0.0.0:*
LISTEN     0        4096                 0.0.0.0:33907                 0.0.0.0:*
LISTEN     0        128                  0.0.0.0:ssh                   0.0.0.0:*
ESTAB      0        0            192.168.122.237:ssh          192.168.122.1:51098
ESTAB      0        0            192.168.122.237:ssh          192.168.122.1:59722
LISTEN     0        64                      [::]:nfs                      [::]:*
LISTEN     0        64                      [::]:45223                    [::]:*
LISTEN     0        4096                    [::]:47815                    [::]:*
LISTEN     0        4096                    [::]:sunrpc                   [::]:*
LISTEN     0        511                        *:http                       *:*
LISTEN     0        4096                    [::]:mountd                   [::]:*
LISTEN     0        128                     [::]:ssh                      [::]:*
```

Figure 17-16. *ss -t -a output*

Additional Network Tools

There are a few other tools that can be used for network monitoring tasks, but as they are not installed by default, we will only list them here. In your own time, install and test them to see how they could benefit your day-to-day tasks:

- – "iptraf-ng" is a nice command-line graphical tool to display stats about your network adapter.

- – "iftop" is a simple command-line utility similar to "top" but for interface information.

- – "tcpdump" is a more advanced network packet capturing tool. Very useful and quite important as you become more experienced.

Performance Copilot

The previously discussed monitoring tools are predominantly used for real-time monitoring and viewing stats as they appear. To view more history data and metrics, you will need to use a tool suite like "pcp". To use "pcp," you will need to install the "pcp" package as per the following:

```
# sudo dnf install pcp -y
```

Table 17-3 lists all the utilities that are installed with the pcp package.

Table 17-3. *pcp tools*

Name	Description
pmstat	Lists live information your system, cpu, memory, etc.
pminfo	Lists the metrics that can be queried.
pmval	Views the metric data.
pmlogger	Stores the metric data into files that can be queried later by pmval.

Remote Monitoring

The best monitoring is of course the monitoring that is done from a remote system. You cannot look at local monitoring information if your system is not working; for this reason, having the monitoring information on a separate system makes sense.

There are a number of options available for monitoring, of which the following two are often mentioned in Linux environments. There are many many other options, but these two are worth reading a bit further on.

Nagios

Nagios is an OpenSource project and has another interesting name, it being recursive. Nagios means "Nagios ain't going to insist on sainthood."

Nagios is a server and agent-based deployment, with a few options of what agents can be used:

– The deprecated NRPE that uses scripts hosted on the client systems

– NRDP or Nagios Remote Data Processor

– A Windows agent for Nagios: NSClient++

– The cross platform agent: NCPA

More about Nagios can be found in the following:
www.nagios.com/

Prometheus

One of the more command monitoring platforms used in the OpenSource world is Prometheus. Prometheus is an OpenSource alerting and event monitoring system that stores data in a time series database. Prometheus is a central location for metric data to be stored and is usually paired with other software to provide an overall monitoring solution.

Read more about Prometheus:

```
https://prometheus.io/
```

Finding Help

As an enterprise Linux system administrator, there will come a time when things will go wrong and you will not know where to look for the solution. There are tools that can help, and there are support options you can use.

Tools

There are no tools that will just give you an answer to your problem. The tools in the succeeding text, however, will give you some of the vital information you will need when you are looking for your answer. When you have exhausted all options, only then proceed to ask for help.

strace

To understand what a process or application is doing behind the scenes, you can use the strace tool. strace is normally run as a prefix to a command or application to see what the application is doing. If you wanted to see what a process was doing, you can also attach strace to a "pid":

```
# strace <application or command>
# strace df -h
```

```
[root@rhel9-server ~]# strace df -h
execve("/bin/df", ["df", "-h"], 0x7ffeff32ea48 /* 22 vars */) = 0
brk(NULL)                              = 0x5634914ed000
arch_prctl(0x3001 /* ARCH_??? */, 0x7ffd6cf944d0) = -1 EINVAL (Invalid argument)
access("/etc/ld.so.preload", R_OK)     = -1 ENOENT (No such file or directory)
openat(AT_FDCWD, "/etc/ld.so.cache", O_RDONLY|O_CLOEXEC) = 3
newfstatat(3, "", {st_mode=S_IFREG|0644, st_size=15779, ...}, AT_EMPTY_PATH) = 0
mmap(NULL, 15779, PROT_READ, MAP_PRIVATE, 3, 0) = 0x7fc48d9cd000
close(3)                               = 0
openat(AT_FDCWD, "/lib64/libc.so.6", O_RDONLY|O_CLOEXEC) = 3
```

The aforementioned is a reduced output from strace command:

```
# strace -p 799
```

```
[root@rhel9-server ~]# strace -p 799
strace: Process 799 attached
restart_syscall(<... resuming interrupted read ...>
```

Figure 17-17. *strace output examples*

Manual Pages and Help

A few times throughout this book, it has been mentioned to read the man pages or the help. It cannot be said enough how important this is before doing anything else. Often the answer is right there:

```
# df --help
```

```
[root@rhel9-server ~]# df --help
Usage: df [OPTION]... [FILE]...
Show information about the file system on which each FILE resides,
or all file systems by default.

Mandatory arguments to long options are mandatory for short options too.
  -a, --all             include pseudo, duplicate, inaccessible file systems
  -B, --block-size=SIZE  scale sizes by SIZE before printing them; e.g.,
                          '-BM' prints sizes in units of 1,048,576 bytes;
                          see SIZE format below
      --direct          show statistics for a file instead of mount point
  -h, --human-readable  print sizes in powers of 1024 (e.g., 1023M)
  -H, --si              print sizes in powers of 1000 (e.g., 1.1G)
  -i, --inodes          list inode information instead of block usage
  -k                    like --block-size=1K
  -l, --local           limit listing to local file systems
      --no-sync         do not invoke sync before getting usage info (default)
      --output[=FIELD_LIST]  use the output format defined by FIELD_LIST,
                          or print all fields if FIELD_LIST is omitted.
  -P, --portability     use the POSIX output format
      --sync            invoke sync before getting usage info
      --total           elide all entries insignificant to available space,
                          and produce a grand total
```

```
# man df
```

```
DF(1)                                   User Commands                                   DF(1)

NAME
       df - report file system disk space usage

SYNOPSIS
       df [OPTION]... [FILE]...

DESCRIPTION
       This  manual page documents the GNU version of df.  df displays the amount of disk space available on
       the file system containing each file name argument.  If no file name is given, the space available on
       all currently mounted file systems is shown.  Disk space is shown in 1K blocks by default, unless the
       environment variable POSIXLY_CORRECT is set, in which case 512-byte blocks are used.

       If an argument is the absolute file name of a disk device node containing a mounted file  system,  df
       shows  the  space  available on that file system rather than on the file system containing the device
       node.  This version of df cannot show the space available on unmounted file systems, because on  most
       kinds of systems doing so requires very nonportable intimate knowledge of file system structures.

OPTIONS
       Show information about the file system on which each FILE resides, or all file systems by default.

       Mandatory arguments to long options are mandatory for short options too.

       -a, --all
              include pseudo, duplicate, inaccessible file systems

       -B, --block-size=SIZE
              scale  sizes  by  SIZE  before  printing  them; e.g., '-BM' prints sizes in units of 1,048,576
              bytes; see SIZE format below

       --direct
              show statistics for a file instead of mount point

       -h, --human-readable
              print sizes in powers of 1024 (e.g., 1023M)
```

Figure 17-18. *Man page and help for the df utility*

Asking for Help

When completely stuck with an issue, you may need to ask other experienced people for help; this could be colleagues or people online. When doing so, there are a few things you should take into consideration.

Before Asking for Help

For someone to help you and give up their time to look at your issue, they would expect you to have done some of your own effort first. The following are some of the basics you should always do before looking for an answer from someone else:

- Tried to fix the problem and failed

- Read the documentation supplied by the software or hardware vendor

- Searched the Internet for examples of what others have tried, and you have checked that no one has already asked the question you need help on

Asking a Question the Right Way

There is also an etiquette on how you ask questions online. If you make your questions too vague or show that you have made no efforts to resolve your issue, chances are that you are going to be ignored and your question will go unanswered.

Here are a few things to keep in mind when you post a question in the future.

Be Very Clear

Your question should always be posted in a way that someone understands clearly what you want and what you have tried to do so far. English may not be everyone's first language, so do not try to be overly expressive; keep your language as simple as possible.

If English is not your first language, then state that in your question; people will then hopefully understand that you are trying your best and look past any grammatical or spelling errors. However, with that said, you should always try to spell-check your work. Google docs is free and has a decent enough spellcheck you can use.

Question Wording

When putting your question together, ensure that you include the following:

- State what you have tried.

- Give the details of all the components. If you are asking questions about hardware, include the make and model.

- Include the Linux distro you are using.

- State that you have read the documentation and read through other examples; keep the links so you can refer back to them in your question.

- Be very specific about your issue in the main body of your question and give a single line on top summarizing your problem.

Example Questions

Knowing where to get help is only as good as your ability to ask the right questions. The following are examples of good and bad questions.

Bad Question

Subject: Hi

I have recently been trying to install packages on RHEL 9; however nothing is working. I'm very new to Linux and not sure what I'm doing.

Thanks.

Good Question

Subject: Unable to install packages on RHEL 9.0

I have recently been given the task of installing an Apache web server on a new RHEL 9.0 server. I am very new to Linux with very little experience. I have read the RHEL 9.0 installation guide, but I cannot seem to find anything that could help.

I have also looked at the /var/log/messages file; the following is the output from the log file:

<extract from log, BUT not the whole log file>

As mentioned, I am very new to Linux, and many of the log file entries are confusing to me. I do however think the problem may be network related but I am not sure. I have Googled and found this article <link to article> that may indicate a problem with a proxy.

Any help you can give will be greatly appreciated.

Thanks.

Getting Support

The likelihood when working in a larger organization is that you will have Linux distributions that are backed by vendor support subscriptions. These subscriptions come with vendor support and the ability to raise support cases.

With Red Hat, support cases can be raised in their "`https://access.redhat.com`" portal. Provided you have valid subscriptions, you should be able to raise support cases. Different support subscriptions do also have different service level agreements. Some will get you 24-hour support with a 1-hour production response; other subscriptions may take longer.

Preempted Support

Something that could be worth doing when you are able to work on a highly critical platform is to open a support case mentioning what you will be doing and when. This could allow the support team to be prepared for any issues they may need to help with. The support teams could also give advice and links to documentation you should read before doing the work.

This support case would also be monitored, and you could then get a faster response, were there to be a problem.

Sosreport

With all enterprise Linux systems, "sosreport" is used to extract information for support teams. Sosreport is a plugin-based tool that can be run with different parameters to export different information. Sosreport's output is often requested by enterprise support teams when support cases are raised and is always worth uploading whenever a new support case is raised.

A sosreport can be created without specifying any parameters as follows:

```
# sosreport
```

As a Linux enterprise administrator, you may wish to use sosreports for your own diagnosis queries. Sosreports can be extracted manually if you wish to look into a user's problem from your own test system. Sosreports are also a good way to keep an historical record of a system's configuration. IE: Once you finish building a new system, before handing it over to the destined user, create a sosreport that you can keep to use for comparison if the system ever were to break.

Summary

In this chapter, you were introduced to the following:

- How Linux logging is configured and where logs can be found

- What options are available to send logs to a remote system and how to configure your own remote logging server

- What local monitoring tools can be used to extract crucial system information and metrics

- Examples of remote monitoring tools

- How to find help when you encounter an issue you are not able to resolve

- The correct way to ask for help

## CHAPTER 18

Recovering from Disaster

When everything is running well, being an enterprise Linux administrator can be quite an easy and enjoyable job. However, when things go wrong, the pressure can build very quickly. Having the tools and knowledge to diagnose system issues is only half of the battle; knowing how to recover a failed system is the other crucial bit that all enterprise Linux administrators should know.

In this chapter, we will discuss how you should approach building systems to avoid lengthy system troubleshooting in the first place. We will discuss why building from code is the way of the future and why so many people are doing this today.

We will continue to discuss different recovery methods for when rebuilds are not possible. We will look at the three main enterprise Linux distributions and how they can be recovered.

Finally, we will look at a few use case examples of why a system might need to be recovered.

Reinstalling

Starting all over or rebuilding is not always something that we want to do, but with today's different operating systems and automation, this is not as big of an issue as it would have been a few years ago.

Things to Consider

When building your Linux estate, there are a few points you should consider.

© Kenneth Hitchcock 2023
K. Hitchcock, *The Enterprise Linux Administrator*, https://doi.org/10.1007/978-1-4842-8801-6_18

Cattle vs. Pets

Do we think of enterprise Linux systems as cattle or do we think of them as pets? Cattle are farmed and are replaceable, often not even given names, just numbers. Cattle are a product and we treat them that way.

With pets however, we put a little more effort in them. We give them names, we love them, and we cannot bear being without them. Pets cost us money and time.

Enterprise systems should not be seen as pets, not if you want to have a flexible robust environment that can recover from disaster quickly. Enterprise systems should be built from code and treated as cattle. This approach increases recovery time when rebuilds are required. New platform and application versions can be deployed quicker; upgrades can be done with less reduction as everything is built from code.

Other than the aforementioned benefits, the "cattle" approach can also reduce concerns around upskilling new staff. New staff can learn how systems are deployed and how systems are configured from the code itself, helping speed up handover and reduce the risk of not having anyone who knows the platform.

Time to Build vs. Time to Troubleshoot

Time spent debugging and troubleshooting vs. rebuilding really depends on the critical nature of the environment. In production, if a system is down, you may need to spend less time reading logs or booting into rescue modes if your system can be rebuilt or redeployed in minutes. In this case, export logs, save configuration files, and rebuild. You can do root cause analysis later when production is running again.

The converse to the previous argument is also true, if your system build is hand-cranked or manual and it will take a long time to rebuild, then you may have no choice but to try to fix the issue. In this situation, it would still be a good idea to attempt to run a parallel build while you troubleshoot, in case you are not able to recover in a reasonable time.

Ideally, you should never have a problem like this in production, but it could be something you encounter in a lab or development testing environment where redundancy might not be a priority. Think carefully about your time and effort when a rebuild can help move you along quicker.

Build from Code

All your enterprise systems should be built from code. Using automation bundled with a repeatable build process that is controlled from a source control platform will allow you to build from code whenever needed. This process can be triggered and run with little to no human intervention. The entire process can also be integrated with change control platforms, allowing a build to be triggered once approval has been granted.

On cloud platforms, this process is managed by redeploying images using automation tooling like Terraform or Ansible, whereas with hardware or virtual machine-based deployments, you may consider using estate management tools like Red Hat Satellite Server that build systems using PXE and kickstart files. Configuration is then generally managed using Ansible, SaltStack, or Puppet.

Knowing When to Start Over

Time is normally the reason why systems are rebuilt. As mentioned, in production, you will be under pressure. Making the decision to start over can save time and reduce downtime, trust your build process has been tested, and that your recovery will resolve the issue quicker than your troubleshooting. If you do not have confidence in the speed of rebuilding, you have a larger problem. In this situation, you need to deal with the current crisis and extend your technical debt. Automated builds are crucial in today's enterprise environments; not being able to build quickly from code will definitely come back to bite you one day. Keep fighting to ensure your organization works this way; in the end, it will be you who will be left resolving issues, not management.

Recovering

With any luck, recovery should be something you never have to worry about if things go wrong as you can just redeploy, but if you ever were unfortunate that redeployment was not possible, knowing how to recover is vital.

Single-User Mode

One of the more important things to know in Linux is how to boot your system into an environment that can help you recover. This is a "safe mode" of sorts where no networking is configured. Filesystems are mounted as read only, and the root filesystem is normally mounted under the /sysroot directory.

RHEL

To boot a RHEL 9 system into single-user mode, you will need to reboot and catch your system when the grub menu appears below. You will need to be quick as the system will continue booting into the highlighted kernel if you do not intervene.

Figure 18-1 shows the grub menu where the up and down arrows were pressed one after another to halt the boot process.

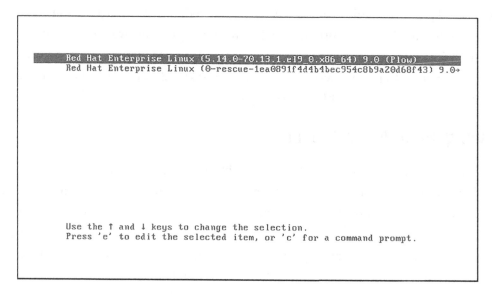

Figure 18-1. *Stopping the boot process*

To enter single-user mode, the highlighted kernel line earlier needs to be edited. To do this, press the "e" key on the kernel line you wish to edit.

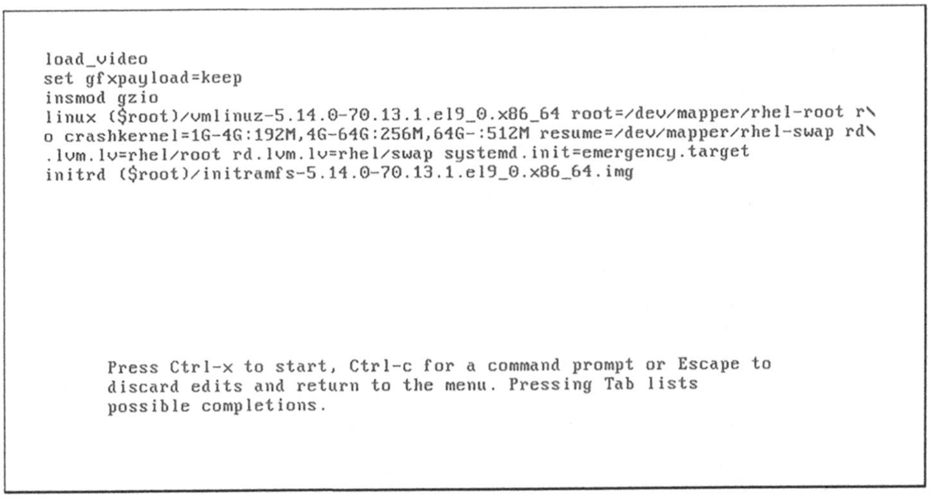

```
load_video
set gfxpayload=keep
insmod gzio
linux ($root)/vmlinuz-5.14.0-70.13.1.el9_0.x86_64 root=/dev/mapper/rhel-root r\
o crashkernel=1G-4G:192M,4G-64G:256M,64G-:512M resume=/dev/mapper/rhel-swap rd\
.lvm.lv=rhel/root rd.lvm.lv=rhel/swap systemd.init=emergency.target
initrd ($root)/initramfs-5.14.0-70.13.1.el9_0.x86_64.img




       Press Ctrl-x to start, Ctrl-c for a command prompt or Escape to
       discard edits and return to the menu. Pressing Tab lists
       possible completions.
```

Figure 18-2. *Editing the kernel startup parameters*

Look for the line starting with "linux". At the end of the line, add the following text:

```
systemd.unit=emergency.target
```

Tip   You may want to press the "end" key on your keyboard to get to the end of the line quicker.

Once you have added the text to the "linux" line, press "Ctrl x" keys together to boot into the edited kernel line.

```
[    4.828149] systemd[1]: Stopped Switch Root.
[  OK  ] Stopped Switch Root.
[    4.829655] systemd[1]: Stopped target Switch Root.
[  OK  ] Stopped target Switch Root.
[    4.830861] systemd[1]: Stopped target Initrd File Systems.
[  OK  ] Stopped target Initrd File Systems.
[    4.832271] systemd[1]: Stopped target Initrd Root File System.
[  OK  ] Stopped target Initrd Root File System.
[    4.838281] systemd[1]: Started Emergency Shell.
[  OK  ] Started Emergency Shell.
[    4.839789] systemd[1]: Reached target Emergency Mode.
[  OK  ] Reached target Emergency Mode.
[    4.841163] systemd[1]: systemd-fsck-root.service: Deactivated successfully.
[    4.842100] systemd[1]: Stopped File System Check on Root Device.
[  OK  ] Stopped File System Check on Root Device.
[    4.848161] systemd[1]: Starting Journal Service...
         Starting Journal Service...
[    4.873027] systemd[1]: Started Journal Service.
[  OK  ] Started Journal Service.
You are in emergency mode. After logging in, type "journalctl -xb" to view
system logs, "systemctl reboot" to reboot, "systemctl default" or "exit"
to boot into default mode.
Give root password for maintenance
(or press Control-D to continue):
[root@rhel9-server ~]#
```

Figure 18-3. *Booting into the edited kernel*

Enter the root password to log in to emergency mode.

In single-user mode, the filesystem will be mounted as read only. To correct this when needing to make system changes, run the following commands:

If the root filesystem has been mounted to /sysroot:

```
# chroot /sysroot
```

To remount the root filesystem as read-write:

```
# mount -o remount,rw /
```

```
[    4.838281] systemd[1]: Started Emergency Shell.
[  OK  ] Started Emergency Shell.
[    4.839789] systemd[1]: Reached target Emergency Mode.
[  OK  ] Reached target Emergency Mode.
[    4.841163] systemd[1]: systemd-fsck-root.service: Deactivated successfully.
[    4.842100] systemd[1]: Stopped File System Check on Root Device.
[  OK  ] Stopped File System Check on Root Device.
[    4.848161] systemd[1]: Starting Journal Service...
          Starting Journal Service...
[    4.873027] systemd[1]: Started Journal Service.
[  OK  ] Started Journal Service.
You are in emergency mode. After logging in, type "journalctl -xb" to view
system logs, "systemctl reboot" to reboot, "systemctl default" or "exit"
to boot into default mode.
Give root password for maintenance
(or press Control-D to continue):
[root@rhel9-server ~]# df -h
Filesystem               Size  Used Avail Use% Mounted on
devtmpfs                 1.8G     0  1.8G   0% /dev
tmpfs                    1.9G     0  1.9G   0% /dev/shm
tmpfs                    745M  8.1M  737M   2% /run
/dev/mapper/rhel-root     17G  1.9G   16G  11% /
[root@rhel9-server ~]# mount -o remount,rw /
[root@rhel9-server ~]# touch /test2
[root@rhel9-server ~]# _
```

Figure 18-4. *Recovery mode*

In the preceding output, you can see that the filesystem was remounted as read-write and a new "test2" file was created on the root filesystem.

Ubuntu

Booting Ubuntu into single-user mode requires a quick reaction time. As soon as your system shows its post messages, press and hold the left shift key on your keyboard. If you do not see a grub menu similar to the one shown in Figure 18-5, reboot and try again.

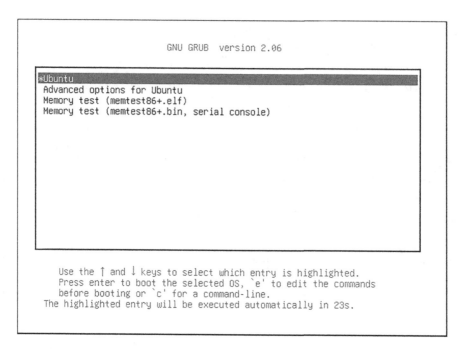

Figure 18-5. *Stopping the Ubuntu boot process*

Press the down arrow key and select the "Advanced options for Ubuntu".

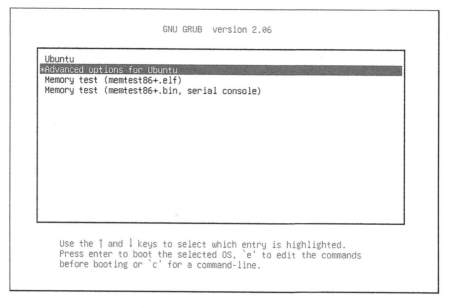

Figure 18-6. *Ubuntu Kernel options*

Select the recovery option for the kernel version you are having an issue with.

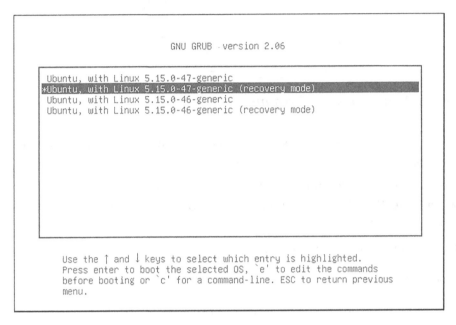

Figure 18-7. *Ubuntu recovery kernel option*

Recovery mode will give you a menu with some options to choose from. Unfortunately, on virtual machine manager consoles, the menu appears like the following:

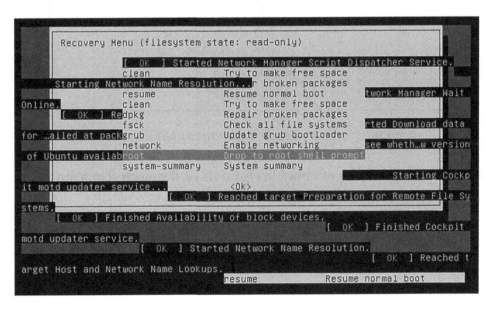

Figure 18-8.

Feel free to run some of these when you have a chance, but to continue, we will select the "root" option that will drop us to a root shell prompt.

```
Give root password for maintenance
(or press Control-D to continue):
root@ubuntu-server:~# _
```

Figure 18-9. *Root password required*

To log in to the root prompt, you will need to know the root password. Make sure to not only set a root password on your systems but also restrict the root account to only console. That is, root should not be able to log in via ssh.

As with the RHEL filesystem, you will need to run the following commands to enable your filesystem to be read and write:

If the root filesystem has been mounted to /sysroot:

chroot /sysroot

To remount the root filesystem as read-write:

mount -o remount,rw /

```
Give root password for maintenance
(or press Control-D to continue):
root@ubuntu-server:~# df -h
Filesystem                      Size  Used Avail Use% Mounted on
tmpfs                           393M 1000K  392M   1% /run
/dev/mapper/ubuntu--vg-ubuntu--lv  9.8G  6.7G  2.6G  73% /
tmpfs                           2.0G     0  2.0G   0% /dev/shm
tmpfs                           5.0M  4.0K  5.0M   1% /run/lock
/dev/sda2                       1.8G  258M  1.4G  16% /boot
root@ubuntu-server:~# mount -o remount,rw /
root@ubuntu-server:~# touch /test
root@ubuntu-server:~# _
```

Figure 18-10. *Logged into recovery mode and remounted filesystem as read-write*

As you can see from the output shown in Figure 18-10, the touch command to create a new file called test on the root filesystem has succeeded.

SLES

To boot your SLES server into a rescue mode, you will need to do very much the same as what was done with RHEL and Ubuntu.

Start your SLES system; when you see the following screen, move your up and down arrows to pause the boot process:

Figure 18-11. *Stop the SLES boot process*

```
                         GNU GRUB   version 2.06

    ┌─────────────────────────────────────────────────────────────────────┐
    │     if [ x$feature_platform_search_hint = xy ]; then                 ↑
    │         search --no-floppy --fs-uuid --set=root --hint-bios=hd0,gpt2 -\
    │-hint-efi=hd0,gpt2 --hint-baremetal=ahci0,gpt2  c1c266d2-e2fc-4339-933c-\
    │042438c86079                                                          │
    │     else                                                             │
    │         search --no-floppy --fs-uuid --set=root c1c266d2-e2fc-4339-933\
    │c-042438c86079                                                        │
    │     fi                                                               │
    │     echo            'Loading Linux 5.14.21-150400.24.18-default ...' │
    │     linux           /boot/vmlinuz-5.14.21-150400.24.18-default root=UUI\
    │D=c1c266d2-e2fc-4339-933c-042438c86079  ${extra_cmdline} splash=silent r\
    │esume=/dev/disk/by-uuid/a60fa200-dee1-4f83-a243-cf3108cc9175 mitigations\
    │=auto quiet security=apparmor crashkernel=228M,high crashkernel=72M,low \
    │single_                                                               │
    │     echo            'Loading initial ramdisk ...'                    ↓
    └─────────────────────────────────────────────────────────────────────┘

    Minimum Emacs-like screen editing is supported. TAB lists
    completions. Press Ctrl-x or F10 to boot, Ctrl-c or F2 for a
    command-line or ESC to discard edits and return to the GRUB
    menu.
```

Figure 18-12. *Press the "e" button when you have highlighted the version of SLES you want to edit*

In the new screen that appeared after pressing the "e" key, find the line that begins with "linux". Go to the end of the line and add the word either "single" or "1".

Once done, just like what was done with RHEL and Ubuntu, press the "Ctrl x" keys on your keyboard.

```
You are in rescue mode. After logging in, type "journalctl -xb" to view
system logs, "systemctl reboot" to reboot, "systemctl default" or "exit"
to boot into default mode.
Give root password for maintenance
(or press Control-D to continue):
```

Figure 18-13. *SLES rescue mode*

Figure 18-13 shows that the SLES 15 server has now booted into rescue mode. This is the single-user mode.

Emergency vs. Rescue Mode

With the three examples discussed so far using RHEL, Ubuntu, and SLES, we have used a combination of emergency mode and rescue mode.

With the RHEL 9 example, the steps to boot into a recovery mode, we added the following line at the end of the line beginning with "linux":

```
systemd.unit=emergency.target
```

This would have taken the RHEL 9 system into emergency mode. Instead of using the aforementioned, by adding the word "single", the RHEL system would have booted into rescue mode.

Why does it matter?

For some rescue operations, it does not matter too much as you can still do what you need to do. The difference between the two is that emergency mode is basically a single-user environment with a read-only filesystem, whereas rescue mode starts a few more services and mounts the root filesystem as read-write.

Using Rescue Disks

There may come a time when your system has been damaged to the extent that it will not boot. Normally this means a system rebuild; however if a rebuild is not possible, you can try one more recovery option. The use of a recovery disk.

For this, you will need to download the ISO media for your operating system. The ISO will then need to be made bootable on a USB drive, or you can mount the ISO directly on a virtual machine, if you are using a virtualization environment.

With RHEL 9, you will have a screen similar to Figure 18-14 when you install the operating system. You can also use the same media to recover a system if required.

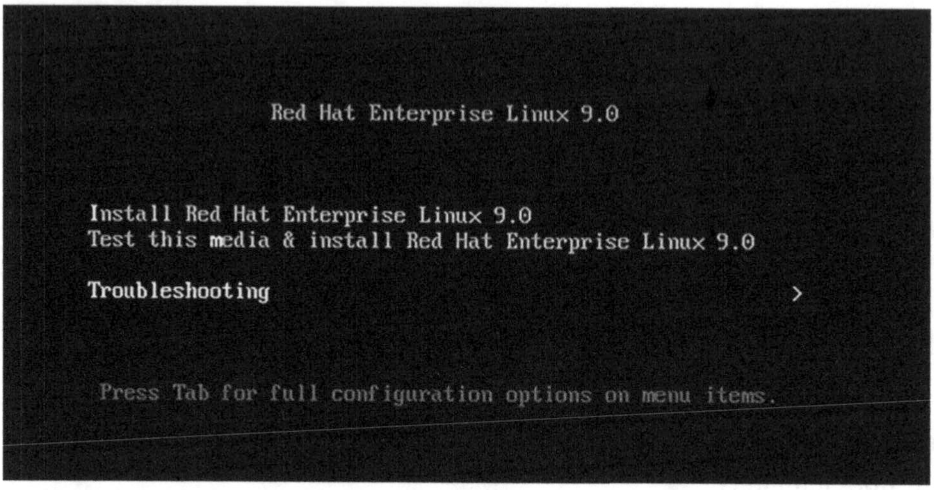

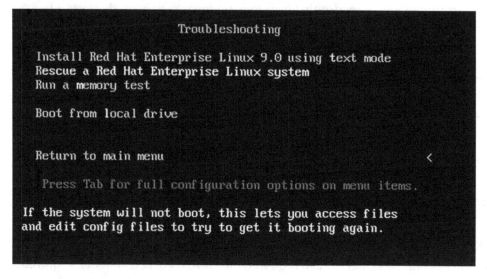

Figure 18-14. *Using RHEL install media to boot*

Figure 18-15. *Selects the Troubleshooting menu item*

Follow the instructions from the RHEL rescue disk in Figure 18-16.

```
Starting installer, one moment...
anaconda 34.25.0.29-1.el9_0 for Red Hat Enterprise Linux 9.0 started.
 * installation log files are stored in /tmp during the installation
 * shell is available on TTY2
 * when reporting a bug add logs from /tmp as separate text/plain attachments
================================================================================
================================================================================
Rescue

The rescue environment will now attempt to find your Linux installation and
mount it under the directory : /mnt/sysroot.  You can then make any changes
required to your system.  Choose '1' to proceed with this step.
You can choose to mount your file systems read-only instead of read-write by
choosing '2'.
If for some reason this process does not work choose '3' to skip directly to a
shell.



1) Continue
2) Read-only mount
3) Skip to shell
4) Quit (Reboot)

Please make a selection from the above:
```

Figure 18-16. *RHEL install media rescue options*

Once completed, you should see the shell prompt appear for you to use.

```
Rescue Shell

Your system has been mounted under /mnt/sysroot.

If you would like to make the root of your system the root of the active system,
run the command:

        chroot /mnt/sysroot

When finished, please exit from the shell and your system will reboot.

Please press ENTER to get a shell:
bash-5.1#
```

Figure 18-17. *Rescue mode from RHEL boot media*

Your Linux system should be mounted under /mnt/sysroot. To make changes to your
Linux environment, run the following command:

```
# chroot /mnt/sysroot
```

With your environment now set and provided you have network connectivity,
you will be able to install and remove any packages. You can fix boot issues and any
misconfigurations you may have.

Rescue Examples

The following are a few examples of why a system may need to be recovered or rescued.

Root Password Reset

One of the more common reasons someone may want to boot into a recovery mode for a system is to recover the root password.

However, with the techniques we have used so far, we have a major problem.

```
You are in rescue mode. After logging in, type "journalctl -xb" to view
system logs, "systemctl reboot" to reboot, "systemctl default" or "exit"
to boot into default mode.
Give root password for maintenance
(or press Control-D to continue): _
```

Figure 18-18. *Rescue modes require passwords*

To access these modes, you need the root password. Bit of a problem if we don't know the root password to start with.

Fortunately, there is still a way.

As we did with each of the environments so far, we need to boot the system and edit the grub menu. However, instead of adding "single" or "systemd.unit=emergency.target", we will do the following.

Change the original line beginning with "linux" in Figure 18-19.

```
load_video
set gfxpayload=keep
insmod gzio
linux ($root)/vmlinuz-5.14.0-70.13.1.el9_0.x86_64 root=/dev/mapper/rhel-root r\
o crashkernel=1G-4G:192M,4G-64G:256M,64G-:512M resume=/dev/mapper/rhel-swap rd\
.lvm.lv=rhel/root rd.lvm.lv=rhel/swap
initrd ($root)/initramfs-5.14.0-70.13.1.el9_0.x86_64.img
```

Figure 18-19. *Original kernel linux line that needs to be edited*

to the one shown in Figure 18-20.

```
load_video
set gfxpayload=keep
insmod gzio
linux ($root)/vmlinuz-5.14.0-70.13.1.el9_0.x86_64 root=/dev/mapper/rhel-root r\
w_crashkernel=1G-4G:192M,4G-64G:256M,64G-:512M resume=/dev/mapper/rhel-swap rd\
.lvm.lv=rhel/root rd.lvm.lv=rhel/swap init=/bin/bash
initrd ($root)/initramfs-5.14.0-70.13.1.el9_0.x86_64.img
```

Figure 18-20. *Updated kernel linux line*

In Figure 18-20, the linux line had two major changes done to it.

The "ro" was changed to "rw" to allow the filesystem to be mounted as read and write.

The second change was that at the end of the "linux" line, "init=/bin/bash" was entered.

Both of these changes would allow you to boot directly into an interpreter with access to the filesystem.

```
                Starting Cleanup udev Database...
[  OK  ] Stopped Create Static Device Nodes in /dev.
[  OK  ] Stopped Create List of Static Device Nodes.
[  OK  ] Stopped Create Volatile Files and Directories.
[  OK  ] Finished Cleaning Up and Shutting Down Daemons.
[  OK  ] Finished Cleanup udev Database.
[  OK  ] Reached target Switch Root.
         Starting Switch Root...
[    4.840833] systemd-journal[255]: Received SIGTERM from PID 1 (systemd).
bash-5.1# _
```

Figure 18-21. *Rescue mode without a password*

Now you are able to change the root password.

```
bash-5.1# passwd
Changing password for user root.
New password:
BAD PASSWORD: The password fails the dictionary check - it is based on a diction
ary word
Retype new password:
passwd: all authentication tokens updated successfully.
bash-5.1# touch /.autorelabel
bash-5.1# exec /sbin/init
```

Figure 18-22. *Root password changed*

From the output in Figure 18-22, you can see that the additional command "touch /.autorelabel" was run. This command is vital to a system with SELinux running in enforcing mode. Without running this command, users will not be able to log in, as SELinux will block access to the passwd and shadow file.

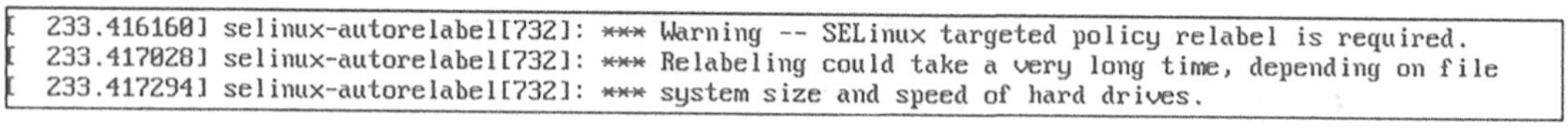

```
[  233.416160] selinux-autorelabel[732]: *** Warning -- SELinux targeted policy relabel is required.
[  233.417028] selinux-autorelabel[732]: *** Relabeling could take a very long time, depending on file
[  233.417294] selinux-autorelabel[732]: *** system size and speed of hard drives.
```

Figure 18-23. *SELinux relabelling on reboot*

If you do not see the preceding output in your reboot, redo the steps, and this time, don't forget to run the "touch /.autorelabel command."

Kernel Issues

Another potential reason to boot into a rescue mode would be to resolve any kernel issues. Resolving kernel issues can be problematic if you cannot boot into a working environment. To fix this kind of issue, you need to do one of the following.

Use Old Kernel

Reboot your system and boot into a working kernel. Reinstall the defective kernel. It is always advisable to keep two kernels installed on your system at all times.

```
                    GNU GRUB   version 2.06

 *Ubuntu, with Linux 5.15.0-47-generic
  Ubuntu, with Linux 5.15.0-47-generic (recovery mode)
  Ubuntu, with Linux 5.15.0-46-generic
  Ubuntu, with Linux 5.15.0-46-generic (recovery mode)




        Use the ↑ and ↓ keys to select which entry is highlighted.
        Press enter to boot the selected OS, `e' to edit the commands
        before booting or `c' for a command-line. ESC to return previous
        menu.
```

Figure 18-24. *List of kernels available in grub*

In Figure 18-24, you can see that there are two kernels available for this Ubuntu server. Select the older kernel, make your changes, and reboot into the new working kernel.

Rescue Disk and Install New Kernel

With no second kernel installed, you may need to resort to installing a new kernel through the use of a rescue disk.

Resolving Mount Issues

The final use case example for having to rescue a system could be through a disk mount misconfiguration.

To resolve boot issues, boot your system into rescue mode using the steps shown earlier.

Investigate the /etc/fstab or kernel parameters with any misconfigurations. Worst-case scenario is that you will need to remove your kernel and reinstall a new one. This can sometimes occur if you have made a mistake with compiling new configuration into your kernel configuration.

```
#
# /etc/fstab
# Created by anaconda on Fri Aug 12 21:26:13 2022
#
# Accessible filesystems, by reference, are maintained under '/dev/disk/'.
# See man pages fstab(5), findfs(8), mount(8) and/or blkid(8) for more info.
#
# After editing this file, run 'systemctl daemon-reload' to update systemd
# units generated from this file.
#
/dev/mapper/rhel-rooti   /                        xfs     defaults      0 0
UUID=3c0d8b4e-ac6d-4a74-8920-58fa659d5260 /boot             xfs       defaults      0 0
/dev/mapper/rhel-swap    none                     swap    defaults      0 0
```

Figure 18-25.   */etc/fstab file with an error*

With the output in Figure 18-25, you can see that someone accidentally added an extra "i" next to the name of the "rhel-root" disk name. This would cause the system to not recognize the name and fail to mount the filesystem.

Using a rescue disk, this can be quickly corrected to restore the system to working order.

Exercise

For some hands-on experience resolving system issues, run through the following exercises.

Boot into Emergency Mode

Boot a RHEL 9 system into emergency mode. Ensure that the filesystem is read-write and create a new file on the root filesystem "/" to test.

Boot into Rescue Mode

Boot a RHEL 9 system into rescue mode and observe the difference between the two modes mentioned so far.

Fix the Root Password

Using any of the enterprise Linux distributions in this book, reset the root password as though someone changed it without letting you know. Remember, you do not know the password.

Boot into a Second Kernel

Assuming that you have experienced a kernel issue, boot into a second kernel. If you do not have a second kernel, install one.

Summary

In this chapter, you were introduced to the following:

- What to consider when troubleshooting a system issue, when is the right time to reinstall, and when is the right time to keep digging for the issue

- How enterprise systems should be viewed, as pets or as cattle

- What the different system recovery options are and the difference between them

- How recovery options cannot help resetting a root password

- What the different recovery use cases are and how to resolve them

CHAPTER 19

Backup and Restore

The final chapter of this book is a sweet and short discussion around system backups. Most large organizations have a good idea on how to back up their environments, and chances are that you will most likely use what is in place. However, if you ever are stuck with having to plan and design a backup strategy, there are a few basic considerations you should bear in mind.

In this chapter, we will look at backup methods that can be used to back up Linux systems. We will look at what on the Linux filesystem should typically be backed up and some of the things you should be thinking about where you back up to.

We will end the chapter and the book by just briefly discussing system restores and the importance of testing backups.

Backups

One of the most important topics for any organization when it comes to platform planning is recovery and backup. More often than most organizations would like to admit, this does get neglected.

As an enterprise Linux administrator, you should be aware of your recovery options and how to implement them if nothing is in place. Backups should be high on your priority list if you are responsible for a platform.

Backup Methods

There are a number of ways that systems can be backed up today. The backup method will depend heavily on the platform. If your Linux system is a physical server, the backup method can't exactly be a virtual machine snapshot. You most likely will need to have a filesystem backup or an image created from the physical system that can be used to revert a system in the event of disaster.

© Kenneth Hitchcock 2023
K. Hitchcock, *The Enterprise Linux Administrator*, https://doi.org/10.1007/978-1-4842-8801-6_19

Filesystem Backups

The first backup method that comes to most of our minds when thinking about backups is file and directory level backups.

On a Linux system, there are a number of directories that are important that should be backed up, and there are a number of utilities that can be used to back these files and directories up. They will be discussed in the following.

When to Back Up

Ensure backups are scheduled to run as often as feasible. The general rule of thumb when planning backup schedules is to ask yourself how much data can be lost without losing money or time. This also has to be weighed with how much storage you have and for how long you want to retain backups. Depending on your organization, this could be a week or years. Storage is no longer as expensive as it used to be, but this can quickly ramp up if a proper plan is not in place.

Tools

Backing up a filesystem can be as simple as manually copying files to a mounted backup location or using a third-party tool to automate the process for you.

Table 19-1 lists some recommended tools that can be used to run backups.

Table 19-1. *Tools to use for backups*

Linux utility	Description
rsync	A very powerful command-line utility that can replicate files and directories including their permissions.
Amanda	An OpenSource enterprise graphical tool that can be used to back up multiple Linux environments from a central location.
Bacula	Another enterprise backup solution that can manage Linux backups centrally.
Timeshift	Largely used for desktops but a useful tool to know about if you are running Linux desktops in your environment.

Note   There are many other OpenSource backup solutions that can be used; some are community based and some provide enterprise support. Remember to look at the best solution for your organization.

What to Back Up

If you are going to back up files and directories on your Linux systems, you will need to make sure you back up the following.

Table 19-2 lists important directories that should be backed up if doing a filesystem backup.

Table 19-2. *Directories to back up*

Linux directory	Description
/boot	Boot-related files, kernel, initrd, and grub files.
/usr/local	Contains the bin and sbin directories that could contain scripts and binaries required by your system.
/etc	Configuration files for the host. Important to have the configuration backed up
/home	User home directories. Contains user-related data.
/opt	Third-party vendor installation files and data.
/root	Home directory for the root user.
/srv	Can sometimes have data for services like httpd.
/var	Can contain important database files, web sites, or other vital data for your environment.

Where to Back Up

Where you back up is as important as what you backup. Understanding how your storage systems work is vital to ensuring that you do not put your environment under too much pressure. You do not want to overload the storage controllers of your production environments with backups running during the day. Work with your storage administrators to understand if there are segregated storage systems that can be used for backups that will not impact live systems. Potentially look at alternative storage solutions that can be scaled based on usage. Backups are important but so are your live systems. Finding the balance between budget, capacity, and performance can be tricky.

Network Considerations

Remember to also consider your network when designing your backup solution. If you are backing up to network-based storage, you will need to ensure that you have a separate network for backups that will not interfere with your main network. This network typically does not need to be bonded but should be monitored to ensure that backups succeed. Remember, if backups are not succeeding and a restoration is required, you will be responsible and will need to justify why the backups were failing. This is not a conversation you wish to have.

Network Mounts

When backups have completed, it is advisable to unmount the backup location. This is advised as it is not impossible for someone to delete everything on a filesystem including the mounted backups. Automate your backups and automate the mount/unmount tasks. Do not risk the chance of your backups being wiped out accidentally.

Virtual Machine Backups

Depending on your environment, there could be a few options for your virtual machine backups.

Snapshots

When using virtual machines, you can have the option of creating virtual machine snapshots. These should not be seen as long-term backups but more to get you back to a working state if you are testing or upgrading your server and you experience a problem.

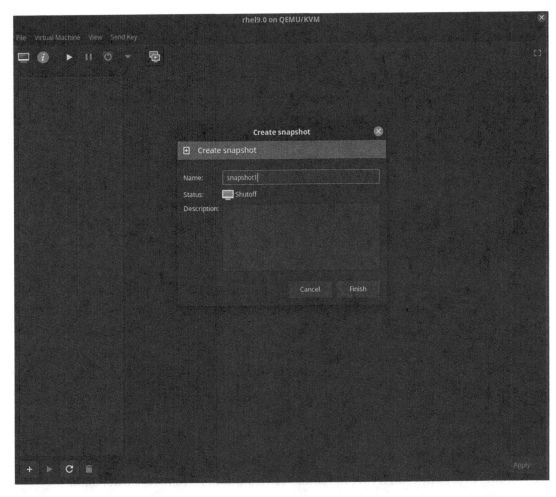

Figure 19-1. *The snapshot window for a virtual machine running on KVM*

Figure 19-1 is the snapshot window for KVM. This can be found by clicking the view menu and clicking snapshots. To create a snapshot, click the "+" in the bottom left.

Backup VM Files

Virtual machines themselves are run from files and directories. When a virtual machine has been powered down, it often is a single disk image file that has a few metadata files that store information about the virtual machine itself. These files can be backed up and restored just like regular files.

Using a backup tool mentioned previously with well-scheduled system shutdowns could be one way to ensure your virtual machines have a way to recover.

Storage Backups

Backups can also be done at a storage array level. By snapshotting the storage, you can create a quick recovery option for your data. Virtual machines can have their entire image snapshotted, or physical systems can have their external storage snapshotted.

Storage snapshots are normally done by your storage administrator and should be planned by a storage specialist. Work closely with them to ensure there is a well thought-out strategy for your backups if this is going to be your preferred backup option. Remember to discuss automation and backup restore testing and how often backups are done.

Backup Reports

Having access to backup reports or some kind of alerting tool for backups is a very useful way for you to stay on top of your system backups. If they cannot be provided, you will need to have some mechanism to scrap this data so you can do something yourself. Consider building a monitoring platform or logging system that can grab this information and display it for you. This should be one of the first things you look at when you start your day and should be right up there as one of the most important things you do as an enterprise Linux administrator.

Remember, if backups are failing and you ignore them, you will have problems down the line and could make more work for yourself. It is easier to make sure your backups are working every day than trying to rebuild environments and reconstruct data.

Restore

The other of backups is restoration; without a testing strategy of your backups, you won't know if they are any good. We never realize how important backups are until we need them and find our backups have been failing.

What to Restore

What we restore is solely dependent on what you need. It goes without saying but you would, for instance, not restore old log files or tmp files. Plan your backups and only keep the data that is vital to your systems.

You do not need to restore binaries as they can be reinstalled. For example, if your system runs a database, back up the database files using the recommended database export tool but do not back up the actual database binaries that can be reinstalled.

Test Restore

Restoring a system from a backup typically means you have encountered a problem and you have reached your last resort. You don't want that last resort to fail for you either. Test your backups on a regular basis and confirm that they are working as intended.

Important   Design and plan your restore test using automation that can be run on a regular basis. As an enterprise Linux administrator, you will be responsible if a system is not able to be restored. Make sure your backups are working as a priority at all costs.

Summary

In this chapter, you were introduced to the following:

- What backup methods can be used to back up your Linux environments

- What tools can be used for backups

- What content on a Linux filesystem should be backed up

- A brief note about system restores and the importance of testing backups

Index

A

AllowGroups and DenyGroups
  parameters, 164, 169
Ansible, 563
  collections, 504
  configuration
    ansible.cfg, 507
    control node, 504, 505
    creating content, 507
    documentation, 513
    Galaxy, 511
    inventory file, 508
    package module, 510
    playbook, 509
    ssh keys, 506
    variable files, 511, 512
  control node, 503
  definition, 502
  directory structure setup, 513, 514
  inventory, 503
  managed node, 503
  modules, 504
  playbooks, 503
  plug-ins, 504
Ansible Automation Platform, 526
Ansible Tower, 356
"apache2" package, 395, 396
Apache httpd, 313, 392, 393, 397
Apache web server package, 316
AppArmor, 402
"apt-get" utility, 197, 198

"apt" utility, 198, 199
Arduino, 34
Asymmetric multiprocessing systems, 22
ausearch command, 438

B

Backups
  definition, 583
  directories, 585
  methods
    directories, 585
    filesystem, 584–586
    storage, 588
    virtual machine backups, 586, 587
    virtual machine snapshot, 583
  reports, 588
  tools, 584
"blkid", 307
Boot process, 8, 57, 70, 126, 366, 568, 571

C

Canonical, 18, 35, 41, 43, 384
Chcon, 435
"chkconfig" utility, 313, 314
"chmod" utility, 182–184
Chown, 184, 185, 188
Cinnamon, 20
"Cinnamon Desktop", 147
Cloud technologies, 23

Cluster
  definition, 465, 467
  enterprise Linux
    components, 467
    Corosync, 468
    pacemaker, 468
    RHEL, 468
    troubleshooting, 485, 486
  types, 466
  web server, 487
Cockpit web console, 133–135,
    316–320, 427
Command line
  distributions, 145, 146
  editing files
    change directories, 138
    command-lie editing, 141
    command mode, 142
    commands, 139
    desktop utilities, 141
    edit mode, 142
    finding files, 139, 140
    listing, 136, 137
    pwd utility, 138
    vi or vim, 142
  exercises, 146, 147
  main pages, 135
  OpenSUSE, 146
  parameters, 135
  shortcuts, 143, 144
Command-line and graphical tools, 269
Command-line graphical utilities, 266
Command-line interface (CLI), 6, 161, 489
Command-line Ubuntu package, 198
Command-line utilities, 147, 202, 240, 267,
    270, 274, 277, 382, 422, 551
Common Open Software Environment
    (COSE), 15

Communication, 28, 459
Community-based distributions, 40, 336
Community-based Linux
    distributions, 219
Community graphical Ansible tool, 526
Community Linux distributions
  definition, 42
  Fedora, 43
  OpenSUSE, 43
  Ubuntu, 43
Computer memory, 8
Computer networking, 6, 7, 9, 11
Computers
  free online courses, 10
  hardware
    components, 8
  hardware/software courses, 11
  network, 9
  networking, 11
  paid-for online courses, 11
  software, 9
  storage, 10
Corosync, 468
Cryptsetup, 454, 455

D

Debian, 19, 31, 32, 41, 197, 209, 214
Debian forked Linux distributions, 209
Deployment method
  definition, 515
  exercise, 521, 522
  image cloning, 520
  kickstart, 516
  vs. cloning, 521
Deployment tools
  automation, 525–528
  build and configuration flow, 522

enterprise deployment tools
Foreman, 523
Red Hat Satellite Server, 523, 524
SUSE manager, 525
Uyuni, 524, 525
parts, 522
Desktop
enabling/disabling, 156
Fedora server, 157
installation, 147–155
Device management, 28
df command, 550
DHCP-configured network address, 126
Disk management
disk layers, 268, 269
exercises, 292, 293
graphical tools, 280–288, 290–292
local disks, 267
LVM, 294
partition tooling, 274–279
storage, 267
tools
disks, 270, 272, 273
Disks, 280
Distributed cluster, 466
"dnf", 148, 194–196, 198, 202, 207, 209, 212, 220, 226–228
"dnf" and "yum" utilities, 226
"dnfdragora" utility, 197
"dpkg" utility, 198, 202, 209
du command, 550

E

Encryption
definition, 450
encrypt data, 450
Linux

SSH keys, 451
public key, 451
Enterprise Linux
Canonical, 41
Red Hat, 40, 41
SLES server/desktop, 42
SUSE, 42
Ubuntu, 41
Enterprise Linux clustering
definition, 487
Enterprise Linux distributions
Red Hat, 335
reinstallation, 561–563
Enterprise Linux system administrator, 6, 156, 357, 382, 490, 533, 553
Estate management tools, 356, 381, 386, 563

F

"fdisk" utility, 274–277, 293
Fedora, 32, 33, 37, 43, 52, 63, 66, 119, 212, 226
Fedora server
configuration, 94, 95
customizations, 95
definition, 81
installation
create virtual machines, 82–85
default options, 81
installation media, 81
optional custom exercise, 96
File and directory permissions
ACLs, 186–188, 190, 192
chmod, 182–184
chown, 184, 185
directory listing, 181
File management, 28

File server
    disk share, 414, 415
    firewall configuration, 411–413
    Linux installation/configuration,
        408, 409
    NFS server
        configuration, 415–418
    NFS server package, 410, 411
    NFS *vs.* Samba, 407
    SELinux, 413
    test NFS server skills, 418, 419
    use case requirement, 408
Filesystem management
    checking disk, 307
    creating file, 307, 308
    directory, 310, 311
    exercise, 312
    mounting disk, 308, 309
    resizing, 309, 310
    system reboots, 312
    types, 307
"find" command, 139, 140, 143
Firewall
    command-line utilities, 422
        firewalld, 423
        iptables, 422
    definition, 421
    ruleset tools, 429, 430
    web UI configuration, 427–429
firewall-cmd commands, 427
Firewalld
        package, 394, 395, 410, 423
    cheat sheet, 427
    definition, 423
    ports/services, adding, 425, 426
    removing ports/services, 426
    services, 423
    status, 423, 424

FreeIPA, 176, 177
Free Software Foundation (FSF), 17,
    19, 29, 40

G

"gateway" parameter, 244
getenforce, 432
"getfacl", 186, 187
GNU, 17
groupdel command, 175, 176
groupmod command, 175

H

Hardening
    CIS, 441
    CIS report, 450
    compliance scanning, 442–446,
        448, 449
    RHEL 9 system and subscribe, 449
    security authorities, 441
    standards, 441
    STIG standard, 442
Hardware consoles, 125
"httpd" package, 316, 317, 321, 325

I

Identity management (IdM), 176
"ifconfig" tool, 238, 239
Information management, 28
Information technology (IT)
    hardware, 4
    Linux, 3
    networking, 6, 7
    software, 5, 6
Initial ramdisk, 28–29

"initrd" or "initramfs"
    methodology, 29
Installation media
  Burn, 63
  network, 64
  USB drive, 63
"ip" and "ifconfig"
    commands, 240
"ip" utility, 239

J

journalctl utility, 325, 540
  commands, 542, 543
  definition, 540
  real-time messages, 541
  run command, 540

K

"ken", 393, 409
ken_cluster, 475
Kernel, 16, 17
  architecture, 26
  definition, 25
  functionalities, 26
  initial ramdisk, 29
  layers, 26
  map, 27
  monolithic modular, 26
  system calls, 27, 28
Kernel-based virtual (KVM) machines,
    50, 51, 53, 58, 65, 66, 79, 80, 95,
    124, 338, 361, 383, 478, 587
Kickstart
  build new system, 517–519
  copy file to web server, 517
  creating file, 516, 517

L

Libvirt, 231, 234
Linus Torvalds, 25
Linux
  access, 123–125
  Android/Ubuntu, 22
  Debian, 19
  definition, 16
  Dell/Oracle/Red Hat, 21
  desktop, 20
  desktop wars, 20
  distributions, 32, 33
  enterprise, 18
  FSF, 17
  installation, 64, 65
  kernel 2.0, 20
  kernel 3.0, 21
  kernel 4.0, 22
  kernel 5.0, 22
  OpenSource, 17, 18, 23
  operating system (*see* Operating
    system, Linux)
  Systemd, 22
  Torvalds, 16
Linux administrator, 1, 3, 5, 12, 13, 27, 64,
    171, 176, 194, 262, 269, 295, 356,
    392, 393, 423, 465, 501, 533, 588
Linux distributions
  definition, 39
  enterprise Linux, 40
  Fedora, 119
  OpenSource and Free Software, 40
  OpenSUSE, 119
  Ubuntu, 119
  upgrade *vs.* migration, 117
  upgrading, 118
  upgrading processes, 119–121

Linux logging system
    debugging, 533
    directory, 534
    errors, 537, 538
    journalctl, 540
    log files, 535
    remote logging, 543, 544
    Rsyslog, 535, 536
    Rsyslog server, 545
    tail logs, 538, 539
    verbosity, 536, 537
Linux system monitoring, *see* Monitoring
Load balancing cluster, 466
Local users and groups
    commands, 171
    configuration files, 171
    creating groups, 175
    password management, 174
    removing users, 173
    setting password, 172
"ls-al" command, 137, 180
"lsblk" utility, 270–272
"lvcreate" utility, 294
LVM-based utilities
    commands, 295
    create logical volumes, 295–297, 299
    exercises, 306
    increase storage, 299, 301
    package, 294
    physical volumes, 302
    RAID, 305
    recovery options, 303, 305
    remove logical volumes, 302, 303

M

Manjaro, 32
MediaWriter tool, 63

Monitoring
    disk related tools, 549, 550
    network tools, 550, 551
    PCP tools, 551
    process-related information, 546–548
    Prometheus, 553
    remote, 552
Multiplexed Information and Computing
    Service (Multics), 14

N

Nagios, 552
"netplan", 243
netstat command, 263, 550
Network configuration
    desktop
        Fedora, 253, 254
        OpemSUSE, 257–261
        Ubuntu, 254–256
    exercises, 261, 262
    ifconfig, 238, 239
    interface, 240–246
    ip, 239
    network manager, 240
    textutal intefaces
        NetworkManager, 250–252
Networking, 3, 6, 7, 11, 26, 237
Network tools
    dig, 264
    Linux system administration, 262
    ping, 262
    ss, 263, 264
    testing, 265
Newtestusers, 180
nfs-utils package, 411
Nginx, 392, 393
"nmtui", 250

O

OpenSCAP, 443–448
OpenSource technologies, 35
OpenSUSE, 43
  customization, 116
  definition, 96
  installation, 97
  installation media, 97
  server, 116
  server installation
    configuration, 112–114
    customizations, 101
    disk partition, 109
    install media, 102, 103
    keyboard type configuration, 104
    online repository activation, 106
    online repository configuration, 105
    online repository updating, 107
    type selection screen, 108
    user account creation, 111
    user login, 114
  virtual machines
    ISO image, 98
    KVM, 97
    setting, 99–101
  virtual machine specifications, 115, 116
Operating system, Linux
  desktop, 35
  IoT, 35, 36
  IT-related problems, 36
  kernel, 25
  mobile devices, 35
  servers, 35
  utilities
    desktops, 30
    shells, 30
    software, 29

OSI model, 7, 9
"out-of-the-box" repositories, 211, 216

P, Q

Pacemaker, 468, 487
Package installation
  deb, 209, 210
  package management systems, 194
  repository configuration
    Fedora, 212, 213
    OpenSUSE, 216–218
    packages, 211
    Ubuntu, 214–216
  RPM, 207, 208
Package management systems, 32, 193
  Fedora
    command line, 194
    definition, 194
    desktop, 196, 197
    dnf utility, 194–196
  Linux distributions, 194
  OpenSUSE
    command-line, 202–204
    definition, 202
    desktop, 205, 206
    install packages, 206, 207
  Ubuntu
    apt utility, 198, 199
    deb, 197
    definition, 197
    desktop, 200, 201
Package management tool, 506
"parted" utility, 277–280, 283, 293
"pcp" package, 551, 552
pcs cluster setup command, 475
pcs cluster status command, 477, 485
"pcs status", 477, 480, 481

"pid", 553
ping command, 263, 265
-p or--password parameter, 172
POSIX, 180
"ps" command, 547
"pstree" command, 548
Puppet, 382, 386, 527, 563
Putty, 127–128
pvmove command, 302

R

Raspberry Pi, 34, 41
"Realmd", 177
Recovery methods
    boot, 580
    emergency *vs.* rescue mode, 573
    kernel issues, 578, 579
    mount issues, 579, 580
    rescue disks, 573–575
    root password reset, 576, 577
    single-user mode
        RHEL, 564, 565, 567
        SLES, 571, 572
        Ubuntu, 567–570
Red Hat, 40
    community upstream products, 336
    definition, 335
    estate management tools, 356
    RHEL, 335, 358
        account, 336
        installation, 341–349
        installation media, 337, 338
        virtual machines, 338, 339, 341
    subscription/support
        attaching subscriptions, 353, 354
        community packages, 349
        packages, 349

        register Red Hat, 351, 352
        unregister, 355
        verify subscriptions, 350, 351
    training/certification, 356, 357
    virtual machines, 357
Red Hat Certified Engineer (RHCE),
    357, 382
Red Hat Certified System Administrator
    (RHCSA), 357, 382
Red Hat Enterprise Linux (RHEL), 18, 21,
    33, 40–43, 81, 133, 165, 194,
    335, 467
Red Hat package manager (rpm), 207
Red Hat Satellite Server, 64, 356, 442,
    523–525, 528, 563
Remote users and groups
    FreeIPA, 176
    ipa-clinet, 177
    system administrators, 176
    Windows Active Directory, 176, 177
Restoration, 588, 589
"rhel9-node1", 470–472, 485, 508, 511
RHEL cluster
    cluster installation
        firewall rules, 473
        install packages, 472, 473
        services, 474
        setup, 474, 475
        status, 476
        user account, 473
    configuration requirements
        hostname, 470
        nodes, 469, 471
        NTP, 470
        static IP addresses, 470
        subscription, 471
    fencing
        definition, 478

KVM, 478

node, 479, 480

fixing cluster issue

group resources, 484

remove resources, 483, 484

status, 485

installation, 468

network information, 469

nodes, 468

resources

virtual IP address, 481, 482

web server, 482, 483

Rolling back system

Fedora, 226–228

installation tools, 226

Linux environments, 235

OpenSUSE, 229

snapshots, 231–234

Ubuntu, 228, 229

virtual machine snapshots, 230

RPM-based packaging, 32

"rpm" package, 208, 209, 212

Rsyslog, 535–537, 543–545

S

"safe mode", 563

SaltStack, 382, 524–527, 563

"sda", 277

"sdb", 278

Secure shell protocol (SSH)

configuration file, 126

configuration files, 128–133

definition, 126

log in, 126, 127

putty, 128

WinSCP, 128

Secure socket layer (SSL), 460

Security

definition, 421

firewall, 421

Security Technical Implementation Guide (STIG), 442

SELinux

command line configuration

cheatsheet, 440

context labels, 433–436

mode, 431

parameters, 432

SELinux booleans, 436–439

definition, 430

exercise, 440

modes, 431

Service management

Cockpit web console, 317

command line, 316

enabling/disabling service, 319–321

new service, creating

enable/start service, 330

exercises, 331, 332

remove service, 331

script, 326

unit file, 328, 329

new servie, creating

script, 327

unit file, 327, 328

statue of service, viewing, 318, 319

stop/disable, 321

stopping service, 317, 318

utilities, 313–315

setenforce command, 433

"Setfacl", 187–189, 191

setsebool command, 437

$SHELL environmental variable, 491

Shell scripting
before writing script, 492
conditionals, 497
conditionals operands, 498
definition, 489
examples, 500, 501
interpreters, 493
languages, 489
Linux shell
environments, 490, 491
loops, 499
packages, 502
structure, 493
variables
arithmetic, 495, 496
defining, 494
names, 494
setting, 494
special, 495
Socket statistics, 263
Sosreport, 558
sources.list.d directory, 214
Spacewalk, 381, 382, 386, 524
"ss" command, 550
ssh_config.d directory, 162
ssh-copy-id, 453
sshd_config.d directory, 162, 166
sshd daemon, 167, 168, 264
ssh-keygen command, 452
Ssh keys
asymmetric encryption, 451
certificates, 459–462
definition, 451
different algorithm, 452
disk encryption, 454–458
encryption, 462, 463
manual configuration, 454
network encryption, 458, 459

RSA, 452
SSH/SSHD configuration
configuration files, 162
configuration parameters, 163, 164
debugging, 168, 169
default configuration, 164–166
firewall restrictions, 161
parameters, 170
SSH service, 167
SteamOS, 32
strace command, 554
Subject matter expert (SME), 3
Sudo
command, 177, 178
definition, 178
OpenSUSE server, 178
SUSE Certified Engineer (SCE)
certification, 382
suseconnect command, 380
SUSE Linux Enterprise Server (SLES), 96
account, 359
certification, 382
configuration, 383
definition, 358
installation media, 359–361
installation, 364–377
management tools, 381, 382
support/subscriptions, 378–380
upstream, 359
virtual machine, 361–364
SUSE Manager, 381, 382, 525
System buses, 4, 8
"systemctl" command, 319
"systemctl" utility, 314, 324
systemd
configuration files, 321–324
definition, 321
utilities, 324, 325

System patching, 236
    community *vs.* enterprise, 219
    definition, 219
    errors, 219
    rollback, 226 (*see Rollback system*)
    system updates
        Fedora, 220, 222
        Linux distributions, 220
        OpenSUSE, 224, 226
        Ubuntu, 222, 223

T

Terraform, 527, 528, 563
"/test", 312
Testacls, 186
Testgroup, 191, 192
Testpermissions, 191, 192
test.sh, 183, 185, 495
Testuser, 179
"tmux" package, 145, 146, 199, 201, 203,
    358, 502, 509, 512
Transport layer security (TLS), 460
Troubleshooting
    finding help, 553
        asking help, 556, 557
        manual pages, 554
        strace, 553, 554
        support cases, 557, 558

U

Ubuntu, 22, 41, 43, 119, 197, 214
    configuration, 79
    customizations, 80
    definition, 65
    installation, 386
        deployment, 66

        keyboard layout selection, 73
        language type, 71
        network configuration, 74
        package installation options, 77, 78
        physical system, 69
        proxy, 74
        user screen, 76
        version, 72
        virtual machine, 66–69
        virtual machine disk
            partitioning, 75
        virtual machine manager
            console, 70
    installation media, 66
    management tools, 386
    optional exercises, 80
    subscription/support, 387–390
    SUSE certifications, 384, 385
    version, 384
"ubuntu-server", 79, 80, 393, 394
Unix
    definition, 13
    early version Unix, 14
    growth, 16
    limitations, 15
    Multics, 14
    standards, 15
    variation, 15
    version 2, 14
useradd command, 171, 172, 175
userdel command, 173
usermod command, 172, 173
Uyuni, 381, 382, 524, 525

V

/var/log directory, 534, 535, 545
vgdisplay command, 298, 300

"virt-manager", 58, 65, 66, 82, 97, 124, 129, 234, 272, 292

VirtualBox, 46–49, 53–57, 79, 80, 95, 115, 231, 292, 357, 383

Virtualization
  definition, 44
  Linux
    exercise, 50–53
    KVM, 50
  types
    BIOS requirements, 45
    hardware requirements, 45
    VirtualBox, 46–49
    Windows, 45
  virtual machines, 53–58, 60–62

Virtual machine cloning, 522

Virtual machines, 44, 45, 53–62, 65–70, 75, 79, 80, 82, 95, 97, 115, 338, 357, 361, 383, 586, 588

W

Web console (cockpit), 133, 147, 315–321, 428

"webip", 481, 483–485

Web server, 440
  configuration, 392, 393
  configuration files, 396–399
    exercises, 406
  firewall configuration, 400
    ports, 400
    reload, 401
    verify, 401
  Linux installation, 393, 394
  options, 391, 392
  package installation, 394–396
  SELinux, 401–405

Windows
  definition, 33
  vs. Linux, 36
  vs. Linux, 34

Windows Active Directory, 176, 177

WinSCP, 128

X

Xenix, 15

Y

Yet another Setup Tool (YAST), 205

"yum" utility, 194

Z

"zypper" utility, 202–204, 209, 220, 224–226

ices

Printed in the United States
by Baker & Taylor Publisher Services